TRAVELS IN KASHMIR AND THE PANJAB,

CONTAINING A PARTICULAR ACCOUNT OF THE GOVERNMENT AND CHARACTER OF THE SIKHS

Baron Ch: Hügel.

TRAVELS
IN
KASHMIR AND THE PANJAB,

CONTAINING
A PARTICULAR ACCOUNT OF THE GOVERNMENT AND CHARACTER OF THE SIKHS,

FROM THE GERMAN OF

BARON CHARLES HUGEL

WITH NOTES BY

MAJOR T. B. JERVIS, F. R. S.

Published under the patronage of the Honourable the Court of Directors of the East India Company

Together with Characteristic Illustrations, and a Map of Those Countries Constructed by Mr. John Arrowsmith, from the Best and Most Recent Authorities.

GYAN

Published by

GYAN

Gyan Publishing House
5, Ansari Road
Daryaganj, New Delhi-110002
Phone: 011-47034999, 9811692060
E-mail: books@gyanbooks.com

Distribution Network
gyanbooks.com
India, USA, Canada, UK, Australia, France

ISBN : 978-81-212-4149-6 (PB)
First Published, London, 1845

2nd Impression 2020

Printed at: Gyan Press, Delhi.

Travels in Kashmir and the Panjab, Containing A Particular Account of the Government and Character of the Sikhs
Author: Baron Charles Hugel with Notes by Major T. B. Jervis, F. R. S.

THE EMPIRE OF EUROPE IS NOW EXTENDED TO THE UTMOST BOUNDS OF THE EARTH, WHERE SEVERAL OF ITS NATIONS HAVE CONQUESTS AND COLONIES. THESE AND MANY MORE ARE THE ADVANTAGES DRAWN FROM THE LABOURS OF THOSE WHO EXPOSE THEMSELVES TO THE DANGERS OF THE VAST OCEAN, AND OF UNKNOWN NATIONS; WHICH THOSE WHO SIT STILL AT HOME ABUNDANTLY REAP IN EVERY KIND; AND THE RELATION OF ONE TRAVELLER IS AN INCENTIVE TO STIR UP ANOTHER TO IMITATE HIM; WHILST THE REST OF MANKIND, IN THEIR ACCOUNTS, WITHOUT STIRRING A FOOT, COMPASS THE EARTH AND SEAS, VISIT ALL COUNTRIES, AND CONVERSE WITH ALL NATIONS.

LOCKE. HISTORY OF NAVIGATION.

THE EDITOR'S PREFACE.

The German original of the present publication has deservedly procured for its illustrious author the reputation of a diligent and faithful observer of nature, who possesses the happy talent of expressing his thoughts with a taste and perspicuity which imparts peculiar interest to his narrative. Independent of the entertainment which is derived, by readers of every age, from the varied incidents of personal adventure and foreign travel, the appearance of a work thus recommended, is calculated at the present moment to throw great light on the important question which now occupies the public mind, as to the proper line of policy to be pursued by the Government of India, in relation to the Panjáb; and although the principal personages in the scenes, so strikingly depicted in the author's progress, have been swept away by the hand of death, or the murderous contests for supremacy which have followed each other in quick succession, the country itself and its prominent features, which, in a military point of view, are of primary consideration—the circumstances and constitution, the habits and peculiar character of the mixed population subject to Sikh rule, are still the same, unaffected as to any ulterior purpose by the numerous political changes which have occurred since the death of Ranjít Singh.

The system of disclaiming all interference in the internal affairs of the Native Powers has invariably had the opposite effect to that which was in the contemplation of the Home Authorities, and in the ordinary course of events provoked dissensions, which have occasioned their overthrow and accelerated the aggrandizement of dominion so strongly deprecated by the British Legislature, on every ground of humanity and justice. The extension of this mighty Empire, to judge from its history and the experience of modern times, is obviously entailed in the designs of an Allwise Providence, irrespective of any choice or human councils, by the natural impulse of conflicting interests; and the great desideratum seems rather to be, how to bring to the administration of a trust of such magnitude all the energy which should actuate an enlightened Christian Government; how to give to every department of the State that increased efficiency which shall ensure the integrity of our territories on any emergency; in what way best to promote the fullest inquiry into their natural resources and capabilities, and admit these possessions to an equal participation in the commercial privileges which are enjoyed by other colonies of the British crown, without detriment to the interests of the state.

The principal objects of the undertaking are succinctly stated in the Preface. The Introduction further specifies the best authorities to which the oriental scholar may refer for information respecting the former state and history of Kashmír, with a brief notice of the several European travellers who preceded the author. The cost of the original*, independent of the

---

* The German edition was published at Stuttgart, in four parts, 8vo., at distant intervals, and is procurable in this country at the high price of 2*l.* 16*s.* unbound. The first and third parts comprise the entire narrative, or journal, of which the present volume is a translation; the intermediate part contains a summary account of the ancient and modern history of Kashmír, abridged from Professor H. H. Wilson's papers published in the Transactions of the Asiatic Society; with sundry miscellaneous particulars, geographical and physical; also an account of the productions, resources, and inhabitants of the mountain regions. The fourth number is a sort of glossary and gazetteer, including miscellaneous matters relating to the various political, civil, and military affairs of Government, the history of India, &c.; from all which much useful information may be gleaned.

difficulties of a foreign language, would necessarily preclude a very extensive circulation, and the expensive form* in which Jacquemont's Travels have been published by the Committee of Public Instruction, under the auspices of M. Guizot, will limit the perusal of that work to a very small number of those who are conversant with the French language. Under such circumstances, the present translation, together with the valuable map which accompanies it, by Mr. John Arrowsmith, will form a most acceptable contribution to the geography of Asia, and be welcomed by those who have looked forward to its publication, as an earnest of the selection and style of an extended series, which is in abeyance only for want of proper encouragement. In any case the reader will receive it as an additional proof of that spirit of inquiry which is abroad in the world, of the liberality with which every desire for information is met by the Government of India, and the testimony borne by an impartial spectator to the intervention of British rule, and the management of the East India Company.

With regard to the Orthography, I have been at great pains to ascertain the true names of every geographical object, and rendered them, as well as all Oriental terms, according to the system observed by the Asiatic Society of Calcutta, and the Royal Asiatic and Geographical Societies in this country, in which I have to acknowledge the friendly aid of its three greatest scholars, Professor Horace Hayman Wilson, the Rev. G. C. Renouard, and the Rev. Dr. John Wilson, Honorary President of the Asiatic Society at Bombay. If the reader does not find every word written exactly according to his taste, I crave his

* Jacquemont's Voyage dans l'Inde is published in royal 4to., of which the first and second volume only have yet appeared. The want of plates, or maps, of any sort, renders the details of natural history and general description far less interesting than they otherwise would be to most readers.

indulgence, and can safely assure him, that it would be far easier to express the varied intonations of the musical notes by literal signs, than the complicated sounds of Oriental alphabets, by the manifold sounds of the English language, varying as Eastern letters do, not only with the great national divisions of languages, but the characteristic distinctions of pastoral, nomade, military, and agricultural pursuits, as if the several avocations of people and tribes had induced peculiarities, which were the true distinguishing tests whereby all were to be traced up to one ancient original. The vowels of Turkey, of Persia, of Arabia, and of India, in one and the same word, *Bokhara*, for instance, are perceptibly different in all, and the interchange and sound of the consonants, the liquids especially, varies indefinitely. Whether we should spell *Mohammedan*, *Turkisthan*, and such like words, according to one or other system, it matters not, provided it be as near as any other to the true pronunciation and mode of spelling. Where uniformity can be attained without any great departure from received usage, it is better to agree to adopt some standard; and although there are objections to Sir William Jones's system, as well as to Gilchrist's—the two principal authorities with Oriental scholars on such subjects—the learned bodies have decided in favour of the former, to which the reader is at once furnished with a perfect key, by remembering that all the vowels are sounded as in the Italian, the accented vowels, *á*, *í*, denoting the broad sounds, and for the rest, the *ch* only supplying the place of *c* before *e* and *i*, the *g* being invariably hard; lastly, the *j* and *z* pronounced simply as in English.

In respect to the notes interspersed through the volume, such as they are, I am alone responsible for them. They were such as an experience of many years' residence in India, and a long acquaintance with the Hindú character, suggested. Many more might have been added with great advantage, and promoted some inquiries of much interest. The value of good geographical works, as is the case in an especial manner with respect to Marco Polo's Travels, edited by Mr. Marsden, is, in fact, to elicit inquiries and comparisons—the basis of all exact knowledge. It is in simplicity and originality of thought that Baron Hügel's merit as a traveller chiefly consists; and the playful, unpretending way in which he touches upon any fact gives an expressive picture of a heart naturally thoughtful, but full of generosity, frank, high-minded, and sincere. To appreciate its worth, the original may be consulted; to divert a leisure hour, the present work, which professes to give the spirit rather than a cold servile translation of the German text, may claim a place by the side of Heber's delightful narrative, and be safely recommended to young people. For any presumable claim to public favour in regard of its style, I would advert with grateful recollection to the unwearied solicitude of the accomplished friend whose assistance I have received throughout.

I have reserved the consideration of recent Political events, and a detailed description of the Panjáb, its resources and principal Geographical features, for a future volume, the materials for which have been supplied by those distinguished and intelligent persons who are most competent to form a sound and correct judgment of its relations, capabilities, and prospects.

T. B. JERVIS.

London, 1*st November*, 1844.

LIST OF SUBSCRIBERS.

HIS ROYAL HIGHNESS PRINCE ALBERT.
HIS ROYAL HIGHNESS THE DUKE OF CAMBRIDGE.

The Honourable the Court of Directors of the East India Company, forty copies.

Her Majesty's Commissioners for the Affairs of India, two copies.

The Most Noble the Marquis of Northampton, (President of the Royal Society.)

The Right Hon. Lord Prudhoe, (President of the Royal Institution.)
The Right Hon. the Earl of Auckland.
The Hon. Mountstuart Elphinstone.
The Right Hon. Sir Edward Ryan.
John Ayrton Paris, M.D., (President of the Royal College of Physicians.)
The Royal Asiatic Society.
The United Service Institution.
Captain F. Beaufort, (Hydrographer to the Admiralty.)
Professor H. H. Wilson, (Director of the Royal Asiatic Society.)
W. R. Hamilton, Esq.
Major-General Sir Henry Pottinger.
Admiral Sir Charles Malcolm.
H. T. Prinsep, Esq.
Admiral Sir Wm. Parker.
Lieut.-Colonel Sir Claude Wade, three copies.
James Farish, Esq.
Lieut.-Colonel Malcolm.
Colonel Wm. Miles.
Colonel Dickinson.
The Rev. Dr. Wilson, Bombay.
Colonel Bonnar.
The Rev. G. C. Renouard, (For. Sec. Royal Geographical Society.)
Louis Hayes Petit, Esq.
Colonel Sabine, Royal Artillery.
Richard Woosnam, Esq., (Sec. to Commissioner, China.)
W. H. Medhurst, Esq.
Robert Thom, Esq.
Gideon Colquhoun, Esq.
Archibald Sconce, Esq., (Collector and Magistrate, Chittagong.)
Thomas Thompson, Esq., M.D., (Bengal Medical Service.)
Gideon Colquhoun, Junior, Esq., Bombay.
Robert Warren, Esq.
G. Young, Esq.
Captain Crawford, Royal Artillery.
J. Stark, Esq., (Secretary East India Board.)
Alexander Beattie, Esq.
J. Cooke, Esq., Isle of Wight.
Mr. J. Gardiner, Junior.
W. Fountain, Esq., 8, Regent's Villas.
M. Poole, Esq., 7, Regent's Villas.
G. T. Vigne, Esq.
Morley's Circulating Library, 27, Park Terrace.

CONTENTS.

ILLUSTRATIONS.

BARON CHARLES HÜGEL'S PREFACE.

WHETHER Kashmír was that favored spot, where, six thousand years ago, the Almighty Word called the human race into being; whether it was the seat of that Paradise which man forfeited by his disobedience to the first command ever given, or whether, as Hindú mythology pretends, it was there that, countless ages back, the world was again renewed by the creation of the present race, are questions which throw no light either on the history of mankind, or of Kashmír itself. The clearing up of the mystery, indeed, though it could be accomplished, would be of little real importance to the believing mind. Most assuredly there was an earthly Paradise, what matters it *where it was*, is the simple answer of the reasonable many; yet the excusable curiosity of the few is not, therefore, to be too severely judged. If the labour of years be spent in seeking out the birth-place of some one great individual, may we not extend the endeavour to search for the favoured spot trodden by the common progenitor of all? On this subject the valley furnishes no information. It is almost superfluous to observe, that the idea of making any discovery on this point constituted no object in my own researches; that the same fond fancy, nevertheless, which has persuaded even the Hindú, surrounded on every side by the magnificent scenery of his native land, that Kashmír was in very truth, the Paradise of the newly awakened world, does invest it with a peculiar charm, is an undoubted fact, and the indifferent and most apathetic traveller is full of expectancy when first he views this famous and lovely valley outspread before his eyes. Whatever anticipations I myself had formed of my visit, will be fully and honestly narrated in the following pages; I have endeavoured to describe the valley of Kashmír and its inhabitants according to the best of my ability and judgment; nor have I suffered myself to be led away from this design, either by the fascinations of the romantic, or the love of the marvellous.

Nothing seems so unaccountable to the traveller from far distant lands, after a brief sojourn in a place where he looked for nothing but the wild adventures which crowded his waking dreams, as his own want of surprise at surrounding things; he discovers here, as everywhere, that in the manners of all nations there is a certain harmonious congruity which, in spite of national principles, is founded on the same universal laws of nature. After the first impression has passed away, which exaggerated every object, he beholds beings like himself, actuated by the same motives, animated with the same lofty spirit, equally moved by like affections and enmities; he no longer feels, that he differs from those around him, since there, as elsewhere, the sports of childhood, the industry of man, the tenderness of woman, and the caution of age, remind him that his fellow men are all formed in one common image; whether they be the Hindús, whose gentle qualities are not sufficiently appreciated, or the New Zealander, of whose nature we as yet know only the darkest side. Thus it is throughout the earth. The Múselmán buries his dead in gardens rich with fragrant flowers, and under marble tombs; while the Parsí abandons those whom he has loved most fondly to the rapacious vulture and the inclement elements: the Chinese address their gods in monosyllables; the fire-worshippers turn in silent adoration towards the ocean and the sun: the Jetí of Gújrát, in the one case, covers his mouth with a cloth, lest he should inhale and thus rob some minute creature of life; the New Zealander, on the other, will devour the very remains of his own fellow-creature. Yet one and all these, so opposite, but strongly-marked, characteristics belong to men who have many thoughts and feelings in common with ourselves; and the Vedah, the solitary ape-like creature of Ceylon, who flies to trees to avoid us, and scarcely bears the semblance of humanity, is perhaps the only class from whom civilized man turns away with disgust; with him we seem to have nothing in common, we gaze on his appearance with astonishment, and the traveller, in recording his existence, sighs to think of the depths of degradation into which the human race has been plunged by sin.

With what prolonged delight do we dwell on the breathing form of an animated creature, after amusing ourselves awhile with its picture; precisely such is the interest called forth by a foreign people; it commences, in truth, when the first impressions of strangeness have worn off. It is the different aspects under which human nature is viewed that exercise the attention of the reflecting traveller. Superficial observers are pleased only with objects so long as they have the charm of novelty. The interest in the latter ceases, in fact, where that for the first commences; and this feeling of hopeful expectation can alone compensate for all the discomforts of tedious adventure, for years of travel, and that depressing sense of frequent unbroken solitude, amid strangers, which fills the heart, constantly looking forward for something to occupy it, with unavailing anxiety.

It is often a problem of great difficulty to solve, in what the peculiarities of nations consist and whence they arise; whether from the religious or civil laws in force among them. It may be either of these; for we know that laws do operate powerfully on the daily current of events, and that the very same system of religion will exercise a mighty influence over the minds of nations whose manners and habits of thinking are widely different.

It cannot admit of a question that the changes of government which have taken place in Kashmír must have materially affected many original characteristics of the people. Subjugated in succession by Mohammedans from Central Asia, who subverted their ancient and patriarchal institutions and government; by the Emperors of Delhi, who brought among them, in their search after new pleasures, a voluptuous and luxurious court abandoned to pomp and prodigality; by the fierce Afghans; and finally, by the half-civilized Sikhs, who now dwell in those long-deserted imperial halls, what can remain of originality to these inhabitants of the valley, after so many changes of rulers, each in turn eager to destroy the works of his predecessor? It is, however, important to notice, that Hindúism, once obeyed, is hardly ever to be eradicated from the minds of its followers, even though they may be compelled to exchange their faith for another; nay, even though their conversion may seem purely voluntary and unconnected with political events.

It needs no argument to prove that the civilization of a people depends on a thousand contingencies of place and time, on the mingled influences of external and internal circumstances favourable to its development. Hence the statesman and legislator will exercise little power over institutions and customs unless he has well weighed the causes which have produced what he desires to change or modify; nor will his laws ever endure to after times unless they are framed so as to harmonize with the present state of feeling among those for whose government they are intended.

The following pages contain materials for much interesting inquiry on this subject; they were written during a journey which detained me some years from Europe, and as the country of the Sikhs with which Kashmír is now incorporated, must necessarily be frequently introduced to the reader's notice while describing it, I resolved to give some account of a kingdom which, as being the only state of importance adjoining British India, cannot fail to interest Europe in general.

INTRODUCTION.

The great mystery of language, which by one sound can bring before us not a single image only, but a multitude of objects and events, and fill the imagination according to its capacity, in no case exercises its influence more strongly than in words which express the names of different lands. To the ear of a European, the word England, for example, instantly recals to mind the wealth of that island, and her maritime power; France, is ever associated with the turmoils of ambition and faction; Italy, with sunny climes and poetry; and Germany, with our ideas of a staid conscientious people. True, the images conjured up in the fancy of every individual, will lose much of their truth and charms when experience has shewn him how sorely he has deceived himself in many things; but when the land of which he dreams, is situated far off, his ideas, though equally vague, are less likely to be disappointed. We have no remembrances attached to the name of a New Zealander; we revert only to his character with horror, as a cannibal, while the New Hollanders excite our compassion for the scanty gifts which Providence has vouchsafed them. Compared, however, with these countries, Kashmír is an object of especial interest. We behold, in imagination, a delightful valley sheltered on every side by lofty mountains, with streams of the purest water issuing forth from their declivities, which flow gently on till they fall into the mighty rivers which bend their way majestically through the vale. From their summits, crowned with Alpine vegetation, down to the depths beneath, where the luxuriant products of India predominate, there is a succession of plants, which gradually assume as they descend, the lighter and more graceful forms of tropical vegetation. The same fancy peoples the land with noble human forms, adorns it with the palaces and gardens of the Moghul Emperors, and recals the tales of fairy islets, with their magic lakes and floating gardens. There, exclaims the youthful enthusiast, who is never likely to realize these visions, there, must be happiness; there, thinks the philosopher, might our first parents have been summoned into being. Indians, no less than Europeans feel the charm of this name. The Mohammedan believes Kashmir to have been the earthly paradise; the Hindú has the same tale in his legends of the last Mahá-Yúg, descriptive of the revival of the human race. Fiction, in every case, points to Kashmír, as the land of promise. Even the apathetic eye of the Brahmin, and the cold-fixed thoughtfulness of the Mullah, are known to brighten up at the mention of its sweet retreats.

The last travellers, Jacquemont and Wolff, men of very opposite minds and opinions, have somewhat lessened our favourable ideas on this subject; but the first avows himself nearly blind, and it certainly was not the design of the latter to descant on the loveliness of nature. To examine whether Kashmír would bear the uplifting of the veil which has so gracefully and immemorially hung over her, and see whether the first or the last travellers have drawn the truest portrait, to reach the very limit of Indian civilization, were my chief persuasives to pass several months in this celebrated region; and, why should I deny it? the anticipation of beholding the loveliest spot on earth, had power enough to allure one no longer young, to undertake another tedious and toilsome journey.

Our authorities on Kashmír are very defective before the time of the Mohammedans, though, in fact, there is yet one native chronicle extant, entitled, the Raja Taringini, which has been translated by Professor Wilson, and published in the Asiatic Researches; to this we shall allude further in speaking of the History of Kashmír. The Raja Taringini has always been considered in our times as a complete work; far otherwise: it is a collection of four separate treatises, by as many authors. The first begins with the creation of the valley of Kashmír, and concludes with the year A.D. 1027 (Saka 949). The author of this portion was Kalhana Pandit. The second, or Rajavali, by Jona Raja, carries the history down to A.D. 1412. The third, or Sri Jaina Raja Taringini, was written by Sri Vara Pandit, who brought it down to the year of the Hejira 882 (A.D. 1477). The fourth and last part, called Rajavali Pataka, by Punya Bhatta, concludes with the conquest of Kashmír by Akbar the Great, Emperor of Delhi, A.H. 995 (A.D. 1586).

We shall see elsewhere, how far the Raja Taringini merits that pretension to antiquity, to which it has hitherto laid claim.

The other works are, Baber's Memoirs, which are quite unimportant on this subject of Kashmír.

Goheri Alem Tohfet us-Shah of Badia-ud-din.

Abúl Fazel Ayín-Akberi.

A History by an unknown Persian author, containing a long list of princes and legends.

A History of the Mohammedan Kingdoms of India, by Mohammed Kásim Ferishta.

Hajus de Rebus Japonicis, Indicis, &c.

Les Lettres Edifiantes.

Tarikh-i-Kashmír, by Naráyan Kúl.

The History of Kashmír, by Múllah Hassan Kári.

Ditto, by Hyder Malek Shad-Waria.

Wakiat-i-Kashmír, by Mohammed Azim.

Nawádir úl Akbar, by Mohammed Rafia-ud-din.

Núr Nameh, written by Shekh Núr-ud-din, in the Kashmirian language, and translated into Persian by Múlvi Ahmet Almeh.

History of Kashmír, while in possession of the Afghans, in Persian, by Múlvi Khair-ud-din.

Elphinstone's Kabúl, and Burnes' Journey to Bokhara; very valuable works for the countries they visited in person; but as their information regarding Kashmír was derived exclusively from natives, whose testimony must be admitted with great caution, many errors have crept in.

The most recent work which treats of Kashmír, and contains the most important documents concerning the last sixteen years, is the History of Ranjít Singh, by Mr. Prinsep, Secretary to the Government of India, who derived his information from the Honourable Company's archives. I have taken most of my notes on the Panjáb from this gentleman's valuable work.

Bernier's Travels in India; an Essay in Letters concerning his Journey in Aurungzíb's suite.

Forster's Letters, Journey from Bengal to St. Petersburgh.

Researches and Missionary Labours, by the Rev. Jos. Wolff.

Correspondence of Victor Jacquemont, during his Travels in India.

The Papers in the Asiatic Researches, and in the Journal of the Asiatic Society of Bengal.

Major Rennel's Geographical Memoirs.

Ritter's Geography of Asia; a work containing an immense store of information and learning, greater indeed and more important than any other dedicated to the same objects, though perhaps not strictly to be considered as one of the authorities on Kashmír.

Moorcroft's work, not yet published, though it was sent to me while in the press, I have purposely abstained from reading, that I might keep my mind free from any impressions which I might otherwise in all probability have received from the perusal of a work by another modern author.

The first authentic information concerning Kashmir, which appears to have reached Europe, was through the Portuguese, whose religious zeal prompted them to promulgate Christianity among the natives; for we attach little credit to the tales we are told of their king marching to the relief of Porus, when he was attacked by Alexander the Great, although the later Greek authors mention a country they call Kaspapyrus and Kaspatyrus, and sometimes Kasperia, which would seem to be Kashmír. Setting aside such unsatisfactory accounts, we may repeat, that to Europe, Kashmír was in a measure unknown, till the subjects of Portugal first trod its valleys. The Jesuit Xavier, a Navarese of high birth, is supposed to be the very first European who ever had the glory or the courage to penetrate to this remote region. Another of the same family, Francis Xavier, animated with like fervent zeal to diffuse the light of Christian truth throughout the East, had already gained, and not undeservedly, the glorious title of the Apostle of the Indies. In the year 1572, exactly twenty years after Francis Xavier had fallen a martyr to his high and holy calling, his kinsman landed on the shores where Xavier had been foremost to plant the cross. His apostolic mission carried him first to the residence of the Moghul Emperors, which Father Rudolf Aquaviva had recently visited. Xavier appeared at the court of Akbar the Great at Agra, accompanied by another fellow-labourer, Benedict Goez, a native of the Azores; and by their shortly afterwards attending the Emperor to Kashmír, it would seem that the tolerant spirit of Akbar had actually entertained some thoughts of establishing, or at least of favouring the progress of, the new faith in India. Xavier's remarks on Kashmír, which are published in that very scarce work, Hajus de Rebus Japonicis, Indicis, &c., (Antwerp, 1605,) are of no particular value.

The second traveller who made us acquainted with this country, was Bernier, whose motives for undertaking the journey were widely different from those of his predecessor. Xavier prosecuted what he believed to be a high and holy office; Bernier's sole object was, an increased knowledge of the world; but the bent of his genius as well as the advantages under which he travelled, render his observations on the countries he visited, more valuable than any that had then appeared. He was a young physician, of engaging appearance, of enterprising mind and pleasing manners, qualities which would insure to most travellers a hearty welcome in foreign lands. Urged by an unconquerable desire to see the world, he left his native country, France, in 1654, in his twenty-ninth year, (Voltaire says he was born at Angers in 1625,) and without any settled purpose or plan, wandered first through Syria and Egypt. In the year 1657, during the reign of Shah Jehan, he came to Surat, then a place of some importance in the commercial world, at the very period when the emperor's four sons were contending for the Moghul throne. Aurungzíb was the conqueror, and under the name of Alumgír ascended the throne of Delhi. To that city Bernier repaired, and there entered the service of Danishmand Khan, an Omrah in the court of Alumgír, as his personal physician, with a monthly salary of 300 rupees. In 1665, he attended the Emperor and Danishmand Khan to Kashmír, for the purpose of restoring the health of the former, which had long been declining. Kashmír at that time was in all the plenitude of its glory. For fifty years it had been the favourite summer resort of Aurungzíb's grandfather Jehangír, and his father Shah Jehan, but the latter had more particularly occupied himself in embellishing the valley with palaces and gardens. The wealth thus brought into circulation by the protracted visits of the Court, had produced general abundance; while the grandees vied with their sovereign in every predilection for luxury and extravagance. The patron of Bernier was a friend and protector to science, and afforded him every facility for exploring the country; but unfortunately, speculative philosophy so pre-occupied his mind, that the study of nature and even statistics, had little or no charm for him. This deprived his work of much value, notwithstanding which, it is an interesting record of the history of that time, as its pages have the evident impress of truth; nor is it any slight praise when we say, that Bernier is one of the most faithful writers that ever travelled, a merit the more uncommon in those days, when readers longed to be surprised by the marvellous, rather than instructed by the true, and when, at all events, Bernier had nothing to fear from the superior information of any European.

After twelve years' abode in India, he returned to his fatherland, and fixed himself at Paris, where his travels were published in 1670. I cannot forbear relating the cause of his end, as it seems to me peculiarly affecting and instructive. Befriended by Ninon de l'Enclos, and in the literary coteries where Racine, Boileau, St. Evremond, and other stars of Louis XIV.'s brilliant reign, moved along with him, distinguished as the handsome philosopher, Bernier could not withstand the general corruption around him, and at length died, in consequence of the mortification he experienced at a bitter satire of the President du Harlay, in 1688, a proof that his philosophy, the Epicurean philosophy of Gassendi, was merely a mask to cover the extreme of folly.

As a traveller, however, Bernier surely deserves a high place among those who unite courage to talent, and whose enterprises are undertaken, not from any low or sordid motives, but from an honourable thirst after knowledge and truth. His travels are now almost forgotten. It has, unhappily, been too much the habit of most readers, to expect something wonderful and fantastic from writers on India; his work, nevertheless, is not a whit the less valuable, and is entitled to every confidence as an authority, from which modern writers may well derive much information, and may justly find a place in every library. Nowhere shall we read a more faithful and impartial account of the manners and usages of India; his descriptions are, to this moment, as striking and appropriate as when his hand first penned them*.

* It is the Editor's hope, at no distant period, to give to the public an entirely new and accurate translation of these travels, with notes and illustrative comments.

Father Desideri, a Jesuit, was the third European visitor to Kashmír; he undertook a mission to Tibet, reached the valley in 1714, and was compelled to remain there during the winter. His observations on Kashmír, contained in a letter from Lassa in 1716, are wholly undeserving of notice.

Then came George Forster, in the year 1783, a civil servant in the Company's Presidency of Madras, who journeyed through Bengal, Lucknow, Srinagur, Nadaun, and over the mountains of Kashmír, returning by way of Kabûl, the Caspian, and St. Petersburg, home, altogether a most arduous enterprise, at a period when Northern India and Central Asia were overrun with freebooters, and a number of petty states had arisen on the ruins of the Moghul kingdoms, whose very weakness made them suspicious of each other. Kashmír had then been, for some years, rent from the crown of Delhi, Ahmed Shah Abdalli having conquered the whole province in 1754, and annexed it to Afghanisthan. Originally Ahmed had been Nadir Shah's armour-bearer, and had learned the art of government in the Persian court. In the year 1739, as Nadir Shah gazed from the terrace before the little mosque of Rokn-ud-dáula, on the burning of the plundered houses of Delhi, he exclaimed to those around him, among whom Ahmed stood, "So will I deal with all the kingdoms of India, until the wealthiest of the land shall beg before seven doors, ere he finds an earthen pot to cook his rice in." His threat was not fulfilled by himself, but his servant Ahmed trod in his footsteps in Hindústhan, and plundered Kashmír, which even Nadir had spared. When Forster visited the valley, Timúr Shah, the son and successor of Ahmed, had been ten years on the throne, enjoying the fruits of his father's conquests, in as much quiet as his restless neighbours to the north and west would permit. A despotic viceroy, Azad Khan, then governed Kashmír, and to avoid persecutions, which had nearly cost him his life, Forster was obliged to have recourse to disguises and concealments which, during his short stay there, under a perpetual dread of discovery, prevented him from making any very important use of his time; his little work is, nevertheless, very attractive, and one cannot help feeling interested in the unassuming kind-hearted man, who relates his adventures and dangers so unpretendingly.

Forty years passed away before another traveller went to Kashmír, and, during this long period, many changes had taken place in the aspect of affairs in this part of Asia. The English had begun to aspire to universal dominion in India; the sums of money, yearly expended for the shawls of Kashmír had not escaped their attention, and it had become a question, which engaged their merchants, whether it would not be more profitable to manufacture the wool in Hindústhan or in England, or even, whether it would not be possible to introduce the breed of sheep into their own country, and secure the exclusive produce of that material. Mr. Moorcroft, an enterprising man, who had gone out to India as a veterinary surgeon, was commissioned, by his government, to make a journey through the Himálaya to the table-land of Tibet, and report on this matter. Both regions were then imperfectly known, and made the subjects of many fabulous narratives; but, however important the result of his journey, in a geographical view, he altogether failed in the object of his mission. It is true that he sent a number of goats to Bengal, which were despatched afterwards to England, but they proved to be of a different breed from the finest shawl-wool goats of Kashmír. In 1820, Moorcroft, then officiating as director of a large stud in Bengal, was commissioned once more to visit Central Asia, and with their usual liberality, the East India Company permitted him to make his own arrangements for the journey, and gave him authority to draw upon them for any sum he might require for his expenses*.

Accompanied by two young men, named Trebeck and Guthrie, Moorcroft commenced his adventurous journey at Lahor. Ranjít Singh, the Mahá Raja of the Sikhs, King of Lahor, had just taken possession of Kashmír, and Moorcroft found no difficulty in obtaining the Prince's permission to traverse his dominions on his way from Ladák

* This account is full of mistakes. Mr. Moorcroft had on neither occasion any appointment or commission from government. He travelled with its sanction, but at his own risk and charge.

to Bokhara. In his character of a horse-dealer, attended by a numerous retinue, he passed by Bilaspoor and Mundí, to the strong fortress of Dankar, and reached Ladák in safety. There, however, forgetting that he had nothing to do with politics, he drew up, and signed, in the name of the Company, a formal treaty with the Rajas of Ladák. Although a stranger in an unknown and dangerous country, he might be excused, if, environed with difficulties, he consented to negotiate where he had no authority, and promised without any power of fulfilment, with the view to gain some specific object. But Moorcroft could plead no such necessity, for he was kindly received, and met with no impediments at all; and hence, the treaty which he executed in the Company's name, can be defended on no one ground; and during my residence in Kashmír, it caused the Raja of Ladák to brave the consequences of a war which may cost him the half of his dominions*.

From Ladák he journeyed to Kashmír through the Naubuk-Pansal; and after remaining there nearly two years, proceeded, with a princely retinue, towards Balkh. His baggage, worth several lacs of rupees, was carried by 300 bearers, exclusive of all the animals employed; and this parade being displayed in sight of the natives, induced the Sikh Viceroy, Moti Ram, to offer him a friendly warning, while his friend Mahommed Shah Nakshbandi, of a Turkisthan family, sent him a strong escort to serve him in case of danger. From Balkh he proceeded to Andkhoo. There he felt symptoms of a fever gaining on him; but he wrote to one of his Indian friends, full of hope, that the medicines he had taken to remove them, would be effectual. In this hope he deceived himself; in three days from that time he was a corpse, and the same disease speedily cut off his two young English companions.

---

* The statements made in the text are wholly erroneous, as a little consideration might have suggested to Baron Hügel. Had any treaty been concluded on the part of the East India Company with the Raja of Ladák, his dominions would have been effectually guarded against Sikh aggression. Mr. Moorcroft never executed any treaty at all; he was the channel of a communication from the Raja of Ladák to the government of India, tendering to it that allegiance which his ancestors had professed to the throne of Delhi. The offer, unhappily for the Raja, was peremptorily declined, and Moorcroft was severely rebuked for his interposition, even to the limited extent to which it had been exercised. (See MOORCROFT'S *Travels*, vol. i., 418.)

Naturally enough, the premature death of the three Europeans was ascribed to the half civilized people among whom they were then residing, and their plundering habits, joined to the circumstance, that Moorcroft's baggage was entirely lost, certainly favoured that suspicion; but a strict investigation, instituted among his retinue, has proved it to be wholly unfounded, and every well-informed person in Kashmír, and Hindústhan, is now satisfied, that his death was occasioned by fever; the declaration that Trebeck and Guthrie fell victims to the same disease, does not seem to me, however, quite so well substantiated.

His papers were saved, and transmitted to the Political Agent in Lúdiána, who sent them forthwith to his superior, the Resident at Delhi. The expectation of the Indian public to know the results of a journey, which had cost such vast sums, and terminated so fatally, was long strained to its highest pitch, but in vain; the non-appearance of the papers was attributed to the narrow policy of the government, which desired not to admit the world to a participation in their unknown treasures, and as all things in India are of brief interest and duration, poor Moorcroft, his travels, and his death, were soon forgotten. A fresh and more tragical event, however, transpired, to shew how unfounded were these accusations of the Company. In March, 1835, Mr. Fraser, Assistant Resident at Delhi, was basely murdered by an hired assassin of Shams-ud-din, the Nawáb of Ferozpoor, and on examining his papers those of Moorcroft were discovered, lying forgotten in his desk, and were then, for the first time, brought to light*. What they may contain, I know not; but certainly the long and uninterrupted residence of Moorcroft, in the valley of Kashmír, must have made him very well acquainted with it.

Under what different aspects and governments was Kashmír seen

---

* This account is not strictly correct. From an opinion very generally entertained, that the later and concluding notices of Moorcroft's journey would constitute a very essential addition to those discursive documents digested by Professor Wilson, Mr. Fraser of Delhi made every exertion for their recovery; and all, both journals and the notes of Trebeck and Guthrie, up to the period of their departure from Bokhara, were obtained from his executors and sent home in 1836. (See preface to MOORCROFT'S *Travels*, p. 52.)—*Ed.*

by these three travellers! Bernier knew it as the summer residence of the haughty Moghul Emperors, a retreat they took pride in adorning, though such embellishments could in no way add to its beauty; on the contrary, throughout the East, the builder of a palace cares little what there may be around and beyond its walls, enough, if within, all is pomp and splendor, and indicative of the lavish prodigality of its wealthy occupant. Hence, too frequently, the road leads to it through a dismal series of ruins, or by a narrow street, bounded by half dilapidated huts, and as no one cares to keep such buildings in good repair, in the course of a few years signs of commencing dilapidation appear. Indifferent soever as Indian monarchs may be, whether the precincts of the royal domain be laid out in gardens or destitute of culture, they are no less so to the condition of their people, whether they dwell in comfort, or languish under the most grievous extortions, nor can any thing be more erroneous, than the opinions of many Europeans, that the dwellings of these Eastern Sovereigns were alike splendid within and without. This is very far from being the case, although Kashmír did, perhaps, more resemble the park-like vicinity of our palaces, than most other tropical regions.

When Mr. Forster visited Kashmír, he found it in a measure independent; the governor left behind by the plundering Afghans, considered himself as absolved from all authority, sending only to the capital, Kabúl, whatever tribute he thought proper to spare, and no more. Though he grievously oppressed the people, the extravagant mode of life of this Mohammedan caused the money collected from the revenue and taxes to circulate again into the hands of the natives indirectly, who derived, also, immense profits by the increased exportation of their manufactures. The system of government prevailing on the occasion of Moorcroft's visit was much the same as at present, and will be explained in a future chapter.

Victor Jacquemont was peculiarly favoured by circumstances when his travels led him to Kashmír. He was commissioned by the Jardin des Plantes, to form a collection for them in India, and General Allard, a Frenchman in Ranjít Singh's service, proposing to him to visit Kashmír on his route, he gladly accepted the offer, and obtained Ranjít's permission and every facility for the journey. I was personally acquainted with Jacquemont, who had improved his natural talents by the most persevering course of study. What he really did while in Kashmír has not yet been made known to the world; all that we have hitherto perused are his familiar letters to his family and friends, which have been published contrary to his expressed wish. These letters, as we might naturally expect, throw no new light on science; they shew the man of talent, but they have done immense injury to his memory in India. They who assisted him with advice and their good services, now stigmatize him as an ungrateful slanderer, and many, who really liked and esteemed him, feel deeply hurt and disappointed.

The missionary travels of Mr. Wolff are before the public. Whose missionary was he? From the Propaganda fide? No; first a Jew, then a Papist, converted in Rome, and now a Protestant; Mr. Wolff is not a delegate either from Rome or the Church of England, but according to his own declaration, derives his mission direct from Christ, to spread the knowledge of the Bible among the Jews, and to fulfil this appointment he has undertaken, at the expense of different zealots, various adventurous and hazardous journeys. His conduct is of an extraordinary nature, however, when he finds himself in the midst of those formerly of the same faith with himself; like a meteor he appears, and then deeming it enough to enlighten them with one or two speeches, he straightway departs again. Those who are well acquainted with Central Asia and India find in his little work a good deal of useful information; but, to the uninitiated, it is a confused mass of materials ill put together, in which the ever-present *I* is mixed up in the most familiar terms with the name of our blessed Lord and Saviour*.

---

* But, in extenuation of this celebrated missionary, it is to be observed, that the grand objects which he has had in view in his intercourse with his brethren have been to inquire into their situation and circumstances in the different lands of their dispersion, and to excite them to religious *inquiry*. He has all along professed to be merely a *pioneer*, leaving the work of systematic and continuous instruction to his successors.—*Ed.*

TRAVELS IN KASHMIR.

Preparations for the Journey.

"Which, beyond all controversy, was the earthly Paradise," was the half-muttered reply of my Brahmin, Thakúr-Dás, when I asked him whether he would accompany me to Kashmír, and I understood immediately that his words implied a willing affirmative. In the north of India, a man is considered to betray a total want of respect for the subject, who forgets to add the above-mentioned encomium whenever Kashmír is named in his presence, or the speaker neglects the compliment himself.

I expected, in consequence of what had been told me, to meet with many difficulties in engaging servants to accompany me, at the advanced season when I undertook my journey, but was agreeably mistaken, as not one of the three servants I had brought with me from Calcutta,—viz. a Hindú Sirdar-bearer, a Musselman Khidmatgár, and a Musbálchí,—made the slightest objection whatever. The names and offices of these three important personages in an Indian establishment require some explanation.

A Sirdar-bearer is a personal attendant. Mine was a native of Patna, an excellent and trustworthy man, whom I always found indefatigable and attentive to his duties. The name Bearer (*Kahar* in Hindústhani), given by the English to this class, is taken from the palankeen-bearers, from whom the younger or more economical of the Company's officers generally select their personal attendant: they pay them about three or four rupees a month, a rupee is worth about a silver florin, (2*s*.,) without board or livery; deducting from this sum the value of everything that is lost in the house, or broken by them. But my servant would have been highly incensed if he had been bound by the same terms. The title Sirdar, the real meaning of which is officer, pointed out his rank, contrasting strangely enough with bearer, the name always given him by his European master, while every other person in and out of the house called him Sirdar. Many of these Sirdar-bearers lay claim to Rajpút descent; and in Upper India the word Singh, or in Bengal, Rúp, is not unfrequently prefixed to their name, as a proof of military ancestry. My sirdar usually carried a shield on his back, and a sheathed sabre in his hand, and the expression of his visage was altogether so martial, that I could seldom refrain from smiling as he went about his very unwarlike duties. On the slightest occasion, he would put himself into a violent rage with his companions, and became then, with his dark features, and his black rolling eyes, a proper object to strike terror into his timid countrymen.

The Khidmatgár Hingam, was the best servant I ever had in India. The Khidmatgár holds the place of a butler in Europe, and is properly the only servant who waits at meals. When his master accepts an invitation he repairs to the friend's house also, and waits upon him there. In a large establishment there are often two or three of these Khidmatgárs; the first is then called the steward, and not only prepares the tea and coffee, but is expected to understand the way of cooking the favourite English dishes.

The Máshalchí is properly a torch-bearer, and runs before the palankeen or the horse, when the master travels or pays a visit in the night-time; while in the house he is employed as a domestic servant. Our Austrian lackeys would probably look down with great contempt on these slim light-footed messengers; but in no one of their official capacities are they at all to be despised.

My Brahmin Secretary, or Munshí, Thakúr-Dás, was a native of Delhi. He did not understand a syllable of English; but to make amends for this, he was a thoroughly honest person, well acquainted with Sanscrit, and wrote Persian very elegantly.

I had engaged an interpreter from the Agra College, to accompany me to Kashmír,—a well-educated Brahmin youth, by name Sitaram, perfectly conversant with English, and of most prepossessing exterior; but unluckily he could not bear the motion of the palankeen in which he followed me; and falling ill on the way from Agra to Delhi, I was under the necessity of sending him back. Another interpreter was then recommended to me, a half-caste, who called himself an Englishman, and with much expense, in consequence of the highly favourable terms in which he was mentioned to me, I brought him from Meerut to Simla, when I found he was not of the least use, and was only too glad to get rid of him within twenty-four hours, the man himself declaring that he was afraid to encounter the dangers of a journey to Kashmír. He had heard at first that he was to travel on terra-firma, and now finding that we should have to cross mountains covered with ice, he was sure that so timid a rider as he was, would never arrive there. In fact, the very thoughts of it had haunted him all the way from Pahar to Simla, and he humbly besought me to spare his life, and allow him to depart, with which solicitation I was only too happy to comply.

Purposing that this should be the last journey I should ever undertake, I was additionally anxious to derive every possible advantage from it, and to neglect nothing which could tend to make its results of some value. Unfortunately, I was under the necessity of making the journey alone, and foresaw months of solitude before me, which yet I could not avert. I might readily have found some companions to accompany me among my English friends; but the Government had strictly forbidden its servants to cross the Setlej without permission, which they would in no case grant. So far as physical comforts could be provided, I resolved to want for nothing, for a traveller's life is not such an easy one that he should spare himself any enjoyments that can be procured.

Besides tents for my party, preserved meats hermetically sealed in tin boxes, wines and drinks of various kinds, preserved fruits and sweetmeats, I did not fail to provide myself with the hookah, universally used throughout the East; with some Himálayan ghunts, or ponies, which climb the steepest mountains, and tread firmly on the edge of the most fearful precipices, also with a sedan-chair or *Jampan*, with twelve bearers. Besides my in-door servants, consisting of the three men just mentioned, a Bwárchí or cook, with two assistants, a Hookahburdar, or servant to attend my pipe, an Abdar for the water, a Durzee or tailor, &c., I had a Chobdar or herald, two Chaprasís, or messengers, having my name engraved in Hindústhaní and Persian on their breastplates, two Shikárís, or huntsmen, to slay or stuff beasts, two Paharis, or mountaineers, as butterfly-catchers, two gardeners to collect plants and seeds, two tent-bearers, &c., &c., in all thirty-seven servants, sixty bearers, and seven beasts.

It was in vain that I sought an interpreter, sufficiently versed in English to translate the manifold questions the object of my journey demanded, when my slight acquaintance with Hindústhaní might cause me to falter. A lad of fourteen, Mohan Bír, was the only one I could engage; and although I almost despaired at first of making anything of him, he soon gained my good graces by his quickness and liveliness of mind.

Three different routes to Kashmír lay before me; that over the highest mountains of the Himálaya range; that which passes across the lowest mountains, or a third through the plain of the Panjáb. The first road might be taken either through the Berenda Pass, or by Mundí and Dankar; but for all or any of them, it was necessary for me in the first place to obtain the permission of Ranjít Singh, the Mahá Raja of Lahor, to whom Kashmír is subject, for without it I should not here have found the means of subsistence. I had therefore applied for this in the month of May.

Ranjít Singh is considered altogether independent of the British Indian Government, and in truth is as much so, as his position as a weaker neighbour can admit of; but the best way of surmounting any difficulties or delays in obtaining such leave, is to apply to the Political Agent of the Company for the Panjáb, who resides at Lúdiána, on the borders of the Lahor territory. To all the unimportant requests of the Company, Ranjít Singh lends a very willing ear; and in the present Resident, Captain Wade, travellers find a most courteous advocate. To him, therefore, I applied, and being already furnished with directions from the Governor-General at Calcutta, that gentleman immediately forwarded an application on my behalf to the Raja.

I had hoped to receive his permission very shortly, but a dangerous illness occasioned me and my petition to be equally forgotten; meanwhile I remained in the cool climate of the Himálaya. The English have established two sanatariums, for the benefit of health and of a cooler retreat, in this mountainous region, at Masúrí and Simla, I made my arrangements, therefore, while the permission was preparing, to take a journey through the mountains, from the first to the latter place, and thence commence my route to Kashmír. Masúrí is the nearest station to the plains of India, inhabited by Englishmen. Simla is on the confines of the British possessions and those of the Mahá Raja. Through this desolate plain, where everything was withered and burnt up, I reached Masúrí on the 21st of June, with the intention of remaining there a few days, and on the 22nd, at break of day, I left the hospitable abode of Mr. Hamilton, to view the snowy mountains of Gangotri and Jamnotri from a neighbouring height. Having arrived at the desired spot on the Landor, I had full time to survey the majesty of scenes never to be forgotten. I was riding slowly homewards to enjoy the refreshing shower which fell on the parched land, reviving everything in nature, when finding the rain becoming more and more violent, I urged my steady horse onwards over the mountain paths to Masúrí. This rain, with the intermission of a few hours only, lasted eighty-five days, the monsoon prevailing in this part of India with more continuous wet weather than in any other.

During this long confinement, I heard frequently from Captain Wade, that he was in daily expectation of Ranjít Singh's answer; and no sooner did the season again clear up, than I proceeded to Simla, not over the mountain road as I had intended, for during the rainy season the passage is very insecure and uncertain, but over the plains. On the 19th September I quitted the beautiful and agreeable station of Masúrí, and after encountering some terrific storms in the plain, reached Simla by way of Ambala in six days, not without some difficulty however, for the rains had converted every brook into a torrent, and the roads were completely flooded. The last rain fell as I reached Simla, where I fully expected to have received, from Captain Wade, the long-looked-for reply from the Raja. Disappointed in this, I again wrote in pressing terms. The reply informed me, that I might certainly expect a favourable answer from the Raja, but time pressed and nothing was fixed. Of the three routes, I had taken a fancy to pursue the one which, skirting the highest mountains, led through the Berenda Pass by Ladák into Kashmír, and had never as yet been trodden by any European traveller. The season also was already far advanced. From Simla, the eye is accustomed to look over a splendid panorama, embracing a line of the snow-capped Himálayas, whose average elevation is 15,000 feet above the level of the sea, and which, according to the very lowest calculation, is two hundred and forty miles in length. This line, during the summer, in spite of its immense height, is not entirely covered with snow, except where it faces the north.

One morning I watched a cloud slowly approaching this far-distant chain of hills, and gradually I observed it tracing its onward path with snow, until it disappeared, and the sky was cloudless as before. The sight was beautiful, but it foreboded ill to my contemplated movements. In the course of the following day the snow melted, but the ridges of the Kaílas had put on their winter garments. It was twenty-three days' journey to the Berenda Pass; and long ere I could reach it the snow would have formed an impenetrable barrier against me; and, even had it not done so, how improbable was my chance of reaching Ladák or Kashmír, in this season, by an unfrequented route. The prospect of remaining all through the winter in the table-lands of Tibet was as miserable as it appeared inevitable; and this was all the information I could get at Simla. How far it was well grounded will shortly appear. They told me, also, that the road from the Panjáb into Kashmír was usually blocked up in the beginning of December; and here, for the benefit of future travellers in India, let me advise that no report should be acted upon as correct which does not rest on the personal experience of the informant; and that even in that case the greatest caution should be exercised.

My plans were consequently changed. It was not without great reluctance that I relinquished my purpose of going through the Berenda Pass. A different route was still open to me, and a shorter one, from Bilaspoor through Mandí and Dankar to Ladák; but all agreed in one fact, that the passes would very shortly be blocked up; and the fear lest my great object might fail, and that I should not reach Kashmír before this happened, deterred me from following that road. This finally determined me to take the direction of the lowest range of the Himálaya, and to travel by way of Bilaspoor, Jwálá Múkhí, and Narpoor; from thence, according to circumstances, to move forward to Kashmír either by Kishtwar or the Pír Panjal, preferring this route to the plain country of the Panjáb and Bimber.

My preparations were all made; but, although I had consulted my comforts as much as possible, I had made up my mind to relinquish anything which might in the slightest way impede my onward progress, and expected to be compelled to abandon my large tents, and even to leave my ponies to await my return from Kashmír, at the foot of the mountains, making my Jampan render me good service. The Jampan is a solid sedan-chair, supported between two thick bamboo poles, and borne by four men, twelve being the complement of bearers usually taken on a journey. It is the customary conveyance on a mountain excursion; but, to my own mind, I relied more on my own two legs than on the twenty-four legs of my bearers.

The Departure.

At last, on the 6th October, I received an intimation from Captain Wade that the Mahá Raja had given me leave to travel through his states, and that an officer would be in Bilaspoor on the 14th with the perwana, or royal mandate, addressed to the governors of the provinces through which my way might lead me. This perwana is of as much, or more importance in India than our passports in Europe; for whereas our passports only give permission to travel through the state which grants it, a perwana commands the governors of every place to furnish the traveller with bearers, beasts, provisions, and, in fact, everything he may stand in need of.

On receiving this notice I sent off my people, with all my baggage, on the 10th October, three days previous to my own departure, in order to give them time to prepare everything properly, ordering them to pitch my tent on the 12th, at the third station from Simla; and, in order to give them as much rest as possible, I did not leave Simla until the 13th, when I rode on one of my kind host's, Major Kennedy's, horses to Saree, breakfasted there, and then proceeded by Kunyar to Sahikoti. Kunyar is the residence of one of the Rajas of the Himálaya, who resides under the protection of the English. It is not my purpose to describe here any place on the left bank of the Setlej; I shall, therefore, only pause to observe that the situation of Kunyar is charming, that the residence of the Raja scarce deserves the name of a house, that his revenue may amount to a few thousand rupees, and his subjects to the same number. In Sahikoti I found my tents pitched in a picturesque little valley. According to their different religions and castes my suite was formed into small groups; white and black woollen tents pointed out the spots they had chosen, and each man had kindled his own fire to cook his food himself, according to Indian habits. It was evening when I joined them, and a simple but very well dressed repast, eaten before my tent, under the cloudless canopy of heaven, made me sensible of that independence which is enjoyed by Indian travellers especially. Once having furnished himself with what is absolutely indispensable, the European journeys through the land like a king: he can go wherever his fancy leads him; and need not trouble himself either about custom-houses, barriers, bridges, hedges, or turnpikes. Nobody inquires his name or demands his passport; no broken wheel stops his way; no full or intolerable inn by the road-side rouses his choler; every European he meets with is his friend, and every other being is his humble servant.

As soon as night came on I strayed out to visit my little encampment of one hundred and fifty men. To a novice in Indian travelling the variety displayed even in this limited area, the difference in features, manners, and habits, arising from the various castes and religions, would have afforded much amusement and surprise. For me, used to all this, the loveliness of night and the surrounding country, now illuminated with a bright moonlight, had more charms, though the thoughts of my home, far distant, but ever near to my heart, weighed heavily on my spirits.

The next day brought me to Bayoon, under the fort of Malaun, erected on the very highest ridge of a mountain, at least two thousand feet above the valley. Malaun is one of those points in the Himálaya, where, in the Gorkha war of 1814, the English met with a brave resistance. The following evening I reached Bilaspoor, a place under the rule of a Hindú Raja, called Kalur Raja.

From Simla, where this Raja, and thirty-two of the petty sovereigns of the Himálaya besides, have kept an agent since the peace of 1815, which placed them all under the protection of the English, Major Kennedy, the Political Agent in these parts, had forwarded a notification of my arrival to Bilaspoor, that my journey might not be impeded by any want of bearers or horses; and on my coming I found the Raja's own state, or durbar tent, pitched for me, in a lovely garden on the banks of the Setlej river. I was soon honoured with a visit from the Raja in person, attended by his miniature court. Of all the ignorant and unmannered native chiefs on this side of the river, he is, perhaps, the most rude and unpolished. The half hour he remained proved a very tedious one to me. His excesses in wine and spirit-drinking have well-nigh robbed him, though still in the prime of life, of the miserable intellect he might once have had. His favourites are two Bengalees, as unworthy as their lord, who speak a little English. According to the custom of the country, he expected me to return his visit, and receive the presents he had prepared for me; but the impressions I had received were so unpleasant, that through my Múnshí, Thakúr-Dás, I very politely excused myself, and agreed, as a compensation, to accept of seven mules, which were not to be had for any money. The animals were to be sent the following morning; meanwhile, however, a certain officer of Ranjít Singh's made his appearance, by the command of his master, and brought me a letter from Captain Wade, advising me that Mirza Abdul had orders to attend me to Narpoor, where a *Chobdar*, or herald, of the Mahá Raja's had received instructions to be in readiness to wait on me also. The Mirza affixed to his name, which answers nearly to the Turkish word Effendi, made me instantly suspect that he was a spy, and I was happy to find that he was not sent to remain any length of time a burden to me, through the ill-provided regions I was soon to traverse; for this escort or guard has prevented many travellers from seeing a country under its true aspect; and it is ever a most serious disadvantage, moreover, in India, to be obliged to increase the number of one's attendants.

Europeans generally come to India fraught with ideas and expectations of finding nature adorned in her richest garb, and a climate which injures health and shortens life, from the very enjoyments to which it tempts you. These anticipations are rarely realized; and the new comer then falls into an extreme opinion directly opposed to the first, that neither the country nor the climate offers any thing uncommon or attractive. Both opinions are erroneous. During the greatest part of the year, Hindústhan is little better than a wilderness; the Dekhan is a stony unproductive region, and to Europeans the climate is, in general, very trying. There are many parts of India, particularly towards the south-west, where the continual heat and damp act powerfully on the constitution, enervating the body, and making exertion most painful. In the north, the heat of the summer is terrific, the short winter is just as cold in proportion, and the transition from one of these seasons to the other, occupies but a few days. But although these remarks apply generally to the country, I allow that a traveller lights often on spots which leave any picture his imagination may have formed far behind; and if the skies favour him on such occasions, he may well exclaim, How beautiful is India!

Bilaspoor lies in a spacious valley, through which the Setlej winds its long and fertilizing course, while, in the distance, high and waving hills, crowned with villages, stretched for several miles, the snowy peaks of the Himálaya being distinctly visible on the horizon. The valley is extremely fertile, and every tropical plant flourishes in richer profusion here, than in most other parts of Hindústhan, as if the Great Author of all Nature had lavished his gifts on it without any reserve. The sun was sinking when first I gazed on this beautiful scene; the river rolled proudly on beneath the garden where I stood, surrounded on every side by a treasury of fragrant flowers, among which, rich orange and citron-trees entangled with jasmines, and groups of magnolias, wafted their exquisite perfume around, in the descending dews. The stars and moon rose one by one; not a breath was felt; the lofty palms rustled, and gently stirred their leaves, as if some spirit breathed upon them; the trees were lighted up by fire-flies, and within their deep recesses was heard the soft twittering of the birds, and the shriller tones of a kind of mantis, which has its dwelling in the citron-trees; in the distance bright lamps shining through the night, pointed out the temple, where loud voices and noisy drums were sounding to the praise of their idols; the fantastic costumes, the dreamy air, all, all combining together, might well have inspired the coldest spectator to exclaim, as he gazed, This is the very India of which I have dreamed!

But the old traveller in the East knows well that these fair scenes and calm moments are rarely enjoyed; and I wandered long through the broad terraces of the garden ere I sought my tent.

There was no repose for me here. This was the last night for a long time that I should pass in a country under European protection; and bidding farewell to the hope of sleep, I again strayed into the garden, where, except the mantis, everything was now buried in the repose of nature. Long I watched for the first break of early dawn through that lovely night, while all within my tent were sleeping heavily, enjoying the comfort within, and unconscious of the charms without. At length it made its appearance; the servants were soon up and stirring; and amid the din of packing and lading, I had time to survey leisurely the scene around me.

Towards the east, the giant form of the Bondelah mountain was faintly illumined by the first rays of the morning; while in the north, Tayuni, crowned with its solitary castle, caught the newly-awakened sunbeams on its loftiest peak. Tradition says, that in a cave on the top of the Bondelah, lives an invisible Bairagí, or Gosáin, a penitent hermit who, from time to time, shakes the ashes from his locks, when the whole valley quakes; houses are shaken down, and large masses of stone tumble from the mountain: these are the ashes, according to the inhabitants of the valley.

At Tayuni, an uncle of the present Raja has been confined for the last twelve years, for having, in the plenitude of his folly, ventured, after Ranjít Singh's treaty with England had changed the order of things, to pursue the same predatory course to which most of the Rajas of the Himálaya owe their possessions; forgetting that what was all right and proper thirty years ago, is now a criminal offence on either side of the river.

Towards the south, the three fortresses of Bahádurpoor, Futihpoor and Champa reminded me vividly of those knightly castles built on the summits of the hills in my native land. Not only is the likeness in situation to be traced: erected during the last century by the Gorkhas, like our own fortresses they served for the security of the little tyrants who plundered both travellers and inhabitants indiscriminately, and then retreated with their ill-gotten booty within their fastnesses. An end is now put to these robberies in India; regular contributions are enforced by the Company on property on one side of the Setlej; and no sooner does an individual give his portion—however small—to the common stock, than he claims the protection of the government as his right. Throughout his own territory, Ranjít Singh is free to levy what taxes he pleases.

But to return. The shoulders of the bearers, and the backs of the asses were all ready laden, when the Wakíl and the Wazír of the Raja of Bilaspoor came to attend me. These Wazírs, as they were called in the Himálaya, are, in point of fact, the real governors of the land, it being looked on as a disgrace for a Raja to concern himself about the administration of his country, or even know how to read or write. His sluggish existence is dragged out in the *Zenana*, the Indian harem, in eating opium, drinking brandy, and smoking; and in his few sober hours he holds his court or Durbar, or rides from one of his summer-houses to another.

The Raja of Bilaspoor has now attained his thirtieth year,—a period when the understanding and intellect have reached their prime; but Nature has been a niggard to him in these; and the quantities of opium he swallows have rendered him a disgusting object, with staring eyes devoid of expression, and a mouth always half open. The extent of his capacity may be easily divined, from the questions he asks of the persons who attend his levee, which are usually of the following nature:—"Are you well?" "How can I be otherwise than well in the Raja's presence?" To this, his Highness generally rejoins, "How old are you?" And being enlightened on this point, his next question is, "How many wives have you?" If, as in my case, the stranger answers that he is unmarried, the conversation suffers a sudden check; and to all the questions which the latter puts in order to while away the time, the Raja turns to the Wazír, that he may prompt some answer, which by good luck may be brought to light after five minutes' consultation between them*.

The Raja of the Himálaya being thus sunk into a state of stupid imbecility, we need not much wonder if the Wazír is supposed to be an influential favourite of the Raní, or first wife; but it usually happens in these cases, that if the husband's eyes are opened but once to his wrongs, they are soon closed on all things, and for ever. A case of this kind occurred recently in one of the petty states of the Himálaya, under British protection. After the death of the Raja, however, the Wazír so far overstepped the limits accorded to oriental exactions, that the enraged people burst into the summer-dwelling, then occupied by him and the Raní, and burnt it to the ground. The next morning, long after both they and their attendants had ceased to breathe, came a crowd to wail and lament over the accidental death of the Raní; but though the real facts were well known to every one, the crime was

* Shortly after the British had captured the fort of Viziadroog—the famous Gheriah captured in 1756 by Lord Clive and Admiral Watson—I was sent by government in my professional capacity to see to the reparation of its defences, and to take account of its military stores. On entering the inner gateway, I was struck with a little circular flat piece of wood, about three inches in diameter, with a handle, on which were cut in rude relief, Shri Angria. The Brahmin near me smiled at my curiosity, and said, that as his master was very ignorant, and unacquainted with writing, in place of signing passports for the egress of his retinue, they presented themselves before him with a pat of soft clay in their hands, which the chief struck with the instrument in question; which credential they exhibited to the guards at the several gates. Such is generally the state of ignorance of all the princes of India. Their females have often far more learning and sagacity.—*Ed.*

never brought home to any individuals; and the English Government soon gave up the inquiry they had instituted on the subject.

As my way from Bilaspoor led me through a part of the town, I purposed to follow it on foot as far as it skirted the river; but I too soon found out that my jampan was never more needed, for the streets are paved with flint stones about a foot in diameter, and as often loose as not, dislodging the unsteady foot of a luckless wayfarer, and knocking it violently to one side or the other. I was surprised to see the natives step lightly over these stones without once stumbling, until I discovered that long acquaintance with the loose ones enabled them, without much difficulty, to avoid them. The garden walls and inclosed places are well built with the same large round stones. For a mile onwards, the road adjoined the left bank of the Setlej; it then led to a rapid brook, and thence to the ferry boat, which was nothing more or less than a square box of wood, strongly put together, and having different partitions a foot high; I had no sooner come up, than I found about twenty persons had already taken their places; in addition to these, Ranjít Singh's two followers, and their horses; my Múnshí, on horseback, twenty of my people; and after all, the Wakíl and Wazír, with their servants, now stepped in. Against this last addition I stoutly protested, and took the part of the poor natives, who had arrived before us, whom the Wazír was ordering away, to make room for my bearers. It is in such matters that every Indian, invested with power, is an absolute tyrant, and considers all things on earth as made to obey the strongest. The lower classes enjoy a certain degree of independence, attributable to the smallness of their wants, the climate, and their indolent character, which is content with the least possible indulgence; but when a higher than themselves appears, they sink at once into nothingness, and from none do they receive less compassion than from hired servants. On all occasions, indeed, the poor Hindú is made to feel the bitterness of inferiority; and if he sues for the smallest favour, he is often sent back to his miserable hut day after day for many months, before he obtains even an answer; yet he bears all this without a murmur, in hopes of better times.

Frontier Ferry Boat on the Setlej, at Bilaspoor.

Baron Hugel's Travels, page 26

Our heavy cargo was at last set in motion, and we soon crossed the roaring stream, and landed safely on the opposite shore, although our strange vessel was half filled with water. The natives swim across the stream with the help of an ox's skin, inflated with wind, in an ingenious way. Having carried this on their shoulders to the shore, they spread themselves upon it on the water, laying fast hold with one hand, while they strike the water with a piece of timber in the other. The sight of a number of these skins, with the head and feet of the beast left on them as in life, constantly floating across the river, is very amusing. Higher up towards the mountains, where the Setlej rushes over rocks deeply embedded, and with amazing force, the passage is made in a basket firmly tied on each shore with ropes which are swung across the stream.

The Panjab.

We were put on shore near a picturesque temple, where I took leave of the great men, whom the Raja of Bilaspoor had sent as an escort of honour with me. We were now in the Panjáb, the dominions of Ranjít Singh, the Mahá Raja of Lahor, a vast plain bounded on the north by the Himálaya, and lying between the Indus or Atok, and the Setlej, called in this part, after receiving the waters of the Beas, the Ghara. The other three rivers which water the country, *Panjáb* meaning five waters, *Panj* being the Persian for five, and *Ab* water, are the Ravee, the Chinab, and the Jelum. The Setlej or Ghara falls into the Indus, which is called also the Sind, and the Atok; into these five large rivers flow several of less importance, of which the Beas is perhaps the most full.

Each of the districts of the Panjáb which lies between two rivers is called Doab, from *Do*, two, and *Ab*, water, and of these there are five, viz.: the Jalander Doab, between the Setlej and the Beas; the Baree Doab, between the Ghara and the Ravee; the Rukna Doab, between the Ravee and the Chinab; the Jeteh Doab, between the Chinab and the Jelum; the Doab-i-Sindi Sagur, between the Jelum and the Indus.

The three first are by far the most fertile districts; the others being hilly, with many deep ravines throughout. The natives, too, are generally inferior in intellect to those in the more fruitful country. The Doab-i-Sindi Sagur is of much greater extent than the others.

The natural advantages of the Panjáb are very great. Large productive plains, watered by the never-failing springs of the Himálaya, which swell into noble streams, capable of bearing the largest vessels, and favoured with a delightful climate, what has nature not done to make it and all its people contented and happy! I need hardly remind the antiquary, that in the days of Alexander the Jelum was known as the Hydaspes, the Chinab as the Acesines*, and the Ravee as the Hydraotes. To give some idea of the various names under which the same place is known in India, I may cite the Setlej, which in the mountains is called by its Sanscrit name *Satudra;* higher up the country, it receives the various names of Zangti, Naksang, Langzhing, and Samudrung; and nearer the Panjáb it is called Ghara. The Beah is called in Sanscrit *Vipása*†, and in different places by the natives, Beas, Veah, and Béya. The Sanscrit name of the Ravee is *Airavadi*, and it is known also as the Rhoas. The Chinab, in Sanscrit *Chandrabhága*, river of the Moon, is called by the natives Sandabhaga, Jenab, Jenal, Ghenal, and Ghenab. The Jelum, in Sanscrit *Vitasta*, is known also as the Behat; and the Indus is Atok in Sanscrit, Sind in the native dialect, and high up the country, Chu, Sechu, and Lingti.

Journey to Kashmir.

It was early in the morning of the 16th October, when my short passage across the Setlej brought me into the dominions of

---

* From the ancient Sanscrit name, Abi-sin.

† The ancient Hyphasis, from the Sanscrit, Vípása,—the Hydaspes, from Vitasta, and the Hydraotes, from Ravee,—or in its separate Greek form, ὕδωρ, ραοτης, may enable us to form some idea of the changes from the originals of other geographical and proper names, where the absence of certain letters in that language was supplied by the nearest sounds of other combinations.—*Ed.*

Ranjít Singh. My mind was engrossed with the future, which lay before me sad and solitary. Fatigues and dangers seemed to point out the road I had to travel. Though in the midst of a crowd, I was nevertheless a solitary being; in descent and colour, in education and religion, in dress and manners, and more than all these, in mind and heart, in every thought and feeling, I was absolutely alone.

Oppressed with these melancholy thoughts, I seated myself under the shade of a large Indian-fig tree before the temple of Jelakatel, and as my attendants wandered about in the distance, I keenly felt my own isolated state, without one near or dear to me, not one soul to sympathize with me in sadness, or to participate in any emotions awakened by the sight of nature's grandest scenes; not an individual to bear my last wishes to my distant friends, were I forbidden ever to see them more.

Although now in the territories of Ranjít Singh, I had not entirely quitted the Raja of Bilaspoor's country, for he is partly under the protection of the Company, and partly under the dominion of the Mahá Raja. To facilitate my observations in travelling through a country so little known, I had begun a small map on the other side of the Setlej, although I was under some apprehension that Mirza, who I hardly doubted had been sent by Ranjít Singh to act as a spy on my movements, would inform his master of my occupation, and receive instructions to stop any further continuance of it.

As far as the line to which English protection extends, the road is very tolerable for an Indian one, but when the Setlej is crossed, it is hardly possible to conceive that one can be in a country where any communication whatever is carried on. For a mile or more, the only road is over large stones lying loose in the path, which a few workmen might clear away in a day or two, but which are left there as a preliminary torture. On the height of Ladhera, it is alternately up and down slippery black rocks, where at one moment the traveller finds himself precipitated into a deep hollow, at the next, scrambling up the steep sides of the rocks, assisted only here and there by some steps three or four feet high, hollowed out of the stone. The ghunts, or little ponies of the Himálaya, were here in their element, while the mules and horses belonging to Ranjít Singh's officers were sorely distressed, and repeatedly fell down the precipices.

From these heights the Setlej, winding in its deep rocky bed through the mountain passes, had a most romantic appearance, and the country is interspersed with groups of buildings, before which the fields are formed into terraces carefully constructed and kept perfectly level. At each turn, the traveller hopes to find himself at an opening into the fine plain which seems so near him, until the continual ravines and steep ascents, the wearisome difficulties of his way, teach him how to bear disappointments. Near Mansala the road improves. Here I found a crowd assembled round a Bairagí, one of those classes of penitents which admit members of all ranks and castes. There are many such throughout India, but the particular rules to which these subject themselves, render them more remarkable than some others. Their disciples, carefully chosen for their natural talent, are subjected to a noviciate of several years, and poverty is the first vow they take. Then alone, and barely covered, with nothing but one small vessel, in which they cook the pittance of rice charitably bestowed on them by the way, they wander about from one part of Asia to another. The one I saw here was in the prime of life. His hair was strewed with ashes, over which a crown of wild flowers had been negligently placed; and another fresh garland hung low from his shoulders. His only garment was a piece of coarse stuff fastened to a rope girt round his loins, and his body was already almost grey from the ashes constantly rubbed on it. On seeing me draw near, the Bairagí beckoned to the crowd to stand back and advanced to meet me. My attendants all saluted him with the deepest veneration, and a Ram Ram Shahjí, The blessing of God on thee, my lord, and the bearers stood still, expecting me also to shew the like respect. The penitent took the crown of flowers from his head, and would have sent it to me, but as no one offered to take it from his hand, he moved forward himself. I had never seen before, even in the presence of an Indian Bairagí, such an exhibition of religious fanaticism. After he had held the crown outstretched towards me for some time, he replaced it on his own head, and took the garland from his shoulders, waiting for some one to convey that to me; however, not a soul stirred a foot, and I therefore invited him to crown me himself. He did this after a little delay, and, as I remarked, with a certain repugnance and haughty bearing, as though he were doing something to which his pride could hardly condescend. On inquiring who he was, he answered, "My name was Tamú, and I was the Wazír of the Raja of Nadaun. Now I serve a higher master, and my name is Tamú Shah."

These Bairagís are philosophers who neither refuse the necessaries of life, nor assume the manners of a Diogenes. They are of independent habits compared with most other classes, and the traveller who can overcome the first impression of a suspicious sanctity, caused by the strangeness of their appearance, will receive more information from them in one interview, than if he travelled from one court to another throughout the whole of India.

Just before we reached the next village, Dukolee, the country suddenly opened on a plain which seemed to extend between the Tayuni and Panauli mountains, as far as the snowy hills in the north-west, and the Bondelah mountain behind Bilaspoor in the south-west. The view over this plain is remarkably fine. In the foreground lies a forest of splendid Indian-fig trees, under whose shadows hundreds of men and beasts might rest, and whose branches are alive with the feathered creation. The high hills are, in many places, crowned with villages, and the eye ranges over an immense variety of plants, the rich natives of an Indian land. Another easy ascent, and then a gentle declivity, and we reached Kumagaheti, the first day's halt, where my little tent was pitched already in the plain. *Gaheti*, means a Serai or lodging, where the traveller finds what he needs to cook his meals; viz., rice, spices, butter, fruits, peas, beans, and fodder for his beasts, and besides these, some *charpáys*, or beds, are provided. These beds are made of cords stretched tightly over a frame of wood, and resting on four low feet; but wo to the unlucky traveller who reckons on a night's rest on one of them; it requires the thick skin of an Indian, or long habit, to support the attack of the hosts of vermin which swarm in every crevice. The distance from Bilaspoor to Kumagaheti is reckoned at eight coss, I calculate it at fifteen miles, which took me five hours to travel, the heat being most oppressive among the black rocks.

Saturday, October 17th, at six in the morning, the thermometer being at 59° Fahrenheit, there was lightning in the north-west. This day's journey to Meyrí was nine coss, about eighteen miles; a cold morning was succeeded by a day, which, by contrast, seemed warm in the extreme. The thermometer, however, at one o'clock, was not higher than 81°, and remained stationary until five. The country was more open than yesterday, but the ascents and descents endless. An invisible stream which rushed through a little forest of pines until it formed a foaming waterfall, seemed, to my fancy, much more romantic than the reality might have shewn it to be. The high chain of hills, called Mori, with its everlasting snows, was not intercepted from my view by any intermediate high ground, but at times, the clouds, which hung over it, announced that rain, perhaps a heavy storm, was visiting that region. The highest point of the mountains is called by the natives Champa.

At Habliheti, the station for the night, close by Meyri, I found neither wood nor any other provision, and was forced to send the Kotwal two miles, to obtain food for my people; at five o'clock the bearers came up with my baggage. This was a lesson to me to make my attendants always precede me in future, for I felt that my difficulties would probably increase as I proceeded, and that I must make up my mind, either to travel very tediously, or to dispense with my numerous suite. In the first case, I might certainly reach Kashmír, but it would not be before the next spring, for when once the snow falls in the mountain paths, all intercourse with India is at an end for many months.

Some persons may conclude, that after five years' experience in travelling, distance and solitude, whether in India or New Holland, would cease to be painful. Habit, however, which can bring us to endure so much, has, nevertheless, its prescribed limits, and to some men, every day casts a stone more on the weight that oppresses the heart, until, at length, nature can bear no more. A tombstone, in some sequestered spot, eventually points out the place where the lonely traveller has taken up his last sad earthly rest.

Had I only followed the plans I had laid down for myself at Bilaspoor, I should have got on much faster; but now, I was encumbered with the Raja of Bilaspoor's people, and it is always a matter of perfect indifference to these Orientals, whether a traveller is delayed a month more or less on his way on their account.

By night-fall all my baggage was collected together, except the large tents; my people all cried out, that it was the Múnshí's fault, that the bearers would not set out until noon, because they were not sufficiently paid. I was obliged to promise, that I would set the matter right when he arrived. In the mean while I strolled out to watch the sun then going down behind the hills. The scenery was peculiarly wild and romantic. In a deep hollow a stream runs hurriedly along the plain, forming cataracts so closely hemmed in with rocks that it is impossible to approach them; the deep rushing sound betraying their existence long ere they are perceptible. A little further on the river widens; the rocks rising, as it were, into perpendicular walls, the spectator looks down on the water beneath into a deep abyss. Tropical plants wave on either bank, and all looks picturesque and mysterious, not forgetting some little villages reposing peacefully under lofty trees. It was the season of rice harvest, and I was delighted to hear from a peasant, that it had been a very abundant one. I learnt that in this part five seers, about 12½ lbs., of rice cost from three to five farthings*; this

* In the original, "ten German pounds of rice cost from two to three kreutzers;" here, as elsewhere, the reader will find such quantities reduced to English money and weight respectively, which I thought it better to insert in the text. The kreutzer of Vienna is reckoned at the ordinary exchange of 585 to the pound sterling; the pound of Germany, at the rate of 100 pounds to 123½ English avoirdupois pounds.—*Ed.*

seemed to me little enough, but I said to my informant, carelessly, "I see you take me for a European, ignorant of your Indian prices, or you would not ask me so much." The man smilingly replied, "You are perfectly right in your conclusion,—I did so."

My little tent was set up between two citron trees, which were rather insufficient to protect me against the sun while it remained high in the heavens. Towards evening the thunder rolled in the distance, and the lightning was very vivid; I was afraid that a storm of rain was approaching to deluge our little encampment, but as the night advanced, the clouds gradually dispersed, and the air became most refreshing and delightful.

Sunday, October 18, thermometer, at six o'clock, 59° of Fahrenheit. There are certain days in one's life when we seem to ourselves to feel as uncomfortable as man can be, until the issue shews us that our troubles in this world are at least one half of our own creating: such was the result of this day. Apprehension that I should be detained from Kashmír the whole winter, irritated my mind; full of impatience therefore, I was up before dawn, determined to be on my way early. Happily disappointed in my expectation, that the large tents would not be brought during the night, I did not suffer this to interrupt my preparations. In this, however, my followers did not second me, for the bearers and muleteers, mostly the subjects of the Raja of Bilaspoor, one and all flatly refused to accompany me. The latter threw the baggage on the ground, and attempted to drive away the cattle; this I resisted, very uncertain at the same time how the affair would terminate, and very much afraid that, at least, I should have to pass the day where I was. The sixty-four bearers from Bilaspoor had received part of their wages in advance, in order to provide themselves with food; they now demanded the remainder before they quitted the station.

The Panjáb bearers rarely receive any remuneration in return for their services; on the contrary, they are compelled by the government, without whose permission nobody can travel, to perform their duty gratuitously; I had engaged, however, to give the poor fellows a sum, which, according to the low price of rice, their only food, would, in one day, have supplied their whole family for a month. I was now in a critical position. Earlier dangers had warned me, that if these men were at once paid up what they were hired for, they would, most probably, run away to amuse themselves with the money elsewhere, but as my people all assured me, that as soon as they were paid, they would willingly take up their burthens, I at last gave in, and desired the Múnshí, who strongly opposed my resolution, to satisfy their demand at once. Scarcely was the money in their hands, than what I had anticipated came to pass; they decamped, and with them also the Raja's soldiers. Perhaps there are few things more difficult than to know how to deal with ignorant men; last evening the Múnshí had given these bearers an anna, and they had refused, on that plea, to move a step further; now that they were paid their whole wages they ran away. I ordered my Múnshí to make a formal complaint to the Raja in my name, and to insist on the punishment of the soldiers who had abandoned their posts, but no good resulted from my application. At length I found in the little village of Meyrí, ten bearers willing to give their services, and with six who had stood to their posts, being, in fact, bound on a pilgrimage to Jwálá-Múkhí, and an additional dozen pressed, with some difficulty, into the service from the country around, we managed to start. This unwillingness to labour only for one day, to earn subsistence for a month, so often found throughout the East, appears extraordinary. These men were all apparently in the most abject poverty, and yet nothing short of blows would make them industrious. Seeing now that all things were in due train, I mounted my ghunt, and desired that ten of the Jampan bearers would assist in carrying the luggage and follow me. Next came the turn of the five drivers, who refused to budge an inch with the cattle. The foremost, an old man, swore that we might break his head, but that nothing should make him quit Habliheti, and though my servants had tried the effects of blows on all the others, on this stubborn old fellow, being a servant of the Raja's, they dared not lay their hands. I remained, for a long time, a silent spectator of what was going on, but when they all proceeded to seat themselves on the baggage, and thus effectually prevent the packing being continued, I thought it high time to interfere, and seizing a very efficient bamboo, I very soundly thrashed the whole five, not even respecting the person of the Raja's servant. This *argumentum ad hominem*, used very reluctantly, and for the first time in all my travels, immediately put every doubt to flight. I heard not a word more of complaint: the animals were soon in motion; but I observed, with many misgivings, that their strength was quite unequal to their task: in crossing a rivulet, the poor mule, bearing the heavy fly, or outer covering of my large tent, staggered and fell, and the load being made still heavier by the soaking it had received, it became perfectly unmanageable. In vain we essayed the backs of his fellows, not one of them was sufficiently strong; leaving one of my people, therefore, to look after the load, I spurred onward, thinking to find sufficient bearers at the next village; but I was not yet thoroughly acquainted with the Jalander Doab and its inhabitants. Not an individual would stir, out of a very populous village, until he received the orders of the Wazír. I shewed them money, and inquired whether they did not consider a rupee of far greater value than a Wazír's order. They were deaf, notwithstanding, to my remonstrances, till at length the Chaprásis compelled two of them to carry the load. Again I had reason to regret, that I had not hired these bearers by the month, as in some of my former travels.

All these petty annoyances detained me the whole morning, still they could not entirely rob me of the enjoyment derived from the splendid view of the mountains which towered in majestic grandeur high over the plain we were now in. The country, gradually, became more open, and in this part consisted of spacious valleys or of plains, surrounded and skirted by hills, which were sufficiently steep, without costing such infinite fatigue to surmount them, nor were the streams which hitherto had rushed so furiously over their deep rocky beds, so frequently met with. From several points I caught a fine prospect of the snowy hills, which are connected with the Himálaya by a single mountain range. This chain of hills is known as the Mori.

Hamirpoor is about ten miles from Meyri. Here I found my tent pitched under a fig-tree, the aspect of vegetation is still tropical.

The magnificent foliage of the mango, fig, and musa paradisaica plantain, is intermingled with that of the oak of Simla, berberis aristata and bramble. Monkeys are not common in Bilaspoor, but parrots, the beautiful squirrel of the tropics, and many kinds of the dove and the turtle-dove, are abundant.

The water is very pure; in every village, and often in the midst of a wood, I found a spring walled about, generally in a small square, with steps leading down to it, and a paved space, the spring flowing from a niche cut out frequently to represent one of their deities, usually either Ganesha or Lachmí. At these springs the Hindú women are often burnt with the corpses of their husbands. The temperature at six o'clock, A.M., was 59°; at three o'clock it marked 82°; at six o'clock, P.M., 74°. In the course of the evening upwards of a hundred men came to offer themselves as bearers; fifty were hired to go as far as Jwálá-Múkhí, and twenty were sent back for my baggage to Meyrí, and to the brook where the fly of my tent was still left.

Monday, Oct. 19th.—I was up before dawn, and ready to start. Jacquemont never said a truer word in his life than when he called Ranjít Singh's soldiers the most lazy, good-for-nothing rascals on earth. My tent was standing about three hundred paces from the door of the Gaheti, the caravanserai of this country, where Mirza had passed the night, and whence all my messages and commands could not extricate him. The coolies began to rebel also, and refused to officiate any longer as bearers. I was once more therefore under the necessity of taking the law into my own hands; and entering the Gaheti, dragged Mirza very unceremoniously off his charpáy, and sent him to arrange with the mutineers. In customs, form, and dress, these people resemble the natives of upper Hindústhan; but instead of the gentleness and willingness to oblige, invariably found there, the inhabitants of the Panjáb are stubborn and disobliging to a degree I never met with in my life before. Neither entreaties nor threats can make them keep their promises, and this, not from any idea that they shall not be paid, but out of sheer sullenness and stupidity. In three days they can easily earn nine annas, sufficing to support their families for a month. At first, I inclined to the belief that they were afraid of the weight they had to carry, until I saw one of them refuse to bear a small chair and half of a table on his head, certainly not more than ten pounds' weight altogether; and my only consolation, amid these scenes of alternate strife and forced submission, was, that when they were hungry they would work.

I was overjoyed to see my Múnshí return with the rest of my baggage from Meyrí, and related to him all my grievances, desiring his interference to maintain order among my followers. In truth, it was very disagreeable to me to see the constant and yet perfectly useless ill-treatment practised by Mirza and the soldiers of the Mahá Raja on these miserable Hindús. The Múnshí walked away, took his seat under one of their sacred trees, and in the course of a short time had congregated round him a crowd of the villagers, engaged more men than we absolutely needed, besides cattle to carry the heavier loads; and I found myself most happily rid of the Raja of Bilaspoor's useless drones, to whom I made amends, however, for the blows I had given them.

When we were fairly once more under weigh, and I was following the train through a forest of palms, I inquired of the Múnshí how he had managed to make these idlers so compliant on a sudden; he answered that he had opened his dress and shown them his brahminical cord*, reminding them that he was their master, and yet a servant of the great king, the Mahá Raja, who was close by. "And will you presume," exclaimed he, to them, "to refuse to obey for one day, him whom I always serve,—you, who are cultivators, and I a Brahmin!"

---

* The Brahminical cord consists of six or more threads of cotton, called the *poita* or *janwa*, with which every male is invested at the age of eleven or twelve years, and constitutes the sacred distinctive badge of that class. On the solemn occasion of their investiture, the youths are first taught the mysterious words entitled the Gayatrí, "Let us meditate on the adorable light of the sun, the divine ruler, Savitrí, may it guide our intellects." No other class of Hindús is admitted on pain of death, to a knowledge of these mysteries, nor can we wonder at the reverence all others pay to the privileged class.—*Ed.*

This day's march was only ten miles; at first the road led up a gentle ascent through a wood of pines; four or five miles further on, it opened suddenly on a temple, the outer walls of which were entirely concealed by some enormous fig-trees. This edifice is called Samnai, and commands an extensive and lovely prospect over the Kunyar, the large temple of Khagul, and on the other side a smiling country, interspersed with villages, and watered by the Beas. Towards the south rises another hill, crowned with two strong forts; and to the north-west towers the snow-capped Mori, the highest peak better known as the Palam Kidar.

The Khagul temple, lying on the declivity, would be passed by without notice in the south of India, where the immense mass of buildings sometimes covers a space of not less than a quarter of a mile; but here, in this comparatively poor and desolate country, it is considered quite a curiosity. In the centre of the large court, which is surrounded by high walls, and paved with smooth stones, circular steps lead down to the tank, where a spring gushes forth from the mouth of a sculptured cow. The adjoining edifice is for priests, and for the reception of pilgrims.

The road continues along the right bank of the Kunyar, which flows calmly along, in a channel which seems about fifty fathoms in width, but when I saw it, it was not more than one-third filled, and in most places fordable, over the huge stones which form its bed. The road is so painful in many parts, owing to the steepness of the rocks, that I chose rather to ford the stream a second time than brave them. At Ril I halted, taking up my quarters for the night in a deserted garden of the Chiri Raja. In the course of the afternoon some native women came to complain of the depredations committed by my people on their citron-trees, producing, in confirmation, a basket filled with the fruit; and despairing of my influence over the unruly bearers, I was obliged, for peace' sake, to pay them the estimated value of the fruit on their trees, which amounted to no more than two rupees; this settled, I suffered the men to finish the demolition of the crop, which was effected in a very few minutes. I must add that this was the first complaint of the kind that I had heard, and that property in general is nowhere more strongly respected than in India*. The thermometer, at six o'clock A.M., was at 62°, at noon at 82°, and at six o'clock P.M., at 80°.

Tuesday, Oct. 20th.—Thermometer in the morning 66°, at 6 P.M. 78°. Still along the Kunyar, by a hill called Jelalika Tiba, which forms an important object in the landscape; on its side are eight or nine groups of villages which are called Jelalis. The clay hills here, all broken and washed down by the rains, reminded me on a small scale of those deep defiles near Agra, where an army was once entangled and perished. By Jelali are standing detached masses of buildings, like towers, which so much resemble those time-worn Dhagoba near Anarayapoor in Ceylon, that until I approached quite close to them, I imagined I should discover unquestionable traces of Buddhism.

Nadaun is four kos, about seven miles, from Ríl; and is a place of some importance, with two hundred or two hundred and fifty houses, and a resident Raja. I chose my station under some fig-trees on the high bank of the Beas, to which was a handsome flight of stone steps. In former times, Nadaun was the residence of a Raja called Gangra, whose yearly revenue was no less than ten lacks of rupees; but Ranjít Singh very unceremoniously robbed him of the whole of his territory on the right bank of the Beas, and at his death his two sons divided the remainder, acknowledging the supremacy of Ranjít Singh, so that the present Raja Judibeer, a young man not more than twenty years of age, is not supposed to be worth more than forty thousand rupees a year. As soon as I arrived, one of his attendants was dispatched to request that I would cross the river. Naturally concluding that the Raja very politely wished to exchange my present station for a better one, I was on the point of ordering a move, when my Múnshí whispered to me, that the other side of the river belonged to a different Prince. On hearing this, I desired him to go and clear up the matter; but Mirza hastily interfered, and bade me remember that he was the person charged

* What a singularly valuable tribute to the native character, and the influence of British generosity and justice in regulating such feelings, from a German nobleman of high birth and great good sense.—*Ed.*

by Ranjít Singh to manage everything relative to my journey. It was in vain to dispute with him, so turning to the poor messenger, who humbly replied to all the impertinence of my people, "Such were the orders I received," I merely intimated my intention of remaining where I was. I notice this as the first act of positive rudeness ever received from an Indian Raja, and I can hardly now persuade myself that it was so intended by the Raja of Nadaun. If it were, I have little doubt that my companion Mirza, knowing how fully alive he must have been to the necessity of keeping his misbehaviour from the ears of Ranjít, made him pay dearly enough for his promised silence on the subject.

In the evening I strolled out into the plain, which, from the shores of the Beas, surrounds the little town for about two miles. I soon found myself an object of great curiosity to some armed riders, who had probably heard Mirza speak of the great white lord who was the friend of the East India Company, and had sallied forth to see me. That I must be this lord my complexion told them; but that I should be walking alone, or walking at all, seemed rather to stagger their belief in the story, and after staring in my face, they hurried away, I dare say, to relate the incredible tale to the Raja. As I returned, I found the whole town in commotion, and waiting for me with curiosity strongly depicted on their faces, and as every one after staring at me followed my steps, I was accompanied back to my tent by the whole population of the place, my servants all rushing out in the opposite direction, to know what could possibly have happened.

Throughout all seasons, the Beas, here called Beyah, is full of very pure and rapidly-flowing water. Before the entrance to my tent, I found a mendicant, who made his petitions in a song, and on my orders being given that he should receive no money, he seated himself on the ground, and gave me to understand that there he should remain during the night. This was no sooner said than done, and his screams were much louder than before. I was beyond measure annoyed with the fellow's obstinacy, and aware from experience that I must give way, or expect something even worse, I gave him a trifle, on receiving which, he immediately sprang on his feet, and danced out of sight.

The stone steps leading down to their rivers, is the best place for a stranger to observe the manners of the natives of India; for as every Hindú, male or female, must wash three times in the day, it is here that they come, and present to the eye of a stranger a scene of variety which well deserves a more particular description.

Wednesday, October 21st.—Before dawn I was on the other side of the Beas, in the Baree Doab, the immediate territory of Ranjít Singh. The river winds here in so many different directions, that it is scarcely possible to trace its course with any accuracy. The right bank is level, but the left is very hilly, the Josun and Khola mountains sinking in these parts gradually into the plain of the Panjáb. The far-famed Jwálá-Múkhí, the resort of so many fanatical devotees, is near this, and long ere it is reached, temples, tanks, and Fakírs are seen, sure evidences of the neighbourhood of some holy shrine. Before I settled myself in my tent, which was pitched at a little distance from the village, I paid a visit to this remarkable temple. Jwálá-Múkhí is of considerable extent, containing at least five or six hundred houses, and a very large population, among whom a great proportion are Gosáins, Bairagís, Yogís, Játs, and penitents of all sorts. To all who die here a grave is set apart, with a *lingam* on it, signifying a worshipper of Siva, and an incredible number of these occupy almost every vacant space. In the midst of a spacious square, shaded with lofty fig-trees, are set the tents of pilgrims of higher rank, and I was rejoiced to find that my attendants had chosen another spot, as the bazaar was close by; the noise and dust on the one hand, and the certainty of losing sight of most, if not of all of them in the passages of this ever irresistible attraction on the other, would have been disagreeable enough. The collection of images, chaplets, and amulets in the shops seemed quite countless.

The temple stands about one hundred feet up the plain. Two Brahmins, stationed at the door, demanded whether I had received permission to enter, and being answered by Mirza in the affirmative, they escorted me through an outer and high building to the stone bridge leading to the entrance-gate. It is true I should have walked much quicker and more comfortably into the bargain, if they had taken me over the straight broad path usually followed; but then I should not have had the honour of hearing the great drums beat in the first building, which are said to be distinctly audible ten miles over the plain. Once through the great gate, the spectator beholds a vast number of little temples scattered over the rocky height, and with the large one inclosed by a high wall. They are one and all of stone, very solidly constructed, many, indeed, are hewn out of a single stone. The cupola of the principal temple is richly gilt; and before the door stands another tiny edifice, in which I only saw two sculptured tigers lying, richly gilt, but horrible in their appearance. This door only admits one person at a time; and the priests would not permit me to pass through, in spite of the remonstrances of Mirza, who persisted that he had been commanded to take me in. I sided, however, with the priests, to their manifest delight, having attentively surveyed the interior from the entrance.

The same ideas of profanation do not exist in the Sikh as in the Hindú faith, and they admit Europeans into the interior of their temples; thus, although Jwálá-Múkhí is a Hindú place of worship and pilgrimage, the commands of Ranjít Singh often compel the Brahmins to be silent, and facilitate the intrusion of Christians. The interior of this great temple is divided in the middle by a stone wall; in the centre of the fore-court is hollowed out a pit, like our graves, having seats at either end, on which the Fakírs place themselves. A perpetual flame arises from this pit, and I observed, where I stood, that from two places in the smooth rock similar flames were bursting to a height of about eight inches, or less. The worshippers, on entering the sanctuary, deliver their gifts, consisting usually of flowers, into the hands of the Fakírs, who first hold them over the flame, and then cast them into the body of the temple. There I perceived, also, several jars filled with ghee, or melted butter, which I imagined to have been brought by some pious devotee; but I had afterwards good reason to believe this was a little artifice on the part of my friends, the Brahmins. I entered afterwards, without any hindrance, the little temple of Gogranáth, dedicated to the patron deity of the Gorkhas; a circumstance which convinced me that formerly, at least, it must have been a place devoted to the Buddhist worship, which recognises no distinction of castes. The name of Gogranáth, one of the thousand appellations of Buddha, confirmed my first impressions, and I have little doubt that it was once applicable to the whole of the temples inclosed within these walls. I was about to say, that on descending a good many steps I saw flames issuing from two places in the perpendicular wall; and, on examining more attentively, I perceived, where the fire was burning, little cavities in the smooth stones, with just the same appearance as when a burning-glass is made to consume wood; the flame issuing, not from any aperture, but from these minute cavities, emits a scent like alcohol burning with an aromatic and most agreeable mixture, which I could by no means identify. Under each of these flames stood a pot of water, of the same temperature as the atmosphere, the condensed residue of the gas thus deposited, takes fire on the application of a light, and burns for more than a minute. The surface of this water I found in continual motion, as though in a state of ebullition, but it is almost tasteless. The fire is of a reddish hue, and gives out very little heat. Altogether this is one of the most extraordinary phenomena I ever recollect to have witnessed; and, no doubt, in distant ages was one of the spots most thronged by fire-worshippers. The sight of this flame rising out of the earth, perhaps long before any building was near it, would doubtless add much to the influence of their superstition on the minds of the attendant worshippers; for this still seems to be the case, although much of the marvellous is lost by confining the flame within the walls of a temple. In different parts of the building are seated Fakírs of most extraordinary appearance, clothed with the attributes of their deities, and condemned by themselves to pass their whole life motionless as statues. One of them represented Gogranáth himself, but, instead of the folded hands of Buddha, his left arm was outstretched, and resting on a silver pedestal, so cleverly managed that it never can fall off; another was covered with ashes, and looked exactly as though chiselled out of stone, but as he gazed about him with a fearful stare, it seemed to me that his fanaticism had already, or soon would rob him of his reason.

That this temple was originally dedicated to the Buddhist worship I think admits of no question; its proportions within; the four square pillars which support the roof; the fact that no images are to be seen within or without; and that no difference of castes is observed within its walls; the name Gogranáth; and, finally, the graves around it, sufficiently evince to whose honour it was first erected. Very different are they all from the towers of the temple of Jaggernáth, in the desert of Orissa, whose great idol is carried about once a year, on the anniversary of its dedication, on an immense car, drawn by willing thousands; and before whose wheels hundreds fling themselves, firmly believing that such a meritorious death must insure their eternal happiness.

Female dancers are very numerous about the temple of Jwálá-Múkhí, and they are rather fairer and prettier than usual. More than twenty, decked out with lilies, made their appearance before my tent-door in the afternoon, but I was ungallant enough to send them away unrewarded, in spite of their tender ditties and the bells they sounded so invitingly on the tips of their fingers.

In the evening I paid another visit to the temple. The golden roof of both the large and small buildings are most tastefully and richly executed, and were the gift of Ranjít Singh, in testimony of his gratitude to the Devi, goddess, to whom he ascribed his recovery from a dangerous illness twelve years ago. They were both executed in Jwálá-Múkhí. The temple measures eighteen feet square, and under the dome is about twelve feet high. The term *Jwálá*, signifies flame, to which they affix either *Múkhí*, mouth, or spirit, or the syllable *jí*, sir, lord; hence, the place is called indifferently Jwálá-Múkhí or Jwálájí. The whole is built like a fort, and enclosed by a wall about twenty feet high. In the streets of the town itself, many Fakírs have grave-like narrow niches erected, in which they live and die, and when dead, these holes are walled up, and the dwelling of the living fanatic becomes his tomb. I did not see a single old man among them; several have pretty houses and gardens about the place, not acquired, however, by their begging profession, for this barely produces enough to build their tombs; and they may be characterized as a class of men who prefer living either by begging, or on their previous resources, to occupying themselves with the concerns of their country; moreover, as an Indian Raja never permits a subject to decline more than one offered post, this pretence of serving God is often but an excuse for refusing to serve the prince. Some go about nearly naked, others wear an orange-coloured habit, while a third sect may be seen with long strings of berries about the throat, according as they are bound by the nature of their tenets or vows, and many travel from Kashmír to the Indus, from Persia to the Ganges, from the Himálaya to Ceylon, covered with ashes, and beggars in the strictest sense of the word. I shall speak hereafter of another sect which is richly paid, and constrained to habits of the greatest luxury, in order to show the world how beneficent their supporters are.

The temple of Jwálá-Múkhí lies on the right bank of a little stream, over which a slender bridge is thrown. Before the building through which they led me to hear the drums, is a spring in the form of a waterfall, and a tank for those pilgrims who desire to bathe. A wish to improve the little design I had made of the whole, led me to follow the open canal which supplies the waterfall, when I unexpectedly came into a charming valley between the mountain heights. A Fakír followed me in my walk, though at first I heeded him not, until seeing that he had no intention of departing, I turned sharply round and desired to know what he wanted; to my surprise he answered, that he was a Naik, or corporal in the Company's military service, and had obtained six months' leave of absence from his corps in Lúdiána, which he meant to pass as a Fakír at Jwálá-Múkhí. The very thought of such a penitent made me smile, and then wonder at the singular character of the people of this country.

This day chanced to be one of their great annual festivals, and the whole place, not excepting the holes of the Fakírs, was illuminated; from the mountain on which I loitered until late in the evening, I saw all that was going on; lamps hung in festoons on, and before the temple, guns were fired, bells were rung, and fireworks discharged in the air. I found the descent from the mountain rather arduous, but I reached my tent without any accident, and had the gratification of finding every one of my attendants, except Mohan Bír the Gorkha boy and Jwala the Chaprási, gone into the town; indeed, the occasion was one, on which it would have been too much to expect them to refrain from amusing themselves; and having no objection to solitude, I gave these two leave to sally forth also, and amuse themselves amid the din and tumult of the place. Mohan Bír soon returned, ostensibly to know whether I did not want something; but as on receiving my negative he still loitered about, I asked him whether he had anything to say to me; after a little hesitation he said that he should much like to know, why I was so earnest, even to the danger of my life, about things which could not give me any happiness in this world, or any reward in the next. I confess that the boy's question staggered me, particularly as coming from a Hindú; I felt that his wonder was very natural, and not wishing to evade his inquiry or leave matters unexplained, I replied, that in the mingled web of a European's life, it was not easy to say what might or might not have important consequences; that I might perhaps have cause to envy the simplicity of mind of himself and his countrymen, but that in his present station, whenever he saw anything hard to be understood in our characters, he might comfort himself with the reflection, that if we were richer and more learned, we were not for all that a whit the happier. He entreated me then, very earnestly, to go into the town and see the beautiful illuminations, and the hundreds of dancing women accompanying their steps with songs and bells; but although he was evidently grieved, that I alone should be in solitude while everything without was so splendid and joyous, I was immoveable, and he was obliged to return to more congenial scenes and leave me to myself.

Thursday, 22nd.—Thermometer, six A.M., 65°; noon, 81°; six P.M., 78°. Before sunrise this morning we were on our way. The people of Jwálá-Múkhí have such an opinion of the importance attached to their town, on account of the presence of the temple, that they conclude the East India Company must be solicitous to gain possession of it, and the Fakírs begged of me the sum of one rupee and four annas, for which they promised to pray the Devi goddess to prosper the English in their wishes; others were rather more presumptuous in their demands;—"Give me," they cried; "it is the same as giving it to God himself." This day's journey was through a country tolerably open; for although two lines of hills bounded the valley through which we marched, they were so low as to offer but slight impediments to our view, and none to our progress over them. We were approaching the Mori mountains very perceptibly; in the evening we halted at Kabli, one mile from the fort of Mongir; before the village is a small jungle. In my walk through Kabli, I was amused to see the pheasants running about the cottage doors like domestic fowls, and seemingly quite unconcerned at the loud barking of the dogs. It was dreadfully hot during the day, a scorching wind blew from the west, and reminded me of the intolerable heat I suffered between Lucknow and Agra. With the setting sun, it moderated a little, and the view of the beams of the departing orb, reflected on the snowy mountains before us, induced me, from its beauty, to attempt to carry away the remembrance in my sketch-book.

Friday, 23rd.—Thermometer, six A.M., 54°; noon, 80°; six P.M., 68°. This morning was bitterly cold, less owing to the temperature without, than to the situation of my tent, which was pitched by a brook in a hollow. Our road led by several villages, which were so closely overhung with trees, that they were not visible until we entered them. This was not the greatest difficulty I met with in the construction of my map; for several villages, belonging to the same Pergannah, and yet several miles apart, bear the same name, while those belonging to others are so intermixed with them, that one can hardly guess where the boundary lines terminate. The country was generally hilly, wild, and overgrown with jungle; but the road is pretty good, though extremely narrow, barely admitting a man with his load. Haripoor lies in a mountain defile, and is a place of some importance. On a hill, which rises from the valley, stands a fort, but the mountain being much higher behind it, makes it useless as a place of strength, though it might defend the town, except against the assaults of artillery. There is a large bazaar in the town, and the heights around are crowned with watch-towers, probably to give warning to the merchants of the approach of an enemy, that they may take refuge with their treasure and valuables in the fort. On the approach from Jwálá-Múkhí stands a little temple, scarcely ten feet square, dedicated to Mahádeo, which seems very ancient; several decorations on the exterior very much resembling those I had seen on many of the little temples at Salsette, and Ellora*, where the three heads, significant of the Hindú Triad, are found united over the entrance. The other ornaments are representations of sepulchres, significant of Buddhist worship. The Brahmin, who was throwing some of the sacred water of the Ganges over the ornaments within, informed me that the temple was three thousand years old, a date which, coming from one of his class, surprised me by its extreme moderation. Near it are some rocky walls covered with colossal images of the Hindú deities, cut out of sandstone, and evidently by hands unacquainted with sculpture. An incredible number of audacious monkeys abound in Haripoor. I had scarcely entered my tent, when a young Fakír presented himself, and would have forced his way in, had not my Chaprásis unceremoniously pushed him back. I was vexed to see them thus rudely thrusting him away, but they assured me that these Fakírs were the greatest thieves in the world. My strange visitant went away without uttering a syllable, but had no sooner seated himself in the centre of a square than he commenced a series of noises, more like the cackling of a German duck than any thing I can remember. The next moment he was surrounded by monkeys, running from every quarter, in the hope of being fed. Finding themselves deceived in their expectation, three of the largest forthwith attacked the Fakír, who had the greatest difficulty in warding them off with his stick. He was now beset by the people, who began to abuse him for cheating their favourite mon-

---

* Sashtee and Verool, changed by the Portuguese and English into other forms. It is worthy of remark, that the very misnomers of ignorant men are calculated to do good service to geography, by pointing out what are the most ordinary transformations, and thus lead to the identification of places, men, and matters of great interest in history. As here in this instance of Ellora, the letters *r* and *l* have manifestly changed places. And other letters, *m*, *b*, and *v*, are generally convertible.—*Ed.*

keys and then maltreating them. Besides these creatures, the trees are covered with parrots; peacocks also without number parade about the town.

The costume in these parts differs little from what I had observed elsewhere; the trousers are perhaps rather fuller, the turban always black, and the men invariably wear a long dark beard; the women a blue petticoat with a deep red border descending to the knee, and the indispensable veil, which, instead of concealing the face, is worn behind the head, and is always pink. Their houses are clean, particularly the substitutes for inns, called Gaheti, where the traveller finds the wherewithal to cook his meal and lie down; and before them is usually a little garden stocked with lilies, balsams, roses, jasmine, and other flowers. I saw the beautiful China rose growing in the hedges, with the Jasminum grandiflorum, in all its native luxuriance.

Among the crowd of men and monkeys which pressed forward to stare at the stranger were some jugglers, whom I hired to while away an intensely hot hour or two; they exhibited to me their much vaunted trick of making a shrub, three feet high, grow up in half an hour from the seed of a mango. They first put one into the earth, and in a few minutes show it sprouting up, and then again six inches high, always producing the roots; the last time it is a twig cut off, which they leave sticking in the ground; but the manner in which two men, two women, and two children, were all employed in trying to persuade me that the trick was really a truth, made me laugh very heartily, and that alone is a great matter for a solitary traveller to accomplish.

In the evening I strolled through the town, which consists of upwards of two hundred houses, and passing through an exceedingly rude gateway, covered over with huge figures of Hari and Hanúmán, I found myself at the top of ninety broad steps, which lead down to a broad river, the banks, generally, of rock scarped perpendicularly. The fortress on this side had a very imposing and regular appearance, being in the form of a square. Figures, and even the holes of Fakírs, are hewn out of the rocks. On the opposite bank were similar steps and a gateway, and on the stream were several water-mills with horizontal wheels, but they could only be stationed where I saw them, during the dry season, for as both banks are perpendicular, when the stream is full, the entire channel must be filled up.

The Kiladar, or commandant, invited me to inspect the fortress; this I declined, not feeling much interest in a strong post without a single gun. After this came a deputation from the merchants, praying me to accept, from their goods, any thing I might want; and on my declining this proffered kindness with many thanks, they insisted on supplying my people, which I was constrained to allow. The horrible noises made by the monkeys kept me awake till very late in the night.

Saturday, 24th.—Thermometer, morning, 60°; noon, 82°; evening, 76°. At the usual hour of four I was stirring. The last two marches had been so short that I now determined, if possible, to double them, particularly, as every one in my suite had, by this time, become thoroughly initiated into the duties he had to perform, a knowledge which is acquired very slowly throughout India. In fact, what Europeans require from their personal attendants, their groom, their cook, and, in short, from every man about them, is very different from what a native master would expect. The groom, for instance, lifts an Indian into his saddle, and then, as he runs along, keeps fast hold of his master's rein, while no European would suffer either the one service or the other, although he expects the attendant to be as swift as his horse. Again, the attendant on the person of a native has but to lay his master's clothes before him, and to take away what he has done with; the cook prepares two dishes, the rice and its spicy sauce; the table servant takes care to furnish two leaves, one for the plate and the other, generally a banana leaf, for the dish, which is all. What is this compared with the services expected of these poor beings by our vanity, luxury, and fastidiousness?

After fording the river, and mounting the steps on the opposite bank, we found ourselves in a small plain, hemmed in by mountains; on it are three small villages, called Bilaspoor, and a temple shaded with fine fig-trees, designated Bilása; five miles beyond this, is the lowest declivity of the Himálaya, which forms a forest-crowned height.

After passing the brook Koteli, we came once more on the plain, which appears to be divided from the great plain of India by an elevation near Jwali, not much more than sixty or eighty feet in height. Several streams carry off the water from the Mori hills into the plain, and though most of them, owing to their great width, are fordable during the dry season, they were now very full of water. It took me six hours to travel from Haripoor to Jwali, about eighteen miles.

Here I felt the difficulty of filling in my map, without the assistance of some intelligent native guide. No sooner did the people catch a glimpse of my convoy, than they all set off and hid themselves amid the thickets of euphorbia and opuntia, from which my servants in vain attempted to draw them out. My tent was pitched on the other side of the Gardadí, in the garden of a Fakír at Jwali, and in the afternoon the Thanadar, a venerable old man, came to pay his respects. His rank did not allow of my offering him a seat. I received him, therefore, standing outside my tent, and left the chair within if he were disposed to take it.

He accompanied me to the hill before Jwali, which is ascended by a good paved road. Forty or fifty feet above the plain stands a little temple, with two Fakírs and two monkeys; and in a very small pond of crystal water, I saw fish of the same kind as I had seen at Aurangabád in the Dekhan. Here, as there, they are considered sacred, and no living man of the place can recollect to have seen one swimming dead on the surface, a presumptive proof of the great age to which they live. They are in such numbers, that they actually appear to take up more space than the water in which they exist. To a weary traveller the prejudice in their favour is extremely provoking; for it is too much, when languishing after better fare, to cast one's eyes upon the very finest and most tempting-looking fish, and while anticipating a delicious repast, to be told that the creatures are sacred. But, in such a case, one resource is left; the palankeen bearers being generally expert anglers, you have only to order them to fish, without heeding the exclamations of horror uttered by the crowd, who not unfrequently resist the sacrilege by every means short of actual violence. In their distress they rush to the white lord himself to complain of the outrage committed by his orders, and then, sufficient time having passed to enable the anglers to satisfy not only his appetite but their own, he commands them instantly to desist, and on no account to disobey his orders in future.

Near Jwali stands a palace, in a dilapidated state, built by the Raja of Narpoor, which commands a very beautiful prospect of the mountains. At present it is only tenanted by the wives of the late Raja, whom Ranjít Singh drove out of his patrimonial territories. The country around is as destitute of plants as the plains of the north of India generally. Birds, on the contrary, of the parrot, búlbúl, and máina kind, are exceedingly abundant. Wild beasts are also very numerous, but I have not yet been able to procure so much as one specimen, though several are of a considerable size. One very much resembles our fox, and I pointed it out to my huntsman, and sent him in pursuit. He was away so long, that I got out of my jampan, and, gun in hand, proceeded in the direction the little animal had taken. The bushes being high, I had stooped down, in the hope of getting a sight of him in his hiding-place. Presently I heard a rustling sound, and was adjusting my gun to fire, when I saw the red turban of my servant; he, too, had heard me; unconscious, however, of this, he instantly lodged a volley of small shot in my clothes. The poor fellow no sooner saw what he had done, than he was ready to swoon with terror, but I cheered his spirits, and expressed my particular satisfaction that he had missed his game this once, at all events.

In the afternoon I wandered about the neighbourhood, which may be termed one vast wilderness. The soil seems good enough, but the feverish state of this part of India for some years past, has almost depopulated this place and converted it into a desert*.

Sunday, 25th October, thermometer 59°, 81°, 74°. Last night was

* There can be no doubt that a deficiency or total neglect of culture is always attended with the production of malaria; and in countries thickly wooded, or where from tropical warmth the growth of vegetation is illimitable, the decay of the autumnal and evergreen shrubs occasions the stagnant waters collected together by falling timbers and accumulated rocks to send forth most pestilential miasmata far and wide. In such cases there is an excess, as in desert tracts a deficiency of oxygen.—*Ed.*

no night of sweet repose for me. The Fakír kept a dog to guard his fruits and flowers from thieves, and the dog did his duty, barking without one moment's intermission, in spite of the blows he received from all quarters to bring him to reason. After this all the horses set up neighing, the wind rose and blew the leaves of the great fig-trees about my tent, and to finish all, a heavy shower pouring down on my packages, which had been left in the open air, convinced me that the best plan would be to start as soon as possible. The distance from Jwali to Narpoor is ten kos, I estimated it fifteen miles. The road leads into a valley, or rather into a part of that vast plain, which stretches away as far as the distant ocean. The country is pleasant, interspersed with villages here and there, while the immense Mori chain refreshes the eye towards the north-east; the plain is hence very far from being that same dead dull flat, unenlivened by verdure, that one travels over between Khanpoor and the Siwalik mountains; here, undulating hills rise gradually, and intersect each other, groups of trees also contributing to its beauty throughout. At the end of a few miles we came to a pond covered with the nelumbium, and here I tasted the nut for the first time. When unripe it has the taste of a hazel-nut, when ripe, it is too hard to be eaten. That this plant might be much valued in Egypt on account of its majestic flower, as well as its delicate taste, is extremely probable; but we need not go out of our way to seek in the pictures on their walls for a meaning which is very seldom literal; in them we certainly perceive boats filled with pleasure-hunters, enjoying themselves among the leaves of the nelumbium, which, together with the flower, float gracefully on the water, and with reference to this quality, convey a certain meaning in Hindú mythology. Notwithstanding it is not to be concluded that it was planted as food for the people, like our peas and beans. It does not flourish like the nymphæa cærulea both in flowing and still water, but grows chiefly in tanks, and hence can be seen but rarely in Egypt, where the water has generally a brackish taste; but a weightier argument against its general cultivation is the fact, that few flowers of this plant from Ceylon even to the mountains of Kashmír, produce any seed which germinates.

From the tank which has caused this digression, the fort of

Narpoor, on a neighbouring hill, from two to three hundred feet in height, has a very picturesque effect. To the Himaláyan traveller, who is accustomed to see every mountain with a peaked summit, it is strange to meet with one like this, crowned with a tabular space one mile and a half in extent, on which the little town, with its bazars and miserable streets and houses, is situated. I should reckon the population at six thousand souls, of whom two-thirds are Kashmírians, who have been settled here for more than a generation. Whoever has once seen this race of men, will never fail to recognise them by their white skin, their clear though colourless complexion, their long, projecting, almost Jewish features, with dark brown or black hair and beard, which distinctly point them out. The dress of the common people merely consists of a white woollen shirt, open in front, with long sleeves; a cloth hanging down from the head behind, completes this ungraceful and generally very dirty costume. The rich have adopted the Indian dress. Among the crowd that soon beset me, were some pretty girls, still in the age of our childhood in Europe, and on my tent being pitched, the whole crowd followed the Thanadar who came to pay his homage. To my no small astonishment I learnt from him, that the Chobdar appointed by Ranjít Singh to attend me to Kashmír had not arrived, yet so far from opposing my further progress on that account, he promised to give me two soldiers as a military escort in place of the two, who had only received instructions to accompany me as far as Narpoor. I instantly decided on starting the very next day, without waiting for the arrival of the Chobdar, but had now to make up my mind, whether I went direct by the mountains, from Kishtiwar to Kashmír, a journey of ten days over a lofty chain, which my gardener implored me not to take, he having once travelled by that route, knew full well the impossibility of conveying horses or even asses through the paths; or the longer but better road by Jammú. On reconsideration, I chose the latter.

A crowd of persons of both sexes and all ages surrounded my tent, resolved not to move away, until I had shown myself to them, which at length I was absolutely compelled to do, giving directions to the Chaprásis to drive them off by force as soon as they had received this mark of favour. The fort of Narpoor, like that of Haripoor, is completely commanded by a neighbouring height forming the lowest ridge of the Mori, which terminates to the north of the town. Here another commences. At a short distance from my tent I saw several persons praying in a little mosque situated between two tanks; and to judge from such instances, there is neither a superabundance of money or piety among the Mohammedans of Narpoor, for it is generally peculiar to the professors of their faith to adorn their mosques and tombs as richly as their means will permit, though in this instance both were conspicuously mean. They have also the custom of lighting many of the tombs in their cemeteries, which I would gladly see in Europe, since this constant remembrance of death and the dead is calculated to bring many important truths to mind.

Monday, 26th. My tent requiring some repairs, the tailors, all Kashmirians, began this morning, but could not complete their work before evening closed. Thus I was forced to rest, whether I would or not. But I had learned to submit to such trifling vexations in that great school, the world, where experience soon teaches a man patience, and the useful lesson, that very few have the good, or rather bad, fortune, to succeed in the attainment of all the wishes and intentions they had entertained.

One of my Shikarís brought me several very pretty birds, but nothing new; among them was a diminutive species of hornbill; on opening its crop I found nothing but vegetable food, contrary to the opinion of naturalists, who have always conjectured its large bill to be formed for the greater facility of catching lizards, on which it was supposed to subsist.

About noon the Chobdar's servant, whom the Mahá Raja had appointed to attend me from Lahor, made his appearance; he brought me a letter from Ranjít, and a bill for 101 rupees, which, together with four others sent, according to his information, to meet me at Jwálá-Múkhí, Hamirpoor, Haripoor, and Jamba, made up the customary token of welcome appointed by Ránjít Singh to travellers, of 505 rupees. I had fully made up my mind not to accept any present whatever in money, unless presented by Ranjít, or his Viceroy in

Kashmir, in his name, when I should have expended it in their native shawls; but as there was no means of declining this bill, without giving great offence, I put it in my portfolio as a curiosity*.

The man protested to me that his master was following in a very few hours: in the afternoon, however, he admitted that it would probably be four or five days before I saw him; as the day closed in he confessed that no master was coming at all; this is a very fair specimen not only of the veracity of the natives of the Panjáb, but of their manner of bringing out a disagreeable piece of intelligence. Why Ranjít's agent did not make his appearance, I was not to know: meanwhile, Mirza expressed so anxious a desire to proceed with me, that I determined to take him. Since I had been in the territories of the Mahá Raja, he had on many occasions proved himself very useful to me. Were there labourers to be pressed into the service, he was always at hand with money and fair words, and perfectly understood the valuable art of getting rid of the most troublesome of my visitors.

More than twenty of the dancing girls persisted in hovering about my tent, and at last I agreed to admit a party of four only within, to exhibit their skill in the dance. They were all Mohammedans, and could not sing a word of Persian; to make amends for this, they were very richly dressed, and had each, besides a ring passing through the left nostril, another at the tip of the nose, suspending a bright, round, golden ornament exactly before the mouth. All with one exception were tolerably fair, and had beautifully white teeth. At the expiration of an hour, I was very glad to send them away, for they sung worse even than in India, though they managed their voices rather better.

I had already enjoyed a ramble on the nearest hill, on the road to Kangra, which is twenty-six kos distant. They have a peculiar

* The giving and taking presents among Orientals is a mere matter of form, and is a pretty plain intimation, in most cases, that a much greater and more costly acknowledgment is expected from the subject to his sovereign, or the inferior to his lord:—nor is the present from the inferior tendered, in the first instance, without a like anticipation. The motives of men are every where the same, however disguised by custom or circumstance; and the whole subject, as it frequently comes under the notice of the intelligent Christian, in his relations, public or private, in India, is full of instruction.—*Ed.*

manner of grinding the clods that the plough encounters here. For which purpose, after the plough, which is made of two pieces of wood of the simplest structure, and without any iron share, has performed its part, four oxen or buffaloes are attached to a board, on which two men stand to steady it, and drive about the field in every direction. There is a considerable quantity of steel manufactured at Narpoor, and a number of forges, but I did not observe anything remarkable; I was more pleased with the beauty of a young Hindú female, who was walking on the flat roof of one of the houses, wrapped in a splendid gold embroidered veil, and glittering with the golden ornaments in her ears and on her arms. Her black hair, according to the fashion of the country, was perfectly plain, but arranged in a knot behind, and confined to the forehead by a small ornament of gold.

It was quite dark as I returned dispirited and alone towards my tent, with my gun over my shoulder. Something suddenly flew past me over the roofs of the houses, and being just in that sort of humour, when the chance of killing anything is satisfactory to the feelings, I took good aim, and the next instant, a vampire or large bat fell on the ground at my feet. The report of my gun had brought all the people out of their houses, and on seeing the creature, which was just able to crawl along, they set up a piercing cry. These animals, as I well knew, are considered holy by the native Indians, and I expected that their fanaticism would break out in some terrible vengeance on the slayer. Such an act of sacrilege has cost many a European his life, and I confess that the howlings set up on this disaster seemed to predict a similar fate for me. The tragical dénouement of an affair very similar to this, which had taken place recently at Matra, came to my mind. Two officers were attacked there by an old monkey, and instead of conforming to the custom of the country and driving the disgusting creature away with stones, they shot it without the least repugnance. The people instantly pressed on them, in spite of the interference of the magistrate, who protected them until they were enabled to mount the back of their elephant, and pursued them, hurling stones which wounded them so sorely, that, as the only means of saving their lives, they ordered the Máhút to drive their elephant into the Jamna and let it swim across. He did so, but the waters were then at their very highest, and elephant and riders were drowned together. By an equally sad death, two of my friends, Colonel Combes and Black, had given a convincing proof how dangerous it is to rouse the fanatical fury of an Indian mob. The same destiny seemed very likely to be mine within an hour; but the traveller, who wanders in strange countries among stranger people, is habituated to look death steadily in the face in all its forms. As for these things, I had resigned myself, on leaving Europe, to the very probable chance of never seeing it again: at this critical moment I did not feel even a sensation of surprise. They hemmed me closely round, one holding up the wounded creature, whose unearthly cry accompanied the chorus of angry voices, till I gradually gained the shelter of a house, which protected me from assailants in the rear, my gun keeping off the foremost of my complainants. There I remained for nearly a quarter of an hour, until some of the Thanadar's people were seen approaching, as I trusted, to rescue me. Whether, however, they thought their force not sufficient for this purpose, or, that after hearing the crime I had been guilty of, their superstition overcame all compassion, they soon turned their backs on the scene, and left me to my fate.

The noise then became louder, the threats grew more alarming. Fortunately, there were no stones to be found, but the task of forcing back my assailants with the gun became more and more fatiguing, until the light of day wholly disappeared. It was then that, quickly availing myself of the known inconstancy of feeling in the Indian character, and of the circumstance of darkness concealing the form of my sacred victim, I harangued the multitude with such happy effect on my sorrow for this mishap, and the precautions I would take in future, that their hearts were gradually softened, and to my infinite relief, I was permitted to find my way back to my tent, with life and liberty.

Tuesday, 27th, thermometer 55°, 80°, 61°. The road led down the hill I had climbed yesterday. There were little gardens on both sides, principally belonging to Fakírs, and now blooming with flowers. At the end of the paved road is a toll-house, where the poor Indian traveller is taxed for his baggage; the European passes free. We came next to the small river Behobon, which has hollowed out a deep bed between the mountains, and sweeps in a semicircle round Narpoor. The stream not being fordable, the traveller winds along it, sometimes on a level with the bed, sometimes on the mountain-path above. At length, after a wearisome journey of ten miles, we fairly descended into the plain, where my experience was again increased, One of my people shot an eagle. As my bearers were already heavily loaded, I offered a trifling present to a peasant who was working in the field, if he would carry the bird to the next village; but he refused, because his caste forbade him to do it. Upon which, one of the bearers exclaimed, "Thy caste forbid thee to touch the bird,—but it does not forbid the bird to touch thee;" and so saying, put the bird on his back, which of course was sprinkled with the blood; his scruples, however, had been overcome by the logic of my bearer, and he walked along without any further demur*. Four miles after we had lost sight of the river we reached Patankota, a stronger fort than any I had before seen, and yet, strange to say, the only one in ruins. It is in the plain, with regular ditches and a glacis, built of brick, and commanding an extensive view; the citadel within is remarkably strong.

The heat was dreadful, and although the thermometer was not so high as yesterday, I was far more inconvenienced. In the summer, Narpoor, from its position, must be one of the hottest places in India.

The women of the Panjáb are celebrated, and not undeservedly, for the beauty of their shape, their feet, and their teeth. To-day, when I came to the place where my tent should have been already pitched, I found nothing done, and on looking narrowly about for the Kalasí, on whom the superintendence properly devolves, I spied him, in some bushes near, engaged in very animated discourse with one of these fair ones. The man's good taste was as conspicuous as his negli-

* The use of the singular, is a mark of great indignity in India; as in this case, "thy" and "thee" are often coupled with most opprobrious and revolting expressions. How characteristic are such terms of a people, and the associations of thought; the Arab, the Jew, and the Quaker, in the simplicity of affection and nature, use the same style as a recognition of friendship.—*Ed.*

gence, for she most fully bore out the renown of her countrywomen for personal beauty, but I was sorry to be under the necessity of disturbing a conference which appeared to be mutually interesting.

The fortress of Patankota was built by Shah Jehan, when he made war on Narpoor. This last place, now so insignificant, belonged then to the ancestors of Bír Singh, who considered it worth while to overawe it by the construction of the strong post of Patankota. Their successor, driven out of his territory by Ranjít Singh, now lives ten kos from hence, in Katawar, in indigence, his only remaining possession, as far as I could learn, consisting of a lovely garden on the way to Narpoor, called Srikagur.

In the evening I obtained the Thanadar's permission to inspect the fort, but on drawing near, the Sirdar positively refused to admit me, and the Thanadar seeing the dispute between us, very coolly ran away; for which he received one of my Múnshí's choicest reproofs. A European should never believe one of these people, even on their oath, a precaution not more necessary than disagreeable*. After all, I believe my loss was not very great, for it is now a defenceless ruin, and weeds and rank grass are invading every part of it. But the position was admirably chosen, and it lies in an open locality, where not a spot of ground commands it from above.

Wednesday, 28th, thermometer 55°, 79°, 74°. The immense plain of India on the left, and stupendous snow-capped mountains to the right, made this day's march a real treat to a lover of nature, nor was the scene we had left behind less delightful. High thick date-trees overshadowed the spot where my tent was pitched; behind this stood the fort, and through the dawn of a lovely morning, the majestic form of the mountain chain gradually stood out in bold but uncertain relief, the outline gradually growing sharper as the rays of the yet hidden sun

* A disregard of veracity is the most obvious and certain test of an unregenerate man of whatever region or religious profession, nor is it confined to India alone. Was it necessary for those who appreciated all that was estimable in the Hindú character, to plead their love of truth in the face of such principles as a distinguished prelate contended for on pure Christian grounds? Those who know most of the Hindús, and regard them most, say one and all: certainly not.—*Ed.*

beamed forth and gave new animation to the scenery. All nature was soon awake, day displacing night in a moment of time, contrasted with our long northern twilight. First was heard the sweet greeting offered by the bulbul to the fair morn; then the mango bird set up his piteous lament, and the variegated máina with his lively chatter, the screaming parrots, and noisy monkeys swinging from bough to bough, all with one consent filling the air with their joyous cries, were speedily up and alive to the announcement of day. In the surrounding groves, the blue thrush warbled in companies; peacocks strutted about the fields, and skylarks soared melodiously over head, mounting aloft to greet the glorious messenger of light before earth's inhabitants.

The sun shone forth brightly, soon after I had quitted Patankota; and an immense pyramidal mass of mountains soon made their appearance in the north-west, while the country was richly cultivated and more populous than I had seen it for a long time. The people appeared to be chiefly Kashmírians, occupied as tailors and weavers, or in agriculture: it is not possible to exceed them in filth, whether they were poor or not, I really could not decide. They seem well fed, look healthy, and are not wanting in ornaments on their dress. They are very ready to serve as bearers too, but this may be caused either by poverty or the love of gain. The country is amply supplied with rivers and tanks, and the vegetation grows to an enormous size. My evening was passed at Kotoa, where they pitched my tent before the Mohammedan cemetery, under the impervious shade of mango and fig-trees.

Thursday, 29th, thermometer 55°, 80°, 74°. The Fakírs in the Panjáb are quite intolerable; great athletic fellows, and, without exception, the most impudent beggars in the world. This morning one came to my tent with two tamtams or drums; he was accompanied by three men, each provided with a sort of oboe; I thought they would have distracted me outright. In vain I commanded the man to desist and take himself off; he was shameless enough to keep his ground until absolutely driven from it by the blows of my servants.

The road to Jesrod is unvaried, winding among gigantic grasses, which brush the traveller's face as he makes his way through them.

The height may be surmised, from the fact that an elephant may be concealed from view in this grass, and each stem is as thick as an ordinary finger*; nor is it easy to escape from this forest with a whole skin. The tiger takes up his abode here, roaming even as far north as Tibet. The path is formed of large stones also, not that the soil is bad, but that the rich earth is carried away for the cultivated grounds. The day's march, however, did not lead me through any region so well cultivated as I saw yesterday. Swamps were frequent, and during the rains I should suppose the whole country must be completely under water.

The palace of the Raja of Jesrod is built on a hill, and the distance from Kotoa about eight coss. The Uts, a rapid stream, flows through the place. Not far from it is a chalybeate spring having a disagreeable taste of iron. At seven in the morning its temperature was 80°, while that of the air was only 56°. The situation of Jesrod is much more romantic than the place itself: the hill on which the Raja's house is situated, is also ornamented with four little towers. The last prince was robbed of his territory by Ranjít Singh, and his son, a child, is now at Lahor. A huge irregular arch leads to the paltry bazar and to the Raja's residence.

The Bal Dewa, called in the plain Ramnagar, a single lofty snowy mountain, is distinctly visible from hence, although at least thirty miles distant: the shortest way from Narpoor to Kashmír is over this mountain.

I had imagined that time would have allowed me to do many things

---

* In March, 1830, I traversed the country at the foot of the Abú mountains, on the borders of Rajpútana, in company with Colonel Sherreff, Bombay army. On our way from the ruins of the celebrated ancient city, Chandrawatí—whence the famous gates of Ghazní really came—in the direction of Girwar, we passed through a large tract overgrown with this high grass, the *Doorba* or *Dúb* grass, which we had the curiosity to measure, and found it fourteen feet high. My friend Colonel Sherreff's perfect indifference, wandering off the unfrequented though beaten route, to admire the beauties of nature and catch a glimpse of the herds of Nilgaís, which are very abundant, occasioned me no little anxiety; as I well remember, both elephant and rider were entirely hidden from my view at a little distance by this high grass.—*Ed.*

during my solitary wanderings, for which now I felt every day much too short. First, the journey itself occupied too many hours; then, there was the difficulty of finding a good guide when I arrived in a strange place; and lastly, the hours necessarily employed in preparing my map, in enriching and arranging my different collections, to say nothing of certain cares for the supply of the necessaries of life, occupied much valuable time. As a consolation to me amidst this never-ceasing anxiety, this restless movement, and ever-changing scene, unconscious what adventures and dangers the next day might bring forth, I had in it all a sufficient antidote against those fancies with which solitude, and separation from all who are dear to him, are too apt to fill the traveller's mind*.

Friday, 30th, thermometer, with rain in the morning, 70°, noon 82°, evening 74°. A very ominous rattling on my tent awoke me this morning; it was the rain, which the oppressive heat of yesterday, and the veil around the Bal Dewa during the day, had given me reason to expect. My people were therefore not taken by surprise, and every thing was under cover. It did not last long, though it prevented us from decamping as early as usual. The road to Aleh is easily missed, and the difficulty we found in following it at all, rendered it more wearisome than nature had made it. A dozen times we got out of the regular track: low jungles like those of the Dekhan, solitary trees of the Butea frondosa, and the most thorny of the Ziziphus species, the Jujube, were among those well known objects, much more familiar than loved. From the mountains of Kashmír to Cape Comorin, the Jujube tree and the turtle dove, the Butea frondosa, and the Maina, the mango and the parrot, with here and there immense fig and cotton-trees, are the surest sign to a traveller that he is in India. The land

* I do not remember to have met a single passage in the course of my life which so perfectly, beautifully, and forcibly depicts the Christian's lot. No sooner has he begun to appreciate his responsibilities and privileges, than he feels life too short, too much straitened for usefulness; the necessary avocations of life, the cares, the duties, and pressing obligations crowd upon him till he perceives the hand of God thus leading and instructing him, and preparing him for those happy abodes where sin and separation shall be no more.—*Ed.*

in this locality is not fertile, and is moreover but poorly cultivated. The people are diminutive, whether from actual want or from the insalubrity of the climate I cannot tell; but it often happens that where jungles extend over the low grounds under a high chain of hills, the country is commonly subject to low fevers, and usually unhealthy. The natives dread such a climate more than the Europeans, for, strange to say, they are more liable to catch intermittent fevers than foreigners, and the reason may very possibly be, that the nourishment they can afford to take is not strong enough to ward off its attacks*. Frequently it issues in death within four days from the first attack: and if the physician cannot cure the third paroxysm, the patient's case is given up as hopeless; he expires generally without pain, from sheer debility.

Aleh is a small fort surrounded with mud walls, and has an inner inclosure of stone: the whole seems now, just strong enough to ensure the safety of a Thanadar. It is the present residence of a Díwan, or minister of the Mahá Raja, who paid me a visit of ceremony: he was a fine-looking man, in spite of the loss of one of his eyes.

I accepted the guidance of a Brahmin in my evening's walk, in order to learn from him the names of the different villages visible from the adjacent hill; but the man refused to name one of them, asserting that he should be severely punished by the Díwan if he did so, since strangers had in other times visited their country and inquired the names of all their towns and villages, of which they had on a second visit taken forcible possession. It needed all my persuasion to satisfy the poor man that I had no design on his fatherland.

The mountains had been dimly hidden throughout the day by thick rain-clouds, and in the evening presented a truly magnificent spectacle. The snow on the Mori had considerably deepened: it now stood dazzlingly forward in its whitest garb, confronting the Bal Dewa. Both mountains described horizontal lines ending in a perpendicular fall, each resembling an immense colossus, while between them the Sánsh mountain projected with its countless peaks, covered as far

* The excitable animal spirits of the European may likewise have something to do with this resistance to the inroads of disease, or rather susceptibility.—*Ed.*

as the eye could follow it, with a complete veil of snow, a proof that it must be higher than either of the others. The greater facility of tracing its outline confirmed me in my former opinion that it stands quite apart from the Mori and the Bal Dewa, but very near to both. My tent was pitched under fig-trees in a newly-ploughed field, very near the Díwan's garden, which consists of long alleys of citron and pomegranate trees, having traces of former beauty, but not a flower was to be seen; the whole place seems encompassed with mountains ranging in every direction without any apparent connection.

Saturday 31st, thermometer 56°, 79°, 68°. This is the temperature as I found it in my tent; but in the morning while it marked 56° within, it was 10° higher in the open air, which I accounted for by the situation of the tent in a newly-ploughed field: thereby absorbing the heat and causing the diffusion of a greater degree of warmth than could penetrate the little protected residence fixed over one nook of its surface.

The road to Samba was the worst and most disagreeable I had yet met with in India, constantly leading through the fatal high grass, and sometimes passing over heaps of stone, at others tending downwards into the soft crumbling soil. The villages, too, with the exception of Thakerdoras, were nothing but miserable huts. I reckon this tedious and distressing day's march at twelve miles; the snow on the mountains was as distinct as yesterday; Trikota, a high hill, about forty kos from Aleh, and a place of pilgrimage, seemed to serve as a guide to our destination; and, at a greater distance, peaks covered with snow lifted up their countless heads.

Meanwhile the Sánsh mountain was gradually shut out, and we were rapidly approaching the chain before us. I had a very good view of its majestic form. Tanks became more frequent in our path; but though rain had fallen so lately, they were almost dry. Near one of them they had pitched the tent for the night, several female forms were peering within; they had been engaged in bathing, an amusement in which large parties appeared to partake together, in this not over pure element, without any inconvenient sense of modesty. With one exception too, they were all particularly ill-favoured in appearance.

I now became eager to turn my back on the plain, and this I trusted to accomplish on the next day but one: that is, provided I should be able to go as far as from Jamú to Rajáor. The difference between the climate of the morning and of the middle of the day is here so great, that it has a decidedly injurious effect on the health: what a terrible calamity would an illness in such a country as this be to my earthly pilgrimage? My lodging chanced to be near a fakír's house, where they were unloading a dozen camels, the property of Gúláb Singh, the Raja of Jamú, laden with the bark of the Deobasa tree, an article used by the Indian women to redden their gums. This bark is collected not far from Samba, on the mountains; and is carried into Persia and Multan, as well as the roots of a species of Scutellaria, and the seeds of a plant of which I could learn neither the name nor use. The camel drivers could only tell me, that it belonged to the Persian merchants, who bought it up eagerly in Kabúl.

Sunday, November 1.—Half a mile from Samba is an uninhabited palace belonging to Sushet Singh, Gúláb Singh's brother. As we proceeded on our way, the roads led over the partially dry bed of the Desentri, where we completely lost the right road. In vain had I repeatedly desired, that a guide should be hired every day, to show us the best and shortest route; for, at this time of year, the men are engaged constantly in the fields; and, in their agricultural avocations, make so free with the usual paths taken by travellers, that it is most difficult to trace them by the ordinary marks. During the day, it is no easy matter to repair the neglect of the morning; for unless the villagers are actually in want of the reward promised them for guiding us, those who know the road refuse to show it, so that one is compelled to carry them along by force. Such a scene took place to-day, near a mill on the Desentri; the man's cries of resistance soon brought out a crowd of forty or fifty from the mill and the huts adjoining, who, armed with bamboo sticks, planted themselves on the banks of the stream. But Mírza and the Chaprasis were in no way daunted by this bravado; and, in spite of their warlike front, they conveyed their friend safely over to the other side. But, alas! the captive escaped from us, and succeeded in rejoining the knights of the bamboo at last. Then ensued a scene of mutual recrimination. My people cast the sand on their enemies, who retaliated with sticks, and others began to advance with spears. As there was no place where my people could fight under shelter, I now judged it high time to retreat. At the next village we were more fortunate, engaging a guide on the promise of a good reward for his services. But this did not make our further efforts more successful; and the reason may be, that these poor men have often been decoyed away from their homes, under similar pretexts, and then made to bear heavy burdens, without receiving the smallest payment in return for such service. The people have been rendered mistrustful; and I much fear that Jacquemont, who travelled at Ranjít Singh's expense, through his territories, did not give them any higher opinion of European honour, than he himself had concerning the Sikh character; we learnt, we must confess, that he took a long time to consider the propriety of paying his native bearers.

The road to-day was really terrible; through a thick jungle; neither mountain nor plain, neither forest nor open field; it is a toilsome, dreary journey, over masses of stones, a zig-zag line from one wretched hamlet to another; little or no cultivation is visible, and what they call fields in tillage are scarcely to be distinguished from heaps of stones. The distance to Ishmaelpoor, a miserable village, is reckoned to be nine long kos; in a straight line, I should think it ten or eleven miles, but we must have made it at least fifteen. As they pitched my tent close to a tank, I had again an opportunity of seeing a large assemblage of females taking their baths. Their costume here differs from that of the women in the Sikh districts on the left shores of the Setlej; the younger ones all wear blue trousers, which fit very close to the leg below the knee, while from the calf to the ancle they fall in numerous folds; over this they wear an ample petticoat, and above, a white cloth hangs down behind, fluttering in the wind.

In a large fig-tree near this tank, dwelt a colony of those large bats or vampyres I before alluded to. One of my Shikarís took the liberty of shooting one of them; but as the misdeed occurred some way from the village, its consequences were not so serious as they had nearly proved to me at Narpoor. The fakír, who lived under the tree, took up the animal, however, and refused at any price to restore it to them. He was, therefore, brought into my presence, and there complained of the death of the creature which belonged to him. I begged to know, whether he could be so silly as to pass his life in looking after vampyres; and he, in return, asked me whether I considered myself doing any better, by permitting my servants to kill one of God's innocent creatures? As I could not give any satisfactory answer to this charge, I solemnly promised him, that neither he nor his dear vampyres should ever be molested again.

Monday, Nov. 2.—Thermometer, morning 60°, noon, 80°, evening, 70°. This day, although provided with a guide, it was difficult to get through the thorny bushes which beset us on every side. Happily, we could almost see Jamú from Ishmaelpoor, so that we were in no danger of losing ourselves. Our course lay over the plain, which in one place I found suddenly invaded by the deep bed of a stream, whence a hill rises almost imperceptibly, on the summit of which Gúláb Singh has lately built the fort of Bala. It does not speak very favorably of his military judgment, for, however handsome its ornamented walls may look, rising as it were, out of the river, from his palace on the other side of the Tohi at Jamú; as a strong place it is quite untenable, being overlooked by other heights most easy of access. Gúláb Singh's palace is a pretty white edifice, built like the whole of Jamú, about 150 feet above the river Tohi, which flows with rapidity, and clear as crystal, over its stony bed, in a deep channel encompassed with waving hills. It is fordable, though not very easily, but as no bridge crosses it, men, women, and children must pass from one side to the other by this means, if at all. From Bala a spacious flight of steps leads down to the river, and another takes the passenger up to Jamú, where, in every direction, the sight of falling ruins and decaying edifices bespeaks its former greatness and present poverty; while the indispensable bazar fills up a large vacant space between the palace and a mass of dilapidated buildings. I sought my tent for some time in vain, and at length discovered it under some acacia trees, in a very filthy neighbourhood of Kashmírian huts. The Thanadar visited me as usual, and promised me impossibilities, but I contented myself with telling him that the station was very badly chosen, and requested him to accompany me to the Raja's garden, which is reached through the once celebrated town. The prosperity of Jamú was at its height under Ranjít Deo, whose mild government extended equal protection to Hindú and Mahommedan, while the Panjáb was overrun with the horrors of war; but no sooner were his eyes closed by death, in 1781, than Mahá Singh, the father of Ranjít Singh, invaded the territories of his feeble son and successor, Brij Raj Deo, and plundered his town; peace was soon restored, but no part of the territories.

The Raja's garden is situated on the bank of the Tohi,* at the foot of a hill; it is prettily laid out in the Indian taste, with a pavilion in the centre, where a variety of animals are kept in separate cages, some on account of their rarity, others for the purpose of being reared. I saw there some enormously fat sheep, and what is almost unheard of among Hindús, some overgrown geese likewise. In this charming garden I was worse off than when close to the wretched hovels; for I had to wait there all day in vain for my large tent and furniture. I had neither table, chair, nor writing materials; and in an attempt to catch a butterfly, for want of something better to do, was seized with a violent pain in my head, occasioned by the burning heat. At last, after eight hours' impatient waiting, two of my servants, who were also seeking me, gave me the pleasing information that the tent was pitched a full mile lower down the river. On my asking them who had ordered it to be put there, they answered with considerable hesitation, that Kháir Singh, one of my chaprasís, was the delinquent. How often I look back to those trifling grievances, which really make up the sum of the traveller's existence, for dangers or misfortunes, in our transit through a strange country, are far less hard to bear than these daily recurring vexatious annoyances. A wretched repast terminated the events of this day of troubles.

---

* The Taúhi or Tohi, rises in the Ratan Panjál mountains, flows by Rajaor, and joins the Chenab above Wazírabad. It must have been between this river and the Chenab that Alexander encamped.—CUNNINGHAM'S REPORT.

Tuesday, 3rd.—Thermometer, 63°, 82°, 70°. The situation of my tent was much better in appearance than in reality. The fig-tree gave shade certainly, but no coolness, and the heat was more intense than I had felt it for a long time. In the river, a troop of females, chiefly Kashmírians, were refreshing themselves by bathing; they are much fairer and more finely formed than the natives of Jamú. A certain amount of trouble attends the arrival of every traveller in India. In the first place, the servants are impatient to hurry out to the bazar and sit gossipping there, and though I considered myself peculiarly fortunate in the character and behaviour of mine, yet in this respect every one was a true Indian; what is still worse than this, it is absolutely necessary to pass much of one's time in the different towns, in order to hire men and animals, which can only be taken from one place to another, unless the traveller engages his suite by the month, a precaution which I continually regretted not having taken myself.

In the afternoon the Thanadar came to offer me a present, in the name of the Raja, which I refused. Mirza, who had been in the town, returned presently with the tidings that a European traveller had just arrived at Jamú, and, after some trouble, I found that the stranger was on his way from Kashmír to Lahor, and was merely resting one day at Jamú to provide himself with necessaries.

I thought this could be no other than Mr. Vigne, an English gentleman, then travelling in India, and as Mirza inclined to the same opinion, I immediately wrote a short note, offering to share my stock, such as it was, with a traveller from Europe, and to pay him any attention in my power. With this note I dispatched Mohan, who soon came back and told me that, instead of an Englishman he had found a Persian, who could neither read nor write. I mention this unimportant circumstance to show how cautious travellers should be in trusting to the opinions of the natives of the north of India. Mirza knew perfectly well that this stranger was not a European, but as soon as he observed that I heartily wished it might prove to be a countryman of my own, he framed his measures, not according to the truth, but according to what he fancied would best please me to hear. In this instance, though he knew I should soon discover my error, he did not attempt to undeceive me, and by this my readers will judge how little those people deprecate falsehood, when the case may be really serious, and the truth more difficult to find out.

Late on the same day I received a letter, very well written, from an Englishman in the service of the Raja, desiring to speak with me, to which, of course, I immediately acceded, and presently a very fine young man, richly attired, made his appearance in my tent. As soon as the servants were out of hearing, without uttering a word, he flung himself at my feet and burst into a passionate flood of tears. In vain I requested him to be seated, and to feel assured that I would do all in my power to alleviate any distress he might be suffering from; for a long time, I could not draw from him any explanation whatever of this strange conduct, although the sight of a European, after so long an interval, and his evident sorrow, filled me with the deepest interest and pity, to say nothing of the natural curiosity which I felt to know the cause which must have brought a man of his appearance into such a situation. He could hardly be an adventurer, and his emotion did not seem the result of any disappointment; besides, he wanted some aid from me—and this aid, to judge from his dress, arms, and jewels, could not be gold. What but the consciousness of guilt could prostrate one man so abjectly before another? This, however, was no place or time to reproach a supplicant with what might be neither crime nor error on his part. Desirous of hearing something in explanation of his visit, I again addressed him, saying—"Speak, whatever you have to say, I promise you my best assistance and pity. How long have you been in Jamú?"—"Many years."—"Are you poor?"—"No, my circumstances are good."—"Then, what brought you to this remote and lonely land?"—"Pity me," he exclaimed, seizing my hand convulsively, "I am miserable, I am guilty, I need forgiveness."—"I must insist on your speaking out more plainly," I said, somewhat impatiently, "how otherwise can I either guess what you may stand in need of, or assist you in any way, as I have engaged, should it be in my power?" Wringing his clasped hands with evident expressions of terror, he suddenly cast a hurried glance at me, exclaiming mournfully, "I cannot, I cannot explain!" and so saying rushed out of the tent.

I asked my people whether they had ever heard anything of this European before, they all denied any knowledge of him; and, as I did not like to excite the curiosity of the Thanadar by making any particular inquiries about him, I remained without hearing anything further of this unhappy person.

Wednesday, Nov. 4.—Thermometer, morning 59°, noon 82°, evening 66°. When I wrote the date of this day in my tablets, I remembered for the first time, that it was a season when, for many years, I had been used to receive testimonies from my friends and family of their love and regard. It is on such days that we think most fondly of those far away; the day was no joyful one for me, and a long toilsome march of twelve kos, accompanied by divers petty annoyances, contributed to depress my spirits. Strange to say, I seem now to be better acquainted with the character of the Indians than my servants, though part of the same nation. I repented more than ever that I had not bought horses, and hired servants at Simla, as the price I had to pay for these necessaries here was preposterous—I was forced to pay down five rupees for each bearer, and ten rupees for a horse for thirteen days' service, beforehand; I had directed the Munshí on no account to let the old bearers depart, until he had made quite sure of obtaining others, but in the morning, trusting to their promises, he had paid those who, under the pressure of want, had hired themselves at Nadaun for five rupees a-month, they now required an addition of at least one and a-half; greatly chagrined I ordered them all to be dismissed, as he had procured substitutes. At 4 o'clock I was prepared to start, but not a single thing was in readiness, and after waiting until 7, I mounted my Ghunt and ordered the Munshí to follow with the rest as soon as possible. About two, I arrived at Agnur, resolved to bear the long fast I anticipated with becoming patience, for there was no means of providing for the wants of appetite at that place.

The road traversed a highly fruitful and well cultivated country, and several clear soft streams meandered through the fields. Jacquemont speaks of the utter destitution of the people, and maintains that in the Panjáb we may best judge of the great happiness enjoyed by the natives of Hindústhan under British dominion. I confess I saw no such signs of misery. When a stranger can only get bearers at a high price, and is forced to pay down the money in advance; when he sees the natives well clothed, and evidently well fed, nay, more independent, even proud in their bearing, how can he conclude that they are so wretched? On the journey, I observed that, instead of carrying the produce of their fields on their heads, as usual, they had horses with them, which were well laden into the bargain.

Agnur has a petty Raja, who is in the service of Gúláb Singh. It lies on the right bank of the Chenab, which is here a strong clear stream, with water of an icy coldness, and is protected by a stately fort, although probably more picturesque than useful. It was built thirty-three years ago by Alum Singh, and plundered by Ranjít Singh, who does not approve of strong places in the territories of his vassals. The palace is in ruins, but the Raja has built a new and charming house behind it. Agnur itself is a place of no importance. The Trikota mountain rises in stately grandeur near it, and a place of pilgrimage lies about half-way up its northern side, with a temple, much celebrated for its beauty and sanctity. It has also a spring, from which the water rises in jerks and falls into a basin; for nine months of the year this water is cold, but during December, January, and part of February, it is too hot to bear touching without pain. This appears to me to be explained by the fact, that, so long as the snow lies on the Trikota, no water can penetrate the protected spring, which, therefore, keeps its own naturally high temperature. Trikota Devi is eighteen kos, or twenty-seven miles from Jamú, and I would fain have visited it, but my time was strictly limited. A new snowy mountain here came in view to the south-west, in the direction of the plains of India. Bimber is eighteen kos from hence, and twenty from Jamú. Our march this day was above eighteen miles. The following is the distance in kos from Simla to Jamú, and the names of the stations—the kos of the Punjáb is about one mile and a half:—

Sarí	7	Habli	5
Kunyar....	7	Haripoor ..	6
Sahikoti ..	8	Jwáli	10
Bayún.....	8	Narpoor...	10
Bilaspoor ..	7	Patankota	10
Kumagaheti	8	Katoa.....	8
Meyrígaheti	9	Jesrod	8
Hamirpoor.	6	Aleh	8
Ráili	5	Samba	8
Nadaun ...	5	Ishmaelpoor	9
Jwálámúkhí	5	Jamú	7

Total accomplished in 22 days, 164 kos.

By degrees my servants found their way to Agnur. About eleven o'clock at night, I was able to break my day's fast, and at midnight to lie down. The servants were the greatest sufferers after all; for their work is only beginning when the baggage arrives, the bearers alone being at liberty to betake themselves to rest.

One of my people shot a rare specimen of the stork on the wing, very like one which I obtained in Ceylon; but not a native could be found to bring the bird to Agnur for us, a distance of three kos, until Mirza resorted to the means, common from Syria to the Himálaya, in such cases—taking off the turban of a countryman, he endeavoured to compel him to lend his services; but the peasant chose rather to put up with his loss, and consoled himself by repeating that he had another at home; and I ordered Mirza, therefore, to let him go, and to hang his turban on the next hedge. While in India, and especially in the Dekhan, I had seen numbers of men scrambling to be hired, at the rate of a pice per kos; here I found it necessary to pay eight annas, or thirty-two pice, for the day's work, surely no proof of poverty in the country. I met with another old acquaintance here, a black cormorant, of that kind so abundant in the South of India.

Thursday, November 5.—Thermometer, morning 59°, noon 80°, evening 64°. The inhabitants were unanimous in their information, that the road was quite level to Rajaor, with the single exception of one ascent near Agnur; and yet I found the day's journey one of extreme toil and difficulty. The distance was reckoned nine kos, that is, between twelve and thirteen miles. It took us from seven in the morning to six in the evening, and their boasted level road led us over two mountains, comparable with those climbed by the traveller in the Himálaya, going from Pahar to Subhátoo, over smooth rocks, and mountain torrents. From the bed of the Kotheri, we began our ascent of the first hill; enormous stones, piled one over another, composed the road to the summit; there a torrent, which has worn its bed deeply into the soil, with sandstone and limestone in detached masses, somewhat varied the route. About one third of the way, we came to the abode of a fakír, near several little stone buildings, and a spring called Dendrah, round which a considerable party of the dwellers of the mountains were spending their hours of rest from work. Many were carrying to Jamú large bundles of rose-coloured wood of the Deobasa, which is found about this spot also; but I could not find any of the trees, though I went out of my way, with one of the collectors, in search of one. Overcome by the heat, my people lay down by the spring, from which the fakír brought them all water, while multitudes of monkeys were leaping from tree to tree, and flocks of parrots filled the air with their clatter. Gigantic trees, round which climbed many a parasite, rose in the little plain near the spring. When the fakír had administered to the wants of all my servants, I beckoned to him, and he quickly drew near with a vessel filled with water. I then perceived that he was a very aged man—"How old are you?" said I. "Ninety-two," replied he. "And how long have you lived at this spring?" "Since I grew to manhood." "And why do you remain here?" "Why!" repeated he, "see you not that I refresh the weary traveller with water, and send him strengthened on his way?" "But he would find it without you." "And when the sand in this lonely spot chokes the spring, who would find the water then? By serving the poor I serve God." "But these same poor feed you, otherwise you could not exist." "He who has abundance gives to the needy, if he values his own happiness. I am the rich man here; for the water is mine: and many a great man travelling this way is bounteous to me, in order that I may live until another comes. Truly there are such good men in this world; for many are the years that I have lived without quitting this spring."

Poor man! Knowing only one small valley, how narrow and confined must God's beautiful creation appear to thee! To thee a tree must be a forest, a hill a division of the world, the spring thine ocean; and yet, who would not give all his knowledge, every worldly advantage, in exchange for this peaceful mind, this conscientious assurance that he commands everything that constitutes happiness.

On the hill which we next reached from Dendrah, I had a beautiful view of the country, conclusive enough to me, that I should soon be in the heart of a mountainous region. This was the last glimpse I had of the plains of India for some time: its native inhabitants also, a perfect host of white monkeys, of peacocks and parrots, as if desirous of taking leave of me, screamed in chorus over my head.

It is curious to observe here, how quickly a little spring becomes a deep stream. At the top of a mountain, it is perhaps like a thread of water, and 100 steps further down, we find it two fathoms across. Over a pretty rivulet called Dalashel, about which are scattered the cottages composing the village of Inghal, we arrived at an extraordinary formation of sandstone; and by clambering first over the great blocks scattered along the bed of the stream, and then up a steep ascent to the second point, and looking back to the first, I became fully alive to the surprising nature of its form. From the valley beneath, spring up, in multitudes, detached sharp points of rocks, while above, the mountain seems to have no end. Until the summit is once gained, the road to Poni appears to be as steep downwards to the banks of the river, as that just surmounted; and then there is another great ascent ere one can reach the town, which is on the opposite side of a river. I lingered on the summit a few minutes, and then commenced the toilsome dangerous descent. Fatigued as I was, it was necessary to descend on foot; but how the poor animals or the bearers were ever to reach the bottom, I could not even surmise. What I might have expected soon occurred; the men would not follow me with the baggage, because they were accustomed to move as slowly as they chose, and to rest whenever they could find any shade, which did not suit my desire to end the day's march as soon as practicable. I had always taken care to send on the small tent, under the care of the Chaprasí, Kháir Singh, that I might find it ready on my arrival; and now, when I reached the river, I found them on the point of carrying it over. As the sun went down, I entered the little town on foot, wearied not a little. Very few of my people were with me, and the night came on, finding me without bed or food. I could not help heartily despising the great broad-shouldered Kashmírians, who carried the Jampan, and let both it and its unlucky tenant fall no less than four times this day, until I began to think my own feet a much safer mode of transport: I am not sure they did not fall purposely. Late at night, when the coldness of the air made me long for warmer clothing, I was favoured with the sight of the *Charpái*, my Indian bedstead, a *Chepáti*, a kind of unleavened cake made by my huntsmen, and a fire.

Friday, November 6.—The servants and bearers were not ready until nine o'clock, and then out of humour at the prospect of a fatiguing march, the bearers threw the bedstead on the ground, breaking two of the feet and the frame. These Kashmírians I take to be an unwilling, ill-tempered, discontented set; and their coarse disagreeable manner of speaking is hardly to be endured. Their exterior is far more pleasing, and some of the old men might have served as models for a patriarch. At Simla, and indeed until I arrived at Jamú, I had seen but two classes, the tailors and shawl weavers, and had fancied the whole race diminutive and insignificant like them. But I knew little of them at that time. About noon I was informed, that my large tent was brought as far as the hill; but that ten men at least were necessary to drag it through paths which were inaccessible to my beasts of burden. Neither fair words nor gold could congregate, out of this populous place, more than half of that number, nor that indeed without great difficulty. I decided, therefore, on climbing the lofty eminence once more, and strengthening the hired force with my eight bearers. Again my trusty Ghunt took me up this arduous ascent, and I was well repaid for my toil; for I discovered by the way many interesting plants. My Shikarí shot a black pheasant, and I enjoyed the fine prospect, and the sweet coolness of the evening. Very lovely was that evening, and the view over the valley of Rás Dhún, at the foot of the Trikota, was magnificent. But I was thoroughly convinced that the road which from fatigue and long watching I had imagined to be more dangerous than it was in reality last evening, was sufficiently perilous: the eye shrinks from the deep yawning chasm below, over which hang grotesque masses of projecting rock, as the road winds round and round, on the very edge of the precipice. One spot we came to, where the rocky wall dropped perpendicularly to a depth of several thousand feet; and, further on, hundreds of steps seem cut out obliquely, and so dangerously projecting over the abyss, that it is almost impossible to descend them. The head swims in passing this fearful place; and as no animal can turn about, on account of the narrowness of the path, I expected every instant to see one or the other of them stumble, and fall into the depths below. Many did flounder about, and nearly lost their footing, trembling meanwhile in every limb; but seemingly aware of their danger, they walked with the most surprising care, and arrived at the bottom safe, their loads being taken off, and carried on men's shoulders.

When I reached my tent again, I found two messengers awaiting me, with a letter from the Thanadar of Narpoor, who sent me, by command of the Mahá Raja, 101 rupees; for which, as I mentioned above, the bill was given at Narpoor without the money. They now demanded Ranjít's note, which I had kept as a curiosity. I desired not to take the money, if this could be done without giving offence to the Mahá Raja; and as part of my suite had already quitted Poni, this gave me the opportunity of declining the money, because the bill of exchange was with my luggage, and could not be returned. I was obliged to remain at Poni another night; and a good meal and rest were doubly welcome to me, after a very uncomfortable night and two fatiguing days, spent almost without sustenance.

Saturday, November 7, thermometer, morning 58°, noon 70°, evening 66°. This morning had nearly seen the last of my earthly excursions; for, while breakfasting as usual before my tent, and some of the servants were taking it down, the rest being seated round me on the grass, it suddenly fell with a crash, shivering in pieces the table at which I was sitting. Had I been but ever so little to the right, the roof of the tent weighing 600 lbs. and the poles, 25 feet high, would have descended on my devoted head. The poor Munshí, who was reading a letter by my side, lay for some time nearly dead with terror; and when I bade him go on, and think no more of the accident, he could find no consolation in my coolness for the fright he had received. I found on inquiry, that the Kalasi had wound up all the ropes, except the principal stay ropes, which were not strong enough to bear the weight of the tent. The pegs were forced out which fastened them to the ground, and the whole gave way together. My people saw the impending danger, and tried to rouse me by their cries; but these things are so commonly heard, that I listened without paying attention to them. The least movement in the direction of the falling load would have brought me under it.

Poni lies in a narrow deep ravine, and the castle, which, at a distance, looks grand and well fortified, is, on a nearer approach, very insignificant. Two roads lead from Poni to Rajaor, the shortest being twenty-four kos, the longest passing by Bal and Noshera, and both, according to the natives, being over a plain country. As I was told that the shortest would bring me in four days' journey to Rajaor, I proposed it on account of the miserable state of my cattle. I made another discovery here, and not an agreeable one. The fatigues and hunger and want of sleep I had lately suffered, made me sensible that I could not, without danger, brave hardships which in younger days I should have laughed at.

The road passes between two rather lofty hills, and up and down through ravines hollowed out by the streams in the rich soil. At Bethyan, we completely lost our way, and Mirza asked a man who was working in the field which direction we should take. He was about to point it out, when they desired him to show it quickly, upon which he stoutly refused to stir from the spot. The usual snatch of the turban from his head, brought on a skirmish, in which three field labourers engaged on his side, and valiantly defended him; one seizing the silver-tipped stick, the sign of Mirza's authority, and another regaining possession of the turban. It was with much difficulty that the stick was wrested from his grasp. During this contest the cowardly bearers had set me down and run off, so that I found myself in the midst of the combatants, quite unprepared to interfere were it necessary, although I looked carefully after my kúkeri or knife. My men being provided with sabres, and the peasants carrying mattocks, I expected that blood would be shed; particularly, when at a loud shout from our four enemies, I saw people rushing out of the village: fortunately the Kotwal was among them, and Mirza laying hold of him without any ceremony, obliged him to guide us to Moghul, the next station. Moghul consists of a few houses only, and has no bazar. It is distant from Poni five kos, or between eight and nine miles, which took us five hours to reach.

Sunday, Nov. 8.—Thermometer 49°, 84°, 68°. The difference of climate was more perceptible from day to day, and I dreaded to think what I should do with my Indians when we reached the Pír Panjal, on which, doubtless, the snow was then lying, for they were hardly to be driven forth this morning on account of the cold. The road was uninteresting and bad; the country is intersected in every direction by ranges of hills; and the people seemed very poor, the villages being paltry and built in valleys, or scattered in small patches about the hills; the vegetation is still tropical, and the Mango, Banána, Parrots, and Máina, abundant as ever. The Nerium Oleander abounds in the river beds, and the stunted Phœnix farinifera or date palm, on the rocks.

We were seven hours going eight kos, or fourteen miles, to Dharmsala, a larger station, which has a bazar. Near it we fell in with a company of Banjárís,* or corn merchants, with 100 or 150 oxen laden with grain. I was forced to pass the evening in the little morning tent, having vainly waited for the larger one.

* The Wanjarís, or Banjarís, are the great grain and salt carriers throughout India, from Tibet to Cape Comorin. They claim to Rajput descent, and constitute one of those remarkable aboriginal races, which in the progress of the early Hindu conquests, betook themselves to a wandering life, thus to avoid the tyrannical yoke of their conquerors.—*Ed.*

Monday, Nov. 9.—Thermometer 46°, 74°, 66°. A very cold morning. There was no getting my people up before 7 o'clock, and the day's route was over steep hills and very rugged paths. Here the houses are built close together for security; each, as in Syria, resembling a little castle. The owner enters his dwelling by a ladder, which he draws up after him, a proof of the fear entertained of the Sikh and Mohammedan troops, and of the few means of defence possessed by the inhabitants, since a day would suffice to pull down every house in the neighbourhood.

On leaving Dharmsala we had a fine view of the Pír Panjal, covered with snow to a considerable extent; many streams of cold and clear water descended towards us from the mountain; of these, the Naritari, dashing over immense stones in its progress, is the most considerable. In order to ford it we were forced to jump from stone to stone, a feat by no means agreeable or easy, on account of their slipperiness and the depth at which they lie. The vegetation still continues tropical. The Barberry and Pine, which commence here and seem to confer their character on this region, are both abundant.* The harvest was just over. The day's journey was six kos, which occupied us five hours.

Tuesday, Nov. 10.—Thermometer, 42°, 72°, 64°. From yesterday's station, I had dispatched a letter to the Raja of Rajáwar, requesting that six horses might be sent to convey my tent to that place. The night was bitterly cold, and my tent was pitched on the heights of Safedar, in a very unprotected situation, where the wind had full liberty to pierce every cranny. In the morning it was covered with a white hoar frost. From a rising ground by the way, we had a fine

* If the isothermal lines which determine the vegetation of any region, depended absolutely on latitude alone, we might understand the purport of such expressions as the above; certain plants indicating a determinate absolute degree of elevation above the level of the ocean, taken at the rate of 300 feet for each degree of latitude; but, as these isothermal lines depend on a variety of circumstances which modify the temperature throughout all parts of the earth, the existence of any vegetation must always be considered in connection with such complicated natural system, or as well established points through which the isothermal curves might be traced.—*Ed.*

view of the Bimber valley which we were soon to descend. We were met by the horses which I had applied for, and their leader informed me that the Raja himself was only four miles off. By Moradpoor we came to that ancient road by which the Emperors of Dehli went from Lahor to Kashmír, and of which Bernier gives so entertaining a description. Moradpoor was one of the resting-places on the route, and under the Moghul rule was a place of some note, but the Serai is now a very unpicturesque ruin, its narrow rooms are converted into stables, and a fine clump of trees is all that remains of the garden. It is five miles from Rajáwar. I had just quitted the village when a party of men rode up to me, and requested that I would there await the Raja's arrival. The idea of standing still at this spot, under a hot sun, was not very agreeable, but politeness demanded the sacrifice of comfort; so, taking my glass, I soon espied a gaily accoutred cavalcade engaged in sporting; as soon as the partridges were on the wing, they threw after them their large sparrow-hawks, but in such a direction that they could hardly have shot the game without wounding their hawks likewise; the gun is, therefore, rarely used: they did not take more than half-a-dozen. The Raja of Rajáwar is an extremely prepossessing and honest-looking man. Surrounded by his little court, he received me standing, and I, having alighted also, took his hand. On declining the offer of his horse or elephant, we took our way together to the town, he on his horse, I in my own favourite conveyance. My new friend was evidently very well informed, and had a good and fitting answer to give to every question. Originally a Sikh, he had now gone over to the Mohammedan creed, and had acquired Rajáwar since the expulsion and imprisonment of the restless Raja Agur Khan, who was seized by Gúlab Singh, during the second and fortunate expedition of Ranjít Singh into Kashmír in May, 1820. For this service he received Jamú as a jaghír. The present Raja Sultan Khan was formerly Raja of Bimber, and in 1812, joined the other Mohammedan princes against Ranjít, but they were subdued, and he spent seven years in captivity at Lahor. Ranjít Singh thought that his acquaintance with Kashmír might be useful to his army on his second march, and Sultan Khan being set at liberty, performed services which gained for him, on the return of the expedition, the jaghír or fief of Rajáwar.

The Raja led me into the once beautiful, but now ruined garden, where the Emperors used to rest on their progresses. Its chief ornaments now are the plane trees, two of which measure between five and six feet in diameter near the ground. There is a fine view from one of the ruined aqueducts over the river and the town, which is protected by walls and towers, and surrounded on all sides with hills. The Raja pointed out to my notice, with great pride, a high point, which is distant about five kos, called Azimgurh, as a very strong fort. After leaving me alone for half-an-hour, which he spent in the garden, he returned to my little tent, where there was but one chair, which he would not accept. After a mutual series of complimentary apologies, we concluded by starting forth again, and seating ourselves on a stone balustrade overlooking the Tohi. I informed him, through the Munshí, that I proposed to return his visit, but he replied, that if I came to his Durbár he should make me a present in money, and that, as he had been informed of my refusal to accept such gifts, he preferred rather to decline receiving me than to endure the affront of seeing his offering rejected. He stayed the whole day in the garden, and ordered his servants to bring me flowers, fish, and fruit: a sheep and several fowls were, moreover, liberally furnished for the wants of my followers. In the evening he came again, and I assured him that, on my return from Kashmír, I must disregard his wishes, and pay him a long visit, at all hazards.

About Rajáwar tropical plants are still seen, as, the Cotton and Banana, but the climate is much changed. Snow storms are frequent in January, and the snow often lies two whole days on the ground. The country is generally flat and uninteresting, but there is a torment for every traveller, whether on foot or horseback, or other conveyance: the Ziziphus or Jujube thorn, tears everything to pieces, and renders the journey to Rajáwar extremely troublesome and tedious. The thorns of the plant are so curved that when they catch hold of anything it is no easy matter to get clear of them, the damage they occasion both to clothes and skin is by no means trifling.

I travelled this day about seven kos in five hours. Unluckily, I found my cook one of the most quarrelsome fellows that I had met with; notwithstanding the softness of his name, Guláb Khan, or rose-water lord, none of the Musselmans could agree with him, and there was no end to his disputes and quarrels with the Hindús. After I had heard him vociferating loudly for some time, he came and complained that he had not time to prepare my curry, and that he was over-worked, his labour consisting of the preparation of my dinner, for the khidmatgár always got the breakfast and tea ready. I soon turned him out of the tent, with an order never to let me see his face or hear his voice again. By the time I had forgotten all about this, Jwali, the most active and useful of my chaprásís, ran in, took off his badge of office, laid it on the table, and declared that he had been too much insulted to feel justified in bearing such a mark of my confidence any longer. I then perceived that his hand was bleeding, and it turned out that in a sore fight, the cook, Gúlab Singh, had bitten the hand of the Chaprásí, Jwali Singh, who, on this occasion, had not maintained the honor of his name of the *fiery lion*. I was, therefore, obliged to send the former about his business forthwith, and took on myself the office of doctor to the injured Jwali, whose wound, however, was of no material importance.

Wednesday, Nov. 11.—Thermometer, 48°. 70°, 59°. Before my departure I took another view of the garden, and admired anew the large Plane trees,* a Plum and Magnolia Champaka, before which were lying, in this Mohammedan garden, some Hindú images; large rose-bushes, bearing the rosa-semperflorens; Indian crysanthemums, white and yellow, and a number of white jonquils with yellow cups, filled the

---

* The Platanus Orientalis, or plane tree, the Chinár of Persia, has a very extensive geographical range from this elevated region westerly; and is admirably characterised by its derivative πλατυς, *ample*, significant of its palmate leaves, its spreading branches, and shady foliage, the pale green colour of which last contrasts beautifully with the silver bark of its lofty stem. Its value in a hot climate has been appreciated by those who looked no higher, to the beneficent goodness of the Creator, and in this favoured spot, the plane tree attained, under the fostering attention of royalty, to the greatest age and perfection.—*Ed.*

whole garden with their sweet perfume. The road lay along the Tohi, which rushes over rocks and stones, to Thana, a place about twelve miles off. The valley of the Tohi, to judge from its situation, ought to be very delightful; as it opens to the mountains on the south, and seemingly cultivated; yet it is not so, the hills, to a great height, are cut into terraces and converted into rice fields, but wherever irrigation is impracticable, the whole country is overrun with briars and wild shrubs. Two of these last, and a very remarkable creeping plant were new to me, the others were all natives of the Himálaya. I am indebted to this day's journey for a large collection of seeds. It is curious to observe the gradual change from the vegetation of the tropics to that of the north, as we approach in that direction. At Berode, the son of the Raja of Rajáwar was waiting to receive me, under a group of splendid lime and chesnut trees. The small distance between Rajáwar and Berode made so great a difference in climate, that these trees, belonging to a northern region, were now substituted for the Magnolia and the Banana. The son was shooting also, and I thought it probable, with the view of having a present to offer me, in the shape of game. To meet a person with a gift is the highest courtesy an Indian can show, and both father and son availed themselves of the pretext of shooting, to do me this honor, without in the least derogating from their own dignity. Falcons were the destroyers employed. Curious to follow the tactics of these little birds of prey, I accompanied the party on their way. They sat as tamely as possible on the sportsman's hand, their feet being fastened together, as in our country, with a silken lace which was held tight, and on each foot was a little bell which betrayed its presence, if the sportsman was not alert in taking it off as he slipped his bird. The falcon usually catches the prey instantly, and seats himself on the ground with it; but a fine black partridge baffled its pursuer for a long time. At length it was brought to me alive and little injured. I reached Thana before nightfall. The ruined Serai is tenanted by a little colony of Kashmirians.

Thursday, Nov. 12.—Thermometer, 44°, 60°, 49°. I have traduced nature in this part. As we journeyed northwards to-day she assumed again a richer attire. The majestic form of the mighty trees, tinged with the most splendid tints of autumn, reminded me forcibly of the forests of my own country, with their garb varying from the golden yellow to the dark deep brown. Between Thana and Perhamgala we scaled the Ratan Panjal, a mountain more than 9000 feet high, following the banks of the Tohi to its source. The road is not invariably precipitous. From the summit of the Ratan Panjal the view is splendid, stretching over seven mountain ranges, to the great plains of the Panjáb. As we ascended, the vegetation around reminded me of Simla and its neighbourhood. I discovered a stunted Vaccinium, a well-known native of the Himálaya, and in the course of the day observed two of the Rhodondendron arboreum. But these grow on the south side of the Ratan Panjal, and on the north side of the Himálaya. There is hardly a foot's breadth of level ground near the summit of this mountain, and Ratan Sháhí, not forty feet below its highest peak, is a resting place, consisting of three houses and a tower. A party of soldiers belonging to the Maha Raja are stationed in the pass throughout the year. Shaded by the finest oaks, limes and chesnuts, unlike those found in European forests, we descended the northern side, taking our downward course over a hard stony path. The larger pines clothe the highest ridge, and blocks of ice, which the noonday's sun had not power to melt, were lying about. The thermometer at this time marked 60°, but the wind blew keenly, and the cold was very piercing. The unmelted piece of ice was a better thermometer, in fact, than the quicksilver, a phenomenon to be attributed to the extreme rarity and dryness of the air.

The Perhamgala on which the little town is built consists of two small streams, over which a bridge is thrown. The principal stream is a clear rapid mountain torrent, which has its source fifteen miles from the town, in the Pir Panjal, where there is a tank and place of pilgrimage; the Damdam flowing thence to Kashmír, and the Perhamgala taking a southward course.

My tent was pitched about a mile up the stream, close by the ruined Serai; the road was singularly romantic, the mountains closely hemmed together, and towering aloft towards the sky, scarcely admit one beam of sunlight to pierce the deep and narrow dell below. A beautiful waterfall on the right would have attracted many a traveller in Europe from a great distance to admire this so magnificent a scene.

Friday, November 13, thermometer 40°, 58°, 50°. The Thanadar made his appearance this morning, and demanded my Perwána, or permission to travel, which I had received from the Maha Raja. I found that the man was only doing his duty, and therefore referred him to my Múnshí, that the Perwána might be produced. It was in the possession of the Chobdár's servant, and he was still snugly lodged in a house, whence, however, he was quickly summoned. When he did come forth, I ordered him to take care in future that he produced the Maha Raja's permit whenever it was necessary, that I might not be importuned by such inquiries; and the man assured me that he had done so the preceding day. The Thanadar then came in for his share, and he was asked what he meant by such impertinence. He could only answer that he was entitled to ask a certain sum from any one who went by this mountain pass, and that he hoped I would not refuse to give the accustomed toll. I desired him to be told that he had chosen a wrong method of asking for a present, and that he might turn his back on my tent as soon as possible.

The snow, which often lies to the depth of a hundred feet at Perhamgala, occasions the place to be entirely abandoned during winter. The road continued to wind down to the valley, which is still closely hemmed in by vast overhanging mountains, and is so low that the presence of daylight is in some places almost unknown. Strange to say, the south side of this valley is everywhere wild and dreary, while fine trees grow up to the very summit of the mountain on the north face. The reason may possibly be found in the fact, that, on the south side, the repeated action of alternate freezing and thawing destroys every kind of vegetation, except a few grasses. Wherever a little open space is seen in the valley, it is crowded with chesnut trees of enormous size in which troops of large white monkeys with black faces have taken up their abode; these live on the fruits as they ripen. The chesnut, oak and holly, the pine and the fir, are the only natives of this region, The trunk of the first, which is very unlike the European tree, sometimes measures as much as six or seven feet in diameter. When the tree is old, the bark peels off in a remarkable way, and stands away from the trunk, in pieces, at a distance of two feet; the outer shell of the fruit has no excrescence. On one spot I saw a tuft of the gigantic lily, and robbed it of as many seeds and bulbs as I could get possession of from the steep rock in which it grew. One stalk measured nine feet, and had six seed capsules. The Shikarí was by far the most active of my attendants in climbing the declivities; and as this lily grew on a slippery soil, which gave way under the feet, there was some little difficulty in obtaining it. When he had succeeded, the next feat was to slit off a part of the stem in an oblique direction, which he then formed into a musical instrument, on which he played after the manner of the shepherds of Switzerland and the Tyrol. This rustic pipe is much in fashion among the Himálayan shepherds also. Early recollections made the sound of this wild music so charming to me, that my attendants imagined they could do no better than provide themselves each with a similar instrument; but the discord that ensued was so terrible, that I was obliged at length to put a stop to their trials, not one of them understanding how to draw one proper sound from the reed except the Shikári.

The pretty village of Dobran is three kos distant from Perhamgala. The women, according to the custom of these mountains, were all on the flat roofs of their cottages, and greeted my arrival with songs. In the valley I was visited by a man, whom I took for a common beggar. I asked him the name of the place ; but misunderstanding me, he told me his own, adding, that he was the Sirdar, or lord of the whole. I made him a present of a rupee, which he thankfully accepted. My next visitors were a large party of monkeys. Two of immense size began fighting together, without taking the slightest notice of us ; and when, I tried to separate them, by throwing stones, they took my mediation very ill, and springing to a rock hard by, amused themselves and us by making the most hideous grimaces.

Two miles from Dobran, a steep road continued up to the hill on which is the ruined Serai of Poshyan. It is inhabited during the summer by traders in provisions, &c., who betake themselves in the winter to Rajáwar. The whole range from Ratan Panjál to Pir Panjál belongs to Guláb Singh. I found my tent spread on the roofs of several houses, the only level place to be found on the mountain, which as far as the eye can reach, is without tree or bush. I arrived at noon, but the sun gave no warmth, and a chilly west wind which at sunset veered round to the east, and blew direct from the snowy mountains, made the air piercingly cold.

Saturday, Nov. 14.—It was late when the servants crept out of the houses, and I was obliged to have a fire lighted to dispel the chill which I also suffered. The thermometer, in a southern aspect, was 50°, at 7 o'clock; at one it fell to 45° in the mountains. The day's march however, was of much interest; at every step the vegetation seemed to dwindle, until we attained the region of perpetual snow, when it disappeared altogether. This was on the north side of the mountain; on the south flank immense naked rocks towered one above the other, in whose deep clefts the snow was piled up. The gradual transition from the vegetation of South Germany, the chesnut, lime, ilex, elm, and alder, to that of Norway, with its stunted firs and birches, as all we met with here, differing however in form from the productions of Europe, gave room to much and most interesting observation and reflection. My company of followers were often forced to quit the straight road and follow the devious paths in every direction, that I might satisfy my strong desire to possess some plant, insect, or stone. My booty in new plants and seeds exceeded my expectation, and the autumn had even spared a few rare flowers. Among the firs on the north side of the mountain I espied a Daphne, at least so I judge from the bud, and a little further on, a Vaccinium, much resembling our own; and, still onwards, on the other side of a ravine amid some birches, a new shrub like the Rhododendron, whose branches were mostly bent earthwards by the snow. Its hardy appearance, however, convinces me that it would flourish in our cold climates. With infinite fatigue and trouble I reached a clump, but could find neither bud nor seed, and returned quite exhausted to the road. Later in the day I perceived a second and larger group, growing on a steep place on the opposite side of the ravine, and I promised to give a couple of rupees to the man who first brought me some of the seeds. In an instant they were all rushing down the precipice, without heed or precaution, springing from rock to rock, until I trembled to look after them; the steep bank was soon gained. My glass showed me that they were breaking off all the branches at hazard, but they were gone too far for my voice to reach them, and I could only hope that by good luck they might bring me one slip, at least, on which a fruit might be found. On their return a small wood was laid before me, but not what I wished, and I retained the rupees, thinking we might be more fortunate presently. With the Rhododendron was intermingled the Elm, and a species of the Evonymus, or spindle tree, both with trunks lying along the earth, and sometimes reaching to a length of forty feet. The Juniper is the highest bush found on the north flank of the mountain; the Barberry and Currant on the south. The snow, which had been falling for a fortnight, prevented me from searching for anything higher. Clay and mica schist are found on the west side of the Pir Panjal up to its summit, and single pieces of hornblende are lying about, as though some way-worn traveller had cast them down, unable to endure the trouble of bearing them along. The ascent is dreadfully steep. With a volume of Bernier in my hand, I gazed around and recalled in imagination the time when the gorgeous suite of the Emperor of Dehli clambered up these perilous and difficult paths. In many parts the soil is so loose and crumbling, as to afford no safe footing; and large masses falling from above, block up the usual road, and force the traveller to find out a new one as he best can. It seems to me impossible that elephants could ever tread such a pass, not so much on account of their unwieldy size, for they climb steep places with incredible facility; but that their weight is so enormous, and I find in Bernier an account of a number of elephants which were precipitated into the depths below, as they proceeded with the Zenana on their backs. A small tower is built on the highest point, where a party of the Maha Raja's troops are stationed throughout the year; and hard by is the grave of a Mohammedan fakír, named Pír Panjal, from whom the mountain takes its name. There is a fine prospect in the direction of the Panjáb, and the eye stretching over unnumbered ranges of hills, loses all further view in the dimmer and warmer atmosphere of the south. A little further on, we passed into a gorge of the mountain. On the north, or right side, was a vast wall of snow above us. The south was a naked rock ; in vain I essayed to catch one glimpse of the long-looked-for valley, the limits of my wanderings in Asia in this direction. Towards the east stretched a barren plain, through which flows the Damdam, a river now partly frozen ; and in many spots were deep holes, evidently dug by bears; I saw none of these animals, but their traces were very perceptible. One creature we saw climbing up the naked rock, which I imagine must have been a leopard : it was nearly white, with a long tail, and of large size. Finally, after another hour of toilsome way, my anxious eye descried the huge mountain masses of Tibet, beyond the valley of Kashmír, their highest peaks, Mer and Ser being plainly visible. I saw them but for an instant, a turn of the road again hid them from my view, but never rose any more proudly than they, with their two pyramids, the one black, the other white, close to one another, and apparently of the same altitude. The valley itself could not be seen from any point.

It seems natural to all nations to experience more or less of fear in passing over these wild mountains. After my Indians and Kashmirians had all prayed at the tomb of Pír Panjal the devotee, they sacrificed some cowries and muscle shells to his namesake the mountain ; these represent the smallest Indian money : the bearers also asked me for some little present, as a thank-offering for my safe conveyance through the dangerous mountain pass. Alihabad Serai, or, as it is usually called, Padshahí Serai, is completely hemmed in on every side by high snowy mountains, and is the only abode kept up for the reception of travellers in this part. The desolate tract between Rajáwar and Kashmír is so thinly inhabited that, if it were not for this station, which is occupied by a corporal and a few sepoys, who are not relieved until they have passed several years in this wilderness, travellers would, indeed, be sadly off. In October, they lay in their winter stock of provisions, wood, &c.; at the end of November the snow storms begin, and from that time the men do not even venture into the yard, where the snow remains piled up for months. My little tent was pitched in the middle of this yard, and the cold was certainly most piercing. I wrote and amused myself with my map until my benumbed fingers refused to serve me any longer. At six in the evening the thermometer fell to 39°.

Sunday, Nov. 15.—Thermometer 48°, 52°, 46°. The night was dreadful. My poor Indians kept up a chorus of coughs, and some of the stoutest, instead of sleeping, sat up all night round a large fire, and tried to while away the cold by singing. In vain I courted sleep under my thick coverlets. In spite of the fatigues I had undergone, I could not close my eyes, and that painful feeling that generally accompanies want of sleep, brought before me, sad and sweet recollections as if from a past world, of all that I had felt and endured in this. How wearisome such nights appear! With the dawn my mind became more tranquillized; images of the future, and hopes all full of home, dispelled the troubles and fancies brought on by cold and fatigue.

From this military post to Hirpoor, the distance is ten long kos,* over the steep side of the Pír Panjal. The road first took us through a deep ravine; and then, just as I expected to get at last a glimpse of the valley, came another hill, and another. We skirted, for some time, a wall of rock, which was built as a safeguard, by order of Shah Jehan. The superstitious inhabitants of these parts have a tale concerning Ali Merdan Khan, the builder of this wall, and of all the Serais between Lahor and Kashmír. According to this fable, as the architect marshalled his workmen along the road, he came suddenly to a tower, which they one and all refused to pass, because a man-eater called Lál Gúlam dwelt there, who was accustomed from the tower to seize upon the passengers, as they stole one by one along the narrow path, and hurl them down the precipice, when he devoured them at leisure. The brave Ali Merdan Khan went into the tower first, but Lál Gúlam had just quitted it. He found his son there, however, whom he instantly hurled down the precipice. Since that time, nothing more has been

---

* The kos of the Hindús, strictly speaking, is about 13,000 feet, or 2 miles, 5 furlongs, 153 yards. The Mohammedans having introduced the itinerary measures of their various native countries, we have a great variety of such measures to which the Hindú term kos is indiscriminately applied—and this accounts in some measure for the discrepancies between the statements furnished by Hindús and Mohammedans. The Mohammedan kos may be taken at 35 to the degree.—*Ed.*

heard of Lál Gúlam, and the remembrance of the murders he committed is gradually dying away, but the tower still bears his name, and was certainly a fit place for the dwelling of a robber. That the Pír Panjal has ever been dangerous enough, without the needless addition of cannibals, is shown by the countless skeletons of horses and oxen, and the whitened human bones, which remain, melancholy evidences of the fate which has overtaken many a wanderer in these terrific passes. The sudden transition from great heat to excessive cold, had brought a fever on many of my servants; and as there was no better physician at hand, and I had often seen the beneficial effects of calomel in similar cases, I gave them doses of twelve to fifteen grains on this occasion. Poor fellows! it was with the utmost difficulty that they could pursue their way, laden as they necessarily were; they were forced to lie down for awhile at the top of every level spot, from sheer exhaustion. I would gladly have thrown away a part of my baggage, if that would have availed them; but they had loaded themselves very absurdly with a weight, on their own account, at least twice as great as what they carried for me.

Four kos from the Padshahí Serai, we arrived at the picturesque fortress of Inganali Kilah; two branches of the Damdam river unite here, and the mountain sinking abruptly to a hill, discloses also two detached towers defending the entrance of the mountain, which towards the north, from the right bank of the stream, might be easily mastered. At all other points, it may safely be deemed impregnable. The Serai now in a ruined state, from the frequent falling masses, which have destroyed the former approaches, lies at the base of the mountain, and near the river.

From this ruin we again directed our steps to the highest of the towers we had previously observed, which is perched 1000 feet above it. The valley of the Damdam was on the route, enriched with beautiful firs, pines, &c., and giving somewhat the appearance of a park to the various points where these little forests have long grown and flourished, far from all human dwellings. Here nature seems to have reigned perfectly free and uncontrolled by the ingenuity of man, since its first creation. I strolled into the forest for some time; and, lost in the interest of such a scene, gazed untired on the myriads of strange birds which were flying about in this oasis; and the large squirrels, which were merrily bounding from branch to branch. How much of life, of happy life too, was there in this lonely spot!

Hirpoor was a miserable place, over which towers the snowy head of the Pír Panjal. The Thanadar came to see me; but I could procure nothing for my servants, although I tried, by every means, to restore their wasted strength by more generous nourishment, and diligently, though in vain, enquired for a sheep. Hirpoor lies in the mountains, and in an elevated situation; but from no point is Kashmír discernible, and amid the continued and devious hill ranges, one can only now and then distinguish the outline of the high chain of Tibet.

In the course of the evening, a fakír, almost naked, crawled to my tent door, and began to sing. The weather had become so bitterly cold, that, wrapped up in vests and shawls as I was, I could not hold a pen in my fingers. Compassionating his wretched appearance, I ordered the servants to give him a rupee, and to bid him shelter himself where he liked, or at least to take as a gift one of my blankets; but no, his vow bound him to add nothing to his present scanty garb. His voice was remarkably fine; and in his song, which was all in praise and honour of God, were mingled wishes for my happiness and peace. He kept me awake till the night was far gone; and when I awoke in the morning, there was the singer still, his voice only hoarser than before. If I had pitied the poor fakír yesterday, how could I help admiring, at the same time, the firm devotedness, the deep conviction, however mistaken, that he was expiating worldly sins, by this endurance of pain and destitution.

Monday, November 16, thermometer 20°, 48°, 52°. I had erroneously anticipated that, on turning my back on Pír Panjal, I had passed the limit of extremest cold. I suffered much from it this morning, and my uneasiness increased, when I considered that as Hirpoor could not be more than 500 feet higher than Kashmír, the cold there must also have robbed nature of her loveliest charms. At sunrise the fakír ceased, and my people began a chorus of complaints. The water-bearer did not know what he should do, his leathern sack was turned into stone, and not a drop of water could he squeeze out; the khidmatgár brought me a broken bottle, in which the water had frozen hard, as something which he thought as new and strange to me, as it was to him; and the bearer who attended to my toilet, after he had got water from the river, did not understand what use he could make of it, everything being hard as iron; gradually, however, the novelty of the sight diverted their minds from these grievances, and a sparkling fire helped to cheer them still more. The cold of northern Europe had never swollen my face and lips as now; and that we might all have as much rest, and as little travelling as possible, I limited the day's journey to Chupayan, which is not more than seven miles further. Our route was over another hill, to the narrow valley of the Damdam. Everywhere I was reminded of the great difference between the poverty of a warm climate, and of a cold one. Where the heaven is cloudless, and the temperature high or moderate, the very first want of life, warmth, renders misery, if painful, at least endurable; but when man cannot protect himself against the pitiless climate he inhabits, and wants, at the same time, every proper necessary of life, then indeed is poverty terrible.

Just before reaching Chupayan, we passed two houses belonging to Pírs, Mohammedan saints, which are surrounded by large plane trees, and decorated with the beautiful iris. I was curious to find in this part the forms of many of our European plants, without recognising anywhere the same exact species.* Except the red clover, the blue chicory and the sweet scented violet, I could gather nothing which grows in Germany. Apples were plentiful, and of many sorts, but neither were they what we cultivate. Grafting or improving their trees in any way seems unpractised among them, probably unknown; hence propagation by layers or offsets is their only means of increasing the

* In examining the various species of plants on the Nilgiri Mountains of Coimbatoor and Malabar, in company with the Rev. Bernard Schmid in 1833, I was often led to remark the same singular anomaly in some one or other circumstance of about 350 different plants, in their general characters closely resembling their congeners of Europe. The altitude of Dodabetta is 8750 feet above the sea, and the table land about 7300 feet on an average, the latitude between 11° and 12° north.—*Ed.*

species. Two small villages preceded the larger one, which cannot be said to lie in the plain, although the declivity is very slight. I sent to the Thanadar for a sheep, which he provided, with an entreaty that I would not allow it to be killed on this day, which was holy; as it was for my attendants I suffered them to do as they pleased with it; and they obeyed the request, depriving themselves of the animal food they really stood in need of. Leprosy, which I had seen continually in the Himálaya mountains, and on my route hither, seemed to disappear in the valleys.

The wind was so piercing, that we were forced to quicken our pace, to keep ourselves from suffering dreadfully from its effects. The sky was clear, with the exception of one little cloud, which seemed to take its stand, seemingly to hide the sun from us until the afternoon, when it had sunk too low to afford us any warmth. In the evening, a change of weather came on; clouds obscured the sky, and the cold abated.

Tuesday, 17th, thermometer 36°, 52°, 47°. The bed of the Damdam at this place is not much less than a mile in width; but at the present season is a shallow stream, certainly not more than a foot deep, and flows in the middle of the channel. Large stones fill up the bed of the watercourse, on which the drought of last season has favoured the growth of a luxuriant vegetation. It was my wish to reach Kánakpoor to-day, and though rain in the morning had somewhat retarded our journey, there was still plenty of time before us; but, at the distance of a few miles, I was met by the Thanadar of Ramú. Our road traversed a beautiful country; two fine mosques, now in ruins, indicated its former prosperity. His welcome consisted of two delicious pears, and a few rupees, the first of which I accepted most willingly, the latter I declined. He confidently assured me I should do well to spend the night at Ramú, where I should find all that I could require, instead of proceeding to Kánakpoor, where I might solicit in vain, even for water. I took his advice accordingly. Ramú is situated at the foot of a hill, whence they told me that the city of Kashmír or Srinagur, the first being the Mohammedan, the last the ancient Hindú name, was plainly discernible. In anxious expectancy to catch a glimpse of the goal of my long journey, I climbed to the top, but saw nothing but smoke and dust. In the evening I was visited by Mirza Abdul Rahim from Kashmír, a native of Túrkestan, who, as my Múnshí informed me, had been a teacher in the Gymnasium at Agra. His glittering dress and green turban designated a descendant of the prophet, and his first act was to offer me half a dozen rupees, which I touched, according to custom, and then returned. He next gave me a letter written by Mr. Vigne, an Englishman, who had extended his Asiatic travels as far as Kashmír, to certify that he was an agent of the East India Company. I was surprised that Captain Wade should neither have spoken nor written to me about him, but doubted not Mr. Vigne's authority; and accordingly treated him with great distinction, that is, I allowed him to take a chair. As he intended to spend the night here, and accompany me to Kashmír on the morrow, I made arrangements that he should share my smaller tent with the Múnshí. Meanwhile, no less a personage than the Kázi, or Mohammedan judge, made his appearance, to salute me in the Viceroy's name; but ere he uttered a syllable, forth came a handful of rupees, which, on my declining, he distributed among my people. I was much pleased with his manners, although I did not think fit to take his advice, which was, that I should divide the ten kos which lay between me and the capital, into two days' journey. My bearers, who were all well lodged and provided for by the Thanadar, at first refused to go all the way to Srinagur in one day; but they, who in the heart of desolate mountains might have laid down the law with impunity, when they reach well-peopled regions, are forced to yield their will to their master's, unless they wish to quit his service. Wednesday, November 18.—For two miles our path led over gentle hills, whence there was a lovely view of the valley beneath, about five or six miles across and beyond it, to the mountains of Tibet. We passed the ruins of the Serai of Kának-poor; and thence, winding over another hill, we came to the banks of the Dudh Ganga, ornamented with villages and rice fields, amid which grew the plane and poplar tree, with many others, bearing rich fruits. All round, and as far as the eye could reach, the land appeared highly cultivated and populous. A little way further, a body of soldiers was sent to escort me; these, with my own suite, and that of the Kázi, formed a considerable, and to me, a most incommodious party, for the dust they raised in the loose soil was perfectly suffocating.

There is nothing in the approach to Kashmír to remind the traveller of the vicinity of a place of note; the Takht-i-Sulimán and fort being the most prominent features. We followed the windings of the Dudh Ganga, and were in Kashmír before we were aware of it. Fine avenues of plane and poplar are the first signs of the former beauty of this favourite and lovely abode of the splendid Moghul emperors; and then comes the square, where the soldiers of Ranjít Singh practised those European tactics which gained him possession of his large dominions. Two of his regiments, disciplined by Europeans, are stationed here; their uniform consisted of a red jacket, with yellow facings, and blue trousers and turban, blue being the favourite Sikh colour. The subalterns wear white turbans. The whole would have had an excellent effect, the men being evidently carefully selected for height and carriage, if their fine dresses had not been in so ragged a condition. The muskets are made after the English fashion, and manufactured in Lahor.

At the same moment that I reached the eastern suburb of the city of Kashmír, near Sháherghur, the viceroy's palace, I saw him coming out at the gates, attended by a numerous retinue, and approaching the spot where I was. The Kázi pointed him out and requested me to stand still till he came up. I was so covered with dust, however, that a basin of water would then have been the most desirable of earthly conveniences. I therefore insisted on the bearers proceeding. From the left bank of the Jelam, we crossed a bridge erected over a canal, and, passing through a great portion of the filthy ruinous suburbs we came at length to the house which had been allotted for my abode. The exterior, dismal and unclean as it appeared, was anything but satisfactory; however, I made no remark, but proceeded to take a fuller survey of that part which some of my servants had occupied since the preceding evening. Approaching a lower window, therefore, I discovered that I was a lodger in the second floor of a house elevated far above the river, which it overlooked. The Jelam, at this spot, forcibly reminded me of the Arno at Florence, but is much deeper and remarkably still: it winds most picturesquely through the city, and was covered with boats of various form and fashion.

Exactly opposite, on the left shore, within a walled inclosure, was that quarter of the city containing the residence of the viceroy, and the several retainers of the court, civil and military. The principal entrance to the viceroy's palace is from the shore, whence a broad flight of wooden stairs leads to a terrace and pavilion, adorned with curiously carved woods. I next visited every part of my new dwelling, which, instead of the spacious clean palace I had too readily anticipated, was filthy in the extreme, and divided into a great number of small mean rooms. It was not in the nature of things that I could fail to express my discontent at such a place; I, therefore, inquired, whether I could not find a garden, in which I might pitch my tent. I recollected the Diláwar Khán Bágh, where Jacquemont and Mr. Vigne had taken up their residence; and as the wishes of a European are commands in Kashmír, on making inquiry, whether there was not some place for me there or elsewhere, I was quickly provided with a boat, which conveyed me to the Shah Hamedán Masjid, whence I proceeded on foot to the garden, in which, surrounded by fruit trees, vines, and the beautiful syringa Persica, I observed two little low square buildings, erected by the side of a large sheet of water. One had been already taken by Mr. Vigne. Of the other I took possession, and ordered my tent to be pitched in front of it. While everything was preparing for my reception, I quietly took my seat at the window of my apartment, where I was visited by many of the principal inhabitants. A party of Kashmírian females in boats drew up also beneath the window, and sang me their Wonimún, or song of welcome. The men of this country were handsome. Let me not be deemed ungallant in asserting that the women, on the contrary, in the plainness of their features, were far inferior to any I had ever before cast eyes on in Asia; their singing, moreover, was little better than a dreadful yell.

After they had all taken their departure, satisfied with a few courteous expressions and some trifling presents, I sat down to write; but was interrupted again by the entrance of the Múnshí, who came to inform me that a man, most wretchedly clad, without doubt some Englishman, desired to speak with me. On being ushered in, he presented the most whimsical figure I ever beheld. His long red and white face, prominent nose and eyes, with matted red beard, constituted his chief personal peculiarities: his filthy tattered garments were partially arranged according to the Tibetan costume. In the strongest Scottish accent, he begged my pardon, and said he expected to find Mr. Vigne there. I exclaimed involuntarily, "Who on earth are you?" To which he replied, "You surely must have heard of Dr. Henderson?" I told him I had, and immediately offered my hand, bidding him welcome to clothes, or anything with which I could provide him. Dr. Henderson's character is well known in India. His restless mind could not be satisfied with the quiet routine of his professional duties. Bent on travelling, he had formed various plans, the most important of which, however, was the publication of newspapers and articles, deprecating the policy of the Indian Government. These he edited in so violent a spirit, that the Commander-in-Chief expressly forbad him, as a Company's officer, having any further connexion with the press. Some months ago, he obtained leave of absence from the station at Lúdiana, to travel on foot to Calcutta, a journey of some three or four months. The greater portion of his time was taken up in wandering from Mandí to Ladák, to trace the Atok to its source; after which he hurried back on his way to Calcutta, hoping to arrive there in time to escape the heavy consequences of exceeding his leave of absence.

Meanwhile the Government had received information that an Englishman in disguise had been seen in the dominions of the independent hill rajahs. All this I had heard in India. I now learnt from Dr. Henderson, that he arrived in Ladák at the very time that it was invaded by Zerávar Singh*, Guláb Singh's general. The Raja of Ladák, who was still there, received Henderson very kindly, having soon discovered that he was an Englishman, in spite of his Mohammedan garb, and his fictitious name of Ishmael Khan, firmly persuading himself that he had come to ratify the treaty which poor Moorcroft had entered into with him, in the name of the Company. Vainly did Henderson

* Zeráwar Singh—the Lion of Strength.

protest that he was mistaken, the Raja shewed him the original document. When produced, his astonishment evidently satisfied the Raja, that Henderson was hitherto utterly ignorant of its existence; and that he had no authority, moreover, to confirm it. Determined, however, to turn the appearance of an Englishman to his own advantage, he now refused to suffer him to quit Ladák; hoping thereby to make the invading general, Zeráwar Singh, believe that he was an envoy, sent from the East India Company, with proffers of assistance. For three months poor Henderson was detained in durance; and, on making an effort to escape, was seized, wounded, and re-imprisoned. During this interval, Zeráwar Singh's military operations were suspended, and he advised Guláb Singh of the supposed envoy's arrival, requesting fresh instructions. Guláb Singh, on his part, applied to the Maha Raja, who, without a moment's delay, addressed the political resident at Lúdiana, to ascertain the meaning of such proceeding.

The resident satisfied Ranjít Singh with an assurance, that Dr. Henderson, the traveller, had passed the Setlej in direct violation of the orders of his Government; and that there was not the slightest idea of interfering with Ranjít's plans of extending his conquests northwards. Zeráwar Singh, after this explanation, was desired to proceed with his operations; upon which, the Rajah of Ladák suffered Henderson to depart, and he lost no time in making his way through Iskardú, the smaller state in Tibet, usually marked in our European maps, Balti, to Kashmír, where he had just arrived. Thus did three Europeans meet, two of whom had entered Kashmír, almost at the same hour, from exactly opposite directions.

Dr. Henderson described Tibet much as I had expected, as a remarkably poor country, except in precious stones and metals. His road led him over vast mountain passes, the highest of which marked 188° Fahr. boiling point; but these again were so overtopped by still loftier peaks, that the prospect, even from these stupendous heights, was still very limited. On a journey such as his must have been, escaping from Ladák in disguise, and in constant fear of detection, it is not to be wondered at that he did not go out of his way to visit any of the mountain heights around him. But as he was provided with instruments, and had some tact for observation, we may confidently trust that he will be able to give us many valuable particulars on a part of the world so imperfectly known as Tibet.

My tent being ready, I now took possession of it; and was most reluctantly compelled to accept from the Kázi the 525 rupees sent me by Ranjít Singh. An important question now arose, whether the Viceroy or I ought to pay the first visit. As I had no intention to stay many days in the city, I simply required his permission to see everything remarkable. I resolved not to run the risk of any delay, but to pay him the first visit on the following morning. Mehan Singh, the present governor, is a general in Ranjít's army, and has been in Kashmír about sixteen months.

Mirza Ahmed, the Múnshí, or rather secretary, of Jacquemont, paid me a visit, and brought the testimonial to his faithful services, which he had received from Jacquemont and General Allard, in whose employ he had formerly been. I could not look upon the well-known writing of poor Jacquemont without deep emotion on this identical spot, in this very garden, in which he had passed so many months. Fondly did he look forward to a futurity of happiness and independence in his own native land. He little dreamed, when he penned those lines, full of health and life, how soon he would be called away. Alas! how nearly are hopes and dreams allied! The dawning day disturbs our fairest visions as time swallows up the cherished anticipations of earthly felicity; wishes, perhaps, are never, or so late, fulfilled, that the bitter disappointment, the hope long deferred, robs them at length of the power of conferring happiness. I felt, myself, the same longings which ever haunted his mind, without expecting the same fruits from my wanderings; and who knows whether the yearning of my heart towards home will ever be gratified; or, if so, under what circumstances?

Mr. Vigne had gone to the mountain behind the city, called the Takht-i-Súliman, to take some sketches. I wrote him a few lines apprising him of my arrival to share the garden with him, and invited him to dine with me in the evening. I found him an agreeable companion, of a lively, open disposition. This invited intimacy from our first interview. He had returned from Iskardú about three weeks since, and prided himself on having accomplished a journey which Jacquemont described as perilous in the extreme.

None but a traveller can understand the delight of visiting a country which is scarcely marked on our maps. The interest he feels as he treads on this terrâ incognitâ, hoping, perchance, to discover something new at every step; nay more, the very expectation of coming dangers and events tends to exhilarate and occupy his mind: to say nothing of the possibility of his name being handed down with honour to futurity. There are few men without their share of vanity. Some such feeling, it may be, accompanies the lonely traveller through the remote mountains and valleys of Tibet, and supports him during months of hardship and solitude, in his labours to effect what others have failed to accomplish.

Ahmed Shah, the reigning prince of Iskardú, is at present in a situation of some embarrassment. The Sikhs, who within the last forty years have sprung up in the north-west of India from comparative obscurity to command the greater part of the country, are now united under one powerful head, to whom all the petty Mohammedan states are subject. The hill chieftains east, west, and south of Kashmír have become his tributaries, and those who refuse his terms are deprived of their possessions without any protracted ceremonials.

The north is now to be the scene of his triumphs. Ladák has fallen. Ahmed Shah sees the storm gradually advancing towards him, without any means of opposing it; he is still preparing himself for the worst. Iskardú had so long been at peace; its poverty seemed to defend it so well against the plunderer; all its neighbours seemed to consider its territories so worthless, that the people are perfectly defenceless against warlike talent. An alliance with the Company would have gladdened Ahmed Shah, and set his mind at rest. Mr. Vigne's visit at this juncture, was highly acceptable. I know not how far he may have given him some hopes of an alliance with England, which assuredly never will be entered into, but I am well aware that a confidential servant of Ahmed Shah accompanies Mr. Vigne for the purpose of taking a reply to his application for aid from the Governor-General back to Iskardú.

Ahmed is not an enemy to be despised even by Ranjít Singh, notwithstanding his lack of regular troops, or the poverty and scanty population of his dominions. His subjects are of a hardy frame, expert in the chase, and would soon acquire dexterity in the use of any weapons necessary for their own defence. Their country is protected by deep ravines and lofty mountains. The troops of Iskardú, unaccustomed to war, which they carry on after the oriental fashion on their own account, would not withstand the well disciplined forces of their enemy, Ranjít Singh, in the open field for a single hour. Well acquainted, however, with the inaccessibility of their mountains, they might bid defiance to an advancing army, nay, destroy it to a man, if only they were resolute. The Sikh soldiery, mostly composed of natives from the plains, are proof against the heat of the Panjáb, or India, but altogether unfitted to resist the variable climate of a mountainous and northern region, or the fatigues inseparable from warfare carried on amid these rugged scenes. The bad effects experienced by the army of a general marching into India from the north, owing to the difference of climate, would be felt equally, though in another way, by an Indian army in Tibet; possibly even more, for the climate of India, by exciting a new comer to increased activity, often affects him injuriously; but the cold climate entirely demoralizes those who dwell near the tropics. The easy conquest of Ladák by Ranjít Singh's army is no proof of anything to the contrary. The faith of the people of Ladák is Buddhism, while that of Iskardú is that of Mohammed.

The direction of the rivers prove that Iskardú, Ladák, and Lassa belong to the Indian side of the mountain chain. The valley of the Atok forms the chief possession of the first and second of these states, and the valleys of the Samper and the Goljao that of Lassa. It is not certain whether the highest mountain chain lies midway, or to the north of these rivers, but the highest table-land is certainly on the other side of them, and is much farther north than we have hitherto supposed.

In the evening I received a message of welcome by Samed Shah, the deputy of Mohammed Shah Nakshbandi, a person of great consequence in Kashmír, who is said to feed two hundred poor men daily. He requested permission to visit me. In return, I sent him the letter of introduction which Captain Wade had given me to him. All that I saw during my first day's stay in Kashmír, was the ruins of what once had been palaces, old dilapidated houses, streets of unexampled filthiness; a population strictly corresponding with them, a large boat full of old fishwomen, who stunned me with their inharmonious voices when they screamed out their wonimún, or song of welcome, from the canal.

Such were my first impressions of this long-dreamt-of fairy land; thence, as I gradually turned my disappointed gaze from the works of man to the glorious mountain scenery above, with their thousand peaks of snowy whiteness, their graceful outlines, the harmony and sweet repose which seemed to characterize the calm, motionless valley; the contrast between simple, majestic, Nature, and enterprising, ambitious Man, filled my heart with emotions which imprinted the beauties of the first on my memory, and made human works lose every shadow of significance.

Dr. Henderson and Mr. Vigne were my guests; I begged them to remain with me during their stay, and thus Hingam, my khansaman, and the two cooks hired at Rájawar, had a fair opportunity of displaying their culinary skill. How delightful it was, after so long an absence, to find myself once again in the society of men, who, although strangers, seemed like dear friends under present circumstances. The Governor had sent me a capital dessert of fresh fruit, grapes, apples, nuts, and pears, all excellent, having in the earlier part of the day most liberally supplied me with sheep, fowls, and other provisions.

That I might feel the cold less severely, I had ordered my bed to be arranged on the carpet of my tent within the pavilion. Unfortunately, this pavilion was constructed for a dwelling place during the great heat of summer; the walls, to the height of two feet, were composed of the beautiful open lattice wood carving for which Kashmír is so celebrated; through this the air entered at every crevice, and windows were pierced on all the four sides. It is superfluous to state that what is delightful in July is exactly the reverse in November, especially to very thinly clad travellers. I fell asleep, indeed, from sheer exhaustion, but the piercing cold soon chased slumber away, nor could I again close my eyes during that long night. How busy was memory the while, calling back the long past events, and the more recent incidents of my pilgrimage, until positive bodily suffering brought up the account to the present. Reluctantly I acknowledge that my arrival in Kashmír had not afforded me any satisfaction. It had neither contributed to my pleasure nor to my repose. Such, methought, is this chapter of my travels, or rather, of my life. I have attained the object of my desire, compared with which every other has appeared insignificant. Have I been sufficiently grateful to God, who has permitted me to reach this place? How great occasion have I for thankfulness as well as for serious reflection! Here am I, in the very land presumed to be the loveliest spot of the whole habitable earth, by many considered the terrestrial paradise:—crumbling ruins attest the instability of human greatness; everything made by man is in course of destruction, without the accompanying loveliness of decay; while nature blooms on for ever in the same youth, energy, and life, as heretofore. In that life all is truth, every promise fulfilled, every hope gratified, since Earth is the obedient child of the Allwise Creator. Man is governed, how often! by his own wayward fancies, his mind tossed to and fro, his fears conflicting with his wishes, nor can the wisest of human philosophers rightly explain or understand what moral truth is. That is a knowledge we must discover in our own hearts, and it will address us with a mighty voice; let us take heed not to turn a deaf ear to it. It tells us that we were made to be the living temples, not of the world, nor the world's vanities, but of our Father in heaven. Does not every situation of life satisfy us of this fact? When we can no longer enjoy the pleasures of youth; when the deceitful views of happiness are abandoned; when man feels how swiftly years roll over his head, never to return; when many sorrows have bowed his spirit, does he not turn for consolation and hope to Heaven, and search, whatever may be his creed, for those promises which religion holds out—retribution, reward, forgiveness, in a happier futurity. Yes! even they whose objects are limited to earth, its fame and honours, aspire to that which they never can attain there—Immortality! and fools who raise not their thoughts above this transitory scene, vainly flatter themselves that their memory will live for ever on earth; these lift up the pyramid, Sesostris-like, destroy one of the world's wonders with an Eratostratus,* or themselves, like Cato. Vain man! thou forgettest that the ever-

---

* In the German text it is erroneously ascribed to Eristothemus. Eratostratus was a native of Ephesus, who burned the celebrated temple of Diana in that city, that he might immortalize his name. A decree was therefore passed by his fellow-citizens, forbidding the mention of his name; nor, indeed, would it have been handed

rolling tide of time carries away all thy boasted deeds and works—even thy very name also is soon blotted out and forgotten!

Thursday, November 19. How strange is the feeling of finding oneself at a place which it has cost much time and trouble to reach. If it is unconnected with any still more distant object, we have at first a sensation of unnecessary fatigue, which might possibly have been spared; the only remedy for this is activity, whereupon I began my day with employment of various kinds. In the first place, it was an important matter to ascertain the situation of Kashmír for my map. The quadrant to-day gave 72,4, by the artificial horizon for Dilawar Khan's garden. I neglected the index error, as Dr. Henderson had noted it, my visit precluding my taking any observation with the sextant. I reckoned on seeing everything worthy of observation in the course of four days, at the expiration of which I purposed to take my leave of the city. At ten o'clock the Kázi came to attend me to the presence of the Governor, Mehan Singh. He had brought the state boat, an unshapely affair, sixty or seventy feet long, and only six feet wide, manned by thirty rowers. The seat was at the upper end, and covered with a Kashmír shawl, or Páshmina, for by that name articles made from their goats' wool are known here. Mr Vigne and Dr. Henderson wished to accompany me, but by the time the breakfast was over, and we were ready to start, it was noon, and the Kázi told me it was then too late. I was vexed that he had not reminded me of the hour before, and declared my intention of not going at all. The Kázi was horrified: he sent an officer off to inform the General that I was coming, and he was only to be pacified on my consenting to pay my visit on the following morning; upon this he overwhelmed me with praises and thanks until he was quite out of breath. The fact was, that Mohan, my little interpreter, who thought a vast deal of my dignity, and was not very careful of his expressions, heard the Kázi say it was too late, and hastily exclaimed, "If I were in my master's place, I would not go to visit any man half so uncivil: he should come to me." The Kázi whispered in his ear, that the Governor, desiring that I should see him in all his

down to posterity, had not Theopompus casually alluded to it in his writings. The reader is referred to Valerius Maximus, viii. 14.

glory, had held a grand levee, or durbar, at ten o'clock, and that the company, after waiting two hours, had been dismissed; the Governor being accustomed daily, at that hour, to drink two bottles of Kashmír spirits.* When Mohan reported this to me, I most readily deferred presenting myself, not wishing to visit a viceroy and find him in a state of drunken insensibility.

I took advantage of this afternoon's leisure, and with my new European companions, went to see the famous Lake Dál. It is partly surrounded by a ditch, to prevent its waters mingling with those of the Jelam, and causing an inundation, for the houses near the lake are built on the same level with it. Exactly under the Takht-i-Súliman is the sluice called Drogshuh, the only outlet of the lake, which flows into the Zand, an arm of the Jelam. A channel which is lined with stone, connects this great river with the lake, and is the only means of getting at the latter, without making a circuit of more than two miles by water from the inhabited part of the town. In olden times, the flood-gate was much nearer to the city, but was removed to the place where it now is, in consequence of the water of the lake discharging itself too rapidly from the direction it was allowed to take. A large white stone, lying in the great canal which leads to the Shalimar Bagh, is of much importance as a mark; when the water covers it, there is danger from the waters of the lake, and the flood-gate is so constructed, that it then shuts of itself. It is about two or three miles from the Dilawar Khan Bagh, under the Takht-i-Súliman.

---

* This is the only part of India where wine is made from the juice of the grape, a fact to be attributed rather to its acescent quality, than to any scarcity of the fruit. It is described by Forster as resembling that of Madeira: and, with what judgment in such matters we know not, he presumes it would be found to improve greatly in quality by age. To the proper radiation of the heat in this elevated region, and its vicinity to the lofty mountains of Tibet, it may be reasonably concluded, much of the acidity would be found in all the fruits which so greatly adds to their taste and flavour in the temperate climates of the north. As there is a limit beyond which the vine cannot pass, or rather, where the acid properties exceed the limits necessary to the perfection of the fruit, there is also an excess of the saccharine principle in tropical countries, which precludes the application of the fruit to the manufacture of wine. In such instances, the vinous particles are concentrated, and fruit of every kind is fit for spirituous liquor only.

The lake is divided into several distinct parts. Gagribal, the first and least division, is separated from the rest by a narrow tongue of land: the second, called Ropelang, has a little island in the middle, on which we landed. A building, now levelled to the ground, formerly stood on it, and the regular form of the whole certainly shews that it was the work of human ingenuity. In many parts the lake is shallow enough to allow of similar contrivances.

There is a charming view of the mountains from the first small lake, and in a semi-circle, a branch of the inferior ridge comes down to the very edge of the stream. High up on the first of these hills, going from the city, stands a very extensive building called Kulimár, founded by Achan Múllah Shah, the major-domo of the Emperor Jehanghír, as a school for Mohammedans. It was never completed, and is now in ruins. The next prominent object is of interest to every Hindú, being a place of pilgrimage called Káli Sangam, built on an eminence projecting far into the lake. Káli signifies *black*, and Sangam the *confluence of two rivers.* These spots are always sacred to the Hindús. With this exception the mountains encircling this lake gradually decrease to a gentle plain, on which villages and pretty gardens have been laid out. There is a beautiful garden in the Ropelang lake, called Nishád Bagh, or Garden of Bliss, made by Jehanghír, after his first visit to Kashmír. The garden is entered by a fine terrace near the shore, leading into an avenue adorned with fountains and basins. Over these are raised small and fanciful buildings on large arches, so as not to shut up the view down the avenue, which is so contrived as to appear much longer than it really is. From the highly ornamented pavilions, the view of the more distant buildings in the back-ground is exceedingly picturesque. The beautiful plane trees are the chief ornaments of this garden at present, which is now almost in other respects, a perfect wilderness. The gardener presented me with a bouquet of the Indian chrysanthemum, yellow, white, and pink, for which he asked me a rupee as an enam or present. Mr. Vigne, who was in this garden during the hot season, found among its tenants a fine hooded snake.

A wealthy Hindú Pandit once built a causeway from Kashmír to this point, which has naturally much impeded the free course of the waters, and only a narrow line was left for our boat to be rowed under a bridge from the Nishád Bágh to the most admired division of the lake, where is the island of Char Chúnar. Under this bridge the water is twenty-four feet deep; in every other part it is but from six to eight feet, allowing the majestic Nelumbium to overspread the whole surface of the lake with its expansive foliage, and rich white and red flowers.

Arrived in the Char Chúnar lake, we were first rowed to the Shalimar garden, which, with its famous palace, was one of the great works of Jehanghír. I do not think he chose the prettiest part of the lake, but the high mountains are here softened down to the plain, and a broad valley afforded more space than elsewhere. A canal half a mile long, but now only capable of admitting a small boat, leads from this lake to the wooden entrance of the building. This entrance has been completely disfigured by the successive Patan Governors, who have erected an ugly flat roof over it, for the convenience of smoking their pipes. According to the style of the period, six inferior buildings, in the midst of an avenue of colossal plane trees, lead, at considerable intervals, to the principal, though not very extensive palace.

A small building is erected over a spring, the roof of which rests on twelve massive black marble columns. The whole forms a square of twelve fathoms, consisting of two covered walks, or terraces, between which are the halls, having on either side partitions of lattice-work, through which were to be seen the once ornamented chambers. It is kept in good repair, as the governors of Kashmír have always made it an occasional resort. The garden is 376 paces long and 220 broad. Compared with the Nishád garden, the view from the hall is very poor. The fine planes are beginning to decay from age, and one had already fallen to the earth. The wood of this tree is highly esteemed by the natives of Kashmír, who think it the best for their gun-stocks. I admired likewise the corn-flag and jonquil, the syringa Persica and chrysanthemum, and a wild plum, which, in the spring, has a flower of delicious fragrance. A little hamlet is gradually extending itself to this royal wilderness.

On quitting the Shalimar garden, we found Mohammed Shah Nakshbandi's boat, and his confidential servant, who presented us with a repast in the name of his master. It was composed of Rewásh, or rhubarb from Kabúl, red partridges, grapes, tea of different sorts, &c. This Sámed Shah is an amusing character, and often cheated me out of a smile, while he keeps the Mohammedans in an incessant roar of laughter with his wit and buffoonery.

About a mile and a half from the garden, and near the centre of this division of the lake, the island Char Chúnar, celebrated by Bernier and Thomas Moore, rises from the waters, a skilful monument of the reign of the Moghul Emperor, who named it from the four plane trees he planted on the spot: two of them are still standing. It has also its building in the centre, surrounded by a deserted garden, and consists of a single open hall, with a little tower, commanding a fine prospect of the lake. Under one of the plane trees is a water-wheel in perfect preservation, made of the incorruptible Himálayan cedar, the invaluable Deodara. It raises the water from the lake to the terrace. Ducks without number live in this lake, feeding on the roots of the water caltrop, (trapa bispinosa), but it is difficult to come within gun-shot distance of them. Formerly, the taking of these creatures afforded a livelihood to numbers of men, but for some reason best known to himself, the present Governor has discountenanced the practice; his protection of the ducks, however, does not extend to a prohibition of the amusement of Europeans, on the strength of which one of the boatmen produced a matchlock, about fourteen feet long, and begged my permission to take one shot for me. With this I readily complied, and furnished him with some powder and shot. At the first discharge, with a single barrel, he brought down eight ducks.

We did not fail, while here, to visit the beautiful wood of plane trees, planted by Akbar, called Názim, or Salubrious, to the number of 1200 trees. They are still in fine preservation, although planted more than two hundred years, forming beautiful walks, whose refreshing shade in summer must be delicious. Near this is a large garden, built in successive terraces, but now altogether in ruins. They say that it was the fancy of Nur Begum, the wife of Jehanghír.

The coming evening warned us that it was time to return homewards. At a mile's distance, we passed the Hirné Parvat Mountain, which terminates the semi-circle round the lake on the west, as the Takht-i-Suliman does on the east, and soon came to the floating gardens, where on a square of about twenty feet, they raise their melons and cucumbers: the surface of earth is scarcely above that of the water. This circumstance alone would seem fully to prove the fact that a perpetual calm must prevail on the lake. So regular indeed, and so gentle, is the movement of the whole body of water, and so very still is the air of the valley, that no flood is ever likely to visit, and consequently to overwhelm, these little islands.

In spite of the exertions of our fifty boatmen, the evening overtook us, and a bitterly cold evening it was. In our garden I found it impossible, even with the assistance of port and sherry at dinner, to make myself comfortably warm. But I preferred sleeping in my tent rather than passing another night of disturbed rest in the pavilion.

Friday, November 20, was a great holiday in the Sikh calendar, and the Governor sent an apology for not receiving me to-day; I therefore decided on ascending the Takht-i-Suliman, whence the best view of the city and the valley is to be had. At this spot Mr. Vigne took sketches for a panorama, which will doubtless be offered to public exhibition in Europe. The road to the mountain was over the bridge of the flood-gate called Drogshuh, alluded to yesterday, and led by a quadrangular tower called Makabara, and through a splendid avenue of poplar trees, which for their age and symmetry, from the trunk to the topmost branches, are most striking. The avenue begins with a group of planes on each side, and the whole separated from the town by an arm of the Jelam, is seemingly planted for the sake of its beauty alone, leading neither to building nor garden of any kind. Beneath the tower is a wretched mosque, built of wood, and known as the Drogshuh Masjid, near to which is a miserable village of the same name. Not far from the tower Makabara is Rústamghur, an unfinished residence built by the late governor Shír Singh as a place for the burning of the bodies of deceased Brahmins. Having with great difficulty clambered up the mountain pompously styled the Throne of Solomon, the first object which presented itself was an ancient Buddhist temple (Deval) composed of masses of rock, with a curious doorway, evidently of very high antiquity. The temple was, in later times, converted into a mosque; a Persian inscription, of more modern date, gives no information as to the original temple, but to Solomon is ascribed the honour of being the founder. It is said, moreover, that a very ancient Sanscrit inscription is now buried under ground. At present the Hindús call the temple Shankar Acharya. The massive construction and peculiar form of this edifice render it well worthy of a visit. The mountain, divided from the Tibetan chain to which it evidently belongs, is 1200 feet high; the view from it, over the whole valley of Kashmír, is indeed most truly grand and beautiful. Motionless as a mirror, the lake lies outstretched below, reflecting the vast chain of the Tibetan hills, while the extensive city is seen spreading along its shores; and the Jelam winds slowly like a serpent through the green valleys, and to complete the scene, the lofty Pír Panjal, with its countless peaks of snow, forms on one side a majestic boundary.

The Mohammedans have a story of that mountain, which they say derives its name from *Panj*, five, and *Pír*, saints; five pious brothers, according to them, having settled on it and performed several wondrous feats around; but to me it seems more probable that the name came from *Pansal*, which, in the Kashmírian language, signifies a pass, and Pír, a devotee. I have before alluded to the tomb of a holy man, which corroborates the probability of this explanation. The Europeans and Persians call the whole mountain Pír Panjal, but the natives restrict this name to the pass. To them mountain chains offer nothing remarkable, while the passes leading through them are of some importance. So also are isolated mountains, when they serve as land-marks, or are deemed holy as places of pilgrimage. In general they give no name to any other.

Some high peaks of the Tibetan mountains tower aloft beyond that dark chain observable from the Takht-i-Suliman, and fancy is beguiled to follow their wanderings long after any continuous form has vanished from the observer's eye. Our friend Samed Shah was already on the hill-top, with a repast for us. In order to animate the scene, Mr. Vigne had desired that he would bring several persons with him; and he took advantage of their picturesque and original appearance, to transfer them to his intended panorama. The Kashmirians had all donned their winter garments, and wore them with a certain air of vanity, peculiar to Mohammedans; while the simple costume of the natives of Tibet, the dark complexion, sprightly animated features and movements of my southern Indians, were all strangely contrasted with another group of strangers from the distant country of Yárkand, who might have been taken for natives of the north of Germany, with their fair hair and red cheeks: these were pupils or guests of Mohammed Shah Nakshbandi, and will be mentioned again. The days were so short, that we did not get back by daylight; the two Englishmen were again my guests, and the evening passed away most agreeably.

Saturday, November 21.—The Kázi and Abdúl Rahim, who gave himself out as the Company's agent in Kashmír, came in the state boat to accompany me in my interview with Mehan Singh. The party consisted of the two English gentlemen and myself, the Kázi and Abdúl Rahim; the Brahmin Thakúr Das, Mohan Bír, Bahadur Singh, and three of my chaprásís. We were more than half an hour on our way to Shaherger, the viceroy's palace, which owes its name to one of the Moghul governors, who belonged to the Shiah sect, called in Kashmír, Shaher. The chief entrance to the palace is by a broad flight of wooden steps outside, and the whole of our way was lined with troops. We were received in an open pavilion on the terrace, which may be very delightful in summer, but on a very cold day is quite the reverse. In the centre stood a square platform, surrounded by a lattice of fine wood, worked like Brussels lace, in which Mehan Singh was seated in an arm chair. The number of his attendants was considerable; and in an outer circle stood his body guard, very richly dressed in red and gold, with red silk sashes; most of them wore a black heron's plume, called in Kashmír a kalga, in their low turbans.

Mehan Singh came forward himself to receive me, and conducted me to the place appointed for me. He has a thickset unwieldy figure; and, though still in the prime of life, his dissolute way of living has given him the appearance of an old man: his hair was white as silver. To judge by his countenance, one would pronounce him goodnatured and kind; but, in many respects, he is not the Governor required in the present critical state of Kashmír. The long unclipped beard announces him to be a Sikh; and his thick lips and but half-opened eyes, indeed every feature, shew him to be an Epicurean in the strictest sense of the word. On this occasion he was wrapped in a yellow silk robe, his head-dress consisting of a simple white handkerchief. On the ground, to his right, sat many of the Mohammedan Rajas, from the Baramúla and Mazafferabád mountains, tributaries of Ranjít Singh. One of every family is detained as a hostage in Kashmír, and from time to time, they are obliged to bring large gifts to the Governor, otherwise their tribute is raised: their present condition is mainly owing to their former habits of independence, which made it necessary for Ranjít Singh to lead his troops against their hill fastnesses. The poor princes, coming from warmer regions, were evidently freezing in their Indian garb; and their eyes sparkled with indignation, at the degradation of sitting at our feet, particularly when Mehan Singh, proud no doubt at showing me the humbled position of half a dozen princes, pointed out each one to me by name. He gave me to understand, with many exaggerated compliments, that the Mahá Rajah had desired my stay in Kashmír to be rendered as agreeable to me as possible, and that I had but to express a wish to make it as effective as a command. In reply to such fine speeches, I said that the advanced season would not permit of my making a long stay in Kashmír, that I perceived in what good hands the government of the valley was placed, and had only to request permission to visit Islamabad, a city at the south-east extremity of Kashmír, and to wander about the valley at pleasure. The Governor assured me in return, that I was master of all my actions, and that his permission was altogether unnecessary.

Besides the princes already alluded to, there were no persons of consideration at this Durbar; in fact the country is so completely subjugated, that the natives, except a few traders in shawls, are nothing better than so many beggars. When the proper time for such visits had elapsed, I took my leave, being accompanied by Mehan Singh to the head of the flight of stairs.

I spent the rest of the day in exploring the city; and, among the things most deserving of remark, I visited the seven bridges which span the Jelam, at once the most enduring and the most dangerous I ever saw. The date of their construction and the material are evidences of the first quality, their appearance and the experience of every passenger sufficiently attest the last. The piers are composed of large cedar trees, fifteen or twenty feet long and three feet in diameter, which are placed one over the other, in the form of a funeral pile, while large lime trees, the seeds having been carried to the place by birds, grow from this foundation, and shadow a part of the bridge. The cross-beams on which one treads are everywhere in a condition to afford an excellent view of the river beneath; and huts and booths have been thrown up, at different periods, on this slippery ground, although nothing is clearer than that one storm would involve houses, bridges, trees, and piles in one common overthrow. A storm, however, or even a wind of any great violence, is a thing altogether unknown in Kashmír.

These bridges were found already laid across the river by the Mohammedans, which gives them an antiquity of at least 500 years. Since the dominion of the last Hindú sovereign, or, more correctly, of the last queen of Kashmír, Rani Kotadevi, which, according to the Ayín Akbari, terminated in 1364, the last partial restoration was undertaken by the governor Ali Merdan Khan, in the reign of the Emperor Jehanghír. The Shah Hamedan Musjid is a modern-looking building, the prototype of every mosque in Kashmír, and if not exactly resembling a Chinese temple, is certainly unlike Indian architecture in general, though some of the same form may be occasionally seen in the British Himálaya. It is nearly square, and within, the roof is supported by slender pillars. Without, and about half way up the wall, are balconies, ornamented with finely carved wood and small columns. The roof of the temple projects over the outer walls and is finished at the four corners with hanging bells; while, on the summit, which rises in a pyramidal form, is a golden ball, instead of the Mohammedan crescent. This form is common throughout the valley of Kashmír, from the simplest village temple, to the richly ornamented mosque of the capital. This, as well as all the mosques of Kashmír, is built of cedar.

The fine stone steps, which in every Hindú city lead down to the river, are in Kashmír without any extensive ornament; but I remarked one novelty in the river in this city, viz., large wooden cages, for I know no more fitting name for them, which stood in great numbers close to the shore, for the convenience of the female bathers. The Jelam is also covered with boats of every size, which gives a pleasant stirring appearance to the whole city. The numerous canals on the right shore of the river, on the left there is but one, have no communication with it, although so close, except through the Drogshuh gate; and hence, from the Dilawer Khan Bagh to the Shah Hamedan mosque, the first being on the great canal, and the last on the Jelam, we were 1½ hour going by water, the distance by land being only a few hundred feet.

Mr. Vigne had left his sketch-book in the Dilawer Khan Bagh, and was obliged to send one of the men back for it; but, in order that we might not lose any time, he waited in his boat while we were rowed to the mosque of Núr Jehan Begum, which is called the new, or *Naya masjid*, and is opposite the one before mentioned. It is unfinished, built of white marble in the best Indo-Mohammedan taste, and is now used as a magazine. Just as Dr. Henderson and I turned from our inspection of it, Mr. Vigne arrived, and with his customary eagerness of movement sprang from his seat towards us. The next moment he had fallen into the river. A cry of terror burst from the crowd of assembled natives on the shore; the boats were all pushed quickly to his aid, and his own boatmen hastened towards the spot. But he was an excellent swimmer; and although the cramp seized him for a moment, as he fell into the water, the temperature of which was at the freezing point, he soon recovered himself; and, to the astonishment of the Kashmírians, who are quite ignorant of the art, he continued swimming about to warm himself before he re-entered the boat. His progress homewards, however, was not very pleasant to him after this accident.

Dr. Henderson and I, acompanied by a very inquisitive crowd, then proceeded to the mosque, where Seynul-ab-ud-Dín lies buried. This second Mohammedan king, or the eighth, according to Abul-Fazl, is worthy, above all others, of a monument to his memory. It was he who first introduced the love of art into the valley of Kashmír: he caused the people to be instructed in that of making glass; and bringing weavers from Turkísthan, he had them taught the weaving of wool from the goats of Tibet, into the shawls since that time so celebrated. The natives have now forgotten his real name, and only remember him as the Badsha or Emperor. The mosque is near to an ancient ruinous Buddhist temple, Wihare, the remains of which are still lying about: a few ornaments, at the door and entrance in the courtyard, shew something of what it once was. The interior is dark and devoid of all pretensions to ornament. Several Mohammedan graves stand in the court around it; and from the appearance of the tombstones I should judge that some inscriptions of interest might be found; but my visit was too hasty to permit any examination into their merits. I was told by a Mullah that Moorcroft lay buried here; but after a long search, I came to a stately marble slab, with a Persian inscription, stating that the servant of that unfortunate traveller lay beneath.

At some distance from this is the Jama Masjid. It is a pity that it is now in a ruinous condition, having once been a beautiful edifice built of cedar, so far back as the time of their own native princes. It forms a large square, each side measuring sixty-three fathoms, and in the centre is an open space with a small building upon it. The roof is supported by large columns, hewn out of a single piece, and with a florid capital and base. The small building in the centre of the court is open on all sides and raised a step. In other mosques a tank for ablution is usually placed in such spots. On my observing that the mosque was not built due east and west, the guides produced from a heart-shaped silver and black enamelled box, a modern needle, which points out the Kibla to them, when they pray, or direction of Mecca. Being ignorant of the fact that Mecca does not lie due west of Kashmír, their needle is worth nothing.

We passed through dirty streets, interminable bazars, and over two canals, to the fort on the Harni Parvat. We observed several large buildings on our route, tenanted in ancient times by the courtiers of the Moghul Emperors, and Kabúl Sovereigns, but, with some few solitary exceptions, where these have been replaced by shawl manufactories, the dwellings are deserted, lonely ruins. At the foot of Harni Parvat the great

Akbar built another city, which he named Nagarnagar, and inclosed it with strong walls and towers. It was about three miles from Shaherghur; the remains, dilapidated as they are, cover a vast extent of what was always considered the loveliest part of the valley. Blocks of stone and large columns, brought from the more ancient temples of Kashmír, lie in desolate grandeur around. A beautiful mosque, built by Achan Mullah Shah, deserves to be mentioned, particularly on account of the finely wrought black marble and stone lavished upon it. The gates are made of one single stone, and polished like a mirror, but the wanton love of destruction during latter wars has torn some out of their places, and others lie perishing on the earth.

There are but two ways of entering this ruined city, viz: by a little doorway under the walls, just high and wide enough to admit the passage of a short thin man, or through a lofty strong gate. Not a living soul lives in Nagarnagar, but my numerous suite peered into every ruined palace and dilapidated mosque and enlivened them strangely for the time. The picturesque grouping and romantic costume, seen through the fallen ruins, would have been a sight for a painter. Mr. Vigne rejoined our party, and Mohammed Shah, having guessed our purpose, had despatched provisions after us. The fort on the Harni Parvat called Ki Maram, is garrisoned by Sikh troops, but as we drew near it we were challenged by the guard and ordered not to proceed any farther, nor to attempt to ascend the heights. It is built on the perpendicular rock and commands the entire city: it might be rendered unassailable but for the total want of water on the mountain. The fortress was built under the Patans by the Governor Ali Mohammed Khan, when he renounced the authority of Kabúl. The Kashmírians and Sikhs presume a great deal on this fort; and even in its present state, it would be a most arduous undertaking to assail it, as the position of the valley ought to preclude the possibility of advance to artillery. On my way homewards I paid a visit to one of the shawl manufactories; and was conducted through one of the most wretched abodes that my imagination could well picture. In a room at the top of the house, sat sixteen men huddled together at their work, which at this time was shewn to me as a Dúshala, or long shawl, valued at three thousand rupees the pair. I made several inquiries as to the nature and extent of their trade, but the master seemed ill disposed to gratify my curiosity. However difficult it may be to arrive at the truth in India, it is still more so here, though for a very different reason. The Indian always accommodates his answer to the supposed pleasure of the inquirer: the Kashmírian is trained to practise the art of concealment, which naturally leads to falsehood, on every occasion. The workmen handled the threads with a rapidity which surprised me, moving their heads continually the while. They work in winter in a room which is never heated, lest dust or smoke might injure the material. Generally speaking, their features are highly intellectual and animated.

My next visit was to an armourer, the most celebrated in Kashmír. As this is a trade in which they are believed to excel, I was disappointed at finding nothing in a sufficiently forward state for my inspection. The appearance of the armourer himself was most venerable; he reminded me of the days of chivalry, when the trade he followed was so honoured in all lands. With more real politeness than I had met with for a long time, he prayed me to be seated, and brought me several half finished muskets and pistols, an Indian matchlock, and some poignards, all elaborately ornamented. Nothing could be much worse than the implements he worked with; particularly his bellows, which consisted of a little box of wood, that forced the wind in, as well as out.

The late dinner of which we three Europeans partook in my tent was better than usually falls to the lot of travellers in Kashmír. It consisted of hare soup, fresh salmon, roasted partridges, and a ham from the wild boar of the Himálaya. The catalogue reminds me of a circumstance relating to the adventures of Henderson. He had gradually lost all his baggage and horses in his wanderings, and entered Kashmír on foot as a beggar. Latterly, ere he quitted Tibet, the guide given him by Ahmed Shah deserted him; the mountain paths were all equally strange, and he lost his way, as might be expected. For two days he and his servant lived on chepatis, or thin cakes of unleavened bread, and as he sat at the well furnished table this evening, and ate of the soup, the salmon, and the chatni, a favourite relish in

India, consisting of a variety of hot and acid condiments, he suddenly exclaimed, "Oh! Chatni, the greatest misfortune that befell me, was when I found my stock of thee exhausted:" this being the only food which has become an absolute necessity to him since his long residence in India. As I was asking some particulars about the Gílpo, or king of Ladák, he went on pouring the hot sauce into his plate until it covered the salmon like soup, and engrossed in the subject, he laid his fork on the table, and taking up the spoon, drank it all without altering a muscle of his countenance. I was apprehensive that he would feel some bad effect from such an accompaniment to a salmon, for such a perversion of taste must surely prove utterly destructive to the stomach, but Dr. Henderson was made for a traveller, never caring about the wants of the body, and never failing in activity either from hunger or difficulty of any kind, it is all the same to him where he sleeps, or what he eats or wears. He never wants water to wash with, and his skin is now proof against the attacks of the fiercest insects. These last peculiarities prevented me from offering him a bed, or any part of my tent, but a pair of Kashmír coverlets, which I afterwards gave away, and a part of the ground floor of my pavilion, were very acceptable to him, so that we were mutually pleased.

I have omitted a few words on Shaherghur, which derives its name, according to the best authorities, not from *Shaher*, City, or *Shir*, Lion, but from *Shiah*, the Persian sect of Mohammedans. The palace was built by Amír Khan Jehan, and was called Narsing-ghur by the Sikhs. It is nominally a walled fort, but altogether unfitted for defence, yet as it has been the residence of the Mohammedan Viceroys for the last hundred years, I expected to find much to interest me within, and was strangely disappointed: the japan work and carved wood, with small compartments filled up with the mirrors of Kashmír, or the specular stones of Bengal, being the objects of chief curiosity and ornament. Not far from this is Chinar Serai, the last on the road from Bimber here, built for the convenience of the Emperors. Their zenanas rested here for the night on the way from India, proceeding on the following morning by boats to the Nishád Bagh or the Shalimar.

The most ancient of the imperial dwelling places was Nagarnagar; Jehanghír, who was very frequently in Kashmír, first built Nishad Bagh, and subsequently, the Shalimar.

Sunday, November 22. The Sikh garrison of the valley consists at present of two regiments of infantry, of some twelve or fourteen hundred men. The Governor assured me that he had been charged by Ranjít Singh to raise two regiments in addition to these, in Kashmír, but could not succeed, and I am sure that even Mehan Singh must be sensible how impossible such an attempt would be. The Patans, who had 20,000 soldiers in Kashmír at one time, vainly endeavoured to discipline the natives. They admit their inability, like the Arab of Egypt, and we may easily credit them. Soldiers in India receive three times as much as any workman would earn by his labour, while here and in Egypt their pay is on the same footing as in Europe, their fatigues and wounds being rewarded only by honour. Abul-Fazl relates, that, in 1594, the fortieth year of Akbar's reign, the number of troops in Kashmír was small, being 4892 cavalry, and 92,400 infantry. We must observe, however, that he comprises in this the whole Súbah, a great part of which belongs to Afghanistan. At present, the two regiments are quite sufficient for all purposes. The people are most patient and inoffensive; from the north and east there is not the least danger of attack; their only enemies, the petty princes of the Mohammedan states in the mountains, being compelled to give hostages for their good behaviour. Moreover, Kashmír has lost all its charms as a desirable acquisition; though it may still be made an important and valuable province. Its riches are all departed, and invaders, such as those adverted to, go in quest of wealth rather than new and productive territories.

At early dawn I broke up my little encampment, preparatory to my excursion to the eastern part of the valley. Three boats were in readiness; one for Dr. Henderson and myself, a second for the guard of honour appointed to attend me, and a third for the Munshí Mirza Ahud. My personal suite was limited to the cooks, a chaprásí, a bearer, Mohan Bír, and the gardener. In the morning an officer paid me a visit, with information that Ranjít Singh had desired him to give an account of my journey in the Akbar, or Gazette: in other words, to act as a spy upon me, and to send a detailed narrative of my proceedings to Lahor. As he knew nothing of writing, he requested me to allow his pandit, or secretary, to attend me, to which I was obliged to reply in the affirmative, determined that the pandit should not take the journey for nothing.

We started in the afternoon, and, to avoid the long circuit which the boats must necessarily take, owing to the windings of the Jelam about the city, I ordered mine to take me from the canal at the bottom of the garden, and sent the horses to the bridge over the Drogshuh canal. For the first time, I saw that this canal empties itself into an arm of the Jelam, called Zand, and that the majestic alley of poplars mentioned above is on an island. Any point may be reached on foot in a third of the time that a boat can go by water, owing to its many turns, and as I wished to see everything on the way, I desired that they would proceed as fast as possible, while I took the earliest opportunity of mounting my trusty little nag.

We followed the route along the inferior ridge of the Tibet Pansahl, which, even here, is piled up in huge masses, thrown one over the other. Having passed the Takht-i-Suliman, we soon came to a deep tank, in the middle of which is a small but complete Buddhist temple, called Pandritan. It can only be reached in a boat. This tank, which the natives believe to be unfathomable, may be about six hundred feet in diameter, and the temple itself certainly not more than twenty-five feet square. Some well preserved Buddhist figures are in the interior, but I did not then get into a boat to examine it, as the evening was drawing on.

From this point we entered the plain. A stone bridge formerly crossed the Jelam at Chok, but, some time back, it fell in. There are many springs in this neighbourhood, all strongly impregnated with iron and sulphur, and which have a temperature something higher than that of the air, at least, during this season of the year. I found the warmest at 70° Fahrenheit, and it seemed as though every frog in Kashmír had found its way to this spot; the whole place literally swarmed with them. The mineral contained in these springs causes them to be overlaid with a yellow pigment, of a beautiful golden tint. A numerous collection of the smaller crustacea, larvæ of flies, and tiny fish, were all of a similar hue, and were moving about busily in the warm water. I had also opportunities of sport, for the birds, foxes, and jackals were in great abundance, notwithstanding which, I had leisure to be impatient for the return of the boat. Pamper, the destination for this evening, is five kos by water, by land two and a half. Several times I went down to the river side, to inquire if the boats were not in sight, but as I was fated to be disappointed, I decided on going on to Pamper at once, and in order that everything might be prepared for us there, I sent off the Pandit, my spy, or rather shadow, during the whole day, to announce my approach.

A mile from Pamper, on a steep place, several huge stones lay about, the remains of a ruined temple. On a closer inspection, I observed that the limestone of which they were composed had muscle shells embedded in it, in a state of petrifaction. The first stroke I gave broke my hammer, and I was obliged to send to Pamper for another. It was brought by the Pandit, who looked anxiously at me while I broke off a piece, and put it carefully away; he then went up to the stone, to see what could possibly have been my object, the result of his observations being an ominous shake of the head, and a speedy record of my misdeeds in his note book. He had a hard day's labour to follow me as I hunted and fished, botanized, or pursued my geological researches, stopped every passer-by with some inquiry, and put all sorts of interrogatories both to him and Mírza Ahud. I had determined not to spare him, and therefore told him all the nonsense I could think of, very gravely, so that his report of my acts and deeds must have been worth looking over. Above all, the Akbar in India was treated most loyally. The spy, or agent, was continually asking what would be agreeable to have introduced into his account, and, on taking leave, received a present, as a testimony that his behaviour had given satisfaction. Pamper is a place of importance, chiefly owing to the saffron which is cultivated in its environs. The fields are laid out with singular care. I made every inquiry into the system of agriculture, and the value of the plant itself. On entering the town, I was received by the proprietor of a large, though scarcely finished house, where I was to lodge, on the first floor of which was a chimney, and a fire without smoke. Chimneys in Kashmír are common enough, but they all smoke so abominably, that no one can breathe in the room, unless he seat himself on the ground. This Pamper fire-place allowed me to work at my table without risk of suffocation, a comfort which made my evening pass away delightfully. The real wants of life are very few, but the discomforts of my present journey may be guessed at by the delight I felt here in a bad room, with a tolerable fire, which did not inconvenience me with smoke. The master of the house brought me some delicious fruit, and not only gave me every information respecting their mode of planting and cultivating, but presented me with a packet of seeds. I found Mírza Ahud also a most useful and intelligent companion. He was General Allard's Múnshí, and was lent by that gentleman to Jacquemont. For his services to him, Ranjít Singh rewarded him, after Jacquemont had quitted the Panjáb, with a village in Kashmír, his native country, which brings him in about a rupee a day. Certainly, this fact is a proof of Ranjít Singh's willingness to give all facility to European travellers through his dominions. I was so warm and comfortable here, that I did not feel inclined to give over my writing and drawing and go to bed until one o'clock.

Monday, November 23. A thick mist hung over the valley, and scarcely suffered me to see half a mile around, and although the sun's rays shone dimly through this troubled atmosphere, and lent to it a warm, yellowish hue, the air was bitterly cold. I left my quarters early, however, much refreshed by the slumbers of the past night, with many regrets on quitting a house which was the most comfortable I had entered for a very long time. Had time permitted it, I should certainly have remained for some days.

Near Pamper is a bridge over the Jelam, under which we passed. It is built on the same plan as those in the capital. It was so very cold in the boat, that we got out at last, and tried to warm ourselves by walking. Tokéna, the end of our day's journey, is ten kos from Pamper by water, and five by land. We took our breakfast on the banks of the river, and then mounted our horses to visit the former capital of

Kashmír, Ventipoor. Two falling Buddhist temples are the most interesting of the ruins; the first called Vencádati Devi, is now nearly level with the earth; the smaller one, called Ventimádati, is still in tolerable preservation. Among the ruins I caught sight of a fox, and as Jwáli, who ran in pursuit of it, was soon at fault, I rode forward myself, in hopes of catching it. My horse carried me up a hill, where I gazed in admiration on the labours of centuries back. Up to a considerable height, this hill was cut out in the form of terraces, each presenting a small level surface for cultivation, and these again were supported by walls of immense strength. We must refer a work so stupendous to a time when the population was so vast as to require every slip of land to be made productive, for its support. Now, if we consider that, on account of this redundant population, very little, if any, rice was allowed to be exported, and that, at a time comparatively recent, 800,000 people dwelt in this valley, we shall not greatly err, probably, if we say that when Ventipoor flourished, three millions of people inhabited Kashmir.

Vainly I wandered through what remained of the city, to find some monument, pillar, or statue, to remind me of Ventipoor: there was not a trace of former greatness, except the two ruins I have before alluded to. The city was built, according to tradition, by Ven, one of the last Hindú Rajas, the hero of many a native song and legend. They relate of him, that his gentle heart could not endure the thought of accepting either money or work from his people; and that he lived on his own private inheritance, and distributed all his treasures among the poor. When he had spent all his fortune, he gained his living by making and selling earthen pots, while his wives sold goods in the open market. There is another tradition, which will not bear the light of a too severe criticism; that is, that this Raja Ven, whose name, by the by, is not mentioned in the Raja Taringini, received a letter from the Prophet Mohammed, enjoining his conversion. This letter is said to have been received in the fourth century of the Hegira; but there is no explanation given where it had been so long concealed. Raja Ven, a true worshipper of Siva, is said to have been so indignant at this requisition to change his religion, that he went on a pilgrimage to Gubukár, on the

Gagribál lake, and there threw the letter of Mohammed into a well. A mosque was afterwards built on the spot, and it is still a favourite resort of pious Musselmen. Zain-ul-ab-ud-Din led the first Mohammedans into the valley, in the fifteenth century of our era, during the reign of Raja Ven. His successor, Raja Ratan, used to converse' it seems, with this Zain-ul-ab-ud-Dín, and he told him he would willingly turn Moslem, but did not know how to begin; whereupon, Zain prayed for him very earnestly, and a noted saint, Bulbul Shah, flew over from Baghdad in a night, and converted not only the Raja, who assumed the name of Ratan Shah, but brought over all his subjects to the Mohammedan faith on the following morning. It is hardly necessary to state, that there is no foundation whatever for this tale in history.

On a charming height, before which the winding Jelam forms a deep hollow, like a haven, stands a mosque, built by Hassan Mán, the son of the first Mohammedan king of Kashmír, Zain-ul-ab-ud-Dín; and adjoining it, is the house in which he lived as a fakír. It is still called Baba Hassan Mán Takiá: Baba signifying an endeared object; Takiá, an abode, or sepulchre.

As I continued to pursue my way on foot and alone, my people having stayed to rest a little, I met a Kashmírian, driving a fellow-countryman before him. The poor fellow stopped every now and then; and, in a pitiful tone, besought the other's compassion, but his entreaties were only answered by blows. I inquired what was the cause of the quarrel, but could not make out what they said; however, when Mírza Ahud joined me, I learnt that the suppliant was a thief; the other, the owner of the stolen goods, who had just apprehended him. The truth being made known, the delinquent waited very humbly to hear what punishment I should decree. Meanwhile, some Sikh soldiers overtook us: the effect was instantaneous: the aggrieved party now stoutly maintained that he had nothing to complain of, the thief put his arm within that of his accuser, and in this amicable manner they hastily walked away together. Mírza Ahud explained to me, that a Kashmírian would put up with any wrong, rather than seek redress from his

Sikh masters, as he is invariably obliged to pay the judge a high price for his decision, without the slightest prospect of recovering his lost property.

Dr. Henderson had changed his Tibetan costume for that of Kashmír; and, if not very magnificent, it was at least clean. On this same road, I met a man with eight horses well laden, and a servant; and having asked him whence he came, I learnt that he was a wool-merchant, and had travelled with much labour from Ladák, through deep snow, for eighteen days. I knew that Henderson, who was hoping to see his baggage and two horses arrive by the same route, would be much interested in this news; and at first was tempted to wait for him and introduce the merchant, but I feared that I should be detained some time, and was sure likewise that the travelling party could not fail to attract his notice. Accordingly when we met, I expected to hear that he had received even fuller information than myself; but, on the contrary, found out that the merchant had pretended to be from Islamabad, travelling with apples. Henderson was greatly annoyed when he knew the truth; and I mention this, as a proof that it is not always to our advantage to assume the native dress. In this case, the merchant was afraid that the Kashmírian, as he supposed him to be, would demand some money from him; he therefore told a falsehood, which it was not necessary to impose on me, a foreigner.

It was dark when we came to the Jelam, where the boats were to carry us over to Tokena, our halting-place; and though the road was well known to Mírza Ahud and the Kashmírians, we had managed to lose our way most completely. I had sent on the soldiers, to put the house in order for us and purchase necessaries, such as wood, milk, &c.; and if I had not, they would have been of no use, for they were as much strangers to the country as ourselves. It was the darkest night I ever remembered, and we were all obliged to grope along with the horses at hazard, sometimes falling over the stones, sometimes into the ditches, and at last, after an hour's wandering through this intense darkness, we all slipped down a steep declivity and heard the river at our feet. But we did not know where the ferry might be, and after calling out loudly without hearing a sound in reply, we stole cautiously along the shore. But this course was not long open to us, for the bank was high and precipitous, and a false step might have carried us into the stream below; we therefore bent our way into the fields again, returning every five minutes to halloo to the boatmen. In this wretched plight we went on stumbling and groping our way, until one of the party espied a light, which happily for us was near the ferry. At last we were safely put on shore to my great joy, for the darkness was next to total, and the little boat was so laden that a single wave might easily have overset the whole party. The khansaman had only just arrived with the boats, and as nothing was ready in consequence of this delay, I had long to wait ere food, fire, or even a chair was set before me.

The house where I was lodged was very dismal; I called out loudly to the guard on finding myself pent up in a square box, the door of which would not admit of my bed being taken through, and which was certainly not half so commodious as my tent, and while deliberating what I should do next, Hingam, the khansaman, came in from a tour of inspection, and acquainted me that the guard had taken all the best part for their own use. This disrespect was not to be borne; guided therefore by Hingam, I ascended to the first floor, and found there two good rooms, with fire-places, where the eight Sikh soldiers were fast asleep, wrapped up most comfortably in warm blankets, and reposing on thickly laid straw. I soon waked the impudent sleepers with the butt-end of a musket, and they all started up in terror, when they saw how seriously I took the matter. I then commanded them to clean the room thoroughly and give it up to me, nor would I suffer them to impose this office on the Kashmírians, as they proposed, but compelled them to take away the very least morsel of straw from the ground with their own hands. This done, I ordered them to go down and keep watch throughout the night in the court-yard, telling them that if they refused to obey my commands, I should make them march back instantly to Kashmír. This was a very moderate punishment, since they had been so regardless of my orders, that not a single thing was bespoken, and we were suffering severely from cold and hunger. It was ten o'clock before the cook could send us anything to eat, and a full hour later before I retired to rest. I then told the Sikh guard, who had remained in the courtyard, all gathered round a large fire, that I forgave them, and permitted them to retire. They expressed many regrets on the occasion, and I took occasion to remind them that implicit obedience was the first duty of a soldier.

Tuesday, November 24. With the exception of a few pretty glimpses of country, where a turn in the road allowed us to catch a view of the snowy peaks, there was little to be admired in the scenery when first we started, but its character changed in the course of the day, and instead of the dull, endless plain on one side, and the bare heights on the other, without tree or bush, the view became delightful. The Jelam was studded with little islands; verdant hills sloped down to its banks, and the country was enriched with a number of small streams which flow into the large one. From Bijbáhar, (the Sanscrit name of this ancient capital of Kashmír must, I think, have been Vidya Wihára, Temple of Wisdom,) a fruitful plain stretches along towards the east, between the ranges of hills which announced our near approach to the lofty mountains of Tibet.

The second bridge up the river is thrown over at Bijbáhar, which may still be considered the next town in importance to Kashmír. Large lime-trees overgrow the piers of this ancient bridge. I landed at this spot in the hope of finding some ruins of the old capital still in existence, but was disappointed, and obliged to content myself with a few coins, of a date prior to the Mohammedan dynasties, which I collected in the bazar. Bazars are the chief attraction in every place throughout India, there the traveller may make himself better acquainted in a few minutes with the productions, the customs and manners, the riches or poverty, and in fact, the general state of the country, by conversing with the Banyans, or merchants, than he could possibly do by living for months in the court of the ruler or nobles of the country.

From Bijbáhar I rode on horseback over a fertile plain to Islamabad. About half a mile from the former place, there is a large plantation of plane trees on both sides of the river, and on the right shore, a ruin. It is called Badsha Bagh, and was the residence of the luckless Dara, the brother of Aurungzíb. A bridge formerly united the spacious gardens which were laid out on both sides. It was my intention to visit Korau Pandau on my way to Islamabad, but so much time had been lost in seeking for a guide, and the day was so near its close when I arrived at the caves of Mattan, that we judged it more expedient to hasten on to Islamabad, the ancient Anatnagh, as fast as we could. I observed with much interest to-day the optical illusions, at this season almost peculiar to Kashmír. There is so little transparency in the air, that places at a mile's distance only, appear to be removed to four times that distance, and mountains only four miles off seem to be at least fifteen or twenty. If the weather be tolerably clear, one can see to this last distance, but the twenty miles appear twice as much. To these peculiarities of the atmosphere, I attribute the exaggerated terms in which many travellers speak of the extent of this country. It was dark when we reached our halting-place, but every thing was in the best order, and a supper of trout from the sacred tank of Anatnagh, was a great relish after the day's journey.

Wednesday, 25. I had an interesting conversation last evening with some Brahmins, who gave me many particulars regarding the belief and tenets of their sect. They promised to ask their brethren several questions which they could not answer for themselves, and bring me the explanation this morning. I never expected them to keep this promise, and the morning passed away without their making their appearance. As the Thanadar, who has the management of the iron and lead mines, five or six kos from this place, offered to shew me any attention in his power, I begged that a boat might be prepared immediately, and some of the ore procured from the mines. These I felt to be objects of great interest from the fact of their having been discovered, as Mirza Ahud told me, by Jacquemont.

The old, dilapidated house I was lodged in, stands between the sacred tank and the spring to which Islamabad, the ancient Anatnagh, owed its celebrity, and which issues from the base of a rock of black marble. The Raja Tarangini has the following legend concerning the spring. About fourteen hundred years B. C. Asoka built Srinagar, his capital, at this day only a heap of ruins. Raja Nara, the twelfth king after Asoka, was one day on his way to the Vitusta or Jelam, for the purpose of bathing according to custom, when he was met by some starving

Brahmins, who entreated him to give them food. Raja Nara promised them what they asked, provided they waited until he had bathed in the river. To shorten the time which must elapse before they were relieved, they told the king they would bring the Vitusta nearer to him, when instantly the river gushed up at his feet. Unmoved by this miracle, the king persisted in continuing on his way to the river. The Brahmins cursed him as he went, and Siva immediately changed him into a serpent, under which form he is still seen, from time to time, in Kashmír. But the spring still gushes from the rock, a warning to all to comply with the demands of the holy Brahmins. A temple is built over the hollow in the rock, whence the water springs in great abundance, filling two small ponds, and then flowing into, and irrigating the adjacent plain. The fish in the basin are sacred, and in such vast numbers, that there is not the smallest point in the water where a head may not be seen. On the steps leading from the temple to the tank, I saw remains of deities of all ages, Buddha, Siva, and the Lingam, some several feet high, of shining hornblende. The temple was probably built by Arya, the king who lived at the date of our Saviour's birth, and was called Sahasralingam, or Thousand Lingams, from the number of those representations of their deity it contained. The Hindú may now approach both the temple and the spring, but in former times, they belonged to the house in which I lodged, and none of that faith were suffered to come near them.

According to Badia-ud-din, Anatnagh was built by the second king of Kashmír, Kasaligham, 3700 years B. C., an ante-diluvian city! It seems that the Mohammedans know how to amplify numbers as well as the Brahmins, though they are rather more moderate in their calculations. About the fifteenth century the name Anatnagh was changed into that of Islamabad, City of the Faith. It long remained the second city in Kashmír, but now the well-built and spacious houses in what we may call the principal streets, are all deserted and in ruins. Many have already sunk into decay, exposed to every wind. The beautiful carved work ornamenting the terraces and windows, is nearly destroyed by owls and jackals, who are the most frequent occupants of the place.

From Islamabad to Mattan, a place exclusively inhabited by Brahmins, the road winds along under the hills, and is shaded by the most majestic avenue of plane trees I ever saw. Towards the plain these hills terminate in steep declivities, and heaps of black marble are scattered about in fantastic disorder; sometimes they decline so gently into the valley that the descent is hardly perceptible. When I entered Mattan my horse was stopped by a Brahmin who seized my bridle and demanded alms. But he had in me no stranger to Indian customs to deal with. The manner in which charity is sometimes asked here shews the degree of misery and despair to which the beggar must be reduced, and though by no means certain of the extent of the present case, I thought it was probable that the man might be in want, and therefore offered him a rupee. My gift, however, was rejected with scorn, and the fellow demanded fifty. I saw in a moment that I had to deal with one of those impudent fakírs who have presumed to demand from a prince as much as a lack of rupees, and have occasionally received it! "Do you tax me so low?" cried I angrily, "drive him away." Another Brahmin now presented his petition to be accepted as my guide to Mattan, and on my consent being given, he ran on before me to his house, whence he brought me a present of fruit, offering it with a very well-turned speech, and then preceded us to the temple of Mattan, under the fine plane trees of Kashmír, which overshadowed the couch where pilgrims customarily rest. I alighted from my horse at the entrance, where sat a venerable old man absorbed in the study of the Veda. Having saluted him and put off my shoes, I stepped into a large square building surrounded by smaller ones on three of its sides. The fourth side is open to the valley. There is a large reservoir in the centre which seemed to me about eighty paces broad. A spring of fine water gushes into it from the rock underneath the building, and is afterwards conducted by channels to irrigate the plain beyond. Here, as at Islamabad, the fish are in immense numbers in this basin or tank, and like them are looked upon by the people as sacred. The spring reminded me very forcibly of that of the Orontes in Syria, more especially of that of the valley of Balbek, though in respect of the quantity of water, both these are much surpassed by the spring at Mattan.

According to a curious old tradition, it was a European physician, Bernier, who was in Kashmír in Aurungzebe's time, who first discovered a spring in the mountains, twenty miles from hence, which was absorbed by the earth. Taking it for granted that the water made its appearance in some other part of the valley, he placed men at all the different springs, and then threw into the one he had discovered some pieces of straw, which came to light again in the Mattan fountain. I was well pleased to find the name of this adventurous traveller still in the recollections of the people of Kashmír. The elucidation of the story is found some way from this spot. Near Buasuan, which lies on the same limestone rocks, and is separated from Islamabad by a bed of clay that unites and partly covers both, are caverns, which serve as aqueducts to subterranean canals. I was particularly desirous to see them on account of the organic remains which it was highly probable they contained. These caves occupy a very conspicuous place in the fables of the timid Kashmírians, and are supposed to have originated from the following causes. In the year Káli 2108 (993 B.C.) Raja Nara succeeded his father Vibhishána. During his reign a certain Brahmin espoused Chandrasáha, the daughter of Susravas, a serpent-god, whose palace was in a lake near the Vitusta, and near a city built and inhabited by Nara. One day, as Raja Nara beheld the beautiful daughter of the serpent on the shore of the lake, moving gracefully through the calm waters, he was struck with the deepest admiration, and endeavoured vainly to inspire the same sentiments he himself felt. At length he resolved to carry her off from her husband, but the plan failed, and the enraged Brahmin called on her father to avenge the insult A storm was accordingly called up, and the earth opened and swallowed up the king and his whole court. The sister of the serpent-god assisted him, and hurled on the city huge stones from the Báman mountain. The caverns of Mattan are said to be on the spot where these rocks were uptorn. The natives believe that they extend to the far depths of the earth, and none will venture within them, lest with the first step they should be seized by the powers of darkness. Mírza Ahud assured me that the largest of them extended ten kos inwards; that from the exterior halls, chambers, and walks, branched in every direction, the walls of which were covered with inscriptions and representations of various deities. He implored me not to venture where no man had ever been known to find his way out again. Raging torrents, he said, deafened every sound, and an evil spirit called Jin, whose breath smote men to death, had his abode there. I told him, as he was afraid, he might stay where he was, which he agreed to, with many thanks, although he still protested he would follow me if I desired it.

I entered first the small cavern, which lies at the extremity of a broad valley. At the projecting angle of the range of mountains which terminate at this point, a flight of steps, hewn out of the rock, leads to the entrance gate, which is from 60 to one hundred feet higher than the plain. Here the traveller enters a room about twenty feet long and twelve high and broad. Beyond, is a little temple in the rock, but the wooden gates were shut, and though most curious to know to what deity it had been dedicated, all my efforts to gain admittance were fruitless. One of my Ghorka companions was more fortunate, and at last we entered, but neither image, nor sign of any kind was there. I concluded that this must be a kind of vestibule to the deeper caves, but could discover no trace of any communication from the place where we now were.

From the hill over this cavern, I enjoyed a fine view of the rich plain of Kashmír, and as far as the Shonibal and Kirwan mountains. Northwards flowed the shallow Lidar, over its stony bed; and, on the heights behind stood the lone fort of Aismokam, while, about a hundred paces below me, was a small square Buddhist temple, in good preservation. I descended from this eminence, and proceeded towards the great cavern. The wild intricacy of the rocks around, together with the dreadful stories I had listened to, induced me to order a great many torches to be lighted. While this was being done I espied some birds, new to me, and desired Jwali Singh, a great fellow, six feet high, and athletic in proportion, to fire at them. One of the Kashmírians stared at me with amazement, and cried out, "Maha Raja, it is impossible." Jwali laughed at his superstition; and taking one of my double-barrelled guns, quickly took his aim; but the gun would not go off, and he turned to me with the greatest anxiety in his countenance. He tried again with fresh powder, but with as little success, when, bringing the gun back to me, he positively declared that nothing should induce him to fire while in this place. To cure them of such superstitious fancies, I determined to take a shot myself; but the wily birds had, by this time, made their escape, so that unluckily their credulity could not be overcome by example. I dare say, if I had succeeded in my aim, they would only have believed me a magician, without feeling a whit the less convinced of the mysterious influence of the place. Mirza Ahud voluntarily offered to follow me into the cavern, the poor Pandit's office compelling him to do the same. We accordingly proceeded to the entrance, which is about thirty feet above the plain, and difficult of access. The first thing that struck us was several little chambers of different forms. I went into all of them but could discover no communication whatever between them. In one was a modern tomb, in another a human skeleton; but when we tried to push forwards into the darkness, we found the roof gradually sloping downwards over our heads; and after we had gone about sixty paces more, of which twenty had been in the wet slippery mud, caused by dropping water, we came to the end of this celebrated cave of Mattan. Mohan Bir, who had followed in some terror, owing to Mirza Ahud's tales, now laughed heartily at the narrator, who took it in very good part, only ridiculing the superstitious fancies of the Kashmírians, of which country he himself was also a native.

I had still Korau Pandau to visit, which is on the high plain that crowns the eminence between the rocks of Buasuan and the mountains of Islamabad. We now travelled along a deep ravine, formed by the violent rains which have gradually washed away the loose soil. This is the only drain for the waters in the plain above. We then ascended a hill, from two to three hundred feet high: it is in some parts perpendicular, in others irregular in its descent, composed of loose mud without any admixture of stone or sand. We made but little progress over this steep and slippery ground, a dead flat being before us, as destitute of vegetation as a desert. The atmosphere peculiar to the country made its dimensions appear of immense extent, while, almost lost in the far distant east, peered the outline of mountains, relieved in the foreground by a dark point standing forth like a sharp black rock.

This was Korau Pandau, and my little ghunt soon galloped away to the temple gate. My first impressions were of gloom and heaviness only; but the dark masses, with their gigantic outlines, are softened down by the slender pillars introduced in many places; and the large round apertures over the doors must have admitted sufficient light to the interior to dispel much of the obscurity.

Korau Pandau owes its existence and name to the most ancient dynasty of Kashmír. The great antiquity of the ruin will be acknowledged therefore when I remind the reader, that the Pandau dynasty ended 2500 years before Christ, after governing Kashmír according to their historians nearly 1300 years. Here no doubt Sri Nagur, the holy city, was first built; in fact the Brahmins still call this place by that name. Just as Solomon is celebrated by the Mohammedans, the Empress Helena in the Holy Land, Charlemagne in Germany, the Cyclops in Italy, and Joseph in Egypt; so every Hindú, from Cape Comorin to Kashmír, ascribes every relic of ancient days to the Pandau dynasty, unless the records of their history pronounce directly to the contrary. That the race really did exist, and in much power, can hardly be questioned, because the ancient Madura, in Southern India, according to history, was subdued by them; and it seems most likely that it was this city to which Ptolemy gave the title Regia Pandionis. Pliny (6. 16) speaks of a city called Panda on the other side of the Sogdus; Solinus (c. 49) gives the same name to a town in Sogdiana, beyond the Bactrus; while, in the same 6th book, Pliny mentions another Panda at the mouth of the Indus. Ptolemy says plainly, "the kingdom of the Pandau is near the Bydaspes," or Jelam. (Circa autem Bydaspum, Pandovorum regio). If the histories of Kashmír and of this race are to be relied on, then these cities may all have been in the possession of the Pandau dynasty, at different epochs. But, after such a lapse of time, all these suppositions must rest in doubt, since the identity of the various places can never be made quite evident to us.

By Korau Pandau is a small house and garden, belonging to a fakír. It is now deserted. The traveller still finds ripe fruit on the trees, which the fakír, who was driven forth by the last famine, will never pluck again. This house was once a place of pilgrimage for Mohammedans; and a well, called Hárat and Márat's Baúri, is yet considered a holy spot. The legend says, that these two good angels were sent on earth by God to reform men by their example; but, alas! they could not withstand the beauty of the daughters of Kashmír; and when conscience awoke, instead of repenting of their errors and hoping to obtain pardon by amendment, they cast themselves down, with their beloved companions, into this well, which bears their name—the Baúri, or well of Hárat and Márat.

To the left is the ruined aqueduct, which formerly conveyed the water from the mountains to the plain, but has long been dry. Mirza Ahud informed me, that the water was carried to a distance of twenty miles: I asked him, if his calculation was as exact as the ten kos of the great cave of Mattan. Having sent on my people towards Islamabad, I turned back again to the great ruin. The more one examines the mighty mass of Korau Pandau, the deeper is the impression it makes on the mind. The time was passing quietly on; the sun sinking below Islamabad, and the mists of the valley still hanging over the snowy peaks of the Pir Panjal, like vast fleecy clouds, as I gazed attentively on the different aspects presented by these ruins. The short twilight soon faded, and I found myself on the lonely road in utter darkness. My good steed, however, retraced the way he had taken once before, in perfect security; and in a very short time accomplished the four miles to our halting place for the night.

No Brahmins came this evening; and I was glad of it, as it gave me leisure to make out a plan and description of Korau Pandau. I was assisted also by a fire which my people had lit; and though it smoked abominably, it prevented my fingers from being numbed by the cold.

Islamabad lies near the end of the valley in this direction; and the Jelam, which flows two miles off, soon ceases to be navigable. Two kos further is Sahibabad, which has a small fort, built by Núr Begam, and three old Buddhist temples, called Wámadevi. Another two kos brings us to Shahabad, a garden of the Moghul emperors; near to this is Warnágh, which was erected by Jehanghír, and boasts of the finest spring in the valley. All these palaces are now in ruins, and the fallen roofs so block up the interior as to leave little room for a wanderer's observation. Sahibabad and Warnágh are built on eminences; Sháhabad is at the eastern limit of the valley of Kashmír. The Jelam, soon after passing Sháhabad, loses its name; and at Banhal, twelve kos from Islamabad, is known as the San-drán. I would fain have gone thus far, but the cold increased daily, and I apprehended a heavy fall of snow might entirely frustrate my intention of visiting the mountains of Tibet. I was, moreover, to speak the truth, nearly worn out with the indifferent food, the piercing cold, the fatigue of body and mind, I had now so long undergone, and was tormented by a constant anxiety to terminate the loneliness of my present position, and bring my journeyings to a close.

Thursday, 26th. The Thanadar was unable to procure me the ore I was desirous of getting from the mountain, and was sadly afraid I should refuse to give him the certificate of good conduct and attention which he was commanded to forward to the Maha Raja. When I assured him to the contrary, his gratitude was unbounded. He informed me that a large animal, of the deer kind, came down from the mountains, in the cold season, and committed great ravages in the fields. The natives pursue and attack them with clubs, and frequently succeed in destroying some. One which has been captured alive has been in Islamabad ever since, roaming about the bazar and adjacent fields; supporting itself on any food it chances to take a fancy to. This tame creature I saw: it was about the size of a fallow deer, but of a greyish colour and had longer hair. It had not shed its horns, which, at their full growth, have as many as twelve antlers. This animal is the Bárasinghi twelve antlers, or perhaps great-antler deer of the Himálaya.

The boats were waiting at Kanibal, where the Jelam ceases to be navigable. Thither we proceeded on foot, the coldness of the morning making the two miles' walk very agreeable. The bridge over the Jelam consists of two arches only. It is the last of any importance in this direction. In no country in the world, perhaps, are there so many bridges as in Kashmír. They span every river and brook, great and small, and are all built and kept in repair by the Government, without the levy of any toll. It was eleven o'clock when we pushed off from the shore, and I saw that it would be late when we arrived in Kashmír. The cold, even wrapped up as I was, was so bitter, that it was painful to write; but I persevered, knowing that, in such a journey as mine, what is not set down quickly is lost for ever, and no longer to be recalled to memory. We came up before dark with two vessels loading with the bark of the birch-tree. It is used in Kashmír to pack up the pears and apples which they export to other parts, the larger pieces are shaped into the long winding pipes of the hookah. Men and women seemed equally busy with the load, which they were carrying through the water, the vessels not being able to approach the shore; they did not appear to be in the least affected with the extreme cold, although their clothing would certainly have afforded them but indifferent protection against it. The bed of the Jelam is everywhere of great depth, but the shores are generally too high to allow of any view beyond them from a boat. Sometimes the river is swollen from twelve to fifteen feet above its ordinary level, and then it overflows, but its motion is so sluggish, that the houses built on the shore are rarely in danger.

The appearance of Ventipoor, as you approach it from Islamabad, is very agreeable. The few buildings and ruins stretching down to the shore, leaning as it were against the mountains, seem to form a safe harbour and landing-place. A fire was lighted on the ground while I took my dinner at seven o'clock in the evening. We then continued our march, and tried every plan to keep ourselves warm. The night, though freezing cold, was fair; the boats glided calmly over the waters, and the boatmen beguiled the time with songs, sometimes in chorus, at other times singly, which they managed with much softness and effect. In summer weather this excursion would have been most delightful, but now the contrast between the keen cold atmosphere and these sentimental strains was rather painful. The lamp burned dimly on the table on which I leaned, while Mohan Bír slept at my feet. Gradually the chaunt of the boatmen lulled me as I smoked my hookah, and I forgot, all associations of the past, Asia, Kashmír, and every present concern in the reveries of my early youth. The hopes and joyous expectations of boyhood, that happiest time, when the heart longs to know a good world, and confides so sweetly in the worth of others; the once-felt sentiments uprose now, as from a better world, in my own heart, and I could have dreamed on, and almost fancied that I was living over again those halcyon days of pleasurable unconcern. The intense cold brought me back to the present, and cruelly reminded me of the truth that I was far from home, alone, the hopes of my youth still unfulfilled, the wishes of the man frustrated, a wanderer, perhaps forgotten, in a region so far away as I then was from every associate, from all my kindred. I roused Mirza Ahud, who was in the next boat, and bade him give me some account of Jacquemont to divert my mind from such idle dreams. By what he related it would appear that he had rather acted a part in Kashmír: he wished to be considered a philosopher, who held money in contempt, and had even been seen to throw rupees out of the window of his lodging; but Mirza Ahud seemed to have seen through this little artifice, and told me that, though his former master did often waste a great deal of money, his first and chief thought seemed always to be, wealth.

I then asked him whether he could not amuse me with some of the old tales of his native land, whereupon he instantly began as follows:— The king Chandranand desired to erect a temple to Siva, and had been long in quest of some suitable place. Having acquired his object he set regularly to work. Now it chanced that part of the ground was in possession of a tanner, but as that trade is followed by none except persons of low caste, they turned him out of the place without ceremony. When the King heard of it, he punished the officer severely and ordered the work to be suspended till the tanner consented to quit the place of his own free will.

I then desired Mirza Ahud to think of something more national, as this manner of dealing was common to all countries. He then commenced a second story.

The Raja Jayanand was the greatest king on earth, and after subduing every country in the seven climates, returned laden with treasures, to his own dominions. Here he lived in the enjoyment of life, forgetting that his successes were all due to the protection and help of God. He had been carousing one night until very late, witnessing the displays of his three hundred nách girls, who had been amusing him with their songs and dances, and quaffing huge draughts of the forbidden spirit, when he lay down; but although he desired his servants to leave him to recruit his strength for the next day's pleasures, sleep refused to obey his call. Presently there appeared to him Máha Padma, a serpent-god, and entreated his aid against a powerful magician of Dravira, who had enchanted him, promising him, as a reward for his assistance, to lead him into a great cavern filled with an incredible mass of gold, which should be wholly at his disposal. The king sent the next morning for the magician, and desired him to point out the serpent-god. The magician accompanied the king to the lake, where the god was lying, and having turned the waters into a cloud, the serpent-god became visible to them in the same form as before. The king then commanded the magician to fill the lake again; and the cloud, at his bidding, sank down, and covered it ten kos in depth; vivid lightning shot from it, and, within half an hour, the lake was a sheet of water as before. Jayanand then rewarded the magician, and sent him back to Dravira. Máha Padma appeared again the next night, and reproached Jayanand for the anguish he had occasioned him; but, in reward for his having sent away the magician finally, he showed him a copper-mine instead of the cavern of gold. The king ordered it to be worked; and, during his reign, 100 kror (990 millions) were coined. He then sent to every monarch in the world, defying them to surpass him in riches.

I asked Mirza whether the Mohammedan writers admitted such sheer nonsense as this into the histories of Kashmír; and his answer was, that if they said nothing about serpent-gods, they related wonders of another kind, but quite as surprising. For instance, they say, that in Daulut Jang's reign, a violent earthquake in Kashmír removed the city of Húsanpur from the right to the left bank of the river, and caused it to change places with Húseinpoor; but I stated to him, that this was but a false statement of a true event, which turned the course of the winding Jelam. The Auk, before which we now found ourselves, comes from the mountains of Tibet. Should the rain fall heavily for a few days, it brings down pieces of timber, which the natives pick up; these shine in the dark as long as they continue moist.

Friday, November 27. It was six o'clock in the morning when we were put ashore at the Hamedan Masjid in Kashmír, so benumbed with cold, that I was obliged to hurry to the garden as fast as I could, to warm my frozen limbs. Early in the day I assembled my attendants, and desired that every preparation should be made for my departure, and at the same time I despatched the múnshi to the Kázi, and begged that the Governor might be informed of my intention to leave Kashmír on the 29th, the day I had appointed before I quitted for Islamabad. The Kázi came an hour after, to tell me that it would require four days to hire the hundred and twenty bearers that I required, but I answered that my múnshí would do it in less time, and that I left that charge to him. This had its effect, and the Kázi promised that everything should be ready on Monday. My next visitor was Sámed Shah, the confidential servant of Mohammed Shah Nakshbandi, who came to remind me of my promise to pay his master a visit. It was agreed, therefore, that I should partake of a supper at his house on the next day, and I was glad of the opportunity of seeing something more of the manners and customs of the country.

I had brought several baskets of potatoes to Kashmír, with the hope of being able to introduce this valuable article among the natives. Mr. Vigne had already spoken of its great utility to Ahmed Shah, the Raja of Iskardú, and I hoped to extend its cultivation to Tibet also. With a view of smoothing the way, I thought of sending the Raja, together with the potatoes, several presents which I judged would be acceptable, among which were three bottles of cognac and some drugs: these were accordingly dispatched to Iskardú, with our letters, in a gold embroidered bag.

I now proposed to my two English friends, that we should erect something like a monument to the travellers who had preceded us in Kashmír; and, at the same time, leave a memorial of our having met, on the present occasion, at this spot. We agreed to carve the following inscription on a black marble tablet, and set it up in the little building on the Char Chúnar island:—

"Three travellers in Kashmír on the 18th November, 1835, the Baron Ch. Hügel, from Jamú; Th. G. Vigne, from Iskardú; and Dr. John Henderson, from Ladák, have caused the names of all the travellers who have preceded them in Kashmír to be engraven on this stone.

"Bernier, 1663. Forster, 1786. Moorcroft, Guthrie, and Trebeck, 1823. Victor Jacquemont, 1831. Joseph Wolff, 1832.

"Two only of all these, the first and last, ever returned to their native country."

I need not remark, that in the list I have included no Catholic missionaries; Forster did, strictly speaking, return home, but he came out again, and died at Madras.

Vigne and Henderson accepted the commission with pleasure; and as it was necessary to get the stone at a short notice, I thought of one of the doors at the mosque of Nagarnagar. This plan I proposed to the Kázi; but he looked grave, and said he must consult the Governor about it, which I desired him to do forthwith. He came back in an hour or two, and informed me that Mehan Singh had thought it right to send off and request the permission of Ranjít Singh before we did so. I expressed my hope that the Governor would not object to the stone being got ready, on my promise being given, that all subsequent proceedings should depend on the Mahá Raja's answer. This was acceded to, and the Kázi said we might take away as many of the stones as we wanted. To guard against any further interruption, Vigne undertook to remove the door at sunset. To another message from Mehan Singh, asking whether it would not be agreeable to me to see the Nách girls, I replied in the affirmative, and they were accordingly ordered to attend and exhibit before us in my tent. Towards evening I went to the bazar, to see whether it had anything particularly worthy of attention, while Vigne proceeded to the ruinous mosque to fetch away the marble tablet. But he had forgotten to take any ropes or poles with him, and the stone was too heavy to be removed without such helps. He had to come back therefore, after making many fruitless efforts, without having advanced our object.

Just before it was dark, a number of the Kashmírian beauties made their appearance, accompanied by musicians, duennas, and divers hideous wretches who usually attend on them, and whose monstrous ugliness makes the features of the dancers, who are almost invariably unsightly in appearance, shew off to greater advantage. After dinner was over, the tents were cleared and lighted, and the whole of our attendants were admitted to view what was going on. There was one among the dancers whose animated cast of features made her much more prepossessing than the rest. The passion of the Sikhs for this amusement is so great, that my chief pleasure was really derived from attending to them, and I believe there is much truth in the proverb, that you may take away the wife and child of a Sikh while he is listening to the adventures of Rústam and Súráb, and he would not miss them. I shall have more to say in another place, on the dancing and song peculiar to Kashmír.

The Nách girls are called sometimes Kanchni, but not by polite speakers; and sometimes Nachwali, dancers, which is more courteous. They are throughout India under the surveillance of the Government, and are, in fact, little better than slaves. These poor creatures are doomed to a hard fate; they are not allowed either to sing or dance without permission, and if they get this, an officer of the Government always accompanies them, who grasps whatever they receive. When I had dismissed the troop, they demanded one hundred rupees for the evening's performance.

Saturday, 28th November. If I had anticipated so long a stay here I should have insisted on Mehan Singh visiting me in the first instance, and I advise every traveller who purposes to remain in Kashmír for any time to do the same, and in case of a refusal, not to visit him at all. He should insist moreover on his own visit being punctiliously returned. For the sake of those who may follow me here, I reproach myself for having swerved from this rule, which I did from my aversion to this ceremonial, which always costs a morning, but principally because I never intended to stay in Kashmír more than a few days.

It was known that I was forming collections of every thing rare, and this whole day I was pestered with men having all sorts of things to sell. About noon came Ganesh Pandit, the first interpreter of the Government, and a Brahmin of some consequence in the place; after a conversation of greater length than learning, he laid an immense roll of paper at my feet, a history of Kashmír, which he presented to me, having heard much of my wisdom and learning. I opened it, and found a list of names, neatly written on the finest Kashmir paper, in the Persian character, which Ganesh Pandit explained to be the names of the different Rajas who reigned in Kashmír before the Mohammedan conquest. I asked, how many kings were there? "Six thousand nine hundred and forty," he replied, evidently with a tone and look of triumphant pride at being born in such a country. His catalogue finished with the year 864 (Hegira 250), to which period he incorrectly assigned the first arrival of the Mohammedans in the valley. "But," said I, "how many years of the Kali Yúg had passed when this event took place?" After a long reckoning he said 3938. This again was a mistake, for the year 250 of the Hegira is the 3966 of the Kali Yúg, an epoch which begins 3102 years before Christ. "Then," said I, "how is it possible that in 3938 years 6940 kings could reign?" To which he replied, that in his list he had included 400 years of the Dwapar Yúg, the epoch which preceded the Kali Yúg. So that his 6940 kings had 4338 years to reign in. I said only in reply, that as Kasyapa, according to their histories, had drained the lake which covered the valley 612 years before the Kali Yúg commenced, he had forgotten the kings of the first 212 years altogether. I however took the list as a curiosity.

At 6 o'clock, Mohammed Shah's state boat was sent to fetch Vigne, Henderson, and myself to dinner. When we had finished, the Shah took us into a room apart; but as the Indian fashion usually demands some appearance of mystery to be displayed in all things, I took this for some empty form, and was rather surprised when the Shah solicited me to do him a great favour. I must premise that the Shah is a Syad—a descendant of the Prophet, and that his surname Nakshbandi is taken from a mystical sect founded by one of his ancestors. His family is of the royal house of Táshkend, whence his ancestors went to Turkisthan, and his grandfather, Khoja Shah Niyás, more recently wandered as far as Kashmír, where he assembled some hundred disciples of his sect around him, from Iskardú, Yárkand, and Turkisthan. Family affairs now render the presence of Mohammed in Turkisthan very advisable, but as the governor declines to allow of his departure on his own responsibility, he has decided on going himself to Lahor, personally to request leave to travel of Ranjít Singh. He had already besought Mr. Vigne to allow him to make one of his party, being influenced in this by another and a very justifiable motive. Every European who had travelled in Kashmír had largely shared in his attentions, and they were particularly useful to Moorcroft during his long sojourn in the valley. He seems naturally to hope now, that the Company may repay this hospitality to him in some way or other; and it is his present object to go from Lahor to Lúdiana, where Captain Wade resides, and get some acknowledgment, from the official resident, of his services to English travellers.

It so happened, that one of the Shah's kinsmen, holding some post in Kishtewar, had fallen under the displeasure of Gulab Singh, and had made his escape to Kashmír; the Shah now begged me to take him as my múnshí, and thus smuggle him out of the country. This was not agreeable to me, for I did not know what fault he had been guilty of, nor what I should do with him in Hindústhan; my answer was therefore evasive, and I told the Shah that I had no power to protect all the suite accompanying me, and that he would be quite as safe and less noticed in his own company. He understood me, and pressed the matter no further, merely asking my leave to introduce his kinsman, which I could not refuse. The young man, on entering, prostrated himself at my feet. His face was remarkable for its expression of stupidity, relieved only by anxiety for the consequences of an offence for which I could not offer much comfort, as I was perfectly ignorant of its nature.

Mohammed Shah has a great many of the natives of Yárkand about him, pilgrims who are on their way to Mecca, which they reach more speedily and safely by way of India and Bombay, than by the considerably shorter route of Central Asia and Persia. This circumstance ought to smooth many difficulties in the path of Europeans travelling in Central Asia; for when the natives return full of the kindness and hospitality they have received from the Company's officers, they will surely requite their generous feeling in the only way they have in their power, by showing them the like. Most of the pilgrims I met in Bombay were men of wealth, and therefore naturally of influence in their own country, and it is to be hoped they will use both for the benefit of fellow-wanderers.

The productions of Yárkand, which were all spread out before me, were highly interesting; thirty-two species of tea brought from the interior of China by way of Axor and Turfan were also shown me. The natives of Yárkand told me, that the caravans go in twenty-eight days from Kashgár to Samarkhand; from Kashgár to Yarkánd in five days; from Samarkhand to Bokhara in ten days. The tea comes from Ili, the Chinese place of exile, by Turfan to Axor. Turfan is on the confines of Turkisthan towards China. It was 10 o'clock when I took leave of my host.

Sunday, November 29.—Mr. Vigne had sent his servant, Mitchell, last evening, with twenty men, provided with every thing requisite, except common sense, to bring the stone away from the ruined mosque. On our return, we heard from him that the guard had threatened to shoot him if he remained there, and that a large crowd had assembled in Nagarnagar to prevent the stone being taken away. This Mitchell was a half-caste, and a confirmed drunkard, and I have some notion that he never went at all, and fabricated the whole story. This morning the Kázi came from Mehan Singh to request that I would visit him, for the purpose of receiving the khilat, or garb of honour, the Mahá Raja's parting gift to travellers. This I would gladly have avoided, for I felt quite sure that Mehan Singh would select some worthless shawls, and expect me to return the gift with something of real value, but I did not wish to offend him, so promised to go speedily. Vigne and Henderson were also invited.

We were received by the Viceroy in a room in the first story in Shaherghur, without any furniture or ornaments suited to an inhabited apartment. A few officers only were present, who retired as soon as we were seated. After the usual oriental fine speeches, I thanked the Governor for the facilities I had enjoyed for seeing Kashmír. He answered that it was nothing more than the Mahá Raja's order. I then told him that it was my intention to travel through the Baramulla pass to Atok. He stared in astonishment, and remarked that the road was a very bad one. I had heard however from many people in Kashmír, that it was the very best, and that the Sikhs always describe it as dangerous, to deter Englishmen from taking that route. I merely said, therefore, that I was prepared to find it so, but wished to travel that way, unless it were displeasing to the Mahá Raja. "Here is a letter to the Mahá Raja," I added, "in answer to one lately received from him. I have informed him that I purpose to enter the Panjáb again at

Hussein Abdul." I stated further that Mohammed Shah Nakshbandi would travel with me. He again enforced on my mind the danger of meeting with parties of Mohammedan robbers by the way; but seeing that he could not move me, he turned the conversation on the beautiful shawls which I had bought. "If you wish for any more," he added, "when you go to your own country, I hope you will commission me to buy them for you."

I now spoke of our inscription, of which we had prepared a Persian translation, and Mr. Vigne obtained his promise that we should not be called to any account if the stone did disappear from Nagarnagar that evening. The khilat, composed of eleven dirty old shawls, was next brought in. I had an opportunity here of observing how well Dr. Henderson had studied the character of this people. When he gave Mehan Singh a gold coin as a mark of his subjection, the features excepted, he might have been taken for one of themselves. When a trifling present was offered him, he declined it, calling himself a poor fakír, and I would have done the same, if my travelling arrangements had been quite secured. Mehan Singh was not so tipsy as at our first interview, but most assuredly was not sober. We took our leave with an embrace.

I had brought letters of credit from Lúdiana on a saráf, or money-changer in Kashmír; and when first I arrived in the city, he had paid me a visit in my tent. I told him before several persons, that when I wanted money I should apply to him, not being then aware that the possessor of ever so little wealth makes the greatest mystery of it, on account of the cupidity of their Sikh masters; and I remember being surprised at the faltering tone in which he answered that he did not know how it would be possible for him to collect even one thousand rupees; when however he paid me a second visit, he explained the reason why, and told me that any sum I wanted was at my command. I commissioned him to buy the best shawls he could find for me, and to-day he brought me some unfinished, which were not of the first class. I suspected at first that this was a trick to impose upon me, but on stricter inquiry I found that it was a very difficult thing to get these shawls complete in Kashmír. More of this, however, hereafter.

Dr. Henderson's servant arrived to-day from Ladák, and alone, having, as he said, lost the horses and every other article in the snow in the Náubak pass. He was dismissed, together with the servant who had come to Kashmír with him: they had subsisted for three days on two chepatis. As I could not find that there was any fault in either, I agreed to take them into my service. The Doctor proposed bending his course now to the Hindú Khosh, and Balkh, and though I tried to dissuade him from such a step at this season, he was bent on it. I therefore fitted him out with such things as instruments, and a second watch, &c., as well as I could, and in this remote land, where a few days passed together make men more familiar, than years would under other circumstances, we both felt much at parting. It was arranged that we should leave Kashmír the same day, the 1st of December, travel westward to the confines of the country together, and there part, hoping to meet early in the following year at Lahor. The rest of the day was spent in packing up the different collections I had made at this place.

Monday, November 30.—My people all informed me, that the whole city was up in arms at the idea of our removing the stone from their mosque, and that nothing but our robbery was talked of in the bazar. We judged it as well therefore to have the Governor's authority for what we were going to do; and when the Kázi came to tell me that every thing would be ready for my departure in two days, Mr. Vigne pressed him for the order, but this he would not give, repeating that if we chose to remove the stone, no notice would be taken. I saw how many difficulties were in our way, and that the Sikhs did not wish openly to offend the prejudices of the Mohammedans, I therefore recommended that we should look out for another tablet, and Mohammed Shah succeeded in getting us a beautiful slab of black marble out of the Shalimár garden.

Several dozen pair of shawls were sent to-day for my selection; I purchased two blue and two white ones, but neither of them was finished. The conduct of Mirza Abdul Rahim highly disgusted me on this occasion, and I was the more confirmed in my original opinion of the man. The first time that Mr. Vigne visited the Governor, he was accompanied by this Mirza Abdul Rahim, who demanded a seat as the Company's agent. It was at first refused, but at last his demand was complied with, although he had no right whatever to the privilege in question. The giving or withholding of this seat, is a matter of vast importance in India, and every European must not only stand firm on his rightful pretensions, but even in his own solitary tent keep up all the etiquette of a court. I passed the day in packing and purchasing, while Mr. Vigne went to complete his drawing on the Tahkt-i-Suliman. I regretted that time would not permit me to ascend this mountain again, for the great antiquity of the ruin gave it additional interest. The erection of the temple is ascribed to Gopaditya, of the Gonerdya dynasty, B.C., 370. Dr. Henderson spent the whole day in the bazar in preparing for his journey. In the evening we all dined together in my tent.

Tuesday, December 1.—The Lieutenant and his guard, who had been stationed before my tent during my stay in Kashmír, were appointed to escort me to Lahor. This was against my will, for such a thing as a guard had never occurred to me during my wanderings from one end of India to the other, and I had no inclination to avail myself of this novel protection.

The servant of Ranjít Singh's chobdar had been dangerously ill in Kashmír, and so had the havildar; several of my attendants had also been attacked with fever. I administered to, and succeeded in curing, them all. Strange to say, the natives of Bengal were of all the least affected by the cold and the fatigues of our journey, and my only surprise still is, how one of the Hindús survived it, seeing that, while they are preparing their food, they throw off every thing except the cloth which is tied round their waist, and that the highest castes all eat in this state of nudity. My múnshí, a Brahmin, never failed to eat his rice thus unclad, even when the glass was at the freezing point, and his health was much better than that of the Mohammedans from the north of India, who could not clothe themselves too warmly. Among others who had heard of my success as a physician, was the Kázi, who came to consult me, but I saw that he suffered from confirmed asthma, so I made him over to Dr. Henderson, his case not being one by which I could hope for any credit*.

Mr. Vigne made a drawing for me to-day of the Dilawer Khan Bágh, and every inhabitant at present in it, servants, horses, dogs, goats, and poultry. My dealings with the shawl merchants harassed me beyond endurance; indeed no patience can stand out against the torments of making ever so trifling a bargain with these people. The mode of their negotiating business is altogether peculiar: the two parties seated on the ground, give their right hand to each other, under a large cloth, without a word being uttered by either of them, the offer and answer are signified by different ways of pressing the hand. Several days frequently elapse in such dealings, without any thing being concluded. My deputy, Abdul Rahim, I had reason to believe equal to any species of knavery; Mirza Ahud however had always proved himself strictly honest and disinterested.

My Indian servants assisted me to-day in packing up my collection of the fishes of Kashmír; and I may remark here, that I found them on all occasions unsparing in their attention and most willing; quite undeserving of the contempt they sometimes receive from their English masters, because they do not comprehend, as it were by instinct, all the petty wants and desires of European fastidiousness.

---

* The natives of India, generally speaking, have very little faith in the medical skill of Europeans. In extreme and desperate cases they will gladly apply, but not till every other resource has failed them. Many such have come to my knowledge during my residence in India, where the most consummate skill, patience, and every benevolent feeling were generously proffered to parties beyond the reach of ordinary cure. In cases of cholera, application was rarely deferred, or in any serious affections of the sight; but in the most dreadful maladies there is a decided aversion to European practice, even with those classes, our soldiery and menials, who come more directly under the influence of authority. Narratives of cases in which diseases of the eye have been successfully treated, would fill a volume with matter of the deepest interest, and discover much of the good quality of the Asiatic—neither wholly destitute of gratitude, good sense, nor feelings of a yet nobler kind. The record of acts of disinterested skill performed by Kemball, Marshall, Duncan, Graham, Jefferson, and many such benevolent members of the medical profession, do honour to this distinguished body, and will long be remembered throughout Western India.

Dr. Henderson and I had reckoned on starting to-day, but the servants he had engaged refused to go when they found that he was journeying to Atok, the bands of robbers being so numerous and daring, that it has at times required the whole power of Ranjít Singh to oppose them. He was therefore compelled to look out for others, while my tents underwent some repairs, and the boats had not yet left the city. The days were so short and so cold, that we did not get through much business.

Wednesday, December 2.—The Dilawer Khan Bágh was like a bazar to-day, not only for me but for my attendants, every one being desirous of taking something to India from Kashmír. Then came the task of examining the múnshí's accounts; and the writing of testimonials of good conduct for all Ranjít Singh's officers, from the Viceroy down to the spy. In the evening a robbery, the first that had befallen me in India, and which was instantly laid to the Kashmírians, was effected in my little territory, the object stolen being a coverlet that Jwali Singh had bought in Rajawar. It was soon discovered, cut into two pieces, in the possession of the Mali, my gardener. He vowed that he had purchased it of a Kashmírian, but the secrecy with which he had offered to sell one half to my bearer as soon as it was dark, proved his criminality. My servants wanted to complain to the Kázi, but I would not permit this, telling them that in my tents I was lord, and entitled to punish any crime committed by my servants; and late as it was, I ordered a formal hearing of the case, assisted by Mr. Vigne. But the evidence was so contradictory and so lengthy, that I was soon glad to break up my court and pay Jwali Singh the value of his property. I must admit that the gardener was too easily let off, as he still had the stolen article in his possession.

The evening was employed in carving our inscription on the stone, Mirza Ahud received thirty rupees to give to the sculptor, and he was to be charged with the care of the stone until permission came from Lahor, with authority to put it up in the Char Chúnar island.

Dr. Henderson set off this afternoon, but divers disagreeable affairs obliged me to remain another night in Kashmír.

Thursday, December 3.—The tents were packed by dawn, and my

baggage, which was greatly increased by the collections I had made at this place, was all carried off to the boats. My stock of provisions was very low, compared with what it had been when first I arrived in Kashmír; the potatoes, wine, and beer, were nearly exhausted, the remains of my cellar consisting of half-a-dozen bottles of port wine, one bottle of brandy, and a very few of other kinds of wine. From Narpoor I had written to Lúdiana for a fresh supply, but it had not arrived. I was obliged in consequence to leave a request with the Governor that as soon as it should find its way to Kashmír, it should be forwarded to me. It was not till two o'clock that we left the garden. The shawl merchant promised that my unfinished purchases should be sent to Lúdiana within four weeks, and took a bill of exchange payable at Calcutta. I mention this as a proof of the facility with which Europeans can receive money in any part of India.

Neither Vigne nor I quitted the Dilawer Khan Bágh without emotion, but it was caused by very opposite feelings: he had many pleasant remembrances connected with his abode in that garden; I had none, and the sufferings of my body almost annihilated every sentiment of pleasure which, in a more genial season, the many beauties around me must have kept alive. At the Hamidan Masjid a little fleet of seven boats was waiting for us, and threading the crowds which were assembled on the shore and the bridge, we found ourselves gently gliding down the stream, and taking our last farewell view of the city. The architecture of the wooden edifices situated on its shores, is peculiar. They are two, three, and sometimes four stories high, but only one window in breadth; being built moreover detached, they appear to invite the wind, if perchance it should ever blow hard in Kashmír, to overthrow them.

When we had left the city behind us, the motion of the boat seemed too slow and tedious in my present frame of mind, and I desired to be put on shore and see whether exercise would not divert my thoughts from melancholy. It was bitter cold, and long ere by dint of hard walking I could get any warmth into my frame. The country is generally marshy, and in many parts uncultivated. The most romantic part of the valley is evidently in the south and south-east, although further west there is a point which the Kashmírians consider by far the most beautiful part of this region, and which has gained the appellation of the Village of Roses, or Gul Mári. I had heard of it before, but it lay far out of my way, and the season of the year altogether precluded my wish to see it. After we left Kashmír, not a flower was to be seen; and the native whom I appointed to search for some, brought me nothing but a few evergreen leaves, the frost having completely destroyed every other description of vegetation.

We came to Koshpára, a village remarkable only for having the largest plane-trees in Kashmír. This tree, as I have often mentioned, is considered of much importance by the natives, who call it the end of misfortune. On its branches criminals are hanged, a punishment of constant occurrence under the Patán sway, when the smallest offence was visited with death, but now only inflicted in cases of murder. Men are too valuable to the present ruler of Kashmír to be lightly spared: penalties and stripes are therefore the usual punishments. The people seem contented with the justice dealt out to them, and admitted to me that not more than one guilty person in every twenty is ever visited with the reward due to his crimes. The dreadful cruelties perpetrated by their earlier rulers, who, for the smallest offence, punished them with the loss of their noses or ears, make the poor Indians well satisfied with their present comparatively mild government; and, in truth, there is very little oppression on the part of the governors or thanadars. The ideas of the Indians on this and many other subjects are also, it may be observed, very different from our own. As an example, I may mention that I had delayed my departure from the Dilawer Khan Bágh until noon, in order to take the sun's altitude once more. The sky was unclouded, and not to lose a moment, I began my observation at half-past eleven. Mr. Vigne meanwhile was sketching in the garden, which was crowded by the natives, who gathered around to see what we were doing. My English friend thought that they must be much impressed with our skill; I, on the contrary, had always remarked throughout India a total want of appreciation for any of our occupations, and rather a contemptible idea of those who were thus engaged. To settle this difference of opinion, Vigne called Mirza Ahud, and asked him what the Kashmírians said of us. Being told that he would not give us any offence, he frankly acknowledged that we were both looked upon as two madmen, who were troubling our heads about nothing better than stones and plants. Even the Governor concluded Mr. Vigne must be a downright idiot, to waste his time in drawing the likeness of an old ruin or a poor native. The Orientals only concern themselves about those treasures which will procure them the enjoyments of this life, or the religion which promises them the pleasures of the next.

At six o'clock the boats stopped, for it was quite dark; and as my people wished to spend the night in Shadipur, I landed, in order to take a survey of the place, which Abul Fazl calls the city of Shahabadipúr, the ancient Phalapur. I found it a wretched village, offering no shelter except that of a plane-tree; but as they told me that there was a beautiful garden on the other side of the Jelam, I desired that I might be taken over to it. This garden, Dab Bágh, Surij Bágh of the Hindús, lies at the confluence of the Siund and the Jelam, the first a small stream, called by us the Chota Sind, or little Indus, a name as little known among the natives as the Indus, which in Kashmír is called Atok, and in northern India, Niláb. The little Indus has been extolled by many writers as one of the chief sources of the Indus, and many have divided this into two branches, and made one of them to flow through Kashmír, the reason of this being the similarity between names, a most prolific source of error, and an occasion of the most absurd theories. In the history of Kashmír it is said, that Sujjya, whose birth and life were both most marvellous, ordained the course of this river about the year 880. The junction of the Siund with the Jelam, which before this, took place further down the stream by the temple of Vainya Swámi, was then removed higher up, namely, between the cities of Parihasapur and Phalapur. The junction of the Siund and Jelam does occur almost at a right angle, which accounts for the story. At the point of confluence is a little island, on which stands a small Buddhist temple.

The garden appointed for our night station, is three-quarters of a mile from the shore; the night was dark, and there was no beaten path. When we reached it, we saw and went over several buildings, until I found at last a very convenient room in a pavilion of marble. I desired one of the Kashmírians to light a fire there, while I went forth again to seek for Vigne; and when we returned together, the fire was kindled on the marble pavement; but the smoke was so unbearable, that we were obliged to throw open every door and window, and the cold was sharper than without. We did not get our dinner until midnight, and then I went to bed perfectly exhausted. Thus ended our first day.

Friday, December 4.—The Surij Bágh, or Dab Bágh, is a large pleasure-ground, laid out in the Indian taste, the chief art of which consists in giving a full view of the whole garden and buildings in it from the entrance gates, which are always of considerable elevation. From these a broad way leads to the basin, where fountains play in abundant variety: large beds of flowers ornament the garden, and the buildings are adorned with all that caprice could desire, or money purchase. The Surij Bágh was made by Surij Báhrí, who was summoned to Kashmír by Moti Rám, the first viceroy under Ranjít Singh, to superintend the new partition of the lands into portions of greater or less size. Several parcels of land were given to him, for which he paid a tribute, and gradually he had charge of eighteen pergannahs, for which he had to pay not less than six lacs of rupees. During the famine he received only five lacs, and prayed therefore to be excused the sixth, but Ranjít Singh refused this, telling him that if he had lost something this year, he had gained largely in the last. On the tribute failing altogether, Surij Báhrí was deprived of every thing, and received for his maintenance two villages, which keep him poorly enough. The consequence of such arbitrary proceedings on the part of their ruler, is, that no man feels quite sure of his own, and that neither in the Panjáb nor in Kashmír, have individuals much credit. For, who would lend his richest subject money, unless at enormous interest, when the Mahá Raja may, by a word, reduce him to beggary*. The garden is

* Such is a correct picture of the proceedings of every native government which, during the last two centuries, has arisen out of the dismemberment of the more ancient Hindú and Moghul sovereignties throughout the whole of India. In contrasting the advantages and comparative immunity from oppression, which the

falling to ruin, though never completed, and many a lac of rupees must all this carving and marble undoubtedly have cost.

The pavilion where we slept, consists of several little rooms, all of marble. The windows are most tastefully ornamented with the glass of Bengal; in the midst of the large square forming the garden, is an airy edifice of wood, with beautiful columns and lattice-work, where the cool of the evening is usually passed by the natives; and the largest of the buildings is close to a piece of water brought from the Siund; the water, when high, reaches to the walls of the buildings, although they are built at a height of forty or fifty feet above it. There are three species of the beautiful rose of Kashmír in the garden, and in defiance of the season, one of the bushes yielded me a flower.

The Surij Bágh is probably on the site of the once famous city of Parihasapur, of the marvels of which the native legends speak so highly. This city was built by the great conqueror Lálitadítya, who reigned from A.D. 714 to 750, and was adorned with many fine temples and monuments; among others, with a pillar cut out of one stone, twenty-four yards high, at the top of which stood the image of Gáruda, half-man, half-eagle. Sikandar Budh Shikán probably destroyed it, but several fragments were seen in 1727 by Mohammed Azim. Immense images of gold, silver, and other metals, also adorned the interior, but all traces of this splendour have disappeared. The point where two rivers meet is called Prayaga, or Sangam, and is always holy. The island at the junction of the Jelam and Siund has been the scene of many a self-immolation, and the Raja Taringini relates that Mitra Serma, the faithful

---

population enjoy under British sway, with the misery attendant on such a disregard of all the higher concerns of legislation by their own princes, there can be no question that the condition of all the industrious classes has been much improved; but this is rather to be ascribed to the concentration of such authority under one head, than to any superior system of administration; as is evident from the mere consideration, that established practice and ancient institutions, are preferred to European ideas of legislation, whenever circumstances will admit of it. The former Hindú, and indeed the Moghul governments, were very much better adapted to the state of Indian society than our own. It was the debasing, destructive, and iniquitous character of their religion, which precluded the full benefit of the former, as Christianity alleviates the bad, and fosters any measure of good in the present administration of this great empire. "Sit Deo laus."—*Ed.*

díwan or minister of the great King Lálitadítya, terminated his life here. The sacrifice is made a matter of much ceremony. The man tired of his life, makes his prescribed ablutions before a vast multitude, repeats the prayers required of his sect, and then seats himself in the water, praying all the while, and remaining there uncovered until he is drowned. The most holy stream for these suicides is the Ganges, where the alligators sometimes destroy the victim before the waters. In the Shástras, suicide, on account of grief or illness, is only allowed at the sacred Prayága at Allahabád, where the Ganges and Jamna unite with the invisible Sáreswati.

We breakfasted in the boat, reached Sambal, where is a bridge near the Jelam, in two hours, and there landed. The natives say that a fine city is here buried under the river, the summits of temples and other buildings having been often distinctly seen. There is no likelihood of this. The deepest part of the river is not more than twelve or fifteen feet, the sounding line finds nothing but earth and slime, and the Jelam carries so much mud along with it, that it would long since have filled up any inequalities of the bed. But the Kashmírians have a legend of this wonderful city, which is sinking deeper and deeper into the earth. I will repeat the story as told me by Mirza Abdul. The city was called Nárapoor from its founder, Buz Nára, a Hindú Raja, who lived 1000 years before Christ, and being on the Jelam, and near the beautiful lake, it soon became the favourite abode of the chief Brahmins, one of whom, Chandrabáha, so pleased Karkota, the serpent-god, that he gave him his sister Nila Bánu to wife. Her greatest pleasure, however, was to visit her brother, and linger for hours beneath the clear waters. It chanced that one day, the King Buz, who often visited Nárapoor, beheld the charming Nila Bánu on the shore, and became desperately enamoured of her. Failing in every attempt to obtain a return of this passion, the king determined to carry her away by force, and accordingly followed her steps with two of his trusty attendants. They were just about to seize her, when her brother Karkota appeared; he hurled a huge wave on the head of the king's servants, drew them into the lake and stifled them. Finding that even this did not put an end to the king's presumptuous hopes, Karkota's rage became unbounded, he raised a storm so terrific, that the king and all his subjects dwelling in Nárapoor, were carried away, and he and his sister even still unsatisfied, took huge masses of rock from the Romanya mountains, and hurled them on the city, causing it to fall in ruins into the Jelam. When all was still as death, Karkota began to be rather ashamed of his anger, and gave the country to his sister and her husband Chandrabaha, after he had turned the lake where he dwelt into milk: hence, the Mansbal Ser is called also Jamatri Saras. The place is still to be seen where the serpent-god dwelt; it is called Amantri, and the milk-white colour distinguishes it from other points. I desired Mirza Ahud to point it out to me as soon as he saw it.

We sent our boats forward from Sambal, with orders to wait for us at the point where the Mansbal Ser runs into the Jelam, our object being to visit the lake. On the south side it is bounded by a sedgy marsh, but in other parts the shores are steep and bare, and the oval form is clearly marked throughout. We strolled along the western shore, which is completely encircled by swelling hills, and reached a lovely point where was a garden inhabited by a fakír. We then passed Sofapoor, and the palace of the Empress Núr Jehán, the beloved wife of Jehánghír, whose name is still revered in Kashmír and throughout northern India, for her virtues and for the noble monuments which she has left of her taste and munificence.

The lake is deep, the mountains of Tibet towering proudly above it, and their deep shadows darkening the waters far beyond the shore. The large building, never quite completed, is now destroyed to the very foundations; but there are remains of three terraces, fifty fathoms in length, which were constructed one above the other.

While Mr. Vigne took a sketch, I hailed a boat, and with some trouble made them take me across to Kondebal, to see the only lime-pits in Kashmír. Their kilns are eight feet in diameter, and it takes sixteen days' labour, and requires 2000 logs of stout wood to heat them thoroughly. The wood, which is from a species of the fir called *kair*, is brought from a distance of twelve kos. There were twenty men, at the charge of the government, working under the superintendence of three sepoys. One hundred and ninety-two pounds (a kurwar) of burnt lime, sells on the average for one rupee.

A small stream, called the Amrawati falls into the lake at the northern extremity. The ground over which it flows is so white, that it looks at a distance like a foaming cataract, and this is the very spot where Karkota is said to have turned the waters into milk. The Hindús smear their bodies with the chalky soil, supposing it to be a means of religious purification.

From the palace a gentle declivity stretches down to the Jelam. This, like the Korau Pandau, only wants irrigation to make it very fruitful. A few little streamlets flow from the mountains and fertilize a small tract, but the rest is a complete waste. In the deep soil of this plain, not a field was cultivated last year, and the blame of this may be charged equally to the indolence of the people, and the carelessness of the government. We saw several villages in the distance, but the population is too scanty in this place to keep the ground in order. We found our boats at Jinpur, which we reached, after many delays and windings, an hour before nightfall, exhausted almost to death. In Hayapur the Thanadar and the most considerable of the natives came out to meet me. I wanted shelter; the Thanadar led me into a palace (for so it might be called in Kashmír) where a man of some consequence was residing with his family, and desired him to make room for me. Luckily for him, neither his doors nor windows would admit my portable bedstead; and though I perambulated every house in the town, not one could accommodate my simple furniture. The way in which a stranger finds lodgings in Kashmír is certainly very strange. He walks through the town and chooses the most convenient quarters, it being a matter of course that the owner moves out for him, without receiving either payment or thanks. At first I felt ashamed to treat any man so, but learnt that it is considered as great an honour to be turned out of one's house here, as it is in Europe to a subject to be put to the immense expense and trouble of a royal visit. In this place there was literally not a house where I could rest for the night; I therefore gave orders for my tent to be made ready.

Mohammed Shah arrived with his suite, and as there was some

difficulty in purchasing food for so many people, I was forced to levy subsidies in the town. Indeed, along this route, the country is so thinly peopled, that a large party cannot expect the villages to supply their wants. They tell me that this state of things will continue as far as Mazafferabad. In other parts of Kashmír, and generally throughout India, every servant and bearer buys his provisions daily in the markets; and a walk through the bazar is always a treat for an Indian, no matter how tired he may be.

The tent was pitched in the tall grass, which at this season is very dry; well remembering how often fires break out in New Holland, and destroy every thing near, I ordered that it should be cut close all about my tent. Vigne thought it would be a more expeditious way to set fire to it at once: it instantly burned with violence, nor was it without the utmost trouble that the destruction of his entire baggage was prevented.

Saturday, December 5.—We followed the course of the Jelam for two hours through an uncultivated district, ending in a marsh, and finally entered the Wallár Lake, into which the Jelam flows in two places. Not far from the shore is a little island called Lankh, a name which might lead us to imagine that the Kashmírians once had an observatory on it, where all their astronomical calculations were made. Here is an extensive building in ruins, formerly, no doubt, a Buddhist temple, which was overthrown by the fanatical Musselman Sikander Budh Shikan. Like the temple of Korau Pandau, it was of a square form, and surrounded by a flight of stone steps leading down to the lake. The view from this island, including the ruins of a mosque built by Báb Hassan Khan, the grandson of Zeynal áb ud Dín*, and of a palace called Zeynlankh, erected by Zeynal himself, is particularly romantic. I observed several boats engaged in collecting the Singhara or water-nut, which is found in abundance in the muddy bottom of the lake, and serves the natives as food in India: it is eaten by the Brahmins on one particular day of the year only.

A veil of mist hung over the motionless lake, and flocks of water-fowl, from the gigantic pelican to the little sea-swallow, were flying

* Zeynul ab ud-din, or Záin ul ab-ud-din. The glimmer of the water of religion.

slowly through the heavy atmosphere. When Mr. Vigne had finished his sketch of the lake, and I had obtained all the information I could from the fishermen, we pursued our way by water to Banderpoor, whence we were to surmount one of the loftiest passes to Tibet. Banderpoor (Haven City) lies a mile away from the shore in a marsh, which the retiring waters of the Wallár Lake have left. We stepped from the boats on planks, which supported us until the soil became firm enough to bear our feet, but owing to its nature, we were forced to take a very circuitous road to the town of Banderpoor, which, from being a large and well-peopled place, is now a comparatively deserted heap of ruins. The Thanadar met me, with the few remaining inhabitants, and brought me a horse, which I very gladly mounted. The saddle was made in the fashion of Central Asia, and very richly ornamented with silver and mother-of-pearl; the seat was embroidered with velvet and gold. In fact, it was a piece of magnificence which was quite fit for a cabinet or a museum, but the pommel being a foot high in front, and half that height behind, it was so very unlike what I had ever been used to, that I much preferred entering the town less ostentatiously on foot, to the honour of feeling so very uncomfortable. The more ambitious Mohan Bir mounted the animal, and soon had a very serious fall. The Thanadar showed me a house which would have suited me for a night's lodging, but time was too precious to me to allow of my stopping so early; I therefore continued my way on foot to Bonikut, the abode of the Malik of Banderpoor. I was met half way by his son, and a number of his followers. Bonikut lies on the banks of a charming rivulet, completely shut in by a range of high mountains. They soon spread out a carpet for me under some large poplar-trees, by a gurgling spring, a delightful spot for a weary traveller in summer, though anything but inviting at the present time. I accepted it nevertheless, as my servants had not yet arrived, and I was thoroughly exhausted.

The Malik, whose office answers to that of a commandant on the frontier, is a fine venerable-looking personage. He had just built a house which was yet unoccupied, and he invited me to lodge in his old one, why I do not exactly know, but I fancied that I should prefer the place where I was. One by one of my party came up, first Vigne, then the attendants. The Khansamán, a Mohammedan, took possession of the mosque, and cooked in the entrance; while the Hindús lighted their fire, and gathered round it in groups. The cold was additionally trying after the previous fatigue I had undergone. Before I settled myself to sleep I ordered some of my people to watch during the night that the fires did not go out.

The place of Malik of Kashmír, first appointed by Akbar, was formerly one of considerable power and influence, and the Malik was almost independent, being subject only to the authority of the distant Emperor of Delhi. By degrees this place has sunk into insignificance, although the present officer, living on the borders of the yet unconquered Ahmed Shah's territory, is a person of some consequence, but his office would speedily be suppressed altogether, if Ranjít Singh were to seize on Iskardú. The Maliks were intended to keep watch on the frontiers; but as Ranjít has already extended his dominions on every side beyond them, this single conquest would render the office quite superfluous. There are nominally 500 armed men in the district of Banderpoor; but here, as in most places about the country, famine and sickness have so depopulated the town, that the Malik could not muster the half of that number. Henderson travelled through this pass, but he did not praise the reception given him by the Malik, nor could he expect any thing better in such a garb as his. He ought to have taken the coldness of his reception as a compliment to the skill with which he played the part of a fakír.

Sunday, December 6.—My attendants were indefatigable in keeping up a good fire during the night; and whenever I waked, I saw the Indians seated about it, and doing their best to maintain the heat on the side where I was lying. We began our preparations for departure at dawn; and yesterday's lesson made me cautious in choosing a horse for the mountains, provided with a saddle-cloth instead of the more picturesque but very inconvenient saddle of Turkisthan, which, at best, is only adapted to a level country: the Malik's son was deputed to be our guide. We commenced our journey by several steep mountains inferior only to the Pir Panjal, to a height which is reckoned to be 4000 feet; here we first entered the pine forests. Through these we continued 1000 feet further until we stopped at a narrow slip of level ground, which was scarped perpendicularly on either side. At 6000 feet we could distinguish the highest summits of the Nanenwara mountain before us. We had still 1000 feet to climb. The ascent was made on horseback, until we were within 300 feet of the top, and thus far I observed the juniper and saxifrage growing, but the peaks were quite destitute of vegetation, and in the clefts snow was still lying in small quantities.

I never shall forget the cold I felt on the summit of that mountain. The north wind cut my face as with a knife, and my very bones seemed turned to ice; my thermometer, notwithstanding, was not lower than 31°. All around me was utter desolation, not a living creature, not a tree, nor sign of vegetation, as far as the eye could reach. Nought else in fact but rocks and ice, and masses of snow-clouds. I had brought every thing necessary to kindle a fire, that I might ascertain the boiling point; and while they were preparing it under a rock 100 feet below the highest peak, I ascended it again to look around me. Diamál, or Nangaparvat, the highest of the chain, rises out of it like a vast pyramid, and was now veiled in clouds, showing little more than its prodigious base. This bounded the prospect towards the N.N.W. and N.E.; further west, and W.S.W. the Gosíeh mountains stretch to the Báramulla chain, and beyond this again was the snowy ridge which joins the Hindú Khosh. Southwards and S.W. lay the valley, only distinguished by a low stripe of mist, above which appeared the snowy peaks of Pir Panjal, which seemed to form but one part of the great Panjal of Tibet. Between 34° and 35° of latitude, the air is generally most transparent, and this, together with the great elevation of my present position, may account for the apparently interminable distance to which the view reached. Towards the S.W. the prospect was bounded by the Pir Panjal: of course the Indian plain beyond it cannot be reached by the naked eye. In every other direction, mountains towering above mountains were seen to an immense distance.

Standing thus on the northernmost point of my wanderings in Asia, my eye involuntarily sought to pierce the veil far beyond those snowy barriers in the west, where Europe and Austria were now so far away, and my heart dreamed of the beloved ones never forgotten there. The mountain tops rose one above the other, like the billows of a stormy sea, and seemed to shut out all hope of escaping from their dreary wastes. How fondly did my thoughts then revert to my much-loved home, with prayer, that this day, hallowed in my recollections as the birth-day of my honoured mother, now in her 66th year, might be blest to her, as well as to her absent, though not forgetful son.

A dreadful headache came on while I was on this high point, but I could not make up my mind to leave it until I had ascertained the height of the boiling point. For this purpose I descended 100 feet, where my people had lighted a fire under a projection of the rock. It was a long time ere the ice in our iron pot would melt at all; the rarity of the air causing it to evaporate, without dissolving into water. At last the boiling point reached 188°, or, by the rectification of the instrument + 1·2 °186·8°. The pains in the head, which had seized Vigne also, and all my people, were now so intense, that we hastened to leave our present situation, and I thought that the horror of the people of Kashmír for these mountain passes, which they suppose haunted by evil spirits, was not so unaccountable after all. This was the farthest limit of my travels, and it seemed a consolation that every step henceforward would take me nearer home.

As soon as we again reached the region of birches, I looked about for the rhododendron, but could not see one; in the pine-woods, however, I saw the titmouse and other birds of our climate.

The descent was even more painful than the ascent, for the poor horses stepped so cautiously down the precipitous paths, that we chose rather to walk, that we might reach Banderpoor before nightfall. It is to be remarked, that neither plant nor bird did we see, except in the pine-forests, and in some ravines where water was heard foaming over rocks.

Three miles before Bonikut, we struck into a foot-path, generally taken by the lime-burners of Kondibal with their loads of fir; it led us over a narrow shelf of rocks as slippery as ice, over which I fell several times. As soon as we were once more in the plain, I dismissed the Malik's son and went on to Banderpoor, where I passed the night in my tent distracted with headache, and unable to swallow a morsel of food.

Monday, December 7.—Later than usual, and long after the attendants and baggage were on their way to the lake, Mr. Vigne and I began our day's work. I gave Mohan a horse to-day, and his rapture was shown in galloping about the marshy plain, and dashing into the canals, unmindful of several tumbles. Vigne stayed behind with his boat, while I crossed the lake in mine in six hours, and in a short time afterwards arrived in Sopoor. There I declined the Thanadar's invitation to his Darbár, and went on to Tuilibal. To this point both shores of the river were covered with muscles, which supply the natives with plenty of unwholesome food.

The Jelam flows rather more briskly on this side of the Wallár Lake. The sun had set sometime before we reached Báramulla. I chose my night's abode in an open hall of the Dharamsála, seeing that the room in which my people had kindled a fire was enveloped in smoke. I was welcomed by the Thanadar of the place, a Brahmin from Delhi, and received letters from Dr. Henderson, whose journey had prospered hitherto, and from Mehan Singh, who wrote to wish me a happy journey, and to express his hope that the arrangements for conveying my baggage and supplying my party with provisions, had given me satisfaction. This they had certainly done hitherto, but the Thanadar assured me now that it would be impossible for him to find the requisite number of bearers (coolies), and carriage (tattoos), by to-morrow morning. I was reluctantly compelled to wait, as the cold became daily more insupportable, and my people suffered much from sickness.

The open hall where I was lodged was spacious, adorned with marble pillars, and paved with squares of the same. True, I fancied more than once that I should have died of cold; but I must admit that I had been most incautious with regard to my wardrobe, and that I possessed neither cloak nor great coat. I drew and wrote until I was quite worn out, and lay benumbed with cold in my charpái. I would not positively affirm that I had not occasionally some dreamy idea how pleasant it might be to be spared ever again awaking to the sorrows, miseries, and labours of this nether world.

Tuesday, December 8.—I was roused before daybreak, by a strange kind of singing. The Dharamsála was properly a Sikh temple, or the residence of a Sikh priest, who is bound to offer a lodging to every traveller of his own faith, and is paid for this hospitable shelter by different sorts of gifts; this is the chief source of his revenue. I had taken possession of the audience hall of a priest of some consequence in Báramulla, and in an open court before it, I remarked a very tasteful building of stone, in which was erected a throne, adorned with red and yellow silk carpets, and hung with richly-ornamented curtains. On this throne was seated the old priest: his beard was as white as snow. In his hand he held a *chāuri* or fly-fan, made from the tail of the Tibet yák. The handle, which was of silver, he moved to and fro incessantly. Over his head there was an oil lamp burning, and before him the Grunth, or Book of the Sikh Law, open, from which he was chaunting in a loud voice. When first I was roused from sleep by the noise, and looked out on the elegant throne, and the venerable old man upon it, I could hardly persuade myself that the whole was not a vision; but the continued pains in my head too soon reminded me of the reality of the scene. The severity of the cold was excessive, yet the old man had been at his religious duties since four o'clock, and every now and then the Sikhs came to ask his advice: he seemed in fact to hold a continuous Durbar.

I was shortly interrupted in the writing I had resumed, by the entrance of Mirza Ahud, who had talked to me so much about a giant's tooth, which was under the care of the Brahmins of Báramulla, that I desired to see it. He now ushered in a deputation from a Brahminical temple near, who straightway seated themselves on the ground, and drawing a large parcel out of a heap of cloths, laid it at my feet. This was the relic: they then commenced a long story about the Jin, to whom it had belonged. It is related that while Kasyapa was living by the Satiser, which formerly covered the whole valley, he happened one day to be praying to the goddess Mata. The Jin tried to disturb his devotions, but he was reproved by the holy man, who desired him to quit the place. Instead of doing this, he made a snatch at the devotee's *pagri* or turban, whereupon Kasyapa gave him so severe a blow, that it knocked out one of his teeth, and sent the evil spirit howling away: this tooth has been preserved in the temple, and shown to pilgrims for thousands of years since*. I begged they would let me see this relic, when, after much unwrapping and ceremonious manœuvring, they produced the upper tooth of an elephant. I ventured to insinuate that the Jin must have been an elephant, to judge by his teeth; but one and all stoutly maintained it was no such thing, but a real giant's, and that this, to boot, was not one of his largest teeth. The tooth was bonâ fide that of an elephant of India, and of no great age, to judge from its appearance. While we were together, in rushed Mohan Bir to tell me that my favourite Ghunt had been stolen, and Osman Khan, to inform his master, Mr. Vigne, that the finest of his Yáks or Tibetan bulls was defunct. I held the Thanadar responsible to me for my horse; and as there was no longer any hope for the bull, I begged Vigne to have his head cut off, and let me take it to Europe. Well versed now in Indian habits, I was curious to see their force on my Shikárí Jonki, who was a native of the Himálaya, and of a good caste; so I sent for him, and desired him to go to the place where it lay, cut the animal's head of, and bring it to me. I shall never forget the expression of the man's visage. He stammered out that he would die for me if necessary, but that this order he could not possibly obey, for that if he only touched the creature, he should assuredly lose his caste. The commission was therefore given to a Mohammedan, to the great satisfaction of poor Jonki, who thanked me very earnestly for not insisting on his obedience.

I could not imagine how my little Ghunt could have been stolen. The stable where he stood, was in an inner court, accessible only through the place where all my servants were lodged, with one entrance door, where a guard was posted. The Thanadar set the whole population on the look out, to get intelligence of it; and though its appearance was so remarkable, no one observed it. At last, how-

---

* The history of all relics is much the same; idle, fanciful, and characteristic of the unsoundness of a faith, which needs such testimonies to the strange marvels of a corrupt and idolatrous superstition.—*Ed.*

ever, it was brought back to me to my great joy; the fact was, that the groom had left him unfastened in the stable, whereupon the poor beast had sagaciously availed himself of the opportunity to take a stroll in the fields. The Thanadar had offered me another horse as a substitute before mine was found, but I refused to take it, which convinced him of the necessity of exerting himself.

Báramulla is the boundary of Kashmír to the westward. On the left bank of the Jelam, near the bridge, and on the road to Prunsh, is a small fort. A gate, close to the town, where the hills approach each other, marks the limit of the territory: here the character of the Jelam changes; from a gentle stream it becomes a broad and rapid river *.

Wednesday, December 9.—We began to move on at daybreak, but I purposed to remain here until noon to take the sun's altitude, and afterwards to follow the people. The day, however, did not promise to be any clearer than yesterday, and I lost my patience and determined to set off at once. The bull's head not having arrived at 8 o'clock, the Thanadar assured me that it should be sent after me, but I put no faith in his promises, and declared my purpose of remaining at Báramulla until it was ready. As the table and chairs had been taken away, and the Dharamsála was bitterly cold, I strolled to the Juma Masjid, a building now in ruins: four magnificent columns of cedar wood are yet standing, which alone are well worth a visit. As I returned, I met a man with the bull's head, and would have made him strip off the skin for the convenience of packing it, but he refused, although I offered him a rupee for the job. With much trouble I found a Mohammedan, who agreed to do it, and for an additional rupee, to carry it to our next station. Such is a specimen of the impediments in the way of those who are forming collections of natural history in these remote countries.

Mirza Ahud accompanied me to the gate of the valley. It was a

---

* The great increase of fall at this point of the valley, gives to the accumulated waters of the Jelam and its tributaries, this prodigious velocity, and fully accounts for the natural passage thus enlarged in the course of many ages, which in earlier times was probably much less considerable. The Kashmírians ascribe the work to Solomon.—*Ed.*

real grief to me to part for ever in this world from this excellent man; he wept bitterly, while the tears stood in my eyes. Mirza Abdul Rahim also ran after me to beg that I would forgive him if he had been remiss in any thing. I walked on with the cold reply, "Ucha hy," all is well, I am satisfied.

And thus leaving this Indian paradise, I passed through a rock, which together with the river forms a strong barrier: northwards, the steep rocks of the Gosíeh slant down to the Jelam; southwards, the Pir Panjal stretches on the other shore as far as the Jelam also, where it forms a steep declivity, the snow-capped peaks of both mountains being but a few miles distant from the river.

If there were any truth in the tradition that the valley has been drained by human ingenuity, that Herculean work must have been undertaken at this part. But the height of the mountain, and the breadth of the bed of the river, preclude the possibility of such a conclusion, except in legendary presumption: others attribute its execution to their gods.

Mounted on my trusty Ghunt, I began my long journey homewards, following the windings of the river, and pondering over the many thousand miles which lay between me and my fatherland, and over all the troubles which might occur during the weeks and months which must necessarily elapse before I could reach that spot. But there is very much to encourage hope and patience in the thought that we are gradually approaching the haven of our hopes, however slowly; it is only when we stop to reflect, that our fatigues are removing us daily from it, or even worse, when we have nothing to look forward to in life, that our hearts sink: we too often forget that when all else in this world shall have lost its charms, there is an eternity beyond it, to which we must inevitably come.

I took my departure from the valley of Kashmír with a heavy heart. The fatigues of mind as well as of body which I had undergone during my residence in this region, had been almost too much for my strength; the extreme cold of my inconvenient dwelling-place, was enough to counteract any benefit from relaxation. Long residence in India had made me doubly sensitive in this colder clime, and I suffered so intensely from pain in the soles of my feet and palms of my hands, that it was a misery to me to walk. When able to add a little to my diary, it needed much care to keep my enfeebled hands under proper control. But I neither experienced uneasiness nor pain when the boundaries of this little kingdom were once passed and we were fairly journeying westward. While my escort loitered behind, I followed for a time the banks of the Jelam; and my attention was gradually called off to the objects around me, and to the impetuous stream, which heretofore, while watering the valley of Kashmír, glided on so gently; now turbulent and rapid, hemmed in by protruding mountains, it brawled under huge masses of rock, or dashed hurriedly over the cataracts. This day's journey was easy, the descents and acclivities being alike inconsiderable. About two miles from Báramulla there is a Buddhist temple in ruins, in a small tank; I judged it to be, most probably, that of Panditran. The plane grows indigenously by the wayside, though in Kashmír this tree can only be propagated from layers. Here, as in the valley, the exhalations and dust obscured the view of the heights, and I could only make out the outlines with extreme difficulty at the distance of a few miles; when at length the sun made its appearance it was just half an hour too late to take corresponding altitudes.

Three buildings in Jempura attracted my curiosity. The first, in the form of a sepulchral monument, was a circular edifice about thirty feet in height, on which stood a square chamber; but to what time or faith the monument belonged, I had no means of discovering, nor had I seen anything at all resembling it elsewhere. The walls were massive, and the whole structure seemed to refer to a race whose monuments were all of the same solid proportions. I examined this mysterious fabric on all sides with great attention, in expectation of finding some inscription which might indicate either the builders or the people to whom it once belonged, or at least its purpose, but could discover nothing to help out my ignorance.

A few miles onward we came to three small forts, Atalgurh, Shenkergurh, and Messekur, which, together with a fourth already passed near Kizenháma, and another by Jempura, were evidently constructed to protect the natives against the attacks of predatory bands. There is a Buddhist temple which is in good preservation, near Guniar, but unluckily it is situated on the left bank of the Jelam: as there was no bridge, and the stream was far too strong to allow a boat to cross, I was obliged to content myself with the view from the opposite bank. At Tátmulla, or Mená, seven kos, about fourteen miles, from Báramulla, I found my sleeping tent pitched, the sun having gone down. The Jelam at this place is 1200 feet lower than at Banderpoor. Thermometer at six in the evening, 52°.

Thursday, December 10, thermometer, 7 A.M. 48°, noon 64°, 6 P.M. 52°. The route continued to skirt the rapid Jelam, and the hills throughout the day's march were of no great height. About five miles from Tátmulla we saw a pretty waterfall, called Shúla. The land between Báramulla and Mazafferabad, was formerly worth six lacks of rupees annually to the Patháns; its value at present is altogether nominal. It is partitioned out between a number of petty Mohammedan chiefs, who style themselves rajas, with the further dignity of khan. This part of the country is thus reduced to the lowest stage of wretchedness, and the unhappy people see themselves stript of everything they possess, that is worth taking. One of these petty chiefs, called Sarfaráz Khán Káker, whose territory extends along the left bank of the Jelam from Kashmír, resides in the fort of Messekur, and as they usually take the designation of their place of residence, he is called the Messekur-raja. Another styles himself Dushina-raja, from the place called Dushina, and bears in addition the title of Zaberdast Khán Ginghel. His country commences on this side of Jempura. Zaberdast Khán is still in his childhood, and is now retained in Kashmír as a hostage for the government of his mother, who resides at Ginghel.

I found my tent pitched five kos from Menah. The ruins of a once important town and temple are visible for some distance along the bank of the river, but at present Diánun cannot boast of so much as one solitary inhabitant. The bed of the Jelam increases in depth. Opposite to Diánun is a Buddhist temple still in good repair, and built in the same style as those of Kashmír. Its situation is its best defence;

Remarkable Suspension Bridge at Uri.

Baron Hugel's Travels, page 175.

its name is Brangutri. Diánun lies 600 feet lower than Menah. At the close of the day my fellow traveller, Mohammed Shah Nakshbandi, paid me a visit of some hours.

Friday, December 11.—The country from Diánun is highly picturesque. The Jelam has hollowed out its bed many hundred feet deep, and roars over huge fragments of rock: it made us quite dizzy to look down from the pathway, as it winds along the course of the lofty precipitous bank. Three miles beyond Kho, the river has forced a passage through the rocks, which hang several hundred feet over it, and almost form a natural bridge. Uri Serai is very near this, and the ruins of its stone bridge are still discernible. These ruins, the bridge, and the serai for travellers, induce me to believe that the high road from India formerly passed by Rajawar, Uri, and Báramulla. What were the stations between Rajawar and Uri, I know not, but the road must certainly have passed Punsh, which is not more than five kos distant. Had I not been deterred by the winter season, I would gladly have explored this road, which at Punsh joins that from Báramulla, direct to Rajawar, and there meets the high road from the Panjáb to Kashmír. I should thus have confirmed my conjecture, that the best route from India to Kashmír must be by Punsh and Uri, so that by avoiding the Pir Panjal, it would be found practicable throughout the year.

The road now led over a mountain, at the foot of which winds the Jelam. On the bank of the river is the fort of Ghorigurh, and over against it, on the perpendicular height, is Uri Kilah; a rope bridge, or sort of ladder, is thrown over the roaring flood, stretching from the deep abyss to the mountain above. I dismounted in order to witness some men pass over this bridge, which in reality is an enterprise attended with considerable peril, it being nothing better than a thick rope twisted together, made out of horse hides. At the distance of every third foot is a loop or knot, which connects the skins together, and prevents the passenger from slipping off; but as it would be impossible to strain this material tight, he finds himself occasionally receding from the mountain across the deep abyss. On each side, however, there is another rope, about four feet above the footway, to lay hold by. In descending as well as ascending this contrivance the utmost precaution is necessary to grasp the hand ropes firmly, and to plant the foot securely on the loops or knots; the weight causing the bridge to fall from Uri as nearly perpendicularly as possible, it requires the greatest presence of mind. Its length is from 500 to 600 feet. The danger when two persons meet is not so great as might be imagined, unless they are both laden with some burden, which certainly increases the difficulty; but I need hardly say that such a bridge is incapable of bearing the weight of any animal, though I did, to my no small astonishment, see one man carrying a sheep on his back across this frail construction.

Beyond Uri Kilah, lie Uri and Dilawara, on a mountain, the surface of which is formed into numberless terraces, which are planted with rice. Behind this, again, one of the loftiest peaks of the Pir Panjal projects aloft, and in every direction the eye follows the line traced out by this snowy ridge. A small river, the Gota, dashes down the steep declivity, losing itself in a deep hollow on one side of the terraces; while the other is bounded by a mountain brook. The whole scene is one of the wildest and most romantic I ever remember to have seen, and the smiling green fields in the midst of the stern natural features around them, render the entire landscape doubly imposing.

From this point the traveller journeys for some time by the mountain side. The masses of rock crumble and fall into the valleys below on the occurrence of every storm of rain, thus perpetually obliterating the road tracks, and making them altogether impassable, till eventually some new path is formed, either above, or often below the former. One horse can only pass at a time, and there are places where it might not unfrequently be supposed to be quite impracticable to proceed a step further. The ground trembles under foot, and the stone which had just borne one's weight, falls heavily into the depths below; sometimes the traveller stumbles and slides downward several feet; my brave horse, as if conscious of the danger, summoned all his strength to extricate himself and his rider from this most imminent peril. The eye has ample opportunity to measure the deep chasm beneath, where the Jelam roars along, a certain grave if once the traveller should miss his footing.

About half way up this high mountain is a village called Nograut, surrounded on every side by terraces. Some rain had fallen during the night, and the temperature was warmer; a few tropical plants also made their appearance. The whole way from Uri the road was bad and uneven, and I had an excellent opportunity of ascertaining how very contrary to fact is the assertion of the natives of Kashmír, that the Sikhs have given a bad name to the road, solely to serve their own political ends. The Jelam at this place is so deep and contracted by the mountains, that approach to the brink is impossible. Shah Dera, my station for the night, was fourteen miles from Diánun. It has a mosque with a beautiful doorway, the carving of which was executed in Kashmír. The thermometer was 58°, 75°, and 52°.

Saturday, December 12.—On leaving this morning, I had been warned to expect a difficult mountainous road, and truly it was so, but diversified with many majestic scenes. The Jelam flowed along under high rocks, so precipitous and deep, that the natives dwelling on its banks cannot avail themselves of the water, and in Shah Dera my people suffered much inconvenience from the want of this necessary, though close to the very stream.

Vigne was very busy with the pretty mosque above alluded to, and its carved work; while I found myself encircled by the sick and poor, to whom, in spite of my best wishes, I could only administer partial relief with my medicaments. We began our long day's march some hours after the tents were struck, and on their road. As for my large tent, we found it a hard matter to light on an even spot of ground sufficiently spacious to pitch it, the mountain on which Shah Dera is built being formed for the most part into terraces, which were too narrow to allow of this accommodation.

About three kos from Shah Dera the river has broken through the hills in a very remarkable manner, and in order to behold the scene I drew as close as I could to the edge of the precipice, and there gazed on the snow-capped mountains on either side, totally destitute of vegetation; and on the perpendicular wall springing upwards of a thousand feet above the river. In the middle of the narrow bed was a solitary rock of the same height as the bank on either side. It resembled the gates of a huge sluice: on the summit of this rock, which is about thirty or forty feet in circumference, lie two enormous blocks of stone, one upon the other, to all appearance brought there in sport. One might almost imagine that the power of the waves had flung them where they are, ages since; for they stand on the very extreme edge of the chasm, as though there needed but a breath to precipitate them from their present situation.

Let not the reader, in transporting himself in idea to this spot, be misled by the legend of the valley mentioned in the former part of this work, nor believe for a moment in the theory that human power ever could succeed in drying the valley. This is one of the spots named as the scene of action; but to form such theories is an easy matter, and many love to entertain them, and to ascribe the works of an Almighty power to ordinary agency. It is very certain that no human exertions ever produced this wonderful scene, nor could the drying up of the Kashmírian lake have contributed in the slightest degree to the formation of such a mighty breach; for the fall of the Jelam is so great, that if the river ran here as high as the road itself, there would be no perceptible difference in its height even at Tatmulla.

Not far from this spot there is a large place smoothly hewn in the rock, evidently intended for an inscription; they told me that it had once borne the name of the Emperor Akbar. The superstitious people of Kashmír believe this spot to be the especial resort of evil spirits, and a Sikh soldier related an adventure of his own which proved to what lengths superstition can carry its votaries. This shall be noticed elsewhere. Another assured me that in this same place, as soon as night draws on, a spirit called Jeja takes his seat, having 5000 leeches on his breast.

This was the place, moreover, where the battle was fought between the sons and successors of Timur Shah and the Viceroys of Kashmír, when the last declared their independence of the throne of Kabúl. These viceroys were unable to maintain their freedom, and the inevitable consequence was, that the fall of the Afghan kingdom, begun by the folly of the brothers, was more and more accelerated.

From this narrow pass the road led through deep ravines and over heights nearly inaccessible to a place where the valley widens, and the traveller arrives at a spot where traces of the most careful cultivation are still perceptible. From the foot to the summit the mountains are formed into terraces, and laid out into rice fields, which in former times were irrigated artificially; but these are now overrun with grass, and bear no vestige of any sort of culture. In truth, anything like agriculture in this region seems quite out of fashion. On every side are mountain torrents gushing from the rocks, and many streams have ploughed so deep into the earth, in imitation of the great river, that it is scarcely possible to conceive anything more laborious than the task of clambering down to wade through them, and then again struggling upwards to reach the level of the wall of rock. At the end of eight long kos from Shah Dera is Kathai. The vegetation on the way, and in the country itself, frequently brought the Apennines to my remembrance. There was the olive and the vine, the pinus longifolia in lieu of the common fir; the myrsine instead of myrtles; the laurel and oleander; about Kathai especially are many olive trees, but the fruit yields no oil; they are very much like the wild olive of Europe, and are probably of the same species. Tropical plants are more and more commonly met with, and the climate was evidently milder, but the consequences of the cold experienced in Kashmír, began now, especially to shew themselves; my hands were inflamed and swollen, and the blood would frequently gush out from the broken skin. My feet were in the same miserable predicament, and both were nearly as large again as the natural size. But worse than this, I suffered from an inflammation in the throat, which had prevented me from taking nourishment since we left Báramulla, and which now extending itself to the ears, rendered me entirely deaf. I had already resorted to calomel, and this morning I repeated the dose of twelve grains. I felt better towards the evening, whether from the remedy employed or the gradually increasing temperature, I could not rightly say. My tent was pitched at Kathai. The fort, or kila, if such a name be permitted, is a simple square inclosure with mud walls, built near to the wretched town, Kathai, and belongs to a Mohammedan prince called by the pompous title of Sultan Zaberdast Khan. Neither houses nor walls can boast of any material more durable than mud and wood; nor is the situation well chosen. A few impudent dependents were seated about the gate, who regarded both the Sikhs and ourselves with the most marked contempt. There was no difficulty in returning this, and I begged to know, as we drew near them, where this Sultan Zaberdast Khan might then be. The soldiers taking my question as an insult, their Sultan being detained in Kashmír as one of the Mohammedan hostages, made me no reply, but immediately retired within their fort, and barricadoed the gate. My people entreated me to break up the encampment forthwith, and journey onward some miles; they fancied the jinjals, or musketry of the place, were already turned against us, and the Mohammedans sallying forth; but I assured them that the affair would have no such fearful consequences, and remained very unconcerned within range of their artillery, without anything occurring to disturb our quiet, unless it were the hideous screams they favoured us with from time to time.

Kathai is the name borne by the Chinese empire in Central Asia, and when I heard in Kashmír that my road would lead me through Kathai, I could not help fancying that it must be a powerful state to which the name had been given for some evident reason. I soon discovered that the place had nothing in common with the Celestial empire, being, in fact, a most insignificant possession, which scarce produces to its king so much as the pay of a captain in the Company's service.

The Deodara, literally, gift of God, the cedar of the Himálaya, is not seen at 4000 feet above the level of the sea, and the Pinus longifolia takes its place; huge masses of petrified or opalized wood are seen on the road between Shah Dera and Kathai, and at the former place the limestone ceases. Kathai is 2200 feet lower than Kashmír.

Sunday, December 13.—Feeling much better this morning, I began to hope that the warmer climate would soon set me free from the ailments brought on by cold.

The garrison within the fort seemed determined to insult us, and took occasion when the Jemidar, or Sikh officer in command of our guard, was near the gate, to hail him with an order not to show himself again at so short a distance. The officer brought his complaint to me, whereupon I dispatched one of my Chaprásís to desire the presence of the Thanadar, who sent me word, with many civil apologies, that he dared not quit the fort. I betook myself, therefore, to the gate, and summoned him to appear, which he did immediately. I assured him that I should be very sorry to receive a bad impression of his behaviour; that being an independent European, and not connected either with the East India Company or Ranjít Singh, but merely travelling for my own pleasure, I was surprised to find a want of hospitable feeling, new to me in this country. The Sikh Jemidar, I added, commanded the guard of honour given me by Ranjít Singh, and without which a man of my rank could not travel at all in India; I was much surprised on my arrival, to find that he had not been apprized of this, in order to strengthen my escort by a party of his own people. Mohan interpreted my harangue so effectually, that the Thanadar immediately poured forth a volley of excuses, begged me to enter the fort, and on my refusal attended me to the tent. I shortly after quitted the place for Khanda, the next station, which was seven kos, or about fifteen miles, off. The Jelam flowed along in a more tranquil stream, and once we found ourselves on its shore; the vegetation on the bank consisted of evergreens. Oleanders grew close to some of the smaller streams; the Linum trigynum* grew in the ravines; the Justicia in drier spots; the Cæsalpinia Sappan covered the bushes, and the máina and bulbul warbled in the deep thickets.

I was once again in India, and the thermometer, which, at six in the morning, was at 58°, rose at noon to 72° in the shade, not falling lower than 64° towards evening. On both sides of the Jelam were deserted villages with their terraces all lying waste. I did not see a single native all the way, although this was no proof that the country was uninhabited, for the people invariably flee at the approach of such a train as mine. The rivulets which fall into the Jelam, in some places rush down in cascades; at others, hollow out channels to a vast depth.

---

* Or probably some other plant, closely resembling it.—*Ed.*

The village of Táni affords an example of the highly cultivated state of this country in former times, the mountain on which it stands, to an elevation of nearly 3000 feet, being cut into terraces for rice fields, now almost entirely abandoned.

In the evening the Shah visited me, and I availed myself of his long stay to make many inquiries about Kashmír and the country I was now passing through. This Mohammedan was evidently a conscientious person, and would admit his ignorance of a fact rather than tell an untruth.

Monday, December 14.—To-day to Hátia, seven kos. The shores of the Jelam are becoming more flat; they are, notwithstanding, very rarely accessible. To the south-east the valley widens, and the eye glancing over the nearest high lands, rests on the snowy mountains which lift their heads beyond in every direction. At Hátia we saw two Hindús, the first we had met with for a long time, and my Brahmin, Thakúr-das, accosted them quickly. It was of great importance to him, as a Brahmin, to ascertain to which class they belonged, and my curiosity was not less than his. When they told him that they also were Brahmins, I bade him get all the information from them that he could, and particularly I wished him to find out how long they had been settled in this place; they were very sparing in their answers, and we could only understand that their forefathers had come there about 150 years since. But it was interesting to see the deep respect with which they received my Brahmin, the first of a rank superior to their own, whom they had ever met with. Hátia is the most northerly point in this direction to which the Hindús are known to have migrated, after their subjection to Mohammedan power, and at present fifteen families are settled in this place. It has a fort, Topata Kila, built of mud only, and garrisoned by Sikhs; a second to the south-west, Shekara Kila, stands on a mountain on the left bank of the Jelam. Near Hátia is a bridge made of goat's skins, one rope serving for the feet, and two others for the hands to lay hold by, like the bridge of Uri; the three ropes are kept at an equal distance from each other by pieces of curved wood, but with this precaution there is no little risk in passing over. At Hátia the banks of the Jelam are low.

Near it stands Petiára, governed by a Raja of its own, called Nasír Ali; this personage, when requested by the Jemidar to see that we were supplied with provisions, refused with the utmost insolence, whereupon my guard proceeded to load their firelocks and direct them against the Raja's house, who took to instant flight, leaving us at liberty to help ourselves. This, however, occasioned a violent dispute between my favourite Mohan and the Jemidar, the former drawing no flattering comparison between the Jemidar's behaviour in the morning towards the Kiladar, and his present violence against the defenceless Raja, reproaching him with not having revenged himself on the man who had really insulted him, but complaining to me instead, like an old woman, and getting out of the way while I conferred with the Kiladar. The Jemidar very stoutly denied this imputation on his bravery, and Mohan getting more and more enraged, gave him a blow on the face, when his antagonist brought his complaint formally to me, and I was obliged to reprove Mohan very severely. In the midst of my lecture he exclaimed, "Is not the Jemidar a cowardly rogue?" "If he were, you have no right to tell him so," I said, "and still less to strike him." "Perhaps not," answered Mohan, "but if he were not a poltroon, he would have killed me rather than come to you with his complaint."

Rain fell to-day for the first time for a long period, but happily for my baggage, it was of no great continuance. My suite enjoyed the unwonted pleasure of a bazar in this place, for so they called two little houses where provisions were sold in such moderate quantities, that ten of my people would have consumed the whole stock; still it was entitled a bazar, and for the first time since they left Kashmír, they sat and smoked for an hour within; most gladly I gave them this treat, for the poor fellows had suffered fearfully from fatigue and cold together, more especially those who were from the Himálaya; my Bengalees were all in perfect health.

Tuesday, December 15.—The distance from Hátia to Mazafferabad is reckoned ten kos, and on the way we passed several villages, but they were either quite deserted or very thinly peopled. There seemed an abundance of the purest water flowing in every direction; the ascents were numerous and steep; but the banks of the Jelam were mostly accessible, and in many places we came to small plains. The country, hitherto uninteresting in its general character, near the somewhat important town of Kosoli, became very pleasing. The Jelam forms a sudden bend, and a pretty island starts from its waters. Kosoli stands in a very favourable situation on an elevated plain on the left bank, and seemed to have several well-built houses; the whole aspect of the place greatly reminded me of an Italian village. From hence the road was very steep as far as Mahra, which is remarkable only for its huge cypress trees and its acacias. The banks of the Jelam continue very precipitous until it meets the river Kishen Ganga, which runs onward to Mazafferabad, having about one third less water than the Jelam. There is a point, about half a mile up the Kishen Ganga, whence we can see the valley in which the united rivers flow into the Panjáb. This valley is surrounded with mountains, and the Jelam flows along it for some distance, in a totally contrary direction to that of the combined streams.

The Kishen Ganga is about twenty-five fathoms broad, and is passed first by a rope bridge, and at a point further down the stream by a ferry. Not far from the right bank lies the Zehela Serai, built by Shah Jehan, and near it the building which tradition calls the palace of Núr Jehan Begum, but which, in truth, was a mausoleum, now in ruins.

Near Thandu I observed granite in large blocks, hurled, as it were, over the trap rock, and about Mazafferabad a considerable quantity of petrified wood. This town lies on a plain about 150 or 200 feet above the Kishen Ganga. The houses, built on this plain beside a wild stream, are surrounded by groups of trees, and have a very pretty, romantic appearance; while behind the plain rises the majestic snowy mountain Kahori-Kataka, a range of stupendous hills forming an amphitheatre around it. My camp was pitched on a natural terrace 150 feet higher than the river, under some large olive trees. The whole population soon collected round my retinue, drawn together by the unusual and no doubt attractive sight of so many strangers in this remote place: curious also to witness the bustle of unpacking and arranging the tents, the various costumes of my followers, and their strange features. There soon came a message from the Raja, begging me to command his services. I thankfully declined accepting anything, however, as Mazafferabad boasts a regular bazar, and I strictly charged the men not to take anything without paying for it. The bearers and animals laden with my baggage had accompanied me thus far from Kashmír. I now directed the Munshí to hire others to-day, that we might be all ready to start on the morrow. In the evening the Shah came; after which I was occupied in writing my journal till midnight.

Wednesday, December 16.—Mazafferabad is nearly 3000 feet lower than Kashmír, and contains 2100 inhabitants, of whom 700 are Hindús of the three higher castes, Brahmins, Kshatriyas, and Shudras. Early this morning the Governor of the place, Sultan Zaberdast Khan, literally, the mighty prince, sent to announce that he was coming to pay me a visit. Shortly afterwards he appeared in person, dressed in the costume of Kabúl, with a mantle of fur, ornamented with gold. His suite was but small.

As he entered the tent I observed, notwithstanding his apparent strength, he needed the help of a servant to reach the chair set ready for him. When we were seated, I inquired the cause of this infirmity, and heard that his eyes were so affected that he could not discern anything in a very strong light.

Having heard that I had great skill as a physician, he hoped I might be able to do him some good. I had the kanát, or wall, of the tent taken down, that I might examine his state more narrowly. I have rarely seen handsomer features; the nose slightly arched, the curved brows, and the lofty forehead, all harmonized with the look of gravity, and with the grey beard which covered the lower part of his careworn face. The light of the eye was nearly quenched, and the optic nerve was evidently fast failing. As the eyes were rather inflamed, I prescribed leeches and abstinence from spirituous liquors, to which the Mohammedans are much addicted in this country. The Khan seemed to have great faith in me, and consulted me about another, but an incurable malady, which must soon put an end to his existence, and for which I could only recommend a temperate course of life. Sad as were his bodily ailments, those of his mind were even more pitiable. He had lost his only son not long before, and the last relative now left, a youth, was detained as a hostage in Kashmír. The poor old grandfather's sole wish was to see and embrace this lad once more; but all his entreaties to Ranjít Singh to grant him this favour were in vain. I promised to add my petition to his own, and during my stay in Lahor to bring the matter before the Mahá Raja.

As the little state possessed hereditarily by Sultan Zaberdast Khan is situated on the high road between Kashmír and Kabúl, it is an independent territory of some importance. The ferry over the Kishen Ganga used to bring him in a yearly sum of a lac of rupees; but since the decrease of traffic and the separation of Kashmír and Kabúl, but especially since the population of this country has fallen off at least one-fifth, the number of passengers has of course diminished in the same proportion, and the whole revenue of the country is estimated at little more than 30,000 rupees, from which we must deduct 6000, the tribute paid to Kashmír, and at this time Mehan Singh contemplates exacting double this sum. I asked the Khan to whom the small house belonged, which is erected high above the wild rivulet, and which was clearly visible from the plain where we were, and seemed inhabited by females, whose forms we were able to distinguish in the distance. It was his new residence, built of wood, the former abode of his ancestors being in a ruinous state, but he was too poor to build another. There was a bitterness in the tone of the poor old man whenever he spoke, which shewed how deeply his feelings had been outraged. I considered which among the trifles I still had in reserve would best please him, and soon excited his amazement by presenting him with some of the little instantaneous lights, which are kindled by a touch, and which he firmly believed to be the fruits of some magical device.

Mazafferabad, or Músafirabad, the abode of travellers, is the modern name of the ancient Hindu-Shikrí, and was given to it, according to the Brahmins, 200 years ago by the Mohammedans. A footway along the bank of the Kishen Ganga leads from the town to the Gures, or Dures, one of its tributary streams, which rises near

Diosay; from this place one road leads to Iskardú *, another for horses from Mazafferabad to Derband on the Atok, and a third goes to Pakeli. Derband is said to be fifty kos from this place, the first ten of which are over a chain of hills. I have no faith, however, in this estimate. Mazafferabad itself offers a rich field for the researches of a geologist; mountains of tertiary formation rise up to the limit of perpetual snow, and on them are piled, in wondrous masses, broken and dismembered heaps of stone. In many places whole mountains look as if they had been riven through and through, and the spectator beholds the vast clefts, one or two thousand feet in depth, as fresh as if the violent convulsion of nature had taken place only yesterday. Nanga Parvat, the famous pyramid, which I observed at Nanenwara, is only thirty kos from this spot.

We were occupied half the day in settling terms with the bearers and drivers; the price they agreed for to go to Lahor was nine rupees. I had only given eight from Kashmír to this place, and as the very same bearers hired themselves again, I was fairly taken in. I might by a little patience have soon found men who would have taken half the money, but time had now become very precious to me; I longed most eagerly to see my own home once more, and therefore I hurried on my departure, until noon saw the bearers on the opposite side of the river in the Zehela Serai. While they were moving off, I strolled about the neighbouring parts, and up the hill where the Sultan's new residence stands, whence I could perceive the kila of Mazafferabad, a regular fort, one mile north of the town, and garrisoned by Sikhs. Having returned from my walk, I had a great desire to shew some little attention to the poor Sultan; but this was not easy, for a visit paid to him would have obliged him to offer me some present or other. I therefore sent the Munshí to tell him I would come and see how he was, if he would dispense with the nazar. The Munshí soon returned with many compliments, but the Sultan excused himself, at the same time assuring me that his house was too wretched to receive me.

* Iskardu is variously written Iskardo, Iskardoo. The Baron's mode is probably most correct. See also Attock, Atok, &c.—*Ed.*

Two boats, constructed of the trunks of trees rudely hollowed out, convey travellers across the river. Each passenger pays a pice for himself, and as much for every load carried either by man or beast. The animals swim across the stream, which is deep and hurried: there are certain fixed places where only it is practicable to land; the bank further down is inaccessible from the steep falling rocks, and our little boats wheeled about in a manner which inspired no great confidence of our reaching the opposite side either safely or expeditiously. After all, considering how they were stranded, the only wonder is that we did not find our way to the bottom. I desired to have one entirely to myself and Mohan, but while the boat was pushing off, and after it had got fairly into the rapid current, three men sprang in, giving it a sudden shock, and half-filled it with water. I sat perfectly still until we came to the other side, and then discovered that our unwelcome companions were ferrymen, who were resolved on crossing with me, that they might share the present, expected as a matter of course.

The Serai is situated on a height a few minutes walk from the shore, and was built by Ali Merdan Khan, by command of Shah Jehan. It forms a large square, and is kept in excellent repair; but my tent, pitched under a thick clump of trees, was far more inviting to me than the closer apartments of the building. Just as I had made myself comfortable, and it began to grow dark, the Shah came to tell me that a party was desirous to see me. His cautious and mysterious manner excited my curiosity; accordingly I requested him to admit them. But he would not bring them through the front entrance where they would be seen, but requested permission to usher them through the back way. Having ordered that no one should obtrude, the Shah went out, and returned shortly with three Mohammedans, who threw themselves at my feet, and laid some trifling presents on the ground. I had the utmost difficulty in finding out from amidst a mass of words, compliments and repetitions, who they could be. I guessed rather than heard, for in spite of my manifold questions as to the name of their master, I could gather nothing but, Málik, Mír, Hakim, Sirdar, &c., which may all be translated, king, prince, lord, and master, that they had been sent to me from Sultan Zaberdast Khan, and described his unhappy situation—the iron yoke imposed on the Mohammedans by Ranjít Singh—the beautiful land of Kashmír—and the peculiar advantages of the Mazafferabad route. I conjectured their object at last; and after they had gone on for half an hour, told them that I was no servant of the East India Company, and that if the Khan wished to enter into any treaty with the British, which would certainly be his best policy, in fact his only chance of preserving his independence, the present time was not the most favourable for such an attempt. They looked at me with amazement; and when I had spoken out thus freely, they drew back, and, perhaps, fearful of compromising themselves, told me that I had not understood their meaning. I answered, that in that case the error was mine; and begging them to assure the Khan of my deep sympathy with him, I dismissed them, whereupon they quitted the tent as mysteriously as they had entered it. Having called my people, Jwala ran in to tell me of the arrival of a fakír, with a letter to me from a European. It was from Henderson, written in Mazafferabad the very day before my arrival there, and telling me that he had been most kindly received by the bearer, and now was thinking of resuming his journey to Derband by an unfrequented path, the route through the valley of Vergund being insecure on account of predatory bands who infested it. Many obstacles threatened to thwart him in this project. He begged me to give the fakír two doses of four grains of calomel, for his sick child, and as the disease was an obstinate ague, I was to order that one of the powders should be administered each day when the fever left him. Unfortunately I had disposed of all my medicines in Mazafferabad, reserving for my own use only a single powder of eight grains, in case of need; but after a moment's hesitation, I handed this to the poor fakír, who had brought me a nazar of a little basket of the pistachio-nuts of Kabúl.

It was midnight before all my retinue crossed to the right bank of the Kishen Ganga, a circumstance which explained to me more conclusively than any mere assertion, how very possible it is for a caravan to be a whole month crossing the Euphrates.

Thursday, December 17.—The last party arrived with my luggage before daylight, just as I sallied forth to superintend the breaking up of my encampment, but many of the men had loitered behind in the bazar of Mazafferabad, and I was obliged to send the Munshí back, with positive orders not to quit the place until he had seen the last of them out of it. This delayed me till nine o'clock, trying my patience most sorely. At last, our long retinue was in motion. The banks on either side of the Kishen Ganga are very steep about this place; and at the narrowest point a bridge formerly stood, which was torn away in a moment by a heavy flood which occurred in 1823, while Hari Singh Nalwa was endeavouring to get possession of the town for Ranjít Singh. It has not been rebuilt. This bridge was a subject of much interest in the war of 1803, between Mukhtyar ud Dáulah and Abdullah Khan.

Below Mazafferabad, exactly opposite the kila, the country is rather flat, and a second ferry crosses the river, but is seldom used; for travellers would not be much disposed to trust themselves so near the Sikh garrison, who are usually not over-nice in taking away what little the defenceless natives may have with them. From this point the Kishen Ganga may be traced for a great distance, until it is lost to the eye behind precipitous hills. The gypsum, here seen in gigantic masses, gives a peculiar character to the landscape. In many places I observed the perpendicular walls of dissevered mountains of a dazzling whiteness, and as often the ground in rear of this is a snowy mountain; the whole resembling in effect a vast avalanche that has slid from the higher range.

From the Kishen Ganga we entered a deep defile leading to the bed of a mountain torrent now dry; thence we proceeded along an immense hill, full 3000 feet above the river. I saw a solitary cow licking the ground on one spot, and alighted to see whether she had found salt there, which turned out to be the case.

While the bearers were toiling up this mountain I stood to gaze at the ruins of a once important fort, called Fatihgurh, or citadel of victory, which lies below the highest point of the hill. At the summit of this is the pass called Dub, formerly the resort of bands of robbers, who struck universal terror throughout the country. Hari Singh Nalwa sent a large force against them, but the robbers knew that they had partisans among the natives who, as Mohammedans, abhor the name of a Sikh. The commander therefore did not succeed without infinite trouble in extirpating a number of the band, and then only by setting fire to the grass in which they lay concealed; thus forcing them to come forth and meet his troops, who slaughtered them without mercy. The bands therefore are destroyed, but for a single traveller the security is not much greater than before, and to-day six of the Sikh soldiers remained at the top of the hill until my bearers had all mounted. There is no great cause of alarm to a traveller with a numerous retinue. It is here indeed as in Europe; to the rich man every trouble of this kind is made light; while the poor, with his cares and sorrows, has to await the just equalization of all things in another world.

At the summit of the Dub pass I saw many birds which were quite new to me, harbouring in the scattered pine trees. I took aim at some of them, but the difficulty of clambering up the steep ascents soon fatigued me, particularly when, after having shot them, there was little possibility of reaching the deep ravines into which the birds fell. Arrived at the highest part, we could see Gárhí, our place of rest for the night, as it lies in the valley of the Konyar. We had no sooner reached it than the natives, who bear the very worst character in the world, surrounded my tent, and as I had heard that their sole occupation was thieving, I made bold to keep their chief as a hostage for their good behaviour, and moreover desired the Sikhs as well as my servants to keep on the alert. The place is situated in a small uncultivated plain: there are neither artisans nor agriculturists to be seen, which was quite conclusive to me that they supplied themselves from other men's property.

Judging by the acclivities from the Kishen Ganga, and the descent into the valley of the Konyar, I should say that the last is at least 600 feet lower than the great river. It was an important point for my map to ascertain whether the Konyar united near this part with the Jelam or not. My observations brought them both to the same level; hence I suspected that such junction must take place somewhere near, and the natives of Gárhí confirmed me in this opinion. A number of these people live in natural caverns hollowed out of the mountains by the waters; others in the filthiest dwellings perhaps in the whole world.

Friday, December 18.—This morning, when I desired the coolies and drivers to take on my small tent as usual, they refused to go without a guard; and as the Sikhs would not divide their party, and Mr. Vigne, who was always tardy, could not be left alone, I was obliged to make a virtue of necessity, and wait patiently until the tents were packed up, the breakfast eaten, and the entire company ready to proceed together. Bearers and natives of the place all agreed that the road to the next night's station was sadly infested with robbers, and that the inhabitants of the different villages by the way, carried on the same profession. The Sikhs seemed to think we were rather in a serious dilemma; they loaded their guns, therefore, and begged me to arm all my servants, intimating at the same time that they could not go on without a present of nine rupees to each man, and double that sum to the Jemidar. I told them that my people wanted no arms, that they themselves were the greatest thieves, and that they might all march back to Kashmír together if they thought proper. Upon this, the Jemidar humbly craved my pardon, and excused the conduct of his soldiers, who he declared were quite unprovided with money. Notwithstanding I had made up my mind beforehand to give them even more than they now demanded, I did not approve of their prescribing to me, and especially as they had made their claims at a moment when my anxieties were sufficiently pressing without any additional cause of trouble. I therefore gave the Jemidar to understand that I remembered quite well how two days before we left Kashmír, he had borrowed from Mr. Vigne a kalga, or plume of heron's feathers, in order to appear in state before the Governor when his services were hired, and that I had also given him 300 rupees, which he could not possibly have spent since we quitted that valley. Until we reached Mazafferabad both he and his men had received rations, and therefore, knowing that he must have money, I could not understand why he should tell me such a falsehood. Not a word more did he say, but got ready to proceed forthwith.

There is a bridge over the Konyar, close to a fort, also called

Futihgurh, where there is a strong Sikh garrison, but some robbers had burnt down the bridge not long before. This in Eurcpe would seem almost incredible, but in Asia it is not the custom to post sentinels on guard, and thus they ventured on this enterprise without much danger. Travellers are forced to cross the remains of this bridge on foot, and it is well for those who do so, not to be subject to giddiness if they ever expect to see the other side; for we found it necessary to stride over half-burnt beams of wood, thirty feet above the surface of the stream, a very perilous undertaking at any time. We got the horses and beasts of burden across the stream not far from Gárhi with much difficulty, as the water reached to the chests of the animals. We then marched on in close column through a narrow valley to a small stream, and there observed some most remarkable natural caves, which I entered, in spite of the remonstrances of my attendants, who asserted that they were full of robbers. Divers kinds of stone, bound together in one mass as though with the strongest cement, form the walls and roof of these caves, the largest of which might hold from forty to fifty people. The height of this cavern in particular was about twenty feet.

The road is diversified at intervals by the Pinus longifolia, frequently a mile apart from each other. On the left bank of the Konyar is the territory formerly held as a fief by Hari Singh Nalwa, at one time Governor of Kashmír. Ranjít Singh took it from him, and granted him another and far more valuable one. By the village of Doga the road branches off into two; one taking the direction of Monsúr to Mángli, the other going direct onwards. I purposed reached Mángli this evening, having computed the distance at ten kos, but the bearers declared that if they travelled without a halt, they could not get there before next morning. In this state of uncertainty I perceived a horseman approaching, who was sent by the Thanadar of Monsúr, to attend me to that town. In consequence of the letters I had written to Ranjít Singh, all the Thanadars in these provinces had been commanded to receive me on the frontiers, as I had announced my desire to return into the Panjáb by way of Mazafferabad and Atok. The man told me he had been expecting me for three days, and that the direct road to Mángli was so bad, that I could not venture to proceed by it with my baggage. Much against my will, I was therefore compelled to relinquish all hope of reaching it this evening; and on his assurance that the road by Monsúr was the safest and best, I determined to follow his advice. I was much vexed, however, at the idea of not being able to arrive at Mangli before the following day. The fact is, the difficulties, the discomforts, and above all the loneliness of my present situation had completely worn me out; and when I reflected on the 2000 miles which yet lay between me and Bombay, through a country where every mile is accomplished with fatigue and trouble of some sort, and then on the long sea voyage of 13,000 miles to Europe, my heart quite sank within me, and I often felt so ill and exhausted, that I threw myself down, and thought it madness to believe I could ever live to meet my friends again.

From Doga the route continued over high lands. The pines were more numerous, the ground seemingly very productive, and the ravines more richly studded with plants, while beautiful cascades fell from the rocky heights. Many birds flew by, which were quite new to me. While the baggage moved forward I remained with Jwala and Mohan only in search of a little sport, though among these abrupt ridges it was attended with much difficulty. Two miles from Doga the road leads over an eminence, whence I had a fine prospect down the valley of Vergund. We descended into it, and found several paths branching off into the thick wood. We ought to have provided ourselves with a good guide, but none was to be found. Our only alternative, therefore, was to march in close column, and not suffer any of the party to straggle or fall in the rear. Following a path which runs in the same direction as that we had been pursuing hitherto, we found, after proceeding a mile, that it terminated at a spring; we then chose another, which took us to a deserted building; finding again that we must have taken the wrong route, we were compelled, finally, to retrace our steps. I was apprehensive that we should have to pass the whole night in this dreary spot, in consequence of the approaching darkness. It set in to rain, and I was already much fatigued, having most unluckily sent my horse on from Doga, that by so doing I might get rid of my anxious thoughts by sheer bodily exhaustion. Thus circumstanced, I was quite at a loss how next to proceed to discover the right road, and at last my companions and I, one and all, sat down thoroughly dejected, to recruit our strength. Jwala alone made an effort to find out some human being in this wilderness. I desired him not to go far way, otherwise he might never find us again; but at the end of half an hour, seeing nothing of him, I felt assured that he had lost his way, and fired off my gun to give him intelligence of our position. Nevertheless he did not make his appearance. It was useless to wait any longer, and with Mohan I struck into the path, which from its being the most beaten, I trusted would lead us to Monsúr. In the course of half an hour we met with Jwala, who had been fortunate enough to get information as to our road, but after receiving this, he could not make his way back again to us to communicate the glad tidings.

Being now in the right track, we proceeded, and soon came to a herd of camels, a glad announcement that we were nearing the plains of India, and almost clear of the toilsome and difficult mountain-roads. There were several hundreds of them, and they presented a curious appearance as they browsed on the acacia and ziziphus thorn. I tried, by shouting and firing off a gun, to bring their keepers to a parley; but no one made his appearance, and they probably kept out of sight from some misgivings of our purpose.

The south side of the plain of Vergund is full of deep and almost perpendicular ravines, hollowed out by the torrents in the soft loamy soil. We came upon them so unexpectedly, that it made the journey excessively laborious. Some of these ravines form, as it were, a valley within a valley, and must furnish a secure retreat to robbers, as no troops could venture to follow them to such coverts. On account of the intricacies of the road, I had joined my party, and for some time marched at the head, entertaining no doubt that the place was a haunt for plunderers. The whole population in fact, must have learned the trade of their Patán masters, as they now carry it on indiscriminately against their Sikh rulers and neighbouring tribes. No village is secure against these inroads, hence every one is defended by a broad thick fence of the thorny ziziphus, through which is an opening that is carefully closed every evening. Nothing can be a more efficacious protection. In the centre stands a little court or building, surrounded with high mud-walls, in which the natives deposit all their valuables.

Another reason for the insecurity of this country may be, that disaffected persons from Kabúl and Lahor have often fled hither, and carried on their petty warfare until some favourable opportunity permitted them to return to the plain. Pretenders also to the throne of Delhi, have made it their refuge when fortune has proved adverse, and from these mountains have witnessed the renewal of operations. It was here the fanatical Syud Ahmed stirred up the Mohammedan population against their new masters the Sikhs; and although he fell in battle against Shír Singh, in 1831, not a year has passed since, without some prince or other having been brought to reason, by force of arms, by bodies assembled in this locality. These continual seditions fully justify the recent measure adopted by Ranjít Singh, of keeping one member of each of these petty royal families as hostages in Kashmír. When the princes are reduced to submission, their subjects are equally ready to maintain the same perpetual strife with each other; and no defenceless traveller is secure from their depredations, nor any incautious neighbour from their aggressions. Often as I drew near their villages, I observed the whole population taking up arms, fearing that my suite might turn out to be a troop of enemies in disguise. Yet the land does not seem poor, and I heard with surprise, that many of these scattered villages produced to their proprietors a revenue of 2000 or 3000 rupees. The country is watered by many streams, among which the Sarn is of some importance, receiving all the tributary mountain rivulets, and supplying in its turn the Atok, or Arub as it is called here. One mile from Monsúr we came to two of those gigantic tombs, so common in Afghanistan. These were fifteen feet long, and nine broad. It was almost dark when I reached them, or I should have examined one or both. Night brought us to Monsúr, where, according to the directions I had given the man who met me at Doga, I expected the two important requisites—wood and milk, would be got in readiness for our party; neither of these however did I find. The drizzling rain which had fallen at intervals during the day, set in faster, and no tent was as yet ready for my accommodation. Completely exhausted, wet through, and heated with the fatigues and haste in getting over our hurried march, I felt that in this state the piercing wind blowing over the snowy mountains had given me a severe chill, my every limb faltered and shivered with cold. The ground was nearly under water; and it took a full hour to get a fire properly kindled: not a stick of wood was to be found in the wretched village, and we did not well know where to pitch our tents. It was, as may be imagined, in no enviable frame of mind, that I stood for nearly three hours in the dark night, leaning against a stone, without so much as a cloak to shelter me from the rain and wind. The Shah was no better off than myself, and his servants were all so discontented, that I invited him into my tent as soon as I had one. At length matters improved, the rain abated, the fire gave out a little cheering warmth; and the clean tent with its pair of lights, seemed to me a perfect palace, in which, after changing my wet garments, I felt myself comparatively happy and comfortable.

Saturday, December 19.—We were now near the frontiers of Ranjít Singh's territories. Arub, a fort about five kos westward, is the entrance to Penda Khan's country. Organized bands of robbers, to the number of two or three hundred, are frequently met in these parts. They plunder the different villages, and have hitherto met with no effectual check; in fact, the power of Ranjít Singh has never been able to keep this country in order, even for a few months at a time. I was greatly alarmed lest Henderson* should fall into the hands of one of these gangs, who, however, in their depredations, rarely proceed to deeds of blood. For my own part, I congratulated myself that I had entered Monsúr at this late hour, as I contemplated leaving it early in the morning, before Penda Khan had received intelligence of the route I had taken, which might have offered a temptation far too great for his cupidity to withstand.

---

* The melancholy termination of this adventurous man's career, by cholera at Lúdiana, while under arrest, pending the determination of Government, has deprived the public of much information respecting Panjáb and Tibet, which at this juncture would have been particularly valuable.—*Ed.*

The valley of Vergund, though it cannot be seen from this miserable village, is, after Kashmír, the largest in the Himálayan range north or west of the Setlej; the mountains, on either side, are low and covered with thick forests; properly speaking, it belongs to the valley of the Atok, or Indus. The heights, by which I had lost my way in descending, divide the waters of the Jelam and Atok.

Vigne had sprained his foot the day before yesterday, in coming down the Dub Pass; and as he could not ride without pain, I had given up my jampan for his use. His ailment was not likely to be cured for several days, an evil which my present condition rendered extremely untoward. In the side pocket of this jampan I always kept my kukeri, one of the most fearful weapons I know, and peculiar to the Ghorkas. They talked so much about thieves, that I resolved if they did attack us, I would not be taken alive, and therefore committed my arms to the charge of Mohan.

At eight in the morning we struck our tents. Long before this, the Thanadar of Kota, whose district I expected to reach in two days, had arrived with a large company to welcome me. The road led about a mile away from the fort of Monsúr, a paltry mud inclosure; the instant we were close abreast of it the gate was suddenly flung open, and the Thanadar issued forth with his followers, all bedizened with the fine trappings of which the Sikhs are so fond; he galloped forward in advance of his troop, and in a moment was at my side, and alighted from his horse to salute me. My party was now as numerous as it was picturesque, the Thanadar of Kota being among us also. Many of the horsemen carried spears fifteen feet long; some wore their Indian costume with the most dazzling colours, burnished weapons, and gorgeous coats of mail; all were splendidly mounted. The Ghunt, on which I was mounted amid this glittering throng, did not look to much more advantage than I myself did, dressed as I was in my plain black suit. While the high-mettled coursers were prancing and neighing about him, he went soberly on his way with the most perfect unconcern, seeming to care very little how ugly or insignificant he might look. I saw the Sikhs looking with infinite contempt on the queer form of my little steed, but ere the day was done they had learned to respect his admirable qualities; the first half of our way lay through a succession of ravines which yesterday's rain had made extremely dangerous to travel, across these my sturdy little Ghunt clambered up and down without making one false step. The Sikhs, on the contrary, were frequently forced to dismount: many of their horses fell down the steep banks, and their splendid dresses, moreover, looked all the worse for the day's journey.

Isolated hills are scattered over the face of the country in every direction, and what in the far distance appears to be a plain, is in fact, a succession of ravines, which begin suddenly with an abrupt fall of 100 feet, and are continued down to a small river. These ravines must have originated in some violent inundations of the plain. Large quantities of water issue from all the rocky eminences.

The famine which desolated Kashmír extended as far as Gárhi only; it is remarkable, that although the cholera did not reach this district, yet all those Kashmírians who fled hither from their own country, fell victims to it. The mountains which had been hitherto clothed with the solitary Pinus longifolia, are here quite bare, reminding me forcibly of the interior of Syria, only that in this place those scattered green patches which grow around the Syrian fountains, are wanting, and the hills are composed of the grey limestone in stiff formations.

About half way on to-day's march we came to a Buddhist monument, called by the natives, Búdh, or Dhagoba, the first we had seen in this direction. Vigne got out of the jampan at my request, to take a drawing of it, while I examined it on every side. One of his servants, a silly fellow, a Patán, called Osman Beg, no sooner saw his master commence drawing, than he seated himself close by to watch his proceedings. The Sikhs followed his example, and gathered round to see what the stranger could be doing with this old ruined edifice. The Thanadar of Monsúr even laid his hand on the piece of paper on which Vigne was sketching. "If you had any manners," cried Osman Beg, "you would know how to be ashamed of such impudence." The Thanadar sprang back in a towering rage, crying out, "*Súr*, hog," the deepest affront he could offer to a Mohammedan. "Down with you, unbelieving dog," cried the Patán vehemently, and at the same moment his sword sprang from its scabbard. The Thanadar and his followers, numbering more than fifty, rushed to their horses, mounted in a trice, and made ready for the strife; some armed with sabres, others with spears or matchlocks. My anxiety may be readily imagined. Their frightful cries made me look every instant for the attack which was impending over Vigne and Osman, but it was quite impossible either to give them any help, or even share their danger. Presently, the whole party dividing itself to the right and left, rushed by the two in the direction of the fort of Monsúr, and the next minute they wheeled round again, and with the Thanadar at their head, rode straight up to me. At a little distance the Thanadar dismounted, strode up to me, and made a low obeisance, I naturally enough concluded that he was going to say something to me, but no; he drew himself up, remounted his horse, and galloped off, quitting the plain with all his cavalcade. Probably he intended to show me that at least he had some idea what good manners were, in spite of the quarrel that had taken place between him and my dependents.

In Amritpoor, a town of some importance, we had the first opportunity of enjoying a bath; bathing is a general custom throughout the Panjáb. The villages we passed were but thinly peopled by Hindús. The broken skin of my face and hands was now almost replaced by a newer and smoother surface, but the absence of bodily heat from which I suffered so much, made me feel the want of wine or brandy most sensibly.

We slept at Náushera; upon my arrival I found my tents already pitched in a wretched situation, in a field as level as a floor. I pointed this out to the Kaláshi, and bade him be more careful another time in selecting his ground. But as the night was clear, and there appeared to be no probability of its raining, which would have fairly imbedded me and my tent in a morass, I spared my servants, already jaded with the march, the trouble of removing the whole baggage to a more suitable spot. A tent should be always fixed on high ground if possible, or at least on sloping ground, to prevent the possibility of water making its way to the interior, in case of rain lodging there.

Sunday, December 20.—With too presumptuous confidence I had

appointed the time when I should be in Atok and Lahor. Spoiled by the continuance of two months' fine weather, I had not anticipated the possibility of rain setting in at this season, and was therefore quite unprepared for the torrent which poured down during the night. If the pelting of the storm on the roof had not aroused me, the disturbance made by the servants would have soon done so; driven by the water from place to place, they at last took refuge just within my tent, though there it was likewise making its way. Towards morning the rain abated, but when I prepared to rise as usual, I stepped from my bed into a complete pool which had collected under the carpet. Having made my way out, I looked abroad on the country, and saw it overspread with a dense fog. It was absurd to think of marching, nor did there seem much prospect of immediate extrication from our situation; the tents were soaked completely through, this added considerably to their weight, and they would moreover require a long time to get dry again. The dismal state of a person travelling with tents in India when these violent rains set in, can only be understood by those who have experienced such a misfortune. The misery, indeed, is aggravated tenfold, when such a mishap befalls him after a long course of dry weather. Indian servants never provide against any accident of the kind; believing that the elements must be as obedient to the Sahib as to themselves. Hence, all my luggage was in the open air, the tent under which they should have been stowed away every night, remained unpacked; and even the *ráuti*, or large tent, intended specially for the accommodation of the servants, was very rarely pitched, as they usually preferred passing the night in the open air with merely some light coverlets over them. This want of energy is the great defect of the Indian character, and in such cases their patience becomes a vice. They will sit, for example, for hours together in a pelting shower, in hopes that it will soon clear off, and then, when they are really in earnest to repair their own want of forethought, and to unpack their tent, it frequently happens that the rain has made it no easy matter to remove the packing cloths, without tearing them to pieces. The water, as I have already said, had made its way through the four-fold covering of my tent, owing to their having calculated on fine weather, and therefore not having tightened the ropes enough to allow the water to run off. The Kalashís now strained the ropes and drove the wedges deep into the ground, but it was so saturated by this time, that the pegs would not hold, and we were forced to let the tent remain as it was. To increase our misery, the field became one large sheet of water, and our sole resource now was, to dig a trench round the tent. Fain would I have gone elsewhere if possible, but knowing the difficulty of removing such a heavy mass, I made up my mind to bear my misfortune with true Indian patience, and lamented not so much the fact of being wet through, as the loss of one day. Assuredly, if vexations are more easily borne, when one observes others worse off than one's self, this consolation was mine; in my large tent I was certainly more comfortable than poor Vigne in his smaller one; his tent, in short, was not habitable after ten in the morning, and his servants not being of the best, he could get nothing done to alleviate his discomfort. Nothing impeded the free entrance of the water, and he was altogether in a worse plight than if he had remained in the open air. When I heard how he was situated, I ventured through the rain to see how he bore it, and found him lying in bed, or rather in a cold bath. I invited him to change his quarters forthwith, and presently he was lodged with all his moveables under my own canvass.

The Shah, unhappily, had nearly thirty men in his company, all crammed into a tent which was scarcely spacious enough for ten. He had gathered them all about his little crib, and there they sat in the water, until a violent gust of wind overturned the whole concern. Nobody was hurt, but it was a very inconvenient accident at such a time, and in spite of my good feeling and sympathy for them, I could not help laughing, as I saw these grave Mohammedans crawling out from under the soaking canvass. The Shah took shelter with me until they had put it in some sort of trim again.

About noon the sky looked somewhat more promising, but the rain still poured down. We could, however, see the mountains covered with snow in the direction of Náushera, which lies in a plain encompassed with hills of no great height. Several small streams intersect this plain, which is quite bare of trees and uncultivated: at this moment it was nothing better than a bog. They told me that it would most probably be quite impassable in a few days, and as my road led through it, this piece of information was not calculated to cheer my spirits. I comforted myself, nevertheless, with the hope that this might be a little Indian exaggeration, and in the evening I interrogated the Thanadar belonging to the fort of Náushera; but he also declared that at this season of the year, travellers were often detained for a whole fortnight together after heavy rains, before the country was practicable. Meanwhile he offered to entertain me in the fort, but I declined his invitation, and not over courteously; for, to confess the truth, I was quite overcome by the intelligence he had just communicated. During the night the rain fell in torrents, and my servants all came to shelter themselves in the outer division of my tent, their own having fallen in at eleven o'clock.

Monday, December 21.—The weather was better than I had dared to anticipate, though the rain had not entirely abated, and at nine o'clock the sky became still calmer. The tents, however, were in such a plight that there was no chance of our departure then, but when the sun came forth at noon, I ordered them instantly to pack up, being most anxious to quit our present position; for it seemed to me that the inclination of the ground towards this plain, must render it liable to frequent rains, and a very few days like the last would detain us prisoners for a long time in this marshy field.

My people knew that I was not to be moved from a resolution once firmly taken, and though my command to quit Náushera directly, seemed to them most extraordinary, they were soon in motion. I had a little more difficulty with the bearers. The Shah also succeeded in stirring up his retinue, though with much trouble; but Vigne, who was so kind and indulgent to his servants, that they did just what pleased them, could not rouse a man from the place. He followed me, therefore, with a single bearer carrying his bed, in the hope that the rest would come after him. I had named Sálat as our night's post, being but three kos from Náushera, or about four miles. For one mile and a half of this distance we had to wade through the marshy valley, which cost us a vast deal of labour and fatigue. After this, the road became higher, and from the plain we came suddenly to the steep declivity on which Sálat is built. The night had come on ere we reached it, nor was it easy for us to find a place of encampment; for Sálat lies, as I have said, on a stony declivity, which leads down to a steep ravine, ending in a rivulet. I examined the vicinity for some time to find a suitable position for the tents, or some dwelling place where we could pass the night; but the night fairly closed in without any successful issue. We were forced, in consequence, to encamp on a height on the other side of the river, at some considerable distance from the village. While here, I was obliged to give Mirza a very severe reprimand. My Sikh lieutenant suggested to me that in the mosque of the town there was a very clean place of shelter at my service. Knowing his religious creed, I asked him whether it was customary in the Panjáb for a traveller of another faith to enter a mosque set apart for Mohammedans, and he assured me that the Sikhs always did it, when there was no Dharamsála in the place. I was just about to decline the offer, when Mirza, who was a Mohammedan, stepped forward, and said that he would not permit the mosque to be so profaned. I desired him to be silent, and to remember that while in my service his duty was to make me as comfortable as possible, instead of starting difficulties, and if this was not consistent with his duty as a good Mussulman, he must cease to be my servant. He understood me, and in order to shew that he was sensible of having manifested his religious zeal at a most unseasonable time, prepared to pack up my baggage himself, and take it to the mosque. I desired him, however, to leave it where it was, as I was quite contented with the tent. Mr. Vigne's people did not make their appearance, neither did the bearer of his bed, and with a little trouble we found a place for him among us. I observed, on this occasion, that the higher castes did not consider themselves defiled by allowing the inferior orders to come into contact with their garments, and my people gave their best shawls and coverings to furnish a bed for my guest, without making the slightest objection.

Tuesday, December 22.—Sálat is 1200 feet higher than Mazafferabad. This morning the weather was tolerably clear, but my limbs were perfectly benumbed with the cold. The thermometer was at 45°. The country for the last few days had been generally bare of trees, but at some distance from every village is a thick grove, which affords a most delightful variety to the general monotony. These usually consist of olive trees, here most appropriately dedicated to peace, for they adorn the graves which lie beneath their shade. Many are famed for encircling the tomb of some Pir, or saint, and surviving friends often bring their dead from a considerable distance to deposit them near the holy man's grave. One of these sacred groves was near Sálat, and afforded us for one night that rest which so many of the inhabitants had taken up for a much longer period. As in other Mohammedan cemeteries, so these are ornamented by the surviving relatives in various ways. At several of the graves there were lamps kept constantly burning.

I was up and out at break of day, and strolled to the nearest high ground, in hopes of seeing the plains of India, but nothing was visible beyond the range of hills, piled one over another. We started soon after, as I wanted to make up for our lost day by a long march. Our route lay through a narrow pass, hemmed in by detached hills, to a wide valley, in which the river Dor, or rather its stony bed, takes its course for half a mile. The rest of the valley is torn up by deep ravines, caused by the rain floods in these low grounds, which force the natives to build their villages on the heights that bound the valley like a wall to the north-west. One may well suppose that a mighty stream has once filled the whole valley, having these steep heights for its shores; at present, no swelling of the waters could ever carry them so far. A species of aqueduct distributes the waters of the Dor at a tolerable elevation; indeed, no region in the world can be oetter supplied than this valley, called the Dhúmtur district. The town itself, which I saw only from a distance, is between five and six kos from Náushera, and there is a second very near to Hussein Abdal, our next station, which leads by it, but I had chosen the shorter route by Sálat. Many books and maps have raised Dhúmtur to the rank of a large city, giving its name to a province, or even to a state; but it is, on the contrary, a very insignificant place. Many small forts are

name of the place where we were to be lodged for the night, I had no resource but to wait patiently till some of my suite returned. I dismounted hastily, and seated myself on a stone by the side of a spring, and held the rein of my horse. They did not make their appearance for about an hour; and remembering the days of hard toil they had gone through with me, I could not find it in my heart to scold them for leaving me alone, while they were snatching at these, to them, so very unusual pleasures.

Here we quitted the Dor, which winds along through the mountain chain, falling into the Atok, seven kos from Haripoor. Three different ways lead from this place to the town of Atok, two of them being shorter than the road by Hussein Abdal, but more hilly, and quite unprovided, according to the information of Hari Singh, who accompanied me, with provisions sufficient for my large company. For that reason only, I decided on going by Kota and Hussein Abdal. The road led at first through deep ravines, where the Haro springs, a river which is at present quite dry, the whole way to Kota.

I desired my tent to be pitched at a short distance from the town, under the walls of a little fort close by the Haro, and where was a mosque shaded by some fine trees. There was a little water in the bed of the Haro at this place in the deepest parts. During my accustomed walk, I examined both the neighbouring heights and the banks of the stream, where I saw many curious caves, as though the Troglodytes had once settled there.

At noon we were met by Khan Singh, an agent from Ranjít Singh, who brought me a most friendly letter from his master, in which neither sun nor moon were spared to attest the stability of his friendship, and no compliments forgotten. He recommended Khan Singh to me as a man who had been of important service to him, and assured me moreover that he was ordered to provide me with every thing I could wish for. To this letter I sent an immediate reply, thanking the Mahá Raja for this additional proof of his kindness, which could only proceed from the firm friendship subsisting between himself and the East India Company, whose friend I also was proud to consider myself.

Thursday, December 24.—As we passed through Kota, I took notice of a house, by far the best built in the place; and inquiring to whom it belonged, I found that it was the property of a fakír, the poor man of the town, and soon after we happened to meet this person clothed in silks, and carried in a palankeen. I thought I must have been mistaken, but no, he told me himself that he was the fakír of Kota; and upon stricter inquiry whether I could rightly have understood the real meaning of the term, I heard further that fakír did actually signify the poor man of the place. What a strange contradiction of things! Every village owns a beggar of this species, who receives something from each inhabitant, or sometimes there is one fakír to so many small villages. I have heard it said, "We are too poor to have a fakír here;" but wherever there is one the people have generally a pride in taking care that he is properly supported. The Kota fakír subsisted on the charity of thirty villages. There is often a spirit of contention between different places most ridiculously carried on, to see which fakír is the best kept; and they seem most desirous that strangers should consider them benevolent in proportion as their own particular object is seen well maintained.

Leaving Kota, I observed some detached mountains, running all in one direction, and evidently members of the same dissevered chain. The formation is singular, and imparts a peculiar character to the locality. They appear like the backs of hills joined together, and like islands in a sea: they lie in the great plain, intersected with innumerable ravines. We passed numerous streams and forts, and the ground seemed remarkably productive.

I eagerly looked out for Hussein Abdal, which is about nine kos from Kota, the spot celebrated by Moore in his Lalla Rookh, and described by Hamilton, whose work has nothing of poetry in it, as a lovely valley, and which in sober truth is neither lovely nor a valley. The place certainly has a mountain behind it; but the elevated lands in all other directions are much too insignificant to give the plain the character of a valley, and too far apart to encompass it. The ruinous Serai, built by Akbar, is striking, not by nature but from the state of the ruin itself, and the cypresses and date-trees, the Phœnix farinosa, near. A tepid spring rises in the neighbourhood, in which a great many sacred fish are kept under the protection of a fakír; he had also in charge a couple of white-headed eagles, which my huntsman shot at, to the consternation of the whole place.

A palace of Jehanghír's, now in ruins, lies a mile from this; it was too late to visit it to-day. The huntsman was guilty of the death of a parrot this afternoon, which excited the rage of the people, though happily it did not explode in any thing worse than abuse. I cannot say whence the erroneous opinion is derived that the Emperors of Dehli always passed through Hussein Abdal on their way to Kashmír. Akbar may have done so, but his father Hamáyun was compelled to relinquish his design of reaching the valley by this route, and none of his predecessors ever proceeded by any other road than that of Rajáwar, and the Pir Panjal.

I had made up my mind to see Atok, the most northern point to the west where the Hindú faith is found. It is two days' march from Hussein Abdal. As I found that I should be obliged at all events to return again to Hussein Abdal from Atok, in order to travel the faster, I resolved to leave my tents here, to proceed to Shujanpoor on the morrow, and thence on the following morning to go on very early to Atok, see the place, and return the same evening to Shujanpoor, thus finding my way back to Hussein Abdal on the third day, and giving my bearers and escort a rest of three days.

There are certain times in one's life, when remembrances of the past are so vivid, as to preclude every consideration of the present. This was the case with me to-day. My situation, as may be readily imagined, is certainly most cheerless, compared with the time, when in the circle of my kinsmen, brothers, and sisters, I customarily spent such anniversaries in the home of my childhood, happy in all the ties of friendship and of love; whereas, now, I am alone in a dreary dwelling-place, with fingers so benumbed, that I can scarcely contrive to trace a few lines by the wretched light of the lamp.

Friday, December 25.—Although I have not mentioned the Shah's name very often of late, I have seen a great deal of him, enough to make me admire and appreciate his true nobility of character, and feel grateful for the repeated proofs he has given me of his kindness and attention, and for the readiness with which he has thought of everything I was most likely to stand in need of. For one thing he would send to Kashmír, for another to Peshawur; and if I asked for information on any subject, every man in the place was employed to procure it for me. Such information, in a country like this, peopled by Mohammedan fanatics, was only to be had through Mohammed Shah Nakhsbandi, whose character for the promotion of the faith made that easy for him to acquire, which to a Sikh would have been impossible, although it were from his personal friend. Probably, I was mainly indebted to the protection of his name for the immunity I experienced in my journey from Mazafferabad to Hussein Abdal, through a country infested with parties of infuriated Musselman bigots. His little tent was always crowded with his retainers, and pitched near mine. When he paid his morning visits to inquire after my health, he never failed to ask my permission to return in the evening. A Mohammedan in the noblest sense of that faith; he was grave, sincere, pious, fearless of men, obliging and polite; always ready to assist others; to feel for their sufferings; and to bear his own with a submissive trust in God, his conduct was truly worthy of admiration.

I set off with a small party of fifteen, at daybreak, on my way to Atok. Near Hussein Abdal we passed over some mounds of a soft slimy earth, which, I think, have been deposited there by the waters, as they were usually preceded by a declivity to a rapid stream. Ten or twelve miles further, brought us to Kokur, and the plain of Atok called Shush, which, although on a larger scale, reminded me of the Dera Dhun, or valley of Dera, in the Himálaya. A range of hills, broken at intervals, shuts it in towards the south, where the valley is inclosed by the Sivalik mountains. The plains of Hindústhan appear to commence with that of Atok, and from Kokur the mountains terminate entirely in a southern direction. These mountains are of limestone, and the marbles are of every shade of colour.

There is not a single tree on the plain of Atok, which is as level as a sheet of water. Ruinous villages are situated on eminences artificially thrown up, like those of the Egyptian Delta. The Indus frequently inundates the whole plain, though not with the same regularity as the Nile. Shujanpoor is eighteen miles from Hussein Abdal, and is a wretched place by the side of a rivulet, with morasses in its immediate vicinity. The course of the Indus may be distinguished thence as far as the mountains, and to the point where it is lost in them, a distance of nineteen miles or thirteen kos from Shujanpoor. The view would be splendid were the plain well cultivated; as it is, however, the scene is devoid of interest, and one only feels surprised at the endless range of mountains seemingly one above the other.

On the plain of Atok, the contest for the possession of that city, and the influence of the Afghans and Mohammedans of the west, was finally decided. It was neither one battle, nor the superior talent of Ranjít Singh, which put an end to that singular train of circumstances which had enabled an insignificant branch from the richest and most populous race in the world, renowned for bravery as well as descent to prescribe laws thus long; the Mahmood power was already on the decline in India, and the unimportant battle of Atok only drove the last bands over the Indus, according to the object always kept in view by Fattih Khan, the Wazír of Mohammed Shah, the last king of Kabúl, before Ranjít made his appearance on the scene; Ranjít has now in view to penetrate into the heart of Afghanistan, and annex the capital, Kabúl, to his own territory; but no one informed of the hatred and contempt felt for the Sikhs by these wild Afghans, could ever dream of the possibility of Kabúl professing allegiance to Ranjít Singh. Nevertheless he has already reached half way from Atok to Kabúl, and got possession of the whole country as far as Jelalabad. I am firmly persuaded that nothing but death or some change in the policy of the East India Company, will deter him from attempting the conquest of Kabúl itself.

Ranjít Singh has been in this part of the country several times, and on such occasions they have thrown up small buildings for his reception, miscalled houses, of one story, consisting of a single room. These houses are rudely built of wood, plastered over with clay, with a single entrance, but without window or other opening of any sort, forming altogether a strange contrast with the magnificent serais of the former Moghul sovereigns*.

Shujanpoor is seen at a great distance, and is remarkable for the six date-trees in its cemetery, where I took up my quarters. I ordered my bed to be put into a mosque most conveniently near, while my dinner was being cooked in another. This caused a violent altercation, for it turned out that the spot we had chosen belonged to the fakir of the town, one of those mendicants who subsist on the bounty of the simple natives. He had just made preparation to feed his falcons on some tame fowls, and was looking forward to the gratification of witnessing the ease with which his birds of prey would kill and tear the poor fowls, when he caught sight of my people kindling a fire with his wood, which the coldness of the evening compelled us to have recourse to. Backed by a number of the inhabitants, who had armed themselves with spears and sticks, the fakír assailed my servants with a volley of imprecations, and soon put them all to flight. I had the greatest difficulty to make myself heard amid this uproar. At length the fakír came up to me, and complained bitterly of the depredation committed on the store of wood he had laid up for the winter's consumption. I told him that we could not possibly remain there all night without a fire, but that he should be amply repaid for what we had consumed. To this arrangement, however, he would not accede, but said he wanted his wood, and remained immoveable in his purpose to keep his property

* The above is an excellent epitome of the Hindú and Mohammedan character. The former, parsimonious, exclusive, bigoted; the latter, thoughtless, extravagant, bold, and luxurious, from the prince to the peasant; or indeed to the very beggar the portraiture is equally applicable; yet let us not therewithal refuse them their proper meed of praise. The Hindú possesses many redeeming qualities,—extreme forbearance, submissive consideration, and a high degree of attachment to his kindred, his relations, his paternal property, and his benefactor. The Mohammedans are brave to a fault, studiously concerned for their faith and its extension, chivalrous and hospitable. These are the necessary results of their political and religious institutions combined. Alas! what a balance is set off against them in the united evils of a demoralising superstition and a naturally depraved heart. In such qualities they are alike; the grossest immorality, the most lax ideas of the sacred obligations of truth, and an utter unconcern for the happiness or eternal interest of the fairest and noblest portion of the human race.

to himself; at length, seeing that words were unavailing, I directed the men to follow me, and proceeded without further to do, to the stack of contested fuel; the fakír standing by and uttering not a word, while we were helping ourselves to the quantity we stood in need of *.

We could get nothing to eat until night, and then partook of our Christmas dinner dismally enough; the cold in the mosque was most intense. For ten days past we had subsisted on rice, mutton, and occasionally a fowl; all other provisions, including wine, being entirely expended.

Saturday, December 26.—The complete subjection of the Mohammedans in this country may be readily inferred from the circumstance of an unbeliever like myself being suffered to sleep in one mosque and use another as a kitchen. Not that I once closed my eyes in reality, for the dreadful howlings of the village dogs altogether prevented my getting a wink of sleep. In Mohammedan countries these animals have no owner; neither have they in the Panjáb. Superstition, therefore, has nothing to do with their preservation; but it would be thought very cruel to injure these inoffensive, watchful brutes; no native could be persuaded to kill one; he would merely content himself with taking up a stone, or possibly stooping in a menacing attitude, when the animal approached too near him. These dogs never become attached to any person or house, however young they may be taken, but associate themselves in a wonderful manner to each other. Woe to the stranger who

* The dilemma in which the traveller often finds himself in India, under similar circumstances, would perhaps demand a larger charity than some might be disposed to allow for this mode of procedure. While the benevolent authorities at the head of affairs in India strictly enjoined that no European officer or subject should compel the natives to serve or supply them with the necessaries of life, the intimation was perversely construed into an opinion that the life and comfort of their own servants was a matter of less concern than the fear of native displeasure, and has always operated most prejudicially to the best interests of Government. Proper and effectual regulations for the supply of everything they might stand in need of by the village officers, and for the fair equivalent in money, would have been the surest means of inculcating the paternal and vigilant concern of a wise administration for all its subjects equally. This, above all other measures, would have had the most salutary effect in conciliating the native army, and raising them and our own Government in the estimation of the people generally.—*Ed.*

should attempt to obtrude into the village compact of this species. With the wolves and jackals they live on a footing of toleration; but the former usually abide in deserted villages or solitary ruins, while the latter prefer the old tenements of inhabited places. The instinct peculiar to dogs which are the companions and friends of men, distinguishes them in every respect from these treacherous and dastardly animals, who can neither defend themselves nor their young; the only quality they possess in common with the domestic dog, is that of watchfulness. As soon as a traveller arrives in a village, half a dozen of them will seat themselves a little way off, and keep up an incessant howl from their mangy wasted skeletons, the prototype of famine and desolation*.

The distance from Shujanpoor to Atok is reckoned five kos. We broke up early to gain time enough to visit the latter place and return before nightfall. The plain of Shush (for so they call the plain of the Atok here) is intersected by some small streams, one of which has been better known since the battle between Ranjít Singh's general, Mokham Chand, and Fatíh Khan. By following its course, the Sikhs were

---

* The Pariah dog of India is, properly speaking, a half-domesticated hybrid animal, and is faithfully described in the above account. A number of these used to come about the Cutcherry at Kaira, where I was then residing (1816), with the Collector, the amiable Mr. Byram Bowles, and his assistants, Captain A. Robertson and Barnwell. The doors of our bungalow being invariably open at all hours, the dogs would come in and receive an occasional bone or piece of meat: and one, a favourite of Captain Robertson, deposited a number of puppies near the house. One of these, when I removed into my own residence in the cantonment, I took away, as most young officers have some such attendant to beguile their lone hours and rambles, and brought it up with great care. Nothing, however, would do; it invariably found its way back to the Cutcherry, and if at any time detained by a chain, would set up such a lamentable howl, that I was obliged eventually to let it go. A number of these troublesome watchful creatures used to collect round the Residency of Baroda, and keep up such an incessant howl as people passed in and out of the town, that at length an officer, who then occupied the corner house, resolved on a general deportation, and sent off two or three cart-loads some eighteen miles away across the Máhí river, rather than offend the natives by killing them. They all found their way back in the course of a week or ten days, and resumed their old station and habit. They have none of the noble traits of the domestic dogs of Europe.—*Ed.*

enabled to recruit themselves constantly throughout the heat of the day, by which great advantage the contest was decided in their favour. As we drew nearer to the Indus, we met with large blocks of granite, thrown up and left on the plain by the waters, at the period of its inundations. I longed to behold this great stream, and looked out impatiently from the jampan in which I had remained, in order to have my sextants and other instruments ready for observation, pressing the bearers now and then to hurry on, that I might reach it before noon. One mile and a half from the city we came to the height on which Atok is situated, and soon after to a small valley, where the Hindús usually burn their dead. According to Hindû law, this people are not permitted to reside beyond the Atok, but many Hindû families, nevertheless, are to be found residing both in Peshawur and Kabúl, and there can be no doubt of the existence, in former times, of a great Hindû empire on the western shore of the Atok.

There is a remarkable Mohammedan mausoleum with a lofty dome about a mile west of the city, where I took my last observation with the sextant. The map taken by the English officers in Mr. Elphinstone's suite being complete as far as Atok; I was delighted to put away my own chart, which occupied me two hours every evening, besides much time spent on it on the journey itself.

The suburbs of the city extend as far as this building, though recent wars have laid everything waste to the very walls of the fort. The Indus at this spot is a clear, rapid, but unimportant stream, seven-eighths of its sandy bed being quite dry at this season of the year. Both banks are steep; on the north they soon become nearly level, but on the southern side, on the contrary, they increase in steepness, and lofty hills arise, to all appearance, from the river itself.

At the distance of half a mile north the point is visible where the Lánder, or Kabûl river, flows into the Atok, in the plain of Shush; while, on the left shore of the Lánder, another plain stretches towards the west, where the fort is situated; the bed of the river is strictly confined between mountains of black clay-slate, and at a little distance beyond the fort is the bridge of boats, formed of nineteen immense vessels, built singularly enough, with fine carved work both fore and aft, in imitation of what we might fancy the ships of the Argonauts to have been when they sailed towards Colchis.

I was greatly surprised indeed at the scene which presented itself. In order to enjoy the view more leisurely, I had mounted the stony bank, raised against the wall of the fortress, where some Sikh soldiers had drawn up respectfully to make room for me. My attention was at first more particularly attracted by the fantastic richly-ornamented entrance to the fort, where I stood for some time, waiting for permission to enter. I was stepping forward to get a better idea of the whole, when the officer on duty advanced towards me, and requested I would not attempt to go further; "And why not?" I inquired. "Because Ranjít Singh has given the Díwan orders to introduce you with all due ceremony to the interior." I was therefore content to look leisurely around me.

Very near the fort was a ruin on some high ground; it was a Serai built by Akbar the Great, which Elphinstone calls a fort; a broad paved road, for cattle, leads down to the Indus between this and the fort, which was also the work of that emperor. From its position on precipitous rocks, it commands a view of the river below; the rapidity of the stream has polished the surface of these rocks like marble. The clear stream itself, its broad bed, with the two huge masses of rock called Jellalia and Kemellia, now standing up dry, and presenting all their dangers, which render the passage of the Indus so perilous when the waters are high, on account of the terrible whirlpools about them; the bridge of boats; the small plain on the right shore, on which stands the fort of Kairabad; the mountains forming a half circle beyond, with their watch-towers on the highest summits; and finally, the strange medley of Hindú and Persian costume and features of the various parties bathing, the very lowest degree of Hindú wretchedness, to the highly polished and richly dressed Persian horsemen with their long lances; composed altogether a very animated and striking scene. But I wished to get down to the brink of this holy stream, the limit of my journey, as it is of many a Hindú pilgrim.

Well, here was I, the first European who had hitherto wandered through this vast empire, from its most southern point at Cape Comorin, to its northern boundary at Atok. I was at the farthest extremity of India, and yet at the nearest point to my own land, had I been but blessed with the wings of a bird to direct my flight thither. Arrived on the shore of the Indus, I looked across to the mountains in the west, and thought of the country hidden beyond them, and of the dangers which attended my homeward return. This feeling of despondency, however, soon left me, and gave place to my customary equanimity as to coming events, the tears which had started unconsciously to my eyes, were dried up, and I hastily crossed the river. The banks, which rise abruptly on both sides from the sandy bed, are about eighty feet high above the level of the water. The bridge and the river in its present state, may be from forty to forty-five fathoms across, and the stream in the middle about three deep, but the breadth between the two shores must be at least 300.

During the rainy season, this river is filled up from bank to bank, the waters at this time rise as much as fifty feet, when the bridge, which is admirably contrived, and made of the very best timber, is taken to pieces, the boats being employed in navigating the stream; the lower classes sometimes make use of the distended ox-hides, which I have already mentioned, but not frequently, because the passage from one shore to the other in the regular boats costs nothing. They have ropes formed out of leaves of some species of palm-tree, unknown to me, twisted together. They told me that this palm grows near Atok. I took away one leaf with me, promising five rupees to any one who would bring me a flower or some of the seeds. Mr. Vigne had taken his post and was sketching on the Kabúl side of the Indus, when presently we both saw a showy troop of horsemen ride down the opposite shore, cross the bridge, and approach the spot where we stood. It was Khan Singh, who was deputed by Ranjít Singh; he came with the Thanadar, in the name of Kashmír Singh, Ranjít's son, who was then governor, to request me to visit the fort. He had ridden forth in another direction in search of me. I accepted the invitation, and quitted Afghanistan, where I had been some five minutes only, and with Mr. Vigne returned to India. The fortress is built on the

Kashmir Singh's Diwan at the Gate of Atok

Baron Hugel's Travels, page 219.

declivity of a mountain, and is very spacious, forming a parallelogram, or rather a polygon, on most uneven ground, in some places reduced to a rectilinear shape, one side of it stretching along the river from north to south. The principal gate is on the north; the walls are high and strong, and surmounted with battlements, but there are no advanced works. In the interior, a third part is rendered habitable for four thousand people, and contains a bazar.

I was received by the prince's Díwan, a Brahmin from Dehli, who came forth on an elephant, from which he dismounted when near to me and in the name of the Mahá Raja proffered me a bag of rupees; in his own, a branch with honey from the wild bees. He was an old man, advanced in years, and could not stand upright without the assistance of two persons. I could not bring myself to give utterance to the usual salutation of "are you well," it seemed so like mockery rather than any compliment. I requested permission to see the building more minutely, and the Díwan declared that he would conduct me wherever I wished to go, but as the day was much too short to admit of such a mode of observation, I begged him to resume his seat on the elephant, while I proceeded on foot.

The reservoir belonging to this fort is well worthy of remark. Its depth is from forty to fifty feet, its circumference about twenty-five feet, and the river fills it as it flows. On the side of the river, the walls are only eight feet above high water; at present they are as much as fifty-eight above the dry bed. I wished to see the largest guns of the place, as in all Mohammedan strong places they are of great beauty; those in position at present were of brass, cast in Lahor, and answering, as I should judge, to the French sixteen-pounders; they are without ornament, but their construction, and the carriages on which they are mounted, seem both very skilfully designed; they are kept under shelter, a necessary precaution where the heat of the sun would otherwise split the wood. I at last completed my survey of this now partly dismantled fort, and not without considerable fatigue. The day was drawing to a close, and Kashmír Singh had not yet returned, but resolving to pursue my original plan, I had declined the invitation of the Díwan to pass a day in Atok, or even to delay my journey for an hour, from the same impatience which had made me refuse the invitation of Ranjít Singh to go on as far as Peshawur.

There was a crush of men and beasts in the bazar, camels terrified, asses kicking, horses prancing, and all this in a place where the closely built stalls scarcely permitted three men to walk abreast. The first sight of the Díwan's elephant put all the other animals to flight, and the boards on which the merchants had displayed their wares were all overset in the tumult; among them were many things which I particularly coveted, and ordered my people to buy for me. The bazar of Atok is excellently furnished with the productions of Peshawur, Kabúl, and Persia, and those of India are to be had in great abundance. My Munshí, Thakúr-das, a Brahmin from Dehli, found in the Díwan a countryman of the same sect as himself, and he requested my leave to eat with him. The longer I travelled in India, the more I was conscious of the great advantage of having a high-caste Hindú in my suite. Almost every business and occupation in the service of the higher orders, being transacted by the agency of Brahmins, the stranger will succeed in whatever he wishes or requires much more readily, should the Munshí be a Brahmin, especially in all communications with other Brahmins, notwithstanding the difference of rank, than if the servant were of any other class.

I had scarcely passed the fort in my jampan, when a man rode up to tell me that Kashmír Singh was approaching, and we met near the field where the Hindús burn their dead to which I before alluded. He was a youth of fifteen or sixteen, with a very clever and animated expression; he was mounted on a white charger very richly caparisoned, and dressed in a long jacket of pink silk, with a belt, in which he carried a pair of English pistols, and a dagger; a loose robe wadded, and made also of pink silk, gave him an appearance of extreme comfort; his trowsers were of blue and white, fitted tight to the leg; his shoes embroidered; his head dress was a low red turban. The complexion of this youth was olive, and the dark beard was just beginning to adorn his chin; a pink umbrella was carried over his head. "You would do well to remain here," he said; I answered, that had I been aware of his presence in the city, I should have asked permission

.o come with all my people, and brought my tents. "They can be sent for; where are they?" "In Shujanpoor," answered I, "and though grateful for the invitation to remain, I must proceed on my way." "I intreat you to stay, the Mahá Raja has commanded me to do everything to make Atok agreeable to you, and I wish to be able to do it." Still I persisted. "You should stay with me two days, then go to Peshawur, and make acquaintance with Avitabile Sahib; after that, the Mahá Raja has written to me that you will certainly stop at Akora to visit Court Sahib, who is stationed there with the French legion, and if you do not like to go as far as Peshawur, you can travel easily to Akora and back in one day*."

I exhausted myself in thanks but took my leave. Kashmír Singh is the only Indian I ever heard speak in short sentences, and he seems to possess more talent than it has hitherto been my good fortune to meet with.

I very soon alighted from my jampan, mounted my ghunt, and attended only by Mohan, galloped over the plain in order to reach Shujanpoor before night-fall. Unluckily, one village is here so exactly like another, that I missed my way, the six palms which distinguish Shujanpoor, being only discernible from this side when one is very near to them. The sun went down while we were crossing the plain, but I had far outridden Mohan, and not another human creature was to be seen. In the distance some villages crowned the small eminences which rise from the level surface at intervals, and I decided on making for one of these and asking my way. While I was considering what I had best do, Mohan came up and assured me we were all right, but I felt equally sure to the contrary, we rode on a little way until the much-longed-for palms started up before our eyes. The darkness soon hid them from us, and we reached Shujanpoor after every ray of light had disappeared. I waited three hours for Mr. Vigne before I began my supper. Just as I had commenced he came in dreadfully

* Kashmír Singh and Peshawur Singh, the two illegitimate sons of Ranjít Singh, allied themselves with Íttar Singh's party. The former met with a cruel death, in the sanguinary contests for supremacy in the Panjáb, in May, 1844.

fatigued. He had stayed behind to sketch, and like me, had lost his way; after many attempts to set himself right, he had been obliged at last to take a guide from one of the villages, which occasioned this long delay.

The plain of Shush produces a species of the goat, which grows to a great size: they have long tails, which they carry horizontally, and no horns: they have a roman nose, and eyes of an uncommon size: their hair is quite black. I purchased the largest male I could meet with, and amused myself, while waiting for Vigne, with watching the motions of this strange caricature of nature by torch light. An old donkey, belonging to the fakír, stood near him, but my goat over-topped him by at least two hands, and the creature at length appeared in my sight like something mysterious. I fancied some Mephistopheles shining out of his great eyes, and turned round to my writing again, the labours of the Danaides to me. For will it ever attain the object I desire? It is true, that is not the meanest design, which expects neither thanks nor reward. To many, labour of any kind is the creative and spiritual life working within them, or the light play of their fancy, assuming form and reality; to others, it is the dull heaving of the heart, in which fate has laid a painful burthen, but which still heaves on for mere existence, which is not unfrequently laid down in this struggle. But after the grave and forgetfulness have long been our portion, when another people are ploughing the field under which we lie mouldering, if no remembrance of ourselves or our actions be left behind, yet will something remain of our labours, if they have been exercised on the realities of life. Such works, however unimportant, contribute to the formation of the minds which succeed their author. Under the most favourable circumstances, mine will repose in my chest, and no kindred spirit will learn a lesson from the sharp experience of these pages*.

* The amiable and instructive spirit which dictated this work, will, we trust, even in the more unpretending garb of a translation, contribute largely to the entertainment of those who are interested in the condition and history of their fellow-men in Asia, and serve, with other travels of a like stamp, to commemorate the parties spoken of, and the author who has so faithfully described the countries he visited.—*Ed.*

More than 2000 years ago, Alexander the Great crossed this plain with his splendid army, and will not this grand idea raise the mind and withdraw it from the every-day repetition of life's toil? Surely it would, if any loftier thought than that of conquest had moved the heart of Alexander, if he had marched to spread benefit instead of ruin over his path. Even then it is not the will that ennobles the deed, but the accomplishment of that will; and what was the great result of Alexander's campaign in India? The death of thousands, the misery of the inoffensive inhabitants, and in the place of tranquillity and order, the unmitigated calamities of war. To me, the idea that brave and adventurous men carried the productions of India over this plain to the west, long before Alexander lived, is far grander than all the brilliant victories of this conqueror of worlds. Their journeys bound nations together in amity, softened the rude manners of the west, and improved all things. Sad is it to think that this same plain has been for the last 800 years the territory where fanatical and furious barbarians, whose faith is a cloak for every crime, have held uncontrolled sway. But these days are now almost at an end, and we may look hopefully forward to the time when expeditions from the east to the west will finally subdue the remains of so baneful a power. To the Sikhs now stretching to the Indus, will succeed the hosts of England, who will unite this country to their enormous empire.

Sunday, December 27.—We started at eight in the morning. I was benumbed with the cold, which had kept me awake all night in an open mosque; and in spite of the fakír's wood, I shivered in every limb. I expected that he would demand some large compensation for his loss, but his pride was too great for this; I therefore told the people to give him five rupees, a sum which would have purchased for me either in London or Paris, a most warm and comfortable apartment.

I began by making use of my feet to bring some warmth into them; but yesterday's journey had so fatigued me, that I soon had recourse to my ghunt, and cantered onward to Hussein Abdal, thinking the day's march would never come to an end. The road itself is altogether uninteresting, and I was obliged to stop in many places and wait for the guide, the path through the ravines being very difficult.

I had no sooner arrived at Hussein Abdal, but I set off at once to visit the ancient palace and garden built by Jehanghír, which is one mile and a half from the town; it is called Wah, the Indian cry of astonishment, It was not a serai, but a regular palace, situated in the best part of the country around, and is now an extensive and imposing ruin. No doubt the great inducement to build a palace here arose from the presence of three beautiful springs, which gush out from the earth, and are encircled by slabs of stone: they spread into large sheets of water, which are full of fish of various kinds. I wandered long about these once splendid rooms, some adorned with specimens of the finest stones, others with rich carvings, but now abandoned to the most perfect solitude. The entrance is still worthy of the residence of an Emperor. At the bottom of the garden stands a little building, the use of which I could not understand; having a beautiful spring issuing from within, and flowing all round it. It is the most richly ornamented part of the grounds, but I looked in vain for some way to enter, and as usually happens, my imagination became vivid in proportion as it remained unsatisfied. I peered into the bushes which surrounded it, and even climbed to the height above, to look for the entrance, but neither door nor window, nor any aperture whatever was visible; and with curiosity ungratified, I was forced to retrace my steps. On my return, I was overjoyed to hear that the long-looked-for stock of provisions from Lúdiana had arrived: they had been sent round by Lahor, Jamú, Kashmír, and Mazafferabad. It was with no little pleasure that I received a supply of wine and brandy, after twelve days' deprivation, replaced my wretched tea and sugar with something far better, and chepatís with biscuit. Instead of the tallow candles of Kashmír, always covered with black grease, I welcomed some wax lights; even the preserved soups and meats had come safe to hand, allowing us a brief respite from the eternal mutton and fowl to which we were latterly restricted *.

* Some idea may be formed of the predilection most men have, especially Europeans, for what comes from their own country: the very name is so associated with early recollections and tastes, that a preference is given at any cost for provisions, which otherwise would be regarded with indifference.—*Ed.*

Near Hussein Abdal stands the ruined Serai of Akbar, in one end of which a Sikh Gurú has established himself. Hussein Abdal owes its name to the grave of a Pír or devotee, who lived in the eminence where the place now stands, and his tomb is still to be seen. This Pír was called Shekh Hussein Abdal; *Abdal* means fanatic, and is applied to a particular tribe among the Afghans*. This individual is a very celebrated person at Kandahar, where he was known as Bába Wali. He chose the place of his abode because a spring comes forth from its summit, and was the resort of pious pilgrims of many creeds. After his death, a fákir took up his place, as is usual, in the case of all the Mohammedan saints. Gurú Nának, the founder of the Sikh religion, coming one day to the hill as a pilgrim, much heated and tired, requested some water of the fakír. The unbeliever's demand was refused; and Nának, laying his hand on the rock whence the spring issued, it ceased to flow, and on the very spot was a bas-relief of that hand in stone, which as soon as the Sikhs became lords of the country, was taken away from the mountain, and placed in the building erected in the middle of the Serai, and there raised as an object of veneration opposite the entrance. The Gurú sings some passages out of the Grunth, or holy volume of the Sikhs, every morning before it.

A tomb, now almost destroyed, stands near this Serai, overshadowed by two large cypresses which, as is frequently the case in Mohammedan countries, grow in a place quite surrounded with massive stone walls. Every account agrees that this is the last resting-place of the well-known Núr Jehán, the wife of Jehanghír. The frame-work of the door retains some vestiges of former grandeur: it is of black marble, as was the door itself, which has been carried off†.

---

* The meaning of the term is referred by others to Abdal, signifying Servant of God; but it is very generally supposed that this race is of far more ancient origin —a tribe of the Huns, known as Abtelites.—*Ed.*

† The tombs and palaces of the once mighty princes and nobles of the East, are highly instructive and affecting as memorials of the character of Asiatic sovereignty, the instability of all human greatness, and the infirmities of humanity. Desirous to stand alone in their lives, they are in the sad trophies of death peculiarly solitary and dishonoured. The rank weed twines carelessly round the fretted

Monday, December 28.—The nights were now extremely cold; the water froze in the bottles, and the ground was covered every morning with hard frost. At noon, however, we had our Indian sun. I had appointed the morning for my visit to the Sikh Gurú, at which ceremony the whole population of Hussein Abdal was present. When I came to the marble steps leading to his Durbar, which was held before the celebrated stone, and saw him there seated on carpets, I took off my shoes, a courtesy which gained for me the loud praises of all present. The Gurú received me with every mark of dignity, and accepted a present, which was certainly well bestowed, if only for the sight of the stone, on which the above-named marvel still remains imprinted.

The great imperial route formerly leading from Hindústhan to Kabúl passes from Hussein Abdal to Lahor, and Serais were built along it at intervals of every six kos from each other. There were three between the former town and Ráwal Pindi, but I purposed making the journey in two days, and started at once therefore from the Gurú's Durbar. Near the first Serai is a small eminence, which has the advantage of a paved road, not remarkable in any way; indeed, why it is there at all is the only singularity, as there are many places where it would be far more useful than here. Perhaps it is owing to its being the only rocky hill between Atok and Lahor, that the honor of a paved road has been given to it; at all events, it is called Múlgala, and an inscription, not very intelligible, ascribes it to Akbar. Just previous to this, I saw a stone bridge in ruins, which is an evidence of the changeableness of the soil in the Panjáb. This bridge spans a rivulet, and is constructed against a hill from sixty to eighty feet high, the formation

---

column, or depends from the massy dome which shelters the owls, and the bats, or affords a temporary refuge to the traveller from the inclemency of the noonday heat or tropical rain. Stone after stone falls, and is carried away with impunity, till at length the name of the tenant perhaps is lost, and the wild beast of the forest, or the scorpion and snake, take up their abode in the ruins,—fit representatives of the court of death. Just such is the history of their illustrious occupants. Fancy throws its ideal charms over the last recollections of Eastern celebrity; till the destructive process of time obliterates the few faint traces of truth, and superstition concurs with fanaticism to supersede reality by fable.—*Ed.*

of which must have originated from the water beneath it. There is another bridge very close to this, which is also nearly destroyed; the traveller is now left to find his way through the ravines and the stream, as he best can. My camels, however, had not learned the secret, consequently their burdens were all cast on the ground. Janikasang, where we halted, is a wretched place, nine kos from Hussein Abdal.

Tuesday, December 29.—The way continued through the plain, where there is very little cultivation, though the soil seems excellent, and must be of a most extraordinary depth, of which I could judge from several parts where it has been torn up by occasional wild torrents. The absence of cultivation is attributable perhaps to the very superiority of the soil; for in this part of Asia, where rain so seldom falls, agriculture depends almost exclusively on irrigation. The country is intersected throughout by numerous streams, which flow from the high mountains, and are so deeply embedded in the earth, that the water cannot be conducted along the plain; hence the country is in many parts a wilderness, producing nothing except stunted acacias and the ziziphus. When the rainy season sets in, the numerous deep ravines must put a stop to all travelling. There is no bridge near at hand, and the water in many places stands sometimes from twenty to thirty feet deep, there is, therefore, no remedy that I know of but patiently to await a change of weather. The ravines being formed by the streams, many of them are well supplied with water in the very driest season.

Just before Ráwal Pindi, there is a river called Sawan, the Swán of the maps, whence a small plain extends to the town itself. By this river I found the Thanadar, with the *Sirni*, (Persian,) or *Míthái*, (Hindústhaní,) the present of welcome, consisting of twenty-one pots of sweetmeats, each enough for one man to carry, a basket of eggs, one of fowls, two sheep, and a bag of rupees.

I went to look about me in the adjacent parts, and then to my tent, which was pitched by the only well in the town, and about a musket-shot from the nearest houses. Ráwal Pindi is called a fort, but it has not even a wall of defence. The place is very populous, and has a large bazar.

Not far from my tent stood a little building, the environs of which were ornamented with a few acacias, the only trees near. On one of these I observed a bird, which was quite new to me, sitting quietly; and sending for the huntsman, Jonki, I desired him to shoot it; but the natives would not permit it, because the house was the residence of the Gurú. On hearing this, I ordered the people to get ready instantly to depart, not because, as I told them, my servants were not permitted to shoot, but because they had entered into a dispute with religious personages. As soon as these last heard my reasons, they came out in a body, and begged me to remain where I was, and shoot whatever I liked. I did remain therefore, but prohibited the shooting.

The same evening I received a letter from General Ventura, and two baskets filled with choice European dainties, an attention not to be forgotten. They were escorted by a Jemidar, who was directed to follow me. I had also to thank the General for some English powder, which he sent me by a Sowár, and for which I had written to him from Báramulla. The man had travelled on a dromedary ninety-six kos from Lahor in three days.

Wednesday, December 30.—It often happens that recent occurrences, however unimportant in themselves, will elucidate questions long put aside from history as something inexplicable. This has more particularly happened in modern days, and perhaps the most striking proof has been afforded by the discovery of the famed Damietta stone, which solved the long-existing enigma of hieroglyphics. Something similar may be found in the journeys of Europeans to the part of Asia where I now am, which have cleared up much difficulty concerning Alexander's Indian expedition, and thrown a broad light on many shadowy paths of history.

It happened one day that an Englishman being in the bazar at Delhi, received in change some of the copper coin called páis, a circumstance only singular in this, that however small the purchase may be, a native always makes the bargain for these lords of India, and is usually paid in larger amounts. It was still more curious, that the Englishman took notice of these small coins, thinking there was something uncommon in their appearance; and I mention the circumstance without any idea of covertly reproving the indolence usually seen in India. Every new comer gazes with more or less curiosity, but always with curiosity, on objects which have all the charm of novelty to him; but this at last wears out, and generally long before the presidency of Bengal is quitted for the upper provinces. I can vouch for the truth of this sensation. Many things on which years ago I should have made an infinity of inquiries, have ceased to awaken the least interest in my mind, and if I, as a traveller, feel thus in matters of immediate inquiry, how much more those whose pursuit is the pleasure to be attained by their large income, or the readiest means of acquiring one. The little copper coins I have alluded to differed from those of India: instead of some legend, as on the Mohammedan; some idol, as on the Hindú coins, they more resembled the money of the West, bearing a bust, a whole figure, and sometimes an inscription engraved round them. A superficial examination pointed them out as Greek coins, or as exact imitations; and a more rigid scrutiny proved them to be either Bactrian or something nearly related to that country. The discovery was no sooner made known than many Englishmen in Upper India hastened to collect as many of the coins as possible, and an immense number were brought in, and at the same time others of silver and gold: the fact was simply this; the workers in those metals had been hitherto in the habit of melting them down, they now kept them to sell to the English. In a short time these ancient coins were all classified, and divided into the ancient Hindú, or Buddhist; the Bactrian, which have been most valuable in illustrating the history of Central Asia; and the Indo-Scythian, which are as precious as the rarest documents.

The last two might be subdivided into dynasties, shewing that Alexander's generals, who shared among them the mighty empire he had conquered, had retained possession of the country of the Indus much longer than history supposes, nay, that it is very possible that some of the dynasties survived to the appearance of the victorious Mohammedans. The last division, forming the transition from the Bactrian to the Hindú, are by far the most remarkable. Like the coins of the West, which during the sway of the Christian Emperors of Constantinople, departed from the noble Greek form to assume the likeness of so many tasteless caricatures; so these degenerate still more, and the beautiful proportions of the original coin are lost in an unconnected jumble of points and lines. In the same way we find, first the Greek Basileos, then the same with Sanscrit letters, then Basileos Raja, then the last only, until, finally, both name and title disappear. This part of India, before the invasion of the Mohammedans, like Italy in the middle ages, had survived all the beauty of the arts.

The strip of country in which the gold and silver coins of Bactria are found is not extensive. It runs down from the bank of the Sawan at Ráwal Pindi as far as the Indus, and from the description as given by the ancient Greek writers, I conclude that Ráwal Pindi may be built on, or near, the site of Taxila. The coins which form the link between the Bactrian and Hindú are found there, and in greater numbers still at Kanoj on the Ganges; the copper money is found from Delhi to Agra. I postpone the inquiry whether there were an Indo-Bactrian kingdom existing in the Panjáb and in a part of Northern India; or whether the coins discovered there were brought by the conquerors, and exchanged for gold and precious stones. I purchased a great many of the Bactrian coins while in Ráwal Pindi, which are called Sítaram País, from Sita and Rama, the first being the name of a goddess, the second that of her celestial lover.

The well-known truth that no place is more unpleasant to a European traveller than one of importance, was quite substantiated here. The bearers refused to go any further; those who carried the jampan left me, the camel drivers demanded their *raza*, discharge, and I was all impatience to get away. I sent therefore for the Thanadar to provide me the means of proceeding on my journey, even should he have recourse to compulsory measures, menacing him with the anger of Ranjít Singh, if I found myself necessitated to pass another night in Ráwal Pindi. Happily Ranjít has given European travellers prodigious power over his functionaries, from the governor of a province down to the village justice. Every man of them was obliged to send in a certificate of my satisfaction to the Máha Raja, and for this, if necessary, they would have given large presents. The consequence was visible in my preparations being completed to-day at 12 o'clock. I was in too great haste to wait for the whole party, and therefore left the Munshí behind to look after the baggage, while I myself journeyed on as far as a ruinous Serai, seven kos distant from Ráwal Pindi, where I halted to give the bearers time to join me before night. A good many travellers were already assembled there. Nothing is left of ancient splendour in this serai, except some portions of the outer walls; but in earlier times there were here, as in most other serais, shaded walks in which persons of the lower ranks found shelter, but the smallest of them, which still afforded some trifling protection against the cold, were all occupied. Although there was room enough to spread my tent in the inner court, the wind whistled round it in every direction, and the walls afforded no defence against the weather: the filthiness of the court-yard was disgusting. I therefore preferred occupying my small tent, which made its appearance towards evening, and pitched it before the entrance to the building, where it was screened from the strong north-west wind; while my servants all lodged near me, in the only unoccupied apartment.

The view from this point was very delightful. Before it lay a large Mohammedan mausoleum, surmounted by a lofty cupola, and surrounded on every side by a multitude of other tombs. The square in which they were erected contained also a mosque and an asylum for pilgrims. The large building was already falling to decay; the cupola admitted the light of heaven through many a rent, and the whole structure had a threatening aspect. Surrounded by rocks of remarkable form, some towering one above the other, some standing out singly and dark from the horizon, this funeral monument is the highest point in the vicinity. In the far distance, and over the lofty mountains, above all these objects, rose the snow-capped chain of which the Pir Panjal is the monarch. The rocks are of sandstone; the direction N.W. and S.E., the strata vertical.

From this elevation there is but one solitary mountain discernible in the south-west, the plain of the Panjáb seeming to extend uninterruptedly in that direction. This appearance however is deceptive, for on a nearer examination the surface is found deeply intersected with ravines and water-courses. Before dinner Vigne and I wandered about the neighbourhood, and soon came to a large tank, round which were some fragments of rock. Here we did our best to furnish ourselves with an extra dish, in the shape of some wild fowl, which were swimming about the water very temptingly. But we were unsuccessful, and on our return I found the Munshí had arrived, with information that my baggage had left Ráwal Pindi on the backs of coolies, in default of proper carriage; that he had seen the large tent poles, usually carried by four men, lying down on the road, and half a dozen other packages belonging to me also strewed about, the bearers having, of course, run away. I immediately dispatched people for the packages, but the tent poles were too far off and much too heavy for the men to fetch them this day; the bearers of the Panjáb, like their fellows in Kashmír, being immoveable at any price after nightfall. The Shah had arrived also, and pitched his tent near mine.

As the sun went down, I saw symptoms in the sky which made me anticipate rain, although I hoped that it might prove only a passing shower. As a precautionary measure, however, I had those things most likely to be injured by wet, brought within the small tent where I was lodged. In the evening I visited the Shah, and seeing that his tent was pitched in a piece of low ground, I warned him of the likelihood of rain; but he did not think there would be much, and so left the tent where it was.

Thursday, December 31.—I had erred in my reckoning as to the time when I made sure of reaching Lahor. A violent sirocco came on last night, accompanied by storms of rain; the wind shifted, and my tent now suffered the fiercest attacks of the tempest. I heard the rain pouring down during the night, and when I left my bed after lying awake for hours, everything in my tent was swimming. My clothes were all saturated with water, and my only comfort in putting them on, in this state, arose from the feeling that it was only an anticipation of what they must be very shortly, at all events. I looked out upon a deluge. The whole country had become one interminable swamp, and the things which had been left outside the tent were scarcely distinguishable. A fire to make our breakfast seemed quite out of the question, and some change of situation absolutely requisite; but where were we to find a better? The ruinous old Serai was filled with a motley assemblage of travellers; and though in my capacity of White Lord, I might have turned them all out of their quarters, without the smallest apprehension that they, though many hundreds in number, would think of disputing my right to rob them of their shelter, backed as I should have been by the Munshí and Khan Singh's authority, humanity prevailed with me, to waive any such method of bettering my own situation. Whereupon I sallied forth to look about me, and about a quarter of a mile in the direction of the cemetery, I found out a place where we could remain for a day defended from the weather, the ruins being surrounded by walls, and having several small vaulted niches, which are still in tolerable repair, the destructive fury of the Sikhs having exhausted itself on the larger tombs and the mosque. Into these niches, therefore, I had all my goods conveyed, and selected a corner cell for myself, very like a dungeon of the age of chivalry, without any window. The entrance was narrow, dark, and very hard to find. There I established myself for the day with my carpet, kanát, and a few immediate necessaries; it was so dark that candles were indispensable, but my greatest discomfort arose from the loss of an entire day, or perhaps many days while this rain lasted. In truth, I could not make sure that I might not be detained in this part of India so long as even to miss the steamer which left Bombay for Egypt, and in this case, it was a question not only of days but of months. So little had I thought of these rains, that I had announced to General Ventura my intention of being in Wazírabad on the 4th of January; an additional proof, if any were needed, of the extreme folly of laying down any definite plan for the future, particularly in a country like this, where a man travelling alone on horseback may get on well enough, but when obliged to have a number of people with him, he is dependent on a thousand contingencies.

After making my own arrangements, I sallied out again to look after my companions in misfortune. I found Vigne in bed, with water all about him, and rain pouring in on all sides. I could not help laughing at his philosophy, and with some trouble persuaded him to get up and share my strange lodging. As for the poor Shah, he was sitting amidst his twenty-five attendants, drenched through; he had lost all his energies, and declined even the trouble of moving when I invited him to share my dry prison-house.

And thus passed the last day of a year which I had purposed to spend on the broad sea. On looking back, I confess that more extraordinary to me than even the wondrous scenes of nature, was the great diversity existing in manners and habits among the various people with whom my travels had brought me acquainted. The last day of the year 1834, I passed on my voyage from Manilla to Canton, upon the stormy waters of the Yellow Sea; and during the succeeding twelvemonths, how much had I been allowed to see! China and India; the most extensive empires in Asia, the most beautiful by nature, offering new evidences of the majesty of creation, and of the high refinement of ancient civilization. From China in the East, where the vast ocean is the only boundary of this mighty continent, to China in the West, or Tibet, I travelled in a very wide and devious course. I had visited the flourishing settlement of Singapoor; the Muluccas now declining; the rich island of Penang; Madras, the theatre of many a European contest; Calcutta, the famous city of palaces; the ancient Brahminical retreat of Benares; Allahabad, Oude, Agra, Gwalior, and Delhi, still magnificent in its fallen greatness; the Himálaya, those giants of our earth; the beautiful but melancholy valley, not impossibly the cradle of the human race; finally, I had had a glimpse of Tibet, finishing with a toilsome journey to the ancient Taxila and the modern Atok. The whole year was fraught with events well deserving my remembrance; and though I had at times experienced a deep sensation of loneliness, I had many days to dream of, full of peace, tranquillity, and friendly intercourse; my strength of mind and of body were unimpaired; yet fatigue and occupation generally silenced every half-suppressed wish for more comforts than I could procure.

And thus, also, ended my fortieth year, without a wish to live over again one of its days, or even hours; that year which, beginning with a storm, and ending in a tomb, presented a true image of our life on earth.

Friday, 1st January, 1836.—Floods of rain ushered in the first day of the new year. I was left alone to welcome it; Vigne had gone early to bed, overcome with fatigue. Some future traveller will perhaps inhabit this same little nook, and should curiosity lead him to creep about it, he will wonder whether he has got into the den of a hyena or a wolf, or if serpents ever made it their abode. But when his researches have led him from the narrow entrance to the dark round tower, and the light of his torch discovers to him the murky walls, and his own laboured breathing tells him of the heavy damp air within, he may with difficulty comprehend how it was possible for a European travelling with a large suite of natives, ever to dream of remaining in such a place for two whole days. The unfortunate conjuncture of circumstances, which brought my tent poles into the power of bearers who were pressed into my service without wages, contrary to my express orders; the folly of leaving them without any one to look after them, solves the riddle but too plainly of their flight and throwing down their burden at four miles distance.

The sky cleared in the afternoon, and I desired them instantly to get ready for a move; the old Serai had not proved a very desirable residence for any of us, for there was no bazar for the natives, and no wood procurable; as for the bearers and camel drivers, they had all taken to flight. Luckily, six camels that my Munshí had picked up somewhere in Ráwal Pindi, arrived about noon; very suspiciously answering to the beasts that had been driven away, and wanting drivers into the bargain; I was anxious, if possible, to get on to Mánikyála to-day, to bring all our affairs into a due train once more, and give the natives the opportunity of thoroughly drying themselves; for this short journey we had yet abundant time.

My first visit, on emerging from my cell, was to the Shah, whom I found in a miserable plight, shivering like a patient in an ague fit, while his servants were so completely soaked with the rain, that I looked forward to nothing else than their serious illness. I offered to administer some brandy to them all, but as staunch Mohammedans they would not listen to such a proposal. The Shah was quite amazed at first when he heard of my intention to recommence our journey to-day, but he soon found himself able to follow my example and get ready, and this being done we started, and after a short progress through a flat country, reached the end of our day's march, a grand monument of ancient times, called by the natives Mánikyála Tóp, or Búrj. According to Elphinstone, this Dhagoba * is 72 feet high, and 450 in circumference. While in Ceylon, where these Dhagobas are frequently seen, I took much pains to find some way of admission into them. They are always strongly built, the exterior being in the form of cupola, but there is nothing else but this; the Dhagoba being, in fact, an edifice raised over some relic, a tooth, a lock of hair, &c., considered sacred, in the Buddhist faith. Near it is generally some Vihára or Temple, and in the neighbourhood of this Mánikáyla Dhagoba, I observed, towards the west, the foundation walls built in the form of a large square, all that remained of a former Vihára. Compared with others which I have seen, this Dhagoba is the smallest in proportion to its elevation that I have ever met with, and the drawing in Elphinstone's work does not give any correct idea of its proportions. It is built of Kankar stone, which is the produce of water, and the softest stone known; the base is constructed of coarse sand-stone, and about six or eight feet high, ornamented with pilasters four feet high, and with decorative capitals. These pilasters are six feet apart. Above this, and about fourteen feet higher than the ground, runs a projecting cornice whence the cupola rises. The building was first opened by General Ventura. From the highest point which I reached, a well descends, twelve feet square and eighteen feet deep, but as the work of opening proceeded, this was soon filled up with stones; and another attempt to penetrate by the lower part of the building was found impracticable. He therefore ordered the workmen to begin at the upper part. In a short time, they arrived at the middle of the shaft, where they met large masses of stones; these were broken through, and near the foundation appeared a small vaulted recess containing

* Or Dagop, (*Dhatúgarbha*, Sanscrit), *Dagonpa*, Tibetan; a name given to all buildings in which relics of Buddha are deposited; generally a hair, a tooth, &c. The remains of these edifices are found extensively scattered throughout the Eastern continent and islands of Asia. The term *Tóp* (*Stúpa*, Sanscrit), also signifies a Buddhist edifice of like character.—*Ed.*

a gold cylinder, with some fluid in it, and some Buddhist coins. Mr. James Prinsep has given a description of these in the Asiatic Journal. According to the natives, 500 men worked for a whole month at the opening of this monument.

Whether owing to their increased weight by being wet, or to the slipperiness of the ground, which always distresses these animals, the camels had carried the tents as far as Mánikyála with the utmost difficulty; they were still too damp to be pitched, and I was obliged to look out for a lodging in the wretched village. The Hindú and Sikh have always their temple to resort to, and the Mohammedan his mosque, the first had often been my refuge, the last but seldom, owing to my unwillingness to shock the Mohammedan prejudices, but on the present occasion it happened that the mosque was the only place large enough to hold my bed. I was, therefore, obliged to take possession of it. Mánikyála is ten kos from Ráwal Pindi, and two and a half kos from the Serai.

Saturday, January 2.—I purposed making the journey to Rotás, twenty-five kos, in two days, Tamák being about half-way. But the poor camels had arrived at Mánikyála very much fatigued, and though I expected that the road would be somewhat drier to-day, yet I feared for the success of my plan. Tamák, therefore, was fixed upon for the end of this day's journey, and after waiting at the *Tóp* until my people had all departed, I followed. The first glance at the unfortunate camels, slipping along the ground, and tumbling down with their burdens, while nothing but heavy blows could induce them to rise or move at all, satisfied me that no baggage would reach Tamák that night, and that if I wanted to keep my people along with me, I must shorten the march. Bisentáur was therefore appointed as the night station, about three kos nearer than Tamák, but this new order only reached a small number of the suite.

About half-way to Bisentáur stands a Serai of large dimensions. I have already said that these buildings were erected at certain distances, and served as lodging places for the Moghul Emperors when they travelled from Delhi to Kabúl. They are not always on the modern traveller's route, nor must the reader even suppose, when I speak of a road, that this is always a broad path kept in constant repair; it is, on the contrary, a mere beaten track, usually found with much trouble, altered by every accident of nature, and, in this part of the Panjáb, constantly broken up by the ravines and hurried waters, and compelling the traveller, no longer invited to shelter himself in the Serai, to swerve very far from the original line. I never passed through a country so devoid of any pretension to beauty. The water has ploughed deep furrows in every direction, and probably owing to the summer droughts, the ground is left without cultivation. Our march was so toilsome that I almost despaired of seeing Bisentáur at all this night, the last hour being consumed in labouring through the deep sandy bed of the Káhan, with precipitous banks on either side of us. Bisentáur lies on one of the highest points, but whether of the right or left bank I cannot say, for the now dry river winds in a thousand directions, and I was so entirely exhausted, that it was with difficulty that I climbed the bank which led us to the miserable dirty village, where the only decent house was the Zenana of the Thanadar. He offered to send his wives elsewhere if I would take up my quarters in it, but this I felt bound to decline. It was in vain to think of waiting for my tent, and I was really at a loss where to go, for neither bearers nor servants were there to assist me. The wretched huts were full of vermin, the whole place seemed under water, in the so-called street, the mud was over my feet; and without warm coverings, or cloak, to pass the night in the open air would have been death. At last, I found shelter in the Dharamsála, the house of the Sikh Gurú, who, seeing me seat myself quite worn out at the threshold of one of the huts, invited me in, on the condition that none of my Musselman servants should enter; to this, however, I refused to accede, and the Brahmin, who joined me at the moment, was eminently useful to me, as the Sikhs hold them in great veneration. He told the Gurú that if he put up with the contamination of the unclean Musselman out of affection to me, a Sikh might safely do the same, and the other being reassured by his tone, opened his dwelling to me, which consisted of one apartment, inclosed on three sides, the other left open. I had neither bed nor chair, and was forced to lie on the ground, so weary and heartsick that life itself seemed a burden. Some of the servants arrived at eight in the evening. For the first time since our companionship, I left the care of providing food to Vigne, but neither khansaman nor bawarchi had arrived. Nazim Khan, Ahmed Shah's deputy from Iskardú, prepared for us a dish much eaten at Kabúl, and which they called kubebi. It consisted of mutton cut into small pieces and roasted; Mohammed Shah sent us a mess of *rewash*, rhubarb, the Brahmin baked some chepatís, and when a bottle of Bordeaux was discovered, though I could not touch a morsel, Vigne's hunger was quite satisfied. The night was cold and rainy, and as the bearers, who had the very things I wanted to protect myself against the weather, were still absent, it passed uncomfortably enough with me. The men who had come, pressed me to take whatever warm covering they had, but I could not deprive them of it, and only entreated to be left undisturbed. Trembling with cold, I watched through the greater part of that wearisome night.

Sunday, January 3.—Long before daybreak I was awakened by the chanting of the Gurú; and suffering from severe headache and cough, I wanted to start; but it was no easy matter to rouse up the poor tired creatures, and I felt how much it costs to put one's self in motion. I had not the least idea what had become of the bearers, the camels, or two-thirds of my attendants. The Brahmin fulfilled his duty of presenting a handsome present to the Gurú, on my part, which he acknowledged with the most profound gratitude, in words and gestures, blessing me in God's name, and wishing me a happy journey. We were passing through the filthy streets, when the confidential servant of the Shah met us with the news that his master was very ill. I reproached myself for having quite forgotten him, since it was to be expected that the cold and damp together would be attended with some injurious consequences to his health. I now dismounted quickly, and went on to see how he really was. I found him very feverish; and after giving him my usual prescription—calomel, advised him to wrap himself well up in his arm-chair, and keep as much warmth in him as possible, until we reached Makreli, eight kos from hence, which place I had fixed on as the station for the night. As soon as we were finally out of Bisentáur, we entered a country entirely composed of hills, running for a long time in every possible direction; and as if to put a negative at once on the Gurú's friendly wishes, a storm came rolling onwards from the south-east, the direction we were taking, and whence, for the last two days, we had heard occasional claps of loud thunder resounding. The hail storm now came on in good earnest, accompanied by repeated and terrific peals, which reverberating from hill to hill, made the noise quite deafening. Not a tree was visible, and my sedan being uncovered, I was wetted to the very skin. The bearers ran as fast as they could to a building at some distance, where the coolies had already taken refuge; but I did not allow them to remain there long, for the place was too small to admit my jampan, and I was consequently exposed all the time to the incessant rain. Our progress now became truly difficult, for the way was so slippery, that the bearers could scarcely keep on their feet; the ravines were all filled with water, foaming and tearing along, and there was not a spot of level ground. It may be guessed that we were by no means in a state to be envied, nor did the piercing wind and rain improve my cold or cough. At length, the road became so bad, that I was obliged to get out and walk. The bearers had chosen to take a bye-way which shortened the distance by three kos, but which was only practicable for pedestrians and horses without any burden, and does not lead by Tamák. Before we reached this place, it was necessary to descend into the bed of the Káhan; and after this we found ourselves more than once in the midst of some swollen mountain torrent; and I was constantly slipping down the deep and insecure paths which skirted the banks. The formation of these is sandstone, of a light grey, very brittle, covered with a red ferruginous earth; the stratum of the sandstone is perpendicular; and on the summit of the hills insulated rocks projected in the most remarkable shapes, the intervening spaces being filled up with the earth above alluded to, which is frequently indurated to stone, and covered with another surface four or five inches thick. Pieces of chalcedony, measuring a quarter of an inch in thickness, are embedded in it; quartz in small crystals, and a whitish substance, unknown to me, is also found in the sandstone. Before we arrived at Makreli, we entered the bed of the Káhan, where the red, yellow, and grey formations towering above each other in masses, were most remarkable. The place is miserable, and very small. I was surprised to see the people and baggage coming in during the evening, but the poor camels were not to be driven so fast. I slept in my little tent, which they pitched in the Mohammedan cemetery, although it was not yet quite dry. For the first time for several days I enjoyed the genial warmth of a fire. Towards evening the Shah arrived: he was much better than when we parted, at least so he assured me; but I think his politeness to his physician carried him a little too far, for he still had a good deal of fever.

Monday, January 4.—I feel as if I ought to be nearer home; for my late exposure to bad weather has given me such a catarrh as I never had before, and my health is evidently affected. A fine sunshiny morning succeeded the stormy weather of yesterday; and before starting, I sent to inquire after my patient, who came to thank me in person, and to assure me that he was quite cured. I was as much astonished as many other doctors are occasionally at the success of their own prescriptions, though I had not quite so many scruples in testifying my surprise.

Our road, in point of hillocks and ravines, was little better than that of yesterday. We had gone about three kos, when we fell in with two Sikh battalions marching towards Pesháwar, fine well dressed men, with long blue coats and turbans. They were irregular troops, and formed no part of the French legion. They marched in good order, and were followed by a body of camp-followers with their tents, also in close column; but I did not think it at all agreeable nevertheless, to be stopped by half a hundred camels in this narrow pass, where it was quite impossible to get out of their way. It was really a pitiable thing to watch these poor beasts trembling with fatigue, toiling up the steep way with their heavy burdens, which threatened every instant to overset them. About a dozen women followed the troops, and one group, consisting of a little woman riding a small pony, with a young girl in front, and a taller one behind her, struck me as quite original. The fort of Rotás, one of the most extensive in the north of India, is visible from a high point at four kos' distance, and encircles, as it were, an isolated hill between 200 and 300 feet high. It is separated into two by a deep cleft in the rock. The fort has an imposing appearance at the end of a fruitful plain, one of the first seen in this part of the Panjáb, with the further advantage of being able to protect the harvest; and it is bathed by the waters of the Káhan, which winds round Bisentáur and Makreli; that is, when it has any water. The Mohammedans have sunk deep wells to supply the plain during the summer season, when the river is always dry; one of these, about two kos on this side of Rotás, is really an immense work. The fortress has long been abandoned as too extensive, and is now all but in ruins, one large portion of the walls having fallen into the depths below. The house of a fakír near the river, was fixed on as my resting-place, but on one side it lay entirely exposed to the wind, which at this season is piercingly cold throughout the Panjáb; I wished, moreover, to visit the fortress, and therefore desired to be conducted to the lodging which Khan Singh told me had been got ready for my accommodation within it. The walls rise in the most singular forms above the river; the entrance gate, 200 feet high, seems to be quite lifted up in the air, so gigantic are its proportions. Other divisions of these immense works, are on a scale equally vast. There are but three gates in the whole fortress: two are almost concealed from view by the ravines and steep eminences close to them. The way to the third is more open towards the river, but still well defended by large towers, which protect the chief entrance, formed by two gates, one within the other. On the second, which is reached by a winding path 100 or 130 feet higher than the first, is an Arabic inscription, which makes known the year of the Hejira, and that of the builder, Shír Shah Lodi Patán, who for five years, until his death in 1545, sat on the defeated Humáyun's throne of Delhi. When Humáyun fled to Afghanistan and Persia, in order to levy forces to recover his kingdom, Shír Shah raised this formidable obstacle in his way. The interior is highly interesting. The ruins of buildings are scattered in every direction. The angular pillars yet standing; the one window in each direction, still traced in the solitary fragment of the ruined palace, struck me forcibly. It seemed unaccountable how it could have survived the ravages which have laid all waste beside it.

But northern India is more fortunate in this respect than the southern parts, where nature soon destroys the most substantial edifices. Here the vegetation is more feeble, and they have not the Ficus religiosa in such luxuriance, as in the more tropical regions, where it frequently takes root in the crevices of the walls. I did, indeed, see one tree of this species growing in Rotás, at the door of a fakír, near the bridge which leads over the ravine to the interior of the town, but this was among the earliest symptoms of my approach to India, and during the cold months of winter the tree is always sickly. The portion of wall above noticed, now standing has been rendered really habitable. Where the deep chasm has parted the mountain in two, a gate and bridge have been erected, which connect the two divisions of the fortress; and on the southern side of the gate a large Indian fig has flourished nearly long enough to overshadow the whole of the entrance in the most picturesque manner. Here the Jemidar deputed by General Ventura to provide for me, had prepared a very convenient little dwelling, and a stock of wood for our use; a necessary article which it occasioned us considerable time and trouble to procure at every station. As I was about stepping in, I was saluted by a puff of smoke, and presently saw three dirty girls squatting round the fire, and warming some bread by it. The poor Thanadar, who was expecting a great many eulogiums on the excellent state of the house, was struck dumb on seeing the children, who had taken the liberty of appropriating to their own use both the wood and the house, calculating that I should not make my appearance for some days to come. He gave the first who came within his reach a slap, which sent her squalling away in a moment, but the others who echoed her screams, did not attempt to move, or to desist from their occupation, in spite of all I could say or do. I really could not help laughing at their horrid noises, and this seemed to have more effect than scolding, for as soon as their bread was done to their liking, they took themselves off.

According to the Thanadar, the detached building which I had been observing with so much interest, is called the palace; Raja Mehan Singh ka Mahál; the people called it Máli Táj or Máli Burj, the Gardener's Tower, and ascribe its construction to Mehán Singh, Shír

Shah's wazír. The Thanadar told me that the fortress, as it now stands, was built in three years, and cost 150 lakhs of rupees. I could believe the last account more easily than the first; but as Shír Shah did not occupy the throne of India more than five years, meeting his death at Kalingarh by the bursting of a bomb from one of his own guns, which rebounded from the walls of the fortress, it is not probable the construction of this great work could have taken a much longer time. It was not until the reign of the third prince in succession to Shír Shah that Humáyun led an army into India to reconquer the throne of his father. The governor of this fortress, Tatái Khan, evacuated it without striking a blow, and gave Hamáyun a good opportunity of seeing to advantage what his enemies had done for him. This fortress has never been well defended. We read in Ferishta's *History of India*, that there was at Rotás an impregnable fortress four centuries before the Christian era, a proof of the high antiquity of the place.

This day General Ventura sent me two packages, one containing some excellent claret, the other some beer, a kindness which I felt most gratefully, and which I quickly acknowledged; for I had caught a severe cold in the late hail-storm, and my poor Brahmin was worse than myself. For his fever I recommended a strong dose of calomel, and I got to his lodging to see him, but no further; for I had no strength left me. In the room where I had to sleep there was no window, and the walls were blackened with smoke, so that as I looked at the bed, and the lights burning near it, the whole had a most funereal aspect.

Tuesday, January 5.—I was very glad when the night was fairly gone. In the morning several sick persons came to ask my advice and aid as usual; among these were two sepoys belonging to the corps we had met yesterday on their march. One who was borne along by two comrades was past all human help, and as my store of medicines was exhausted, I could do little or nothing for any of them, however compassionately disposed towards them. During my journey to Kashmír I was so frequently called upon to act the part of a physician, that I had abundant opportunity of observing the benefits arising from the use of calomel, and in this country I should consider it the only medicine of any service. We passed through a variety of climates in our long marches; sometimes we travelled in companies of some hundreds of persons together; and scarcely a day passed without one or more cases of sickness, and yet, with two solitary exceptions, (where jaundice had preceded the attack of fever,) none of them lasted more than a single day, nor did I lose so much as one of my followers during the whole five months of my travels, neither was I obliged to leave any of them behind me.

The whole company now started for Wazírabad, where a vehicle and four horses, sent by Ventura, awaited my arrival. The distance is thirty-one kos, and we learnt from Ranjít Singh's guides that it was not an easy matter to divide the journey; for, except near the Jelam, there was no house to be met with in those parts, and if I had my tent pitched, it would be necessary to make very short marches. Every six kos there had been serais, and to these Khan Singh proposed to direct me, dividing the journey into five days. To this, however, I objected, determining to put up with any inconvenience rather than thus linger by the way; and for the same reason I declined to take the other but longer route by Jalálpoor, though the country was much better peopled.

I was induced afterwards to let Khan Singh do as he pleased to-day; for I anticipated great delay at the Jelam. He assured me that we could only march six kos. Our first essay brought us into a deep ravine, ending in the bed of the Káhan, through the heavy sand of which we struggled for some considerable distance. After marching four miles, we turned our backs on the high lands, and the plain of India lay stretched before us, without the faintest perceptible swelling in that broad and interminable vista; while behind us lay the grand mountains of Kashmír.

The lofty passes of the Tose Máídán and Pir Panjal glistened and towered upward, like so many giant forms, their snowy mantles contrasting with the dark mountains in the vicinity of the plain. While the eye of the weary traveller rests with satisfaction on this plain, the surface seeming to threaten no further impediment to his onward course, he glances with some surprise in the direction he has just been following, and sees none of those obstacles which made the latter part of his journey so tedious. Scarcely an eminence diversifies the uniformity of the general surface. The salt hills, which occupy much of the distance between this and the Atok, are here lost to the eye towards the south-west, the place where the mineral is found in the greatest abundance. Dádan Pindi Khan is about six kos distant, the natives saying that no salt is found further east. The last hilly ground in this direction is a detached group south-west of Rotás, which is not visible for any distance on the other side of the Jelam.

The town called Jelam is five kos from Rotás, and there we quitted the Doab-i-Sindi Sagur, which lies between the rivers Atok and Jelam, and is here about ninety kos, or from 135 to 140 miles in breadth: a few words on this country in its earlier days before I leave it. Arrian and Strabo call the region between these two rivers,—Taxila, the chief town of which bore the same name. This capital might have been where Ráwal Pindi now stands, in a fruitful plain, no other town being met with further east until we come to Rotás, nor further west until we reach the plain of Atok. Mánikyála, with its vast ruins, which will be more fully dwelt on elsewhere, was fixed on by Burnes as the site of Taxila, but this lies in a poorly watered and unproductive country; whereas the Sawan, which flows by Ráwal Pindi, has some water, even in the driest season. After all, it is not very easy to decide where the course of a river may have been two thousand years ago, in a country where everything shows such amazing changes to have taken place in the soil. But the variety of ruins found in the neighbourhood of Ráwal Pindi is an evidence of the former existence of some large city in its vicinity. In the time of Alexander, Taxiles was the sovereign of Taxila, and when the conqueror passed the Indus, he sent an embassy consisting of 700 persons, all horsemen, to meet him, and attend him to his city, which he surrendered at once, Alexander loading this peaceloving Hindú monarch with presents and favours. Above Taxila in the mountains, Arrian places the kingdom of Abisarus, but whether this stretched to Kashmír we know not. From the accounts given us of Alexander's march, we should believe that he penetrated further into the mountains called

Method of crossing Rivers in the Panjab on inflated Skins.

Baron Hugel's Travels, page 247.

Emoda, since we read that, having passed the Jelam, he had the trees of the pine forests cut down to supply the river with shipping: these forests never extended to the plains. His fleet was composed, in part of the vessels which he had transported from the Indus, in part of those ships built at that city which he founded on either side of the Hydaspes or Jelam, and called Bucephalia, after his horse, and Náikía (victory), from his victory over Porus. Burnes believed Jalálpoor to be the most probable site of these cities.

At least, there is no doubt of one fact, that when Alexander was in this country of Taxila, the people belonged neither to the Brahminical nor to the Buddhist faith; for the priests ate at his table, and did not burn their dead, giving them to be devoured by vultures: who would not at once decide from this to what religious community they belonged? I purpose resuming the subject when I have traversed the whole country of Alexander's conquest.

Jelam is a town of some importance, and the streets are clean, though narrow. At the entrance stands a group of trees and a fakír's dwelling. The whole reminded me of the Delta of the Nile, the Phœnix farinosa, which grows as tall here as the date palms, and the acacias, being of the same species as in Egypt. The boiling point was 21i ($209\frac{4}{3}$ = 1620 feet above the level of the sea). The inhabitants met me in a body, with an invitation to take up my abode there for the night, while the shopkeepers requested that I would take every thing that I wanted, without thinking of any payment. But for no consideration would I have prolonged my stay in the Panjáb for a single day longer than was necessary.

Twenty large boats, excellently built and managed, convey travellers gratis across the river. This river is much wider than the Atok by its town of the same name, but less deep and rapid. The right bank is rather high, the left is flat, and in the rainy season, no doubt, the water overflows it to a considerable extent. One kos from the Jelam lies the ruinous Serai called Nárangabad, the outer walls of which are yet standing, and within them a population of filthy people in still filthier huts. I could not find any place to put up, and though the Gurú of the Dharamsála was ready to receive me, his house was so small, that there was no standing room for my bed. I had therefore to choose, my tent being too wet to be put up, whether I would sleep in the open air, or on the ground. On account of the season I preferred the latter; but the loss of my tent entailed on me so much inconvenience, that I ordered the people, even at the risk of tearing it, to spread it out somewhere, that it might dry the sooner.

The Gurú and his wife reminded me of Philemon and Baucis. They could not have numbered much less than two hundred years between them, and their feebleness prevented either of them from standing on their feet. I confess that I envied the man, not the length of life, for a long life is not always a happy one, but that, having witnessed the humiliation of his countrymen, he now lived to see them amply revenged.

The authorities of Jelam came to request that they might be allowed to supply my people with everything needful, to which I most willingly agreed, well assured that there was nothing to be purchased for any money in the Serai.

Wednesday, January 6.—Having risen from my comfortless sleeping place, and reached the open square, where I had ordered my tent to be spread out, the first thing I saw was my unfortunate tent lying on the ground, and the Kaláshis all fast asleep. It was evident that their laziness had lost me another night's rest, besides increasing the chances that the tent would be entirely spoiled; and more vexed at their neglect of my orders than I ought to have been in reason, I desired them instantly to get up, pitch the tent properly in my presence, and then wait until the heat of the sun had thoroughly dried it, after which they were to pack it properly and follow me. This naturally caused so much delay that I knew I must not expect to be able to sleep under it this night; but it was, at all events, quite useless to me while so wet. Besides, I did not think it was likely that I should have any occasion to pitch the tents again after to-night, and felt anxious to take a farewell look at them as companions with whom I had passed many solitary hours.

Although Khawás Khan is not more than twelve miles, we had a long march, and some ravines which I had not at all expected. The country is indifferently cultivated, but it seems to support a vast number of horned cattle. The flocks of sheep and goats also were numerous, the last growing to an enormous size. We can now perfectly understand a remark of Ctesias, that the Indian goats are as large as asses, an assertion which is quite correct, taken in the sense of Strabo, who by the term India means the Panjáb. The Serai Khawás Khan, which we did not reach till nightfall, was surrounded by high walls smeared with *upla*, or cow dung, which also is the only fuel used by the natives. The town on the plain is built in the form of a fort. It is populous, but has a singular appearance, all the walls and roofs of the houses being covered with upla drying in the sun: stores of the same are also heaped up in the open square in large quantities.

The only resting-place to be found, was an open mosque; and with much difficulty I had obtained a supply of fuel, which I knew would be indispensable during the long cold night. For a rupee each, I had also hired two men to keep it alive while I slept. The cold, however, soon awoke me; nor was I much surprised to find the fire all but out, and the men fast asleep. This would not have happened had they been Hindús. I made them get up, went with them to the nearest houses in search of more wood, got a small supply, and again kindled a fire, by which I remained sitting all the rest of the night, finding it impossible to keep myself warm.

Thursday, January 7.—From Serai Khawás Khan to Wazírabad is twelve kos, through an open, level country, with a fertile though little cultivated soil. Gujrat, a town inclosed by mud walls, is about half way, and is a place of importance to the family of Ranjít Singh. His father, Mahá Singh, whose fortune it was to lay the foundation of that power, which his son afterwards extended over the whole Panjáb, was, in his twenty-seventh year, engaged in an attempt to gain possession of this Gujrat, being at the time in the neighbouring and opulent city of Sohdera. Ranjít Singh possessed himself of it in a manner which I shall refer to elsewhere, but certainly not much to the increase of his honour. Indeed, it was always the policy of this wily chief to press his demand on those who had no power to resist his claims; the helpless, the orphan, and the widow, have ever been the objects he has more peculiarly oppressed.

Between the Jelam and Chenáb, is the Jinhat Doáb, twenty-six kos broad in the direction I took across it. The Chenáb is shallow and rather sluggish, but nowhere fordable; the low bank is no obstacle to its overflowing, and at present it is a good half mile broad, though the waters are not at their usual level. From the left bank it is about an hour's march to Wazírabad; and shortly before our arrival at that place, the authorities made their appearance, with a party of horse sent by Ranjít Singh, and with a carriage and four, for which I was indebted to the kindness of General Ventura. I felt infinitely happy to think that I was at the end of a tedious journey, which requires at this season more strength than I could boast; and had I halted even for one day, so excited was my nervous system, that I doubt not I should have been quite laid up. It seemed like a dream when I found myself really seated in this vehicle, and drawn by four horses to Wazírabad. There the Mahá Raja has built a palace in the midst of a lovely garden, which is a singular edifice, both in its exterior form and its internal decorations. It has two stories, and in the centre is a sort of tower which divides the wings, while the outside walls, as well as the apartments within, are adorned with fresco paintings illustrative of the religion of the Sikhs. Among them are the portraits of the ten Gurús from Nának the first to Govind the last, the size of life; the chief painter of Ranjít's court is certainly not a Raphael. I preferred taking up my quarters for the night in a small pavilion, containing one large and four small rooms, which appeared to me more comfortable than the stately palace. We had to wait for our dinner a long while, for the bearers, who were far in the rear, had all the cooking apparatus and provisions with them. In truth, the distance was too great for them; henceforward, as I had little need of their services, they travelled as leisurely as they pleased.

Avitable, an officer high in Ranjít Singh's favour, and now commanding in Peshávar under Shír Singh, was for some time Governor of Wazírabad; while he resided here he almost rebuilt the town in the

European style, and pulled down the old bazar, making the streets wide enough to admit a carriage and four horses, to the astonishment of the natives, the streets being so excessively narrow in most Indian towns, that a pedestrian can hardly force his way through the bazar. The people are enraptured with the present beauty of the bazar of Wazírabad, and its charms were boastingly represented to me long before I saw it.

Friday, January 8.—I was so apprehensive of coming clouds, that yesterday I took the direction of the mountains with the magnetic needle, for the proper completion of my map. There is no place on the plain whence the form and position of the mountains can be so well ascertained as this; the snow which covered a large portion of them, rendered the task of fixing their relative heights much easier; this, together with my knowledge of the distances between each of the most prominent, combined to make the present a very interesting attempt. My fears concerning the weather proved groundless, the mountains standing forth in all their majesty to-day, though not appearing to the eye so towering as by the twilight of last evening. The prospect from the terrace round the pavilion is a very lovely one. Below lies a soft meadow, covered with the verdant green of the early year; the Chenáb winds along the plain to an immense distance, bathing the feet of the mountain chain, which, with the gentle undulations of the nearest ridge, softened by distance, now forms the misty limits of the plain. From these, the eye is attracted to the mountains rising high behind each other, covered with snow, and seemingly very much nearer than in reality. The plain, without tree or village on that side, stretches out to an interminable extent, contrasting very powerfully with the diversity of form so remarkable in these mountains. I could plainly recognise the double pyramid called Mer and Ser, which is further off than the valley of Kashmír, and could even discern by the distinction of colour, that in that region no snow had fallen very recently.

I had determined on taking only a small number of attendants to Lahor, and sending on the greater part direct to Lúdiana; for at Wazírabad the road branches off to both places, the way to Lúdiana by Lahor being one-third longer than the direct road. This plan required a division of the baggage, a most disagreeable occupation for the whole morning. Indian servants are utterly useless, except as machines; literally obeying their master's orders, without exercising a particle of their own intellect *. I therefore imposed on myself the penance of packing those objects which had cost me much money and trouble, and which their negligence might have entirely spoiled.

The servants having taken their departure at eleven o'clock, I strolled, for the last time, ere I went my way, into the grounds which surround the pavilion; and after my last month's experience of a wild and uncultivated country, I cannot express the delight I felt at seeing this Indian garden, with its regular little flower-beds and fountains. There is something very tranquillizing in these scenes, where the desire of embellishing life is displayed so tastefully; whereas the love for the darker and more terrible in nature, whether occupied by the beasts of the forest, or men scarcely less savage, is one of those unreasonable fancies indulged mostly by persons who have never experienced the dreariness of regions unimproved by industry and civilization. When one gazes from some eminence on such a country, and beholds nothing but forests, unrelieved by field or human habitation, it is then only that a correct idea can be formed of an Indian wilderness. It may be very pleasant to dream of wild countries and simple people, in a well-furnished house or a beautiful garden, surrounded by pleasures, and comforts, and friends: but the reality is very different. For myself, who have seen enough of solitude, sublimity, and the more terrific beauties of nature, I admit that the lot of a European labourer seems to me

* Perhaps there is no more valuable trait in the character of the Hindú servants, than that of implicit obedience. This is just what a good servant should do —simply and unhesitatingly obey. It would be well for European, for English society especially, if such were the *failing of our servants.* A long residence among the people of the East, and a thorough and most intimate acquaintance with their character, led me, as indeed it has led all those who have been similarly circumstanced, to appreciate the forbearance, fidelity, laborious zeal, and good-will with which our Indian domestics and all classes serve those who employ them. They have their failings, it is true, but their good qualities, irrespective of their superstition, will bear comparison with those of any of the most civilized nations in the world.—*Ed.*

more enviable than that of the greatest among Indian princes; and a small garden laid out and ornamented by the owner's taste, more charming than the gigantic scenery of the Himálaya, or the finest view in Ceylon. Perhaps, nevertheless, I may think otherwise, after enjoying for some time the safety and peace to be found in the every-day life of Europe.

In the neighbourhood of Kashmír I had found the Linum trigynum in the ravines where waters were flowing; in this garden the same plant grew as a beautiful shrub four or five feet high, of a spherical form, and covered with a profusion of flowers.

We soon get used to luxury; and in this delightful English carriage I could fancy myself, if not in Europe, at least very near it, and forget that I had ever travelled by a less comfortable conveyance. The distance to Guseráoli is reckoned twelve kos, about twenty miles: the country is poorly cultivated. This is one of the possessions of Hari Singh Nalwa, commander-in-chief of all the Mahá Raja's troops, the French legion alone excepted. Originally it was the property of Ranjít's family, which can be traced no further back than to his grandfather, Charat Singh, the descendant of a common trooper, or Dharwárí. Hari Singh Nalwa has a palace and garden in Guseráoli, which are protected by a mud fort. As we drew near the town, a troop of horse was deputed to escort me; and presently the Díwan rode up, mounted on an elephant. The splendour of the rooms in the palace did not excite my admiration nearly so much as the garden, which was the most beautiful and best kept I had seen in India. The trees were loaded with oranges, of the same kind known in China as Mandarin oranges, but much larger and finer, here called the Santreh orange*; Hari Singh has

* This orange is probably the Cintra orange of Portugal, introduced by the monks, with many other plants, now extensively cultivated, and to which India is indebted for its revenues. Among others may be instanced the tobacco, and various kinds of grain, cotton, maize, onions, and sugar-cane. On the mountains of Aboo, at the extremity of the Arawalli range, at an elevation of 4700 feet, (lat. 25°), I have gathered several varieties of the wild orange, one of which approaches very much in character, size, and external form, to the Cintra or San-

also transported the plane-tree from Kashmír, which seems to flourish exceedingly well in its new locality. An odour almost overwhelming ascended from the jonquils, which were in immense abundance, and of an incredibly large size. Nothing, in fact, could be more carefully adorned with lovely flowers and plants of various kinds, than this garden, which evidently formed one of the chief delights, and sometimes the occupation of its owner: it reminded me of my own at home. As I approached the terrace, where I saw luxurious carpets spread, Hari Singh came to meet me, with a present, consisting of twenty-five plates of sweetmeats, and a dozen baskets of fruit, &c. I tasted some of the former, and found them very good. He then conducted me over the palace, every room of which was hung and covered with the richest carpets of Kashmír and Kabúl, a sight promising comfort and repose, and most inviting in this cool season. When I mentioned the coldness of the last few days, he immediately ordered two portable stoves to be taken to my apartments. Hari Singh's manner and conversation are very frank and affable; and having acquainted myself beforehand with the history of this most distinguished member of Ranjít's court, I surprised him by my knowledge whence he had gained the appellation of Nalwa, and of his having cloven the head of a tiger who had already seized him as its prey. He told the Díwan to bring some drawings, and gave me his portrait, in the act of killing the beast. Hari Singh Nalwa was the person sent by Ranjít to invite Lord

---

tra, and, what is most unusual in the wild state, the fruit was very pulpy; but sour, and in taste coming nearer to the Seville orange. From one bough I gathered nearly two hundred oranges. The trees, which grew out of the clefts of the rocks, were loaded to excess with fruit, in March and April. On the Nilgiri mountains I gathered and described seven perfectly distinct varieties, growing in and near the beautiful dell called the Orange Valley, five miles from Dimhatti. Many persons have concluded that the wild peaches and oranges, have originated in some seeds casually thrown down, or brought hither by birds; but if so, how could they account for the numerous kinds of wild citron, lime, lemon, and orange, found throughout the forests and mountains of Malabar, and other localities in Nipal and Eastern India. The graft of the Portuguese, Spanish, and Chinese fruit on the Indian species, has contributed to the improvement, as in fact the finest Italian fruit is produced from grafts on the bitter wild species.—*Ed.*

William Bentinck to confer with the Mahá Raja at Simla; and as I happened to know most of the persons he had met there, our conversation was very different from the majority of such interviews in India, and really consisted of a due exchange of ideas, and of references to events which had actually taken place. His questions proved him to have thought and reasoned justly: he is well informed on the statistics of many of the European States, and on the policy of the East India Company, and, what is very rare among the Sikhs, he can both read and write the Persian language.

As my stores had not arrived at Guseráoli, I was very glad to accept Hari Singh's offer of providing us with a dinner, which both Vigne and myself dispatched with an excellent appetite.

Saturday, January 9.—The warmth of the rooms procured me the great comfort of rest last night, and for the first time for a very long period, I would willingly have indulged myself with more sleep. While the carriage was being packed, I strolled out into a part of the garden which I had not yet visited, and wondered at the variety of little buildings scattered about it; one of these, called San Padre, is in the form of a square with one side open, and a fountain in the middle, which falls into a broad thick sheet of water. In the three walls I observed several niches made for lamps.

I wished to take leave of Hari Singh, and thank him for his kind reception of us; and on inquiring for him, was conducted to the terrace, where he was seated in the sun, having caught a cold and slight fever. He was able, notwithstanding, to keep up a very lively conversation, and put a variety of questions. He had all my answers taken down on paper. On my departure, he presented me with a beautiful Khilat, accepting in return some trifles as a remembrance of me. He was pleased greatly to magnify their value. Our station for to-night was only six kos from Guseráoli; I had therefore time enough to see the garden and house which was formerly the residence of Ranjít Singh, but it contains nothing remarkable; except a small building erected over the spot, where the remains of his father Mahá Singh were burnt, and another over the ashes of his mother.

Not far from Guseráoli, I was met by Júni Lál, the same Brahmin from Delhi who had accompanied Burnes, and was now sent to me by the Mahá Raja; two elephants, with rich housings and silver howdahs, and thirty men on horseback, attended him. On my approach, they saluted me with military honours, and two trumpeters struck up, "God save the king." The large tent of General Ventura was pitched at a small place called Kámúki. It was a singular-looking Bechoba, (a tent fixed without tent-poles,) which is peculiar to the Panjáb. The servants and baggage all arrived in due time, and we got our dinner before nightfall, which had not been the case very frequently of late.

Sunday, January 10.—The country still remains but poorly cultivated. To-day we had a short march of seven or eight kos to Nángel, where another tent belonging to this General was pitched: this had three separate divisions. We had for several miles enjoyed the view of the lofty mountain chain, and behind the snowy range and the Baldewa, at an immense distance, the Mer and Ser were seen proudly rising.

I can hardly describe how delightful the present mode of travelling seemed to me. Everything appeared to go on with so little trouble, the only drawback being, that I did not come into contact so frequently with the natives, nor learn so much about the country through which I was passing. My present experience taught me how it happens that so few Englishmen know any thing of the manners or customs of that part of India which they have perhaps travelled over the best part of their lives. The truth is, they move from place to place, without giving themselves any concern, and generally by night, unlearning whatever correct ideas they may have brought out with them from their own country respecting India, and in their solitary tents kill time, which with them passes so slowly, by inventing sundry theories, which a just examination of things as they are, would speedily dispel from their minds *.

---

* This is a most erroneous opinion. The intelligence, attention to every thing that passes, the acquaintance that the officers of the army, and indeed a very great many even of the humbler grades of the soldiery possess, of the countries, resources, and people they come in contact with, is far greater than that of any other body of men of like rank and pursuits elsewhere; and that because each individual is thrown upon his own intellectual resources and common sense; but they have not those

The arrival of the Brahmin Júni Lál had cured Thákúr-Das of all his indisposition, and while some of the officers took possession of one elephant, the two new friends occupied the howdah of the second. I proceeded meanwhile at a rapid pace, escorted by the party of horsemen, having taken leave of the Shah at Wazírabad until we should meet at Lahor. He had entreated to be allowed to live with me in that city, but as I did not myself know where I should be on my arrival, it was settled that he should at all events see me often while there. I had determined to do all I could for him in Lahor, but I did not like to promise anything.

Monday, January 11.—This morning I received a letter from General Ventura, telling me that he had the Mahá Raja's orders to come and give me the meeting. It was the wish of Ranjít, that I should halt at Shah Dera, the celebrated mausoleum of Jehánghír, where the General was to announce my arrival to Khalifa Sahib, the marshal of the court, who would forthwith receive me; and I was likewise to remain a day at Shah Dera, that everything might be prepared for my reception in Lahor. Shah Dera is but three miles from that city, on the right bank of the Rávi. I replied to this note directly, that nothing was likely to prevent me from reaching Shah Dera at twelve o'clock, and that he could hardly err in announcing my arrival at that town without waiting for me to address him again. The expectation of residing in Ventura's house while at Lahor, gave me more pleasure than any honour the Mahá Raja was likely to pay me.

---

advantages of carrying out, or studying any subject, that every man can freely command in Europe. With few scientific or literary institutions, with few appliances for investigation, with few experienced master-minds to associate or compare notes with, they do nevertheless frequently make great and most important observations; and what they want in taste or learning, is amply made up by honesty and originality. The civil service was never surpassed for all the high qualities of an effective executive body by that of any state. One and all labouring under the heavy disadvantages, in some respects, of coming out to India when very young; and in point of fact, before the mind is perfectly formed, all the after-work, therefore, is self-teaching, or dear-bought experience—a severe but excellent school.—*Ed.*

The nearer one approaches the Rávi, the more desolate and uncultivated is the country about it. The distance from Nangel to Shah Dera, which lies somewhat to the left of the great road to Lahor, is not more than eight kos, but we arrived before twelve o'clock, though the Basanta, a small river, which was very deep, and had no bridge across it, detained us for some time. Indeed, I was forced to betake myself to the back of an elephant, and the carriage was brought across with a great deal of difficulty. I was surprised to see with what ingenuity the Indians surmounted it, and particularly as they were not at all accustomed to the sort of work now required at their hands.

Shah Dera is a splendid ruin, its beauty consisting not so much in the plan or arrangement of the building, as in the details. Marbles and precious stones were there in profusion. The chief building, placed in a fine garden, forms a square with a beautiful minaret at each corner; these are covered with pietra dura, and appear from a distance as though painted with a variety of colours; they should be seen very near, for the colours have a very poor effect when viewed from any point distant enough to embrace a proper view of the gigantic edifice itself. The ground floor consists of an arcade, raised on several steps, and a lofty terrace, whence, towards the west, the highly ornamented entrance leads to the small vaulted chamber, the tomb of Jehánghír, which is very similar to that in the Táj Mahál at Agra. The light falls on it from above.

There is nothing of the same kind in India more elegant, than the terrace which runs round the roof of the building, formed entirely of pietra dura, and having an open balustrade of marble. I ascended one of the minarets, to gain a view of the long-desired Lahor, which has a goodly appearance from this distance, with its high walls and stately minarets and houses. In the foreground, are the buildings belonging to Shah Dera, which extend down to the Rávi; then comes the river; next, a long line of fields, intermixed with groups of trees, now clad in their fresh livery of spring; beyond these are the handsome edifices built by Jehánghír in Lahor. I had hardly time to gaze on all these attractive objects, when a cloud of dust rolled onwards from the river, concealing for a time a party of horsemen and bearers, the deputation sent by Ranjít Singh to welcome me.

Fakír Khalifa Sahib was accompanied by the commander of the forces in Lahor, and in the name of the Mahá Raja, addressed me in a speech full of the flowers of rhetoric, assuring me that he had made daily inquiries where I was, and had waited for me with the utmost impatience; that now I was in my own country and had only to command; the Mahá Raja desiring that my residence might be made as agreeable to me as possible. After this, Mr. Vigne and I, with the commandant and Khalifa Sahib, entered the general's carriage; the ferry over the Rávi is about a mile beyond Shah Dera, and even in this dry season, there is now in many places not less than eighteen feet of water. On the shore is a large garden made by the Moghul Emperor Dílkusha, with buildings on both sides of the river; the waters have long destroyed everything that stood on the left bank, and carried the massy walls into its soft bed. One side of the great square surrounding the monument at Shah Dera, has met with the same fate, and here the right bank is giving way before the river in a similar manner.

The approach to Lahor by this road is very striking. The fortress repaired by Ranjít Singh, and garrisoned by regular cavalry, is in excellent repair; its great extent notwithstanding, would utterly preclude its defence against the assaults of regular artillery. It was with the most pleasurable feelings that I contemplated meeting General Ventura in his own residence, for his continual attentions to me since I had entered the Panjáb, made me consider him as an old friend. I was heartily tired of solitude, and longed moreover for a few days' rest in a house, and the company of a European host. He met me in the tent which forms the entrance to his beautiful garden, and though we had never seen each other before, we shook hands most cordially, and I attempted to convey all my thanks for his kindness, and to assure him that the pleasure of making his acquaintance, made me less averse to the idea that I should trespass on his hospitality for some days to come. He replied most obligingly that the Mahá Raja expected me to remain at least one month in Lahor; but I had already resolved to limit my stay there to four days, on account of my desire not on any account to miss the steamer which left Bombay in March.

The fakír Sahib now took his leave of me, and was straightway succeeded by his elder brother, Aziz úd Dín, the minister for foreign affairs and confidential secretary, who came from the Mahá Raja to acquaint me, that he had been informed of my arrival by General Ventura, and had laid aside all occupations to rejoice at it. I cannot repeat the fine speeches that followed; soon after this, fifty bearers made their appearance with presents of fruit and sweetmeats, a bottle of his own wine, of which I shall have something to say presently, and a bag with 700 rupees.

The general now introduced me to Mr. Mackeson, the Company's political agent at Bhawalpoor, and to a Frenchman, named Dubuignon. The first is a most intelligent young officer, who has accepted a place in a desert, 300 miles from Lúdiana, where he will have to superintend and protect the English vessels in the navigation of the Indus, a privilege lately conceded to them by a treaty with the Amírs of Sind. I had nearly forgotten to name an old acquaintance whom I also met with. On the left bank of the Ráví, I was accosted by a man with a grey beard, and a uniform somewhat French in its cut, whom I perfectly recollected to have seen before, but could not think where nor when, until he began to talk of Bombay. I then recognized Mr. Forni, the manufacturer of saltpetre, who had come from Bombay to Egypt while I was there. At our richly-covered board in the evening, we were joined also by Mr. Fox, an Englishman lately enrolled in the service of the Mahá Raja.

Before I give any account of my own residence at Lahor, I shall introduce a brief notice of the Sikhs and their king, whose energetic mind has embodied a multitude of disjointed materials, which he, and only he, could ever have succeeded in compacting together. His standard is planted upon the ruins of the Moghul Empire, and he now holds his court in their second viceregal city.

By the victory obtained over the Emperor Ibrahim Lodi, at Pániput, in 1525, India was subjugated, and the dynasty of the house of Timúr established on the throne of Delhi in the person of the illustrious

Báber, whose intellectual accomplishments were in no respect inferior to his genius as a soldier*. Driven from his hereditary possessions, he worked his way by personal exertion, to the sovereignty of his native kingdom, Ferghána, and when he lost this by the treachery of his nearest kinsman, proposed another and a bolder expedition to the south, and, after a sanguinary struggle for the richest prize in the world, ascended the throne of Delhi. All his actions evinced the working of a bold and comprehensive genius, whether we consider his plans of conquest, or his forbearance towards the followers of the different religious persuasions throughout his kingdom; the latter quality was not less extraordinary than honourable, when we take into consideration the age in which he lived. His toleration enabled the sect of the Gurú Nának to spread its doctrines very widely throughout his empire. At first they were but few in number, and assumed the title of Sikhs or Sikhsha, a word which in Sanscrit signifies instruction; yet it is worthy of remark, that the government never considered either Nának, or the Gurús who succeeded him, in any formidable light. It is, in truth, a peculiarity belonging to the many sects in India, that they rarely have anything to do with politics, and that the sectaries care as little what may be the faith of their ruler, as the ruler concerns himself about the creed of his subjects. Very different were the opinions of the Mohammedans in this respect; the propagation of their religion always served as a decent covering for their love of conquest, and they pretended to justify all the misery they brought on India, all their oppressive deeds for centuries, by an ardent zeal for the faith of their prophet. Whatever change the Mohammedan religion may have undergone in these revolutions, experience has always shown, that very few of its followers have been free from that fanaticism which seems an integral part of Islamism. The governing powers

* The autobiography of Báber is characteristic of his talent, and derives additional interest from the taste and fidelity with which it has been translated by Mr. Erskine. To appreciate the character of this great prince, we must read what he has written, and bear in mind the period at which he wrote, the people amongst whom he was living, and the sovereignty he exercised.—*Ed.*

of India take care that the taxes are regularly paid; so that they have his money, they do not trouble themselves about what deity the payer may believe in; in like manner also, the subject does not inquire to whom he pays the impost; and thus matters proceed quietly, except when the fanatical members of a sect, from some real or fancied injury, seek for redress or revenge on their rulers, and thereby attract more particular notice.

The immediate successors of Gurú Nának were: Angad, Amíra Dás, Rám Dás, and Arjun Mal, whose very existence was disregarded by the government. The maxims of the new doctrine, which I have endeavoured to explain in another place, were at first of an ambiguous nature, and chiefly directed against the polytheism of the Hindús, in the same manner as the Iconoclasts of the eighth century sought to purify the Christian religion from the abuses which had sprung up; but they soon began to assume a more definite form, until, under the last-mentioned Gurú, they were sufficiently arranged to allow him to write them down in a book called the Grunth.

Hargovind, Hari, Harkrishna, and Tegh-Bahadúr, succeeded each other as ministers of this sect, and it was in the lifetime of the last that Aurungzíb dethroned his father Shah Jehan, (that Emperor of Delhi who, of all the Moghul rulers, has left the most enduring memorials of himself in the buildings he erected,) and caused the destruction of his brothers and their families, who perished in warring against the usurper. Religion was the pretext used by Aurungzíb in this unnatural contest with those of his own blood: totally destitute as he was of every pretension to it, he invariably proclaimed his ardent zeal for the faith of the prophet, urging on its reception, among other means, by persecuting each separate sect of the Hindús. In the year 1675, Tegh-Bahadúr was put to death in Patna by his commands. His son Govind thereupon swore eternal enmity to all Mohammedans, and changing his religious appellation of Sikh, which, in common with all of his own faith he had hitherto borne, for the name of Singh, or Lion, which is peculiar to the military castes of India, he thus proclaimed openly his change of mind, and was imitated by all the professors of his faith, who assumed a similar title. Govind Singh lost no time in forming a band of predatory troops out of the multitude of religious devotees who flocked to him, whose watch-word was "eternal enmity to the Mohammedans." Neither did they long want a token of recognition; as an open defiance to the Mohammedans, they suffered the hair of their heads and beards to grow, and followed up these conspicuous signs of their altered profession by entering on their new career. Predatory excursions were first undertaken, and when the Mohammedan commanders in the different provinces aroused themselves to check these disorders, Govind Singh summoned every member of his sect to join him in carrying on the contest with energy and determination. The time indeed was not favourable for the success of such an enterprise, for Aurungzíb held the reins of power with no feeble hand, his armies, by uninterrupted exercise, were well trained to battle, and had every advantage against these inexperienced zealots. After a few unimportant skirmishes, the revolters were dispersed, and Govind Singh obliged to flee to the Dekhan, where he is supposed to have died in the year 1708. His followers returned to their former peaceable condition, and resumed those occupations from which the martial ardour of their leader had withdrawn them. The office of the Gurú, however, was not filled up; first, because the Sikhs long expected the return of Govind Singh, of whose death they never received any certain information; and also, when after so long a time had elapsed since his escape, that the fact of his death could no longer be doubted, the whole frame of their society, if I may so express it, had undergone a change. Govind Singh has remained, therefore, up to this time, the last acknowledged spiritual head of the Sikhs.

A Hindú Bairagí, or penitent, called Banda, assembled together a small band of Sikhs soon after the flight of Govind Singh, and commenced a series of hostilities against the Mohammedans by destroying Sirhind. But he was quickly overpowered, taken prisoner, and by command of Shah Alam, the son and successor of Aurungzíb, openly put to death. Delhi was soon the theatre of civil war for the succession to the imperial throne, and the Sikhs ceased for the time to be the objects of much attention or of persecution. Once more they resumed their habits of predatory warfare, but with more impunity than heretofore, and the sect gradually and quietly extended its numbers.

Thirty-two years after the death of Aurungzíb, under whom the Mohammedan empire in India attained its highest pitch of glory, and four years after the Mahrattas from the south had burnt the suburbs of Delhi, a warning so to speak to the great Mohammedan States in the west, not to let the treasures of the Moghul Emperors fall into the hands of the unbelievers, the imperial capital was plundered and reduced to ashes by Nadir Shah, who, however, made no long stay there, but left India most precipitately, returning laden with treasures to his own land, after uniting to his empire that part of the Moghul dominions lying on the right bank of the Indus. Notwithstanding the throne of the house of Timúr was undermined, an able and independent prince had succeeded in propping up the tottering edifice, strengthening and restoring it to something of its original order. But it wanted real stability, and the two powerful governors of the provinces watched their opportunity to avail themselves of the weakness of their masters, who now followed each other in quick succession, and established their own independence.

There was still, however, a spell in the name of the Emperor of Delhi, which averted the breaking out of an open rebellion; nor were there wanting many men of ability who were willing to devote themselves and identify their fortunes with that throne to which they were indebted for their own power; but their loyalty was for the most part but very ill rewarded by the feeble successors of Báber.

Nádir Shah was murdered in the year 1743; his servant and friend Ahmed Khán Abdalli, an Afghan, taking advantage of the confusion consequent on his death, subdued and took possession of that portion of his vast dominions, Afghánistan, which Nádir Shah had united to Persia. He assumed the title of Ahmed Shah, made Kandahár his capital, and undertook the invasion of India, in order to chastise the infidels. A dispute between two brothers for the governorship of Lahor, in 1747, gave him an opportunity of declaring himself the protector of one, and brought him into the very heart of the falling empire. He speedily conquered Lahor, and resolved not to lose sight of his good fortune. He then hastened towards Delhi, but without any successful result, for the brave Mír Mánu gave him battle near Sirhind, and compelled him to retrace his steps beyond the Indus. The second invasion, in 1748, was bought off by Mír Mánu, who, as a reward for his military conduct, had been invested with the Governorship of Lahor; but the third, which took place in 1751, made him master of the city, after a very sharp struggle. The rainy season soon obliged him to recross the Indus, but he left Mír Mánu, who had so well defended Lahor against him, as his representative there; and on the death of this brave viceroy, which happened soon afterwards, his son, a child, and at his death, his widow, were permitted to succeed as governors in his room, a plain proof of the miserable state of affairs at Delhi, that in such difficult times children and women were thought capable of being intrusted with places of such high importance.

In 1755, Ahmed Shah appeared for the fourth time in India, and without encountering any opposition, he advanced from Lahor to Delhi. There he espoused a princess of the house of Timúr, laid the city under a heavy contribution, and returned homewards again, leaving the feeble monarch, who had given him so little trouble, on his ancestral throne. He united Sirhind and the Panjáb to his own dominions, appointed Timúr his son, then only eleven years old, as his viceroy in Lahor, and recrossed the Indus.

In the Panjáb, confusion was now at its height, and the Sikh sect enlarged itself almost unnoticed, and carried on with impunity the profession of regular highway robbery. In order to put a stop to this state of things, and make the Government more respected, the Viceroy Timúr was directed by Ahmed Shah, to require the presence of all his vassals at court, and in particular, Adína Beg, the most powerful Jaghirdár in the new provinces, was commanded to repair to Lahor, and do homage to his new sovereign. Adína Beg, who had long enjoyed his independence in the Jalander Doáb, excused himself on this summons; and when Timúr would have compelled his appearance, he imagined a terrible means of insuring the continuance of his own power; he invited Mulhar-Rao Holkar, the chief of the Mahrattas, who considered all India as their prey at that period, and promised him a large sum of money for every day that he would make the Panjáb the field of his incursions.

Holkar was not slow to profit by this invitation, and the Sikhs served as auxiliaries in Holkar's army, as they had before served in the Persian army against the Moghuls. The Mahrattas entered the Panjáb, expelled the Viceroy, plundered Lahor, captured the baggage of the fugitive Timúr, and retraced their steps towards Hindústhan, leaving a garrison behind them to keep possession of Lahor, while the Sikhs carried on their robberies unmolested.

Meanwhile, Ahmed Shah, assembling a force more numerous than any with which he had hitherto entered Hindústhan, resolved to chastise Adína Beg; the death of this chief, however, precluded the meditated vengeance of the Abdali. The Mahrattas at this period were at the zenith of their power; and intelligence of Ahmed Shah's advance with a large army, was received by the Mohammedan princes of India with a feeling of universal satisfaction. All prepared themselves forthwith to join him with their troops, and make war against the common enemy. Nor was the Peshwa, the chief of the Mahrattas in the Dekhan, indifferent to the gathering storm. He mustered all his forces, well aware that the question now to be determined, was not merely which Mohammedan or Hindú prince was to occupy the throne of Delhi, but which power was henceforth to preponderate throughout India,—which of the two in fine was to be the lord, and which the servant.

On the 7th of July, 1761, the fate of India was once more contested at Pániput; the Mahrattas were utterly defeated; and in the battle and subsequent flight to the Dekhan, they are said to have lost not less than 200,000 men *.

* The carnage and desolation which ensued on all these great revolutions, are very imperfectly measured by the numbers actually slain in the field of battle. In modern warfare artillery has effected a great change—the discipline and skill of military tactics a yet greater diminution of the horrors of war. Medical skill also comes in aid of the claims of civilization and humanity. But in all these early contests, the hatred of the Shiah and the Súní, the rival sects of Mohammedanism; the rooted aversion of the Hindús of every class to the followers of the prophet; inspired the contending parties with motives to implacable revenge and unheard-of

After remaining a few days only in Delhi, Ahmed Shah recrossed the Indus, leaving Záin Khan in Sirhind, and Khája Obeid in Lahor, as his Viceroys. At first sight, it appears unaccountable that Ahmed Shah should not have declared himself at once Emperor of Delhi, as he might then so easily have done. Perhaps he was deterred by the conviction that the separate portions of the Empire had become too powerful to be governed from one great central point. This obstacle chiefly proceeded from the preponderating influence of the Omrah or nobles, who had long considered themselves as so many sovereigns, and hence offered so much opposition to the different Emperors, that the imperial government had scarce more than the shadow of authority over them. The alliance of Ahmed Shah with the house of Timúr, might also tend to predispose him in favour of its fallen greatness, as well as his own disposition, which had more of humanity in it than had been seen in any conqueror of India who had preceded him.

This explanation of the early events which occurred in the north of India, though not strictly connected with the Sikhs, was necessary in order to show the degree of confusion existing there, which was so favourable for the growth and projects of that religious sect. At this same period, the great majority of the Sikhs were agriculturists, or owners of one or more wells, by which the value of property is calculated in their country, and were without exception men who were sighing for an opportunity of taking the spear in hand, and mounting their steeds to endeavour by robbery to increase their scanty means. Whenever the Mohammedans were at war with each other, they

---

cruelties. It is calculated that 4,347,000 persons, perished in the destruction of three principal cities of Khorasán by Timúr, and a very much larger number in the irruption of Chungez Khán into China. The British supremacy in the East has certainly been effected at a comparatively small sacrifice of life; and if it has not accomplished all the good that its advocates might desire, it is well to advert to the discontinuance of such unmitigated atrocities as were perpetrated in Asiatic wars, under the cloak of religion; also to the resources of medical skill and Christian principle in abatement of the disease, suffering, and injustice, which, in the sequel, had heretofore proved more destructive than the sword itself. —*Ed.*

engaged a number of these marauders in their service: they fought against each other in the opposite ranks without the least scruple, being in fact mere mercenaries, using religion as their watchword, when no other pretext served as a decent cloak for their atrocities. The fact of a separate sect of these zealots, called Akáli, having brought themselves into notice from the main body of the Sikhs, shows how greatly they must have degenerated from their original institutions. These Akáli, when fighting for their faith, threw aside their garments with the exception of their turban, and urging on their fleet coursers, brandished their sabres, and with a shrill war-cry compelled their fellow believers to proceed against the enemy.

Ahmed Shah was too much occupied with his conquests in other countries to keep these new provinces constantly in view; and so long as the taxes could be raised, the Governors of Lahor and Sirhind gave themselves very little concern about those disorders, occasioned everywhere by the growing power of the Sikhs; hence, nothing could be more favourable to these fanatics than the posture of affairs at that period. Their confidence and expectation of success augmented in proportion to the impunity with which they were allowed to carry on their depredations, while the peaceful inhabitants of the Panjáb became aware that nothing but their conversion to the new doctrines could insure to them the quiet which they would have purchased at any price. Whenever the opportunity presented itself for an incursion, a small band of horsemen suddenly swelled into an army; and on the approach of an overwhelming Mohammedan force, this army was suddenly transformed again into a body of husbandmen, quietly occupied in the cultivation of their fields. The day of vengeance had arrived for the long-oppressed Hindús against their hard task-masters the Mohammedans, nor could it be expected they would neglect to take advantage of it. The Sikhs wanted some places of security to lodge their booty in, to preserve it from the dangers of a sudden surprise. At this time Nodh Singh became distinguished among the many leaders of the various parties who were carrying on war on their own account. He was the great-grandfather of Ranjít Singh, and the son of Disu, a Jat, whose property as a peasant was very trifling. Nodh Singh was the first of the family who made profession of the Sikh religion. He died in 1750, and his son Charat Singh formed a party of his own. As he was favoured by fortune, he was very soon in a situation to erect a Garhí, or fort, at Guseráolí, which he surrounded with mud walls, and made the storehouse for his booty. In every respect, the place was well chosen: it was situated in the vicinity of Lahor, and in the midst of the Sikh population, to whom, on emergency, it might serve as a rallying-point. From the period when the Mahrattas entered the Panjáb by Hindústhan, this population had been gradually moving towards the most northerly point of Hindústhan and the Panjáb, where the prevailing disorders seemed to offer them a much wider field of booty than any other part of India. In the year 1762, the perpetration of some daring acts of robbery, undertaken from Guseráolí, first drew the attention of the Viceroy of Lahor, Khája Obied, to the place. He marched forthwith to destroy it; but it was a post of great importance to the Sikhs, and they had intimation of the Viceroy's design in sufficient time to throw a strong force into the Garhí. These forts, however unimportant, have at all times been sufficient to present great impediments in the way of Indian armies, and prolong their wars to an indefinite period. The military equipments of Khája Obied were on too small a scale for him to capture this petty fortress within a short time, and the composition of his army caused him infinite embarrassment during the prolonged siege. In his expeditions against the Emperor of Delhi, in Hindústhan and the Panjáb, Ahmed Shah Abdali, like other Mohammedans, had enlisted Sikh soldiers in his service; his Governor, Khája Obied, followed his example, and had a large body of them among his troops. This fact proves plainly enough that the Sikhs thought much more of plunder than of spreading their faith, and were ever ready to take the field with friend or foe, where they had any prospect of acquiring it. So long as the Moghuls had a higher remuneration to offer, they served them; but as soon as Ahmed Shah had become master of the country, several of the Sikhs amassed considerable wealth, and the poorer classes of this sect joined the Mohammedans in hope of spoiling their more fortunate brethren, and dividing the plunder among them.

While Khája Obied was carrying on his slow operations before

Guseráolí, the Sikhs in his service began to negotiate with their brethren in the fortress. On a day appointed, they forsook their posts simultaneously; the other troops, on hearing of this desertion, took to flight; and the combined Sikhs, without striking a blow, got possession of the camp: meanwhile Khája Obied escaped with difficulty to Lahor: nor did he venture to leave the walls of that city. For the first time since the foundation of their religion, the Sikhs found themselves strong enough to have a public assembly, Sarhat Kalsa, in Amritsir. This place, the ancient Chak, was of great importance in their estimation; for it was there that the fourth of their Gurús, Rám Dás, constructed that celebrated tank in 1521, which he called Amrit Saras, or the Spring of Immortality, because they who bathed in its waters were cleansed from their sins. Thence was derived the name of the city Amritsir.

As soon as Ahmed Shah learned what had befallen his general, he prepared, in November, 1762, to recross the Indus, chastise the rebels, and liberate Khája Obied. His approach was the signal to the Sikhs to disperse themselves in different directions, the majority taking refuge in Hindústhan. Ahmed Shah arriving in Lahor without encountering an enemy, commanded Záin Khan, his Viceroy in Sirhind, to observe the movements of the fugitives, and summoned all his Mohammedan vassals or Jaghirdars to send him their contingent of troops. He soon received notice that the Sikhs had assembled in vast numbers at Kos Ráhira, in Hindústhan. Whereupon, he left Lahor secretly, at the head of a select division of his army, and in the course of thirty-six hours was at Lúdiana, on the other side of the Setlej, a surprising march. Here he allowed his troops a few hours' rest, and the next morning reached Kos Ráhira, where the Sikhs, trusting to their superiority in numbers, had just attacked the governor of Sirhind. The appearance of the black fur caps, the well-known uniform of the flower of the army of the Abdali, suddenly changed the aspect of affairs. Seized with a sudden panic, the Sikhs never thought of offering them any opposition, and Ahmed Shah took a bloody revenge on them for all the trouble they had given him. From twenty to thirty thousand Sikhs are said to have fallen on this field of battle, and it was only when his soldiers were tired of slaughtering, that the survivors were enabled to save themselves by flight. The battle is known to the Sikhs by the name of Ghalu Ghára, or the bloody massacre.

An honourable trait in Ahmed Shah's character may be mentioned here. Ala Sing, Sirdar of Patiala, was brought a prisoner to Lahor, and his valour in the field and courage when brought into Ahmed's presence so gained the admiration of his conqueror, that he not only received a pardon, but with it the khilat, or dress of honour, and the title of Raja.

Ahmed Shah then marched towards Amritsir, ordered the temple of Harmanden (Hari), which stood in the centre of the sacred tank, to be blown up with gunpowder, the water to be choked up with sand and stones, and rendered unclean by throwing in the blood and carcasses of cows (a profanation even more terrible, according to the maxims of the Sikh faith, than in the estimation of the Brahmins themselves); and finally, appointing Kábuli Mal, a Brahmin from Kabúl, his deputy in Lahor, he returned at the end of the year 1762 to Kandahar. But he had scarcely time to cross the Indus, ere he received the news that the Sikhs had again broken out into open revolt, seized the fort of Kasur, and appeared before Sirhind with 40,000 horsemen. The governor, Záin Khan, accepted the battle offered by them, which terminated in his death, and the defeat of his army. Sirhind itself, one of the handsomest and richest cities in Hindústhan, fell into their power, and after having suffered much from their devastations so far back as 1707, was now made a heap of ruins. This rage for its destruction proceeded from the remembrance, that in the time of Aurungzíb, the wife and child of Govind Singh had been put to death there, and its ruin was therefore, in their eyes, merely an act of just retribution. Even at the present time, it is considered a most meritorious action for a Sikh to tear out the bricks from some detached piece of wall yet standing, and throw them into the Setlej or the Jamna.

Ahmed Shah entered India in 1764, for the seventh time, and the rebels took refuge in the desert bordering on Rajpútána, and escaped the meditated vengeance of the Abdali, who was compelled to return homewards without having seen one Sikh. No sooner did the insurgents hear of his departure, than they found their way back to the Panjáb. Their first exploit was the capture of Lahor, which Kábuli Mal, feeling himself too weak in troops to hold out against them, evacuated on their approach. The indefatigable Ahmed moved back, marched through Lahor and as far as the Setlej, the cunning Sikhs as usual dispersing before his army. On this occasion, strange to say, a Sikh Sirdar called Amar Singh, the son of the before-named Ala Singh, of Patiala, received from Ahmed Shah the investiture of Sirhind, which his father had exchanged with the Sikh conquerors for a few villages. He was now established in it with the title of Mahá Raja. It is said that Amar Singh appeared dressed for the ceremony in the presence of the Abdali, with the long hair and beard, the requisite distinctions of a Sikh. He was commanded to cut them off directly, and only obtained the privilege of retaining them by paying down a lakh of rupees to Ahmed Shah.

Without waiting for the orders of the Shah, twelve thousand of his soldiers suddenly decamped at this time, and marched back to Kabúl, Ahmed being compelled to follow them. With much difficulty and the loss of his baggage he reached the Indus, pursued by the Sikhs, whom he thus left in undisturbed possession of the Panjáb and of Sirhind, with the exception of some few Mohammedan principalities, which were too well defended to give any hope of their sudden alienation.

The Sikhs were not governed at this period by any one prince, but were divided into twelve fraternities, called Misal, each one acting according to its own interest and ways of thinking. Twice in the year, at the anniversary of great festivals, at the Bysakhi, in April, and at the Díwali, in October, the Sikhs assembled in Amritsir and held a Gurmatta, or general council, where everything relating to their affairs was deliberated, their future enterprises resolved on, and according to their importance, the co-operation of the whole brotherhood or of one or more divisions called for. Without much regard to unity of purpose in such enterprises, every Sikh Sirdar was accustomed to live at the expense of his Hindú and Mohammedan neighbours. When Ahmed Shah ceased finally to interfere in the affairs of the Panjáb, in the year 1764, the twelve Misals numbered as follow:—1. Bangi Misal, 10,000 armed horsemen; 2. Ramgarhia Misal, 3000; 3. Ghania Misal, 8000; 4. Nakia Misal, 2000; 5. Aluwala Misal, 3000; 6. Daliala Misal, 7500; 7. Nishánwala Misal, 12,000; 8. Fáizullapúria Misal, 2500; 9. Khora Singhia Misal, 12,000; 10. Shahíd and Nihang Misal, 2000; 11. Phalkia and Bhekia Misal, 5000; 12. Suker Chakia Misal, 2500: making a total of 69,500 horsemen.

The chiefs of these Misals were, properly, only the commanders of the troops in their general enterprises, but they were always the most considerable men in the Misal. Each individual horseman, however, had some property, whether small or large, and was, in truth, an arbitrary chief, who formed a member of the Misal, just as it suited his own pleasure, or when some common interest was at stake; we need not dwell on the impossibility of any State, governed by 69,500 tyrants, being either supportable to others, or lasting in itself. Its existence was protracted only so long as there was a foreign enemy to oppose, the baggage train of an Ahmed Shah to plunder, or the territory of a Mohammedan prince to enter for spoil and devastation. Peace brought its unfailing consequences; divisions and strife between the different Misals. Ahmed Shah died in 1773, and his son, Timúr, more peaceably inclined by nature, never seems to have contemplated the subjugation of the Panjáb. During his reign of twenty years, the last of the above-named Misals, the Suker Chakia, had advanced in number and power beyond most of the other fraternities. Its founder was Charat Singh, the grandfather of Ranjít, a common trooper, to whom fortune was so kindly disposed, that at his death he left behind him a revenue of three lakhs of rupees. He fell a victim to the bursting of one of his own guns at the assault on Jamú, in 1747, leaving a son, Mahá Singh, only ten years old. The widow placed herself and the lad under the protection of Jái Singh, the chief of the powerful Bangi Misal, until Mahá Singh was old enough, in 1778, to marry the daughter of the Sirdar of Jhínd, and maintain his own independence. His life from that period was one unbroken series of audacious robbery, the plundering of Jamú being the most profitable of his enterprises, though it nearly caused his ruin.

Jamú was at this time one of the richest towns of India, the inhabitants of the Panjáb having made it their usual place of refuge, where they conveyed all their treasures*. It belonged to a Hindú Raja called Ranjít-Deo, a friend of Jái Singh, who was naturally very much incensed when Mahá Singh, who owed even his territories to his protection, now made war without first consulting him, and that, against his own friend, terminating it with the plunder of Jamú, and the exaction of contributions from the richest Sikh Sirdars. The more particular details of this contest, with which the present power of Ranjít Singh's house originated, will be given in the sequel. It produced a war between Mahá Singh and Jái Sing, which terminated in a battle, the rout of Jái Singh's army, and the fall of his eldest son, Gur Bakhsh Singh. This disaster humbled the pride of this chieftain. Old and infirm, he saw himself prostrated before the man who was his debtor for all he had, and forced to accept the terms of peace prescribed to him. The articles of this treaty prove how little the Sikh chieftains of that time understood their own real interests. One of Mahá Singh's allies was a Hindú Raja, called Sansar Chand, who, some years before, had surrendered to Jái Singh the very important hill-fort of Kángra. According to the treaty now imposed on him, this place was restored to Sansar Chand, to the evident injury of the whole Sikh nation.

An important alliance was early formed for Ranjít Singh, who when five years old was betrothed by his father to Mehtab Kúnwar, a female of high lineage, the daughter of that Gur Bakhsh Singh slain in battle against him. Her mother, Suda Kúnwar, was a woman versed in cunning and intrigue of every kind, and laid the foundation for much of the future greatness of Ranjít, by artfully causing the two remaining sons of Jái Singh to be deprived of their heritage in the Bangi Misal, and herself to be made the guardian of her young daughter.

---

* Jamú, or Jummoo, as it is frequently written, was a place of great note, and the resort of the principal merchants in the Panjáb, who made it the great entrepôt for the trade of Kashmír, till the town was plundered by Mahá Singh, when the current of the great shawl trade was distributed in other quarters, chiefly between Amritsir and Lahor.—*Ed.*

Mahá Singh died in 1792, Jái Singh the following year, when this aspiring woman instantly prepared to govern the two powerful Misals, until her son-in-law should be of age to take the reins of power into his own hands.

The intrigues of Ranjít Singh himself, and his fortunate exploits are related elsewhere. Here, it will be sufficient to remark, that the three first years of his minority passed quietly, and that the three following years were distinguished by the renewed incursions of the Afghans. On the death of the peaceably-disposed Timúr in 1793, Shah Zemán ascended the throne of Kabúl. Thirty-one years had elapsed since the Panjáb was disturbed by foes from without, when in 1795, Shah Zemán crossed the Atok, with the avowed object of retaking those Indian provinces which had succeeded in separating themselves from the dominion of his grandfather, Ahmed Shah. But this expedition, as well as a second in 1797, only proved the utter ignorance of this prince as to the real state of affairs. They both occasioned great disorders in the country, where neither glory nor riches were at that time to be acquired; but the invaders had never the opportunity given them to combat honourably, and each separate division, as it marched, found itself encompassed by vast bands of plunderers. Instead of one king, Shah Zemán had to oppose 69,500 chiefs, and as the power was thus subdivided, so was also the wealth of the country: the soldiers of course had little chance of enriching themselves by booty; for the Sikhs fled, each man with his property before the advancing foe, ready at a moment's notice, to turn and fall on them, when he felt himself strong enough, and plunder their baggage or cut off their provisions. Many of the Sikh Sirdars did outwardly submit to the Shah, either for the promotion of their own interests, or in order to be ready for any moment of peril.

In 1798, Shah Zemán made his appearance again in the Panjáb with a powerful force, and possessed himself of Lahor without meeting with opposition. Most of the Sirdars of the Panjáb did him homage in person; others, among whom was Ranjít Singh, who was then governing his own Misal, performed this duty by deputy. A temporary residence there, however, was sufficient to convince Shah Zemán that there was no good reason to believe that the provinces of the Panjáb and Sirhind would ever again form part of his empire. He was forced to return to Afghanistan with all possible dispatch, having received information that his brother Shah Mahmúd had established himself in the western provinces of his kingdom, and had called on Persia to assist him in his projects.

When Shah Zemán captured Lahor, Ranjít Singh withdrew to Sirhind, but had no sooner ascertained that the conqueror was about to leave the country, than he instantly retraced his steps to the Panjáb, and followed the retreating army, undecided how to act, as a friend or as a foe, but quite resolved to be guided according to his own interest, and the circumstances which should present themselves. His ambition grasped at the possession of Lahor, then divided between three Sikh Sirdars.

Shah Zemán arrived at the Jelam on his return homewards. The river was much swollen by the rains, and twelve of his guns sank down deep in the soft muddy soil; but the Shah did not consider this accident of sufficient moment to induce him to wait until they could be extricated; he contented himself with offering Ranjít Singh the investiture of Lahor, if he would send them after him. Lahor, however, as we have observed, had been partitioned between three Sikh Sirdars, both before the invasion of the Abdalis and also after their departure; the proposition of the Shah, in point of fact, simply admitted the right of Ranjít Singh to conquer it on his own account, if he were able; and Ranjít believed that this investiture might be useful to him, not so much to give his conquest a certain apparent right in the minds of his fellow Sikhs, as to bring over the Mohammedan population of Lahor more effectually to his party. He forthwith sent eight guns to the Shah, and in reward received the investiture of Lahor, with the title of Raja. Not tarrying to make his right good by intrigue, he entered the city in 1799 by a gate opened for him by the Mohammedans, took possession of this important post, and forced the three Sikh Sirdars to accept some trifling jaghírs or fiefs, as a compensation for their loss.

The contests which took place for the throne of Kabúl among the sons of Timúr, who had transferred the seat of government to that city, allowed them no time to think of reconquering the Panjáb, and their unhappy dissensions so enfeebled their country, that it assumed towards its powerful neighbour an aspect purely defensive. On this side, then, Ranjít Singh, whom we may henceforth consider as the King of the Sikhs, was quite secure; while the British had too many weighty affairs on their hands to interpose any hindrance in his path. When his power had grown to an unlimited height in the Panjáb, through the suppression and subjugation of the Mohammedan princes and the Sikh Sirdars, who could not comprehend their obvious policy of union against the common enemy; and lastly, through his conquests over the Hindú and Mohammedan Rajas in the mountains between the Panjáb and the Himalaya, then at length the Sikh Sirdars on the left bank of the Setlej saw but one means of saving their possessions, namely, by placing themselves under the protection of the East India Company, lately become their near neighbour. Accordingly, an embassy from these Sikhs arrived at Delhi in 1807, with proposals for a treaty, which was concluded in 1809, and the Setlej declared as the boundary of the British territories towards the north-west.

This treaty was the cause of Ranjít Singh's just displeasure to his brethren of that faith, and it was long ere he could bring himself to yield his pretensions to the command of the whole Sikh nation, or reconcile himself to his territorial limits being removed to the Setlej instead of the Jamna as heretofore. In vain he strove to gain time; the movement of a considerable body of English troops on Lúdiana shewed him that the diplomatic negotiations were brought to a close. Presently he sent a detachment over the boundaries, who occupied Bilaspoor, but was obliged to countermand it on the advance of the British force, and admit the hard condition, that his territories should not be extended to the left bank of the Setlej.

Angry as the Mahá Raja was, he was aware of the necessity of coming to terms with the British Government, whose territories actually bordered on his own; and, after some hesitation, he accepted the treaty proposed to him by their plenipotentiary, Mr. Charles Metcalfe, the conditions of which were as follow:—

"Article I. Perpetual friendship shall subsist between the British Government and the State of Lahor, and the latter shall be considered with respect to the former to be on the footing of the most favoured Powers; and the British Government will have no concern with the territories and subjects of the Rajas to the northward of the river Setlej.

"Article II. The Raja Ranjít Singh will never maintain in the territories which he occupies on the left bank of the Setlej more troops than are necessary for the internal duties of the territory, nor commit, nor suffer any encroachment on the possessions or rights of the chiefs in its vicinity.

"Article III. In the event of any violation of the preceding articles, or of any departure from the rules of friendship on the part of either State, this treaty shall be considered to be null and void."

[The fourth and last article provides for the exchange of ratifications.]

"Lahor, 25th May, 1809."

The following is the proclamation (Itálanáma) issued in the name of the general Government on the arrival of the British corps at Lúdiana, the northernmost point on the Setlej, and addressed by their commander to the Sikh Sirdars.

This is to make known :—

First. That the territories of Sirhind and Malooa, (the designation assumed by the Sikhs of Puteeala, Naba, Jheend, and Kythul, have been taken under British protection, and Ranjít Singh has bound himself by treaty to exercise in future no interference therein.

Second. That it is not the intention of the British Government to demand any tribute from the Chiefs and Sirdars benefiting by this arrangement.

Third. That the Chiefs and Sirdars will be permitted to exercise, and are for the future secured in, the rights and authorities they possessed in their respective states, prior to and at the time of the declaration of protection by the British Government.

Fourth. That the Chiefs and Sirdars shall be bound to offer every facility and accommodation to British troops and detachments employed in securing the protection guaranteed, or for purposes otherwise connected with the general interests of the state, whenever the same may be marched into, or stationed in their respective territories.

Fifth. In case of invasion or war the Sirdars are to join the British standard with their followers whenever called upon.

Sixth. Merchants conveying articles, the produce of Europe, for the use of the detachments at Lúdiana, or of any other British force or detachment, shall not be subject to transit duties, but must be protected in their passage through the Sikh country.

Seventh. In like manner horses for the cavalry, when furnished with passports from competent officers, must be exempt from all tax.

This proclamation, favourable as it certainly was to the Sikh chiefs, ensured the safety of their country from the invasion of Ranjít Singh, and appears to the uninitiated an instance of the rarest disinterestedness on the part of the British Government. He is inclined to believe that the sole object of the rulers of Hindústhan was to bring about a general state of peace, and the extension, nominally, of their frontier to the Setlej. But those better informed on Eastern politics, will soon see how this treaty, according to Indian usage, gave the Company the right to possess themselves of any of those territories when the ruler happened to die childless, a case which, in consequence of the excessively dissolute manners of the Sikhs, cannot fail within a short time to happen in most of the ruling families. The twenty-five years which have elapsed since this proclamation was issued, have already put the Company in possession of a large portion of these provinces.

This cursory notice of the history of the Sikhs may serve to explain the present condition of the Panjáb. Ranjít Singh has now gradually become master of every district on the right bank of the Setlej, excepting some few belonging to petty chiefs, who have possessions also on the left bank. These have been spared out of mere policy. The rest of the Panjáb is subject to his sovereignty, and the Sirdars and chieftains do homage to him as their liege lord.

The ephemeral power of the Mahrattas arose on the ruins of the gigantic monarchy of the Emperors of Delhi, which, as often as it shewed symptoms of decay, seemed destined to rise again. One dynasty succeeded another, but the throne was still filled; institutions and usages remaining unalterably the same. In default of any judicious system of government, and supported by mere individual superiority of intellect, the empire at length went to decay. The more powerful men in the state never contended for the crown in fair open warfare, but had recourse to poison or the dagger to rid themselves of every obnoxious rival. The Mohammedan religion, and the system of invasions and conquest then in vogue, rendered it necessary to depart from the natural order of hereditary succession; the most powerful, enterprising, or favoured prince succeeded to the throne; and these changes necessarily produced in all classes of the people a restless unquiet spirit. The moment that their monarchs ceased to be conquerors, the empire began to languish, and the stronger the single portions of it became, the more irretrievable was the general ruin. The Mohammedan system had, notwithstanding, the spirit of continuance in it; there were among them many deeply-thinking men, who strove for the possession of the world, and took due measures to ensure success; they introduced their laws into the conquered provinces; regard was had to ancient usages; the viceroys upheld the laws of the land; one regular system embraced the whole empire, and the dispositions made by the great Akbar evince a high degree of administrative sagacity. Nothing of this kind can be instanced in the Mahratta Government. Hosts of robbers, like birds of prey, swept over India without any systematic plan, suddenly invading those points where the vast distance might have precluded the least probability of attack. Their sole rule of government seeming to consist in the exaction of the *Chout*, or tribute, which amounted to the fourth part of the revenue of the country, cruel to the defenceless, overbearing to the humble, dastardly where they met with a brave resistance, their power lasted no longer than the alarm occasioned by their inroads. Their nominal dominion, consequent on the disorders which had effected the ruin of the overgrown empire of the Moghuls, was entirely subverted on the first rencounter with a regular power. This also would have been the case with the Sikhs, had not natural limits been set to their territories.

The power of Delhi, which otherwise might have directed all its energies to restrain the growth of the new state to the north-west, was assailed by foes from within as well as without. The Mahrattas in the south were involved in wars which ended in their downfall; under any circumstances it was a matter of indifference to them whom they plundered, or who governed India. Terror of the Afghans kept them away from the north, as well as the conviction that their first appearance in the Panjáb would leave little enough for any after-gleaning, and that they could be no gainers by interfering in the affairs of the Sikhs and Mohammedans. The new Dúrani, or Afghan monarchy, was too insecurely established to make any opposition to the formation of the neighbouring empire. The field, therefore, on which the Sikhs carried on their operations was open, though at the same time comparatively limited. Defined by the right bank of the Setlej, the policy of the British Government had excluded a third part of the Sikh nation from the establishment of the new monarchy. To the west were various warlike tribes who had only to confederate together to crush the rising state at a blow: the boundaries, in fact, were so prescribed both by nature and the state of the surrounding provinces, that no power could have overpassed them, but that peculiar military talent which promptly avails itself of circumstances. Ranjít Singh nevertheless, however ably he went about the work, either did not understand, or did not concern himself to take any further measure to fortify or insure the integrity of his newly-acquired kingdom.

And here I may be allowed to say a few words on the Sikh religion. The Sikhs, not excepting those in high station, make no pretensions to education. Generally speaking, they are the descendants from all the lowest castes of Hindús, from which they have been proselyted. There are few among them to be found who can either read or write: the only language spoken from the prince to the peasant, is a corrupt Hindústhaní—the proper provincial dialect of the Panjáb.

In order to give some notion of the principles of this sect, we may briefly instance the prescribed form of initiation into their religion, which consists in drinking the *Pahul*, a rite established by Gurú Govind. The neophyte and the officiating priest first wash their feet in water, then put some sugar into a basin of water, stir it with a sword or dagger, and pronounce five *shlokas*, or verses, the first of which runs thus:—

Saráwak sidh samoh sidhának dekh phiriyo ghur Jogi Jatike.
Súr saráwak sidh saráwak sant samoh anek matíke.
Sáre hí desko dekh phiriyo mut kohú nu dekhat pránpatike.
Shri Bhagwánki Bhái kripa bin ek rati bin ek ratike.

Which may be thus translated:—

I have traversed the world, Jogi and Jeti, in short all sorts of devotees have I seen.
Holy men and hermits, absorbed in the contemplation of God, of every sort and form.
I have traversed every land, but a truly God-fearing man have I never seen.
Without God's grace, brother, the works of man are not of the least possible merit.

The other verses are all to the same general effect.

In what, then, it may possibly be asked, does the Sikh religion consist, beyond the above ceremony of partaking in the *Pahul*. It would be difficult to answer this question properly without entering minutely into the history and tenets of Hindúism—or the Brahminical faith, as it is commonly termed by Europeans. The Hindú considers none but the Brahmin privileged to discuss spiritual matters. He only may read the Veds or Holy Books, which raise the devout mind thus occupied and withdrawn from the sublunary affairs of this world, to a state of blissful abstraction. The Brahmin alone may presume to supplicate the Deity, or enter within the innermost court of the temple, where no other image is seen but the mystical symbol of their divinity. Hindús of every other caste have only to look forward to their transmigration, and to strive by moral rectitude to emulate the holy character of the Brahmins in this state of being, that they may thus have an opportunity afforded them of advancing their immortality in a new birth. They can worship one only among the particular attributes of God, which are displayed under the strangest forms in the outer temple.

The Sikh faith, therefore, is a modified Hindúism, chiefly differing from the latter in rejecting all distinctions of caste, and the worship of images; in admitting proselytes of every religion, and allowing each individual to work out his own eternal reward, which, in the Brahminical faith, is the prescriptive right of those only who are twice-born Hindús.

Nának, the founder of the Sikh religion, probably desired to divest

Hindúism of its exclusiveness, and to lay down the principle, that every man, no matter how humble his birth, is entitled to address the only Creator in prayer. This idea, in fact, is inculcated by the Brahminical religion, with this only difference, that those who do not belong to that faith, can never attain to the new birth, or in other words, make any progress to the divine character, but by the most excessive ascetic practices. This last was unquestionably the discipline which Nának inculcated on his followers, and which distinguished them from those of other Hindú sects, such as the Yogís, Gosáins, &c. His precept was to be constant in prayer, and to maintain peace with all men. Subsequent political events, however, have given to the Sikh faith its present notoriety.

The Sikhs are not restricted to certain food and water, like the Hindús, but they are forbidden to eat the flesh of beef, or of tame swine, nor dare they smoke tobacco or any substitute for it,—a most salutary prohibition, as the pernicious habit of smoking sufficiently accounts for the want of talent, and indolence so generally observable among all classes of Mohammedans and Hindús.

The Grunth, or sacred book of the religious laws of the Sikhs, is a compound of mystical absurdities; like every other religion grounded on pure deism, the faith of the Sikhs is already deteriorated; image worship and distinction of castes are gradually taking place of the precepts enjoined by their original institutions.

Tuesday, January 12.—The first night which I had passed in the house of a European, for a very long time, was now over. I had scarcely awoke from a profound sleep, when a messenger arrived from the Mahá Raja, to make inquiry after me. I was soon dressed, and found Khalifa Sahib with the commandant of the garrison. They acquainted me that the Mahá Raja greatly regretted he could not see me on that day, which happening to be a grand holiday among the Sikhs, rendered it impossible for him to receive any stranger with due ceremony. He sent me as a present a bed and its furniture, consisting of silk and shawls.

General Ventura's house, built by himself and General Allard, though of no great size, combines the splendour of the East with the comforts of a European residence. On the walls of the entrance hall, before the range of pillars on the first story, was portrayed the reception of the two French officers at the court of Ranjít Singh, consisting of many thousand figures. The second room is adorned with a profusion of small mirrors in gilt frames, which have an excellent effect; the third is a large hall, extending the entire width of the house, and terminating in the sleeping apartments. At a short distance behind the house stands an ancient tomb, crowned with a lofty dome. This is now tenanted by the families of the European officers. Standing in the midst of the garden, which has been laid out with great taste, it forms a very striking contrast to the surrounding sandy plain. This spot overlooks an arm of the Rávi, and eastward the old city and necropolis, with countless dilapidated buildings and tombs, which in parts form small hillocks, without any apparent vestige of regular edifices. The neighbourhood of Lahor abounds in saltpetre, which soon destroys any walls that may be left standing; and not only these, but covered buildings, crumble beneath its influence, and frequently become an unshapely mass of rubbish. Among these ruins, a square has been cleared for the troops to exercise, in front of General Ventura's house; and the bricks which have been dug out from them, have been used not only to erect his dwelling-house, but the barracks for the French legion. These are now unoccupied, as the legion is at Peshâwar, nominally under the command of Shír Singh, Ranjít's son, though actually under Avitabile, formerly an officer of Murat's army and court, a pupil of the Polytechnic School at Paris, who is in the Mahá Raja's service. There are very few Europeans in the Panjáb. Generals Ventura and Avitable, (besides Allard, who is in Europe on leave,) Colonel Court, and Mr. Fox, an Englishman, with some few holding subordinate situations, sum up the entire list. All the troops, regular and irregular, excepting the irregular cavalry, have the French words of command on their being armed with muskets; and the French legion has the eagle and the tri-coloured flag, with the inscription Govind Singh. Each private has eight rupees a month, a red coat and his arms, but he has to feed and clothe himself. The whole army is generally kept a twelvemonth in arrear, Ranjít thinking this a good means of securing their subservience to him. The Jemidars, or lieutenants, have thirty rupees; and with the exception of the French legion, all are allowed to dress as they please, so that there is a strange medley of European costumes with those of the Panjáb.

The house was illuminated in the evening, and twenty-five female dancers made their appearance before us, with their plaintive music. Fireworks were also displayed; and at a late hour another dancer came with her party: she was specially sent for my entertainment, by the Mahá Raja himself, with many eulogiums, as a performer of no ordinary merit. She had performed at the Conference between the Governor-General and Ranjít Singh, from the latter of whom she had received marked testimonies of favour; but this famed beauty of Lahor, though not more than twenty years old, was already faded, if such an expression can ever be applied to a Hindú.

Wednesday, January 13.—At nine o'clock, Khalifa Sahib came to conduct me to the palace. He brought with him three elephants, with European howdahs, in which a person can sit upright and stretch out his feet; a numerous escort was likewise in attendance under the commandant of Lahor. Mr. Mackeson had also received an invitation. We entered Lahor by the south gate. When we arrived at the outer ward of the old imperial palace, the Mahá Raja's officers who formed our escort, all alighted from their horses, while the elephants marched up some steps through a second gate into a garden, in an excellent state of cultivation, and where I observed one of those beautiful little marble buildings, belonging to the pure taste of the Akbar dynasty. The exterior is ornamented with flowers worked in high relief in the marble, and the floor and inner walls are of pietra dura. On making some inquiries, I was told that the Mahá Raja had built it, which is evidently incorrect. A more modern structure of white brick, which has an upper story, abutting on one corner of this pretty edifice, has gained for him the reputation of having built the whole. To the left of this garden, but not accessible from it, stands the great Juma Masjid of Jehánghír, with its three domes of marble. The warlike Ranjít has turned it to the best advantage, the north side of this strong building being made a portion of the city wall, and the mosque itself converted into a barrack. We proceeded through a wide gate straight before us, and opening on a small square, where a company of soldiers was drawn up, and presented arms to us. The Mahá Raja was sitting in a small arm-chair with a low back, in a little pavilion; the walls were covered with gold brocade, and the floor with a large Kashmírian carpet. I had no sooner put my foot on the carpet, than he rose and received me at the entrance, taking my hand and leading me to an arm-chair close to his own. Before I had seated myself, I took a bag containing 750 rupees out of my Múnshí's hands, and giving it a preliminary wave over his head from left to right, handed it to his dependants. This ceremony is considered necessary whenever the Mahá Raja is ill, in order to drive away evil spirits, who are esteemed the sole cause of the royal infirmities.

My uniform had not arrived, and I had no boots with me; I had therefore to appear in shoes: to cross a carpet in them, is considered in India not so much an offence against the king's majesty as the English suppose, as a mark of extreme ill-breeding and rudeness, and the king himself would be considered wholly deficient in politeness, if he were to walk over the carpet of a room with his shoes on, no matter how inferior to himself the owner of the house might be. Knowing this, I left mine outside the border of the carpet. It is the English custom to offer their presents through a Múnshí; but as I knew that the Mahá Raja would feel flattered if I performed that ceremony myself, and I saw no degradation in it, I determined to do so. He asked me if I had served as a soldier, to which I answered in the affirmative, upon which he questioned me about our Austrian army, and our wars with France. Mr. Mackeson was a capital interpreter. Seeing Mohan standing behind me, he inquired about him, and finding that he was my interpreter, and that my former one, the Brahmin from Agra, had fallen ill, he desired Mohan to sit down at my feet, and inquired who he was. Mohan told him that he was a Ghorka, a kshatriya, (of the military caste), and the son of a Súbhedar, or captain. The Mahá Raja then turned to me, and asked me whether Mohan was able to translate every thing that I wished to say; and on my replying that he was, he said he would try him, and forthwith ordered the youth to ask me what I thought of his army, and whether it was in a state to encounter a

European force. I answered that the Sikhs had long been remarkable for their bravery, and the discipline now introduced must no doubt have rendered them quite equal to such an encounter ; "With equal forces?" he asked. "Doubtless," said I. "You have seen the whole world, which country do you like best ?"—"My own native land." "You have seen Kashmír, what think you of it ?"—"That sickness and famine have of late years so depopulated it, that it must produce a revenue of small amount." "I have ordered Mehán Singh to give money to the poor. Think you that he robs me ?"—"I think not." "Do not you think that I should do well to remove him from the government ? he has no intellect."—"I think the Governor a worthy man, and that you will not easily find a better. The country needs indulgence, in order that it may recover itself."

During the time this questioning was going on, and while Mr. Mackeson was translating it into Persian and Khalifa Sahib into the Panjábí, I took the opportunity of surveying the company. On a chair near the Mahá Raja, sat Híra Singh, a youth of sixteen, the son of the favourite, Raja Dhyan Singh, the Prime Minister; all the other great officers of state were seated on the ground. Every one had his eyes fixed on me to guess at the answers I was giving, before they were translated for the Mahá Raja's information. The court colour of the Durbar is yellow or green ; and the chiefs and officers were all clothed in yellow garments of the wool of Kashmír, except Híra Singh, who wore a satin dress of light green and pink. There were also present there, Raja Suchet Singh, the brother of Dhyan and Gúlab Singh, Míyan, or Lord of Jamú; Kúshal Singh, called the Jemidar, a Brahmin, who has been converted some time since to the Sikh faith; this man was formerly a cook in the Mahá Raja's household, and then a Jemidar, or Lieutenant, equivalent to the house-steward in a palace. He has retained this latter appellation, though now next to Dhyan Singh, the most powerful of Ranjít's vassals. The eldest son of the Mahá Raja, Karak Singh, resides at Lahor, but is always overlooked, as his intellect is too feeble to afford any probability of his ever ruling over the scarcely united empire of the Sikhs. His son, Nihal Singh, promises to be a clever active youth, but as he is no more than fifteen, it depends much on Ranjít Singh's health, whether he will be able to consolidate a party strong enough to enable him to succeed his grandfather, in supersession of his father's right. Shír Singh and Tára Singh are twins, who have never been acknowledged by Ranjít as his sons; the former has distinguished himself as a soldier, but was found very unfit for his appointment as governor of Kashmír. He is at present in Pesháwar, with the title of governor; General Avitabile, however, has the entire direction of the affairs and administration of the country; Tara Singh is not of any importance. Kashmír Singh and Pesháwar Singh, are also called sons of Ranjít, but of them I know nothing. One of the great obstacles to the duration of the empire founded by Ranjít Singh, consists in the imprudence of suffering so much power to accumulate in the persons of his vassals. Gúlab Singh, for example, in Jamú, with his brothers, Dhyan Singh and Suchet Singh, possess a large district, which extends over inaccessible mountains from Atok to Narpoor* in the south-east, and thence north to Ladak, besides other large estates in the Panjáb. These brothers, who are powerful in money, troops, cannon and fortresses, would with great difficulty be brought into subjection by the arm of the feeble successors of Ranjít, and several others are similarly circumstanced. Nothing can establish this prince's dynasty firmly, except an alliance with the Company, which his pride and the policy of the latter have hitherto precluded. The Mahá Raja has no throne. "My sword," he observed, "procures me all the distinction I desire; I am quite indifferent to external pomp."

Ranjít Singh is now fifty-four years old. The small-pox deprived him, when a child, of his left eye, whence he gained the surname of Kána, one-eyed, and his face is scarred by the same malady. His beard is thin and gray, with a few dark hairs in it: according to the Sikh religious custom, it reaches a little below his chin, and is untrimmed. His head is square and large for his stature, which, though naturally

---

* Narpoor or Núrpoor, according to others. The former is probably the true Hindú name.—*Ed.*

short, is now considerably bowed by disease; his forehead is remarkably broad. His shoulders are wide, though his arms and hands are quite shrunk; altogether, he is the most forbidding human being I have ever seen. His large brown, unsteady and suspicious eye seems diving into the thoughts of the person with whom he converses, and his straightforward questions are put incessantly and in the most laconic terms. His speech is so much affected by paralysis that it is no easy matter to understand him, but if the answer be delayed for an instant, one of his courtiers, usually the Jemidar, repeats the question. After I had been subjected to this examination for a whole hour, without one moment's intermission to put a single question in return, he turned to Mr. Vigne, and asked: "And what can you do?" To which my fellow traveller, with his usual simplicity, replied, "I can draw." The Mahá Raja did not seem to comprehend how an art so little esteemed by himself, could possibly occupy the time of a great white man, one of the Sahib Lóg. I now took occasion to thank him for the protection afforded me throughout his territories, which made travelling as safe under his vigorous government, as in the dominions of the East India Company. "The strict friendship between the two countries," I added, "is a great source of satisfaction both in Hindústhan and the Panjáb." This was a remark particularly agreeable to him, and in answering his first letter, I had instinctively let fall a few flowers of oriental rhetoric on this same friendship, which procured me in a short time a most flattering epistle, enlarging on my amplifications. He now asked me, "Who writes your letters?" I named Thakúr Dás. He praised him much, adding: "I hope Lahor will please you. Issue your commands, every thing here is yours." A company of soldiers were stationed in the court, and he asked me if I should like to see them go through their manœuvres. To this I bowed assent; he then stood up, took my left hand, and Mohan's right, and stationed himself at the entrance while the men marched past; the word of command was given in French, and the exercise was gone through with much precision. He begged me to excuse anything amiss. I observed, that I was surprised to find his troops so proficient in European tactics. "Are the troops of your Emperor exercised in this manner?" he enquired. I answered, that there was a great similarity in the discipline of all the European States, although in the Austrian army there were some essential points of difference; we, for instance, execute in three manœuvres what the French do in two. "What is your pay?" said he. I replied, that I received none, having quitted the service ten years ago, peace having deprived it of every attraction, and as none but officers on active service and invalids had any pay, I now lived on my own income. "What is the pay of an Austrian Colonel?" said he. I told him that it was less than that of an English Colonel, but that, as they have not to purchase their steps, they do in reality receive more money. "Have you seen Lord William Bentinck?"—"No; he had left Calcutta before I arrived there." "Do you know Mr. Burnes?"—"Only through his works*." "Do you wish to see my troops exercise?" This, I told him, I should consider a great mark of his Highness' favour.

While the soldiers were marching about the little court, he continued his endless questions about the military resources of Austria, France, and England, and the number of disposable troops kept up by the different states of Europe. He then asked me what I meant to do with Mohan when I left the Panjáb and prepared for my return to Europe. I answered that I had not yet decided, but that I would take him with me, if he liked to go, adding that I believed he had a great wish to do so. I guessed what the Mahá Raja was thinking of, and presently he said, "You can make his fortune if you will but leave him behind; send the youth to me, and I will take care of him."

---

* The memory of Lieut.-Colonel Sir Alexander Burnes will be immemorially associated with the fatal occupation of Afghánistan. In the early part of his promising career, the Commander-in-Chief, General Sir Thomas Bradford, whose concern extended to every soldier in the army, was solicitous that the utmost facility should be afforded to Lieut. Burnes for extending our geographical knowledge in the regions he was about to explore, and desired I would instruct him, as time permitted, in surveying and reconnoitring. The service thus rendered for the cause of science, was frequently adverted to with grateful pride by Sir Alexander Burnes, who exultingly exhibited his papers to me on his return, when proceeding by the way of the Nilgiri Hills to meet Lord William Bentinck. "This," he said, "is the highest proof I can give you of my attention to your instructions." In all his change of fortunes, he was never known to overlook a kindness, or forget his early friendships.—*Ed.*

After we had seated ourselves again, he observed that I must be tired with answering all his questions. That, I replied, was impossible, but taking the hint to leave him, I departed, the Mahá Raja accompanying me to the door.

I had nearly omitted the flowery discourse of the Fakír Sahib as we went along. It began to rain, and his elephant marched close to mine. "This will be a rainy day," said I. "When princes meet in the garden of friendship," said the Fakír, "the water-bearers of heaven moisten the flowers, that they may give out all their perfume." I expressed my disappointment at being obliged to appear in a dark suit, on account of the non-arrival of my uniform from Lúdiana, which I had ordered to be sent on to me to Lahor. He then began to tell me a long story about a tiger, who had made his appearance in a city to the terror of everybody, and how the king of the country having heard what the tiger was doing, and found that his actions were all very noble, discovered his real nature in spite of his disguise, and sending for him to his palace, recognised in the tiger a great prince. "What," said I, "do you compare me with a tiger?"—"Under this disguise," he answered, "your noble actions and your talent will betray you." Such, in brief, was the meaning of his prolix tale.

When we returned from this interview I desired to see something of the city, for in going to the palace, which lies in the south-west or west end, we had passed through the south gate and had seen nothing but one very uninteresting street. Throughout India one remarks the strange contrast presented by majestic buildings, round which are huddled together ruins, rubbish, and wretched huts of every description. Lahor may claim a pre-eminence over all other cities in these contrasts. Close to the palace are mounds of dirt and pits of considerable depth, mud walls crumbled down, and unshapely heaps of stones, over which the traveller and his elephant move on wearily, coming oftentimes in this chaos of destruction on the apparition of an elephant, rhinoceros, tiger, or chíta, which the elephant passes very timidly without the slightest token of recognition. Beyond these you at length reach the bazar, where goods of great value are displayed, in streets which form, from one extremity to the other, a perfect slough after a heavy fall of rain; through these the luckless pedestrian is obliged to paddle, and looks in vain for a spot of dry ground on which to rest his foot, his white dress bespattered by every one passing by on horseback, and himself splashed all over from head to foot long before he gets out of the place again. Very strong and moveable awnings project over the shops, and nearly occupy the entire breadth of the narrow crooked roadway, which makes it a matter of no little difficulty to retain one's lofty position on the elephant's back, however desirable in many respects. Stuffs hung out to dry, carts with oxen, horsemen, camels, an elephant coming from the opposite direction, and an endless diversity of objects, fully engage the thought how to contrive to proceed, or get out of their way; while on the finely-carved balconies, almost within arm's length on either side, the wealthy Banyans with their painted faces and red turbans present their low obeisance occasionally, or some of the dark beauties of the place salute the traveller with a "Salam! Mahá Raja!" The streets of this bazar are intricate beyond measure, and I was rejoiced to find myself once more issuing forth from another gate into the external fresh air.

On my arrival at General Ventura's house, I found a messenger of the Mahá Raja's, Azíz-ud Dín, the elder brother of Khalifa Sahib, a diplomatic Minister, who informed me that the Mahá Raja had been highly pleased with my visit, and hoped I should make a long stay in Lahor. He brought me also twelve baskets filled with the finest fruits of Kabúl, Kashmír, and Lahor, and 225 rupees, for the daily pay of my people.

The three brothers, Azíz-ud Dín, the confidential Secretary; Khalifa Sahib, the Marshal; and the Governor of Amritsir, were often in my company; and I may observe here that the Mahá Raja places great confidence in these Mohammedans, who by their talents and honourable character, seem well to deserve it. They are usually styled Fakír Sahib, and seem proud of the poverty nominally assigned them, though they are all wealthy men. Their master, Ranjít Singh, is in every point of view so remarkable a character, for an Indian, that I have elsewhere devoted a considerable space to my description of him.

The days were short, and the evening came on soon after my

visitors had taken their leave. A walk in the plain by the river side and in some charming green fields occupied me till sunset.

Wednesday, January 14.—I was awakened with the intelligence that Azíz-ud Dín had been waiting for me half an hour, with a message from the Mahá Raja. I quickly dressed and hurried into the apartment, when the following conversation took place, after the customary extravagant compliments. The fakír assured me, first, that the Mahá Raja had never conversed with any person, whose talent had caused him so much surprise, and he wished I would consent to remain with him. He was aware that neither money nor any lucrative office could influence my actions, but as he did not wish me to reside in Lahor, and be obliged at the same time to draw any sums of money from my own country, he requested me, supposing that I did make up my mind to reside there, to accept a monthly allowance of 6000 rupees by way of compensation.

I answered, that the Mahá Raja's offer was most flattering to me, and if I had been a younger man, I should certainly have accepted it; but that family reasons made me anxious to return without loss of time to my own home, and that I must be at Bombay in six weeks, or I should most likely be detained in India for another year; in other words, I should lose a year of my life. The fakír strove to persuade me to remain, but finding me resolute, ceased to importune me further, and said that he would take my answer to the Mahá Raja, and that his master had given him a list of questions to put to me, dictated by himself, which he thereupon took from his pocket and read:—

1. The Mahá Raja knows you have travelled over the world; he wishes to hear what in all these countries has seemed to you most remarkable?

I answered, that the object of my travels was manifold; my chief purpose was to make myself acquainted with the most remarkable phenomena, moral and physical, of distant countries: that as edifices, the Egyptian Pyramids and the Táj Mahál: as countries, New Holland and Kashmír: lastly and above all, the manners and customs of the Malabar coast, the greatness and power of the East India Company, the Mahá Raja's ally, and more recently, the kingdom founded by

Ranjít Singh, who, like a skilful architect, has formed of so many insignificant unpromising fragments, one majestic fabric, seemed to me the most wonderful objects in the whole world.

The fakír wrote down my answer, with sundry Wáh! Wáh! as tokens of his amazement.

2. The Mahá Raja is aware that you did not travel for profit, and that in your own country your position is honourable and important. What was your motive for travelling so far?

I answered, that my reasons were already in part explained, and that it was most difficult to make a native of the East comprehend the mind of a European: life in India being limited to two pursuits, namely, physical or moral enjoyments through the attainment of power, which ensures the fulfilment of a man's desires; or, the hope of attaining greater happiness in another world by self-denial and holy deeds in the present. In Europe, the human mind is directed also to a third pursuit, that of scientific inquiry, which affords full occupation on subjects which to the mind of an Asiatic appear altogether unimportant. To this inclination for mental activity must be ascribed all the useful and extraordinary discoveries made by Europeans, and to this may partly be ascribed also my own wanderings, besides other reasons still less comprehensible to men of different habits. It will be well to give the Mahá Raja this answer, that my chief object was to observe the most remarkable customs of different lands, and where such was possible to make these observations subservient to the interests of my own country.

3. The Mahá Raja cannot think it possible, that you undertook such a dangerous journey, without something to protect you against disease. Probably you have brought some life-preserving medicine with you; the Mahá Raja wishes to know what it is, provided such communication should not weaken the force of the spell on yourself?

Without even smiling at this question, which doubtless had occasioned all the others to be introduced, I answered, that in Europe we no longer believed in the power of particular medicines to prolong life, but that I was fully persuaded I owed the preservation of my health to a medicine which I had always successfully used in two forms, either as a pill, and more promptly and efficaciously in a white powder. The fakír wrote my answer down verbatim.

4. The Mahá Raja is aware that Europeans are accustomed to eat a variety of food. How have you been able to obtain this necessary on your travels, and particularly, how did you contrive to get beef?

I answered, that I cared very little about any particular kind of diet, and subsisted on whatever I could get; but that we had a method in Europe of preserving food in tin boxes, which was thus kept fresh for years.

5. What is the surest means of being victorious over an enemy?

In answer to this, I stated it to be my opinion that the best policy of the Panjáb state would be to keep its soldiers under the strong arm of discipline, and when the General had once brought the army to this point, that the whole mass moved like his own sword, as one spirit with ten thousand arms, he might then make quite sure of victory. The Fakír Sahib exclaimed "Wáh! Wáh! Wáh! Amazing! Wonderful!" and turning round, inquired of Mr. Mackeson whether this was my own idea; upon hearing that it was, he again repeated "Wáh! Wáh!" Having straightway recorded the reply in due form, he begged to take his leave, departing with a torrent of the most exaggerated oriental compliments.

I had made arrangements to remain here until I was satisfied that all my people were in Lúdiana, which place I should reach from Lahor in three days. There all my collections were to be packed up, and I intended to hire relays of bearers to convey them with all dispatch to Delhi, and thence to Bombay. To-day I heard that my people had not even arrived at Amritsir, which place, according to the route laid down for them, they ought to have reached the same day that I arrived in Lahor. From Amritsir to Lúdiana is eight marches, consequently I had to make up my mind to stay in Lahor until the 22nd, that I might not have to wait for them at Lúdiana.

A deputation from the family of Mehán Singh, the Governor of Kashmír, with his son at the head of it, came to-day to thank me for the manner in which I had spoken of his father to Ranjít Singh. This was in reference to the Mahá Raja's question, whether he ought not to remove Mehán Singh from Kashmír. As I observed, while in that province, it would be very desirable to have a more active Governor there, but the difficulty would be to replace him with a better. Since his intentions at least are good, I told the youth, who was about thirteen or fourteen years old, that he might assure his father that I should never prejudice Ranjít Singh against him. I had also a visit from the son of the Jemidar, a General of fourteen; notwithstanding his youth, his talents, vivacity, and desire for information promise great things.

The day was bitterly cold, and my fingers were almost frozen as I arranged my papers. I paced the terrace very often to warm myself in the sun's rays. In the evening we had a Nách, and the Mahá Raja did not forget to send his presents, and three of his dancing girls.

Friday, January 15.—The fakír Azíz-ud Dín was here early this morning, to thank me from the Mahá Raja, for my answers to his questions. According to the Eastern fashion, he repeated these thanks three times, adding also that the Mahá Raja wished that I would remain for some time in Lahor; and even if the Emperor of Austria's permission was necessary, he was quite ready to apply for it himself. At all events he hoped I should not quit Lahor for several months, and that I would organize some regiments for him according to the plan I had laid down. If it were not agreeable to me to receive regular pay, some other arrangement might be entered into between us.

The earnest repetition of this offer, which at first I had taken as a mere courtesy, convinced me that the Mahá Raja was serious; and I candidly confess that I reflected for a moment on the opening now afforded to me, so far beyond my utmost expectations. Had I desired to undertake an expedition into Central Asia, it seems it would not have been difficult for me to lead an army formed by myself in that quarter; and the various, though perhaps not profound information I had acquired, would suffice to render me very useful to the Mahá Raja. All things needful were at hand, money and the consent of the reigning authorities: by one man's efforts, civilization might be mightily advanced. But then the image of my mother, aged and expecting my return to her, would obtrude itself. I therefore repeated my thanks, adding, that the Mahá Raja might be assured that nothing but considerations of the most pressing importance would have induced me to decline his proposals. The fakír now informed me, that my answers yesterday had given him so high an idea of my penetration, that he had charged him to ask my advice respecting his health. I replied that I could not but be highly flattered, and though no physician, that I had, like most intelligent Europeans, occasionally turned my attention to the science of medicine.

The Mahá Raja was suffering, as I have said, from a paralysis, which appeared to me, from his general appearance, not so much the consequence of a ruined constitution, as the effect of a temporary state of ill health. I expressed this opinion to the fakír, and questioned him as to the condition of his health prior to the attack. He informed me, that on a very sultry day, just before the rainy season set in, which in the past year was preceded by heats which were unusually great, the Mahá Raja had ridden the whole day on horseback, and had greatly exhausted and overheated himself. With his usual carelessness with regard to food, he took nothing that day but water melons, of which he partook very freely. A heavy storm fell in the afternoon, the rain poured down in torrents, and the piercing wind from the mountains of Kashmír suddenly lowered the temperature to a degree inconveniently cold. The Mahá Raja rode for a long time, and at a foot's pace through this storm, until he reached a hut. There, however, the walls afforded him little protection against the wind, and he sat in his wet clothes, the draughts of air penetrating to him, and of course contributing to chill his frame. He did not reach his tent until nightfall, and nothing could persuade him to take any medicine, or use any sort of remedy. A violent pain in the stomach occasioned him very disturbed sleep; and when he would have called for assistance, his tongue felt heavy in his mouth, and he found his left hand quite powerless. When a servant came and saw him in this state, he called immediately for Azíz-ud Dín, who found him with his face much drawn up, and next to speechless. I could not understand what means were employed to restore him, but according to the Hindú custom, musk was probably administered in large doses. He was brought back to Lahor, and became something better, and Dr.

M'Gregor being called in from Lúdiana, he was placed under his care. He can now mount his horse again, but the motion is painful to him, and causes the hesitation in his speech to increase perceptibly: his eye has also suffered, and is still distorted, giving a stranger an idea that the sight is quite gone. If he wishes to examine any object, he brings it within two inches of his eye in an oblique direction, but at the distance of eight or ten paces he can guess the thoughts by the expression of the face. This account confirmed me in my opinion that the evil was not so deeply seated as is usual in such cases. Azíz-ud Dín requested me to write a prescription for the Mahá Raja. I inquired as to the regimen he pursued, and found it a most pernicious one; for though what he ate was simple enough, and not too much in quantity, he drank spirits in ruinous draughts. He gave me the receipt for a brandy prepared for him, in which were the strongest sauces compounded from the flesh of every kind of animal, beef excepted, pearls and jewels, musk, opium, plants of various kinds, all mingled together into a beverage, which must be nearly as strong as alcohol itself. This devil's drink I had myself tasted the evening before, and found the flavour good enough, but the following morning my spirits were exceedingly depressed. I asked whether he often drank of this royal wine, as it is here called, and he said yes, but that the Mahá Raja had desired him to inquire what I thought of it. I answered, that I considered it a most noxious potation, not improbably the cause of his last attack of illness; but as he had been in the habit of drinking it for many years, I considered that it would be very hazardous to leave it off suddenly, and likely to produce an alarming prostration of strength. The fakír told me that Dr. M'Gregor had forbidden the liquor altogether, but that the Mahá Raja, while obeying the prescription, had been so enfeebled, that he had taken to it again. The fakír asked me how much I thought he could drink without injuring his health, but I confessed my inability to specify any quantity. One wine glass had been a powerful dose in my own case, but as the Mahá Raja had accustomed himself to a larger allowance, perhaps this might do to begin with. The less he took, however, the better.

Ranjít also wished to have some of the medicine I had spoken of as having brought and used; for, whatever I might say, it was evident that I must consider it as a life preservative, or I should never be so foolish as to hazard my existence for no other purpose than the mere gratification of curiosity. I knew that I could not persuade either Ranjít or the fakír that I had nothing like an elixir of life, and therefore answered, that I had sent my stock with my servants to Lúdiana, except a few pills, but that I would send for it thence, and in the mean time, the little I had, was at the Mahá Raja's service. He then wanted some of the hermetically sealed provisions, but of these I had none remaining. I gave him half a dozen blue pills, the last I had, and Mr. Vigne produced a packet of calomel. I explained the dose to him.

The fakír then informed me that the Mahá Raja had ordered a review to take place that day, which he hoped I would attend; that at noon a salute of artillery would give notice that he had left his palace, and Khalifa Sahib would then come to escort me. I told the fakír I should be ready to accompany his brother, and he requested my permission to withdraw, taking his leave with a profusion of compliments.

Long before twelve the fakír arrived with three elephants, two valuable richly clad horses, palankeens, &c. I preferred mounting the elephant's back, for the dust on horseback, or in the palankeen, surrounded by a party of forty or fifty horsemen, would have been quite intolerable. General Ventura rode on horseback, and as the salute was fired, Mr. Mackeson and I took our seats in one howdah, the fakír and Mr. Vigne in another, when we proceeded by the outer walls of the city, by the splendid building, formerly the mosque of Jehánghír, and through a gate which led to the entrance of the palace, with its small fort guarding it, on to the large exercising ground. The warmth of the sun and the opening spring, had given the country the most enchanting appearance; the inimitable green of the earliest Indian vegetation adorned the plain, which was thinly scattered with trees now in blossom; these trees being planted in the European taste, together with a number of pleasure houses here and there visible down to the banks of the Rávi, combined altogether to produce a scene most beautifully diversified. The whole neighbourhood is intersected by canals, which preclude the assemblage of any vast concourse, and it now presented to my gaze, the most brilliant, magnificent, and imposing spectacle which I had ever beheld in my life. Before I proceed to describe the living actors in the scene, I may be allowed to say a few words more on the inanimate features. And first, as we approached towards the city, were seen those picturesque and beautiful buildings erected by Jehánghír, for the winter residence of the empress, and executed with the lavish profusion of a man, who had only to will, and forthwith to show before her whom he loved a perfect world of treasures. Jehánghír built this splendid palace because Lahor was a favourite residence of Núr Jehán: the walls are chiefly of marble, and the different buildings tower one above the other in the form of an amphitheatre. Ranjít Singh has added to it other buildings not less extraordinary or expensive, though in very bad taste. Even this inconsistent work of modern times, corresponding as it does with the uncultivated taste of the suddenly-raised Lord of the country, serves to bring out the back ground, formed of palaces built in the noblest styles. A view of the façades to the west, and the light thrown on them at this hour, mingled with deep masses of shade, formed one of the most enchanting and picturesque sights that it is possible to imagine. Vigne was in raptures, and I urged him not to let a single day pass while he remained at Lahor, without committing to paper some part of this splendid picture, which it would require several days to complete.

Meanwhile we had arrived at the scene of the review. Several regiments of infantry were drawn up in line, having on the right wing two batteries of horse artillery. These began marching upon us, and our elephants were, as nearly as possible, caught by the wheels of the gun-carriages, the clumsy animals having placed themselves in the way, and all the exclamations of the Mahúts were ineffectual to coax them out of their customary step. When we got within thirty paces of the Mahá Raja's open tent, the elephants were ordered to kneel down; this tent was of yellow Kashmír shawl stuff, supported on columns of silver, the inside was covered with a large carpet, another being spread without. Both were the produce of

Kashmír. .Several other tents were pitched behind the royal tent. Ranjít Singh himself was seated in the European manner in a plain arm chair, and by him was Raja Hira Singh; the first was dressed in a simple riding-dress, while the latter was clad in white muslin and pink satin, with bracelets of diamonds, pearls, and other jewels; his accoutrements, turban, and other habiliments were covered with the most expensive stones. Kúshal Singh, the Jemidar, and Raja Súshet Singh, were the only state officers present. The last, a very fine distinguished man, wore a black and gold enamelled helmet with the visor open, and ornamented with three large black herons' feathers. His dress was a green robe of Kashmír shawl, trimmed with red, over which he wore a shirt of mail of glittering steel; an armlet inlaid with gold was fastened on his right arm. The Mahá Raja rose up, came to the end of the carpet, and received me with a clasp of the hand, leading me to an arm chair placed beside his own. Mr. Mackeson and Vigne sat near me, and Mohan stood behind Ranjít's chair.

The troops consisted of some regular infantry; they wore red jackets, and carried matchlocks; they marched by in order. But what particularly attracted me, was the sight of the Mahá Raja's favourite horses, drawn up between the tent and the troops, twenty-five or thirty in number. The breed in the Panjáb is very peculiar, and not unlike that of Spain, but with straighter noses. The animals are large, and their movements are very gentle; they may be trained to execute the most graceful curvettings, and the Sikhs value them according to their proficiency in their movements. But I suspect that they have not much spirit, owing to the state of repose in which they are habitually kept, being from their very birth consigned to the care of a groom, and fastened by means of two ropes round the head, and two on the hind feet, to small pegs. In this manner their life is passed in the open air, and they are very rarely mounted. Many are born white. To the artist, who is not a painter of horses, these animals present a beautiful appearance, with their small bones, flowing mane and tail, and their proud and fiery action, and lofty heads. The passion of Ranjít Singh for horses has passed into a proverb in the East. The bridle, saddle, and other ornaments of these creatures are most costly. The first is overlaid with gold or enamel, and at the top of the head, or else on either side, waves a plume of heron's feathers; strings of jewels are hung round the neck, under which are the *Sulimans*, or Onyx stones, very highly prized on account of the superstition attached to them. The saddle is also of enamel or gold, covered with precious stones, the pommel being particularly rich. The housings are of Kashmír shawl, fringed with gold; the crupper and martingale ornamented very highly, and on each side of the favourite usually hangs the tail of the Tibetan yák, dyed of various hues; the saddle, moreover, is covered with a velvet cushion.

After a profusion of compliments, the Mahá Raja poured out a torrent of questions of every kind, and it became quite evident to me, that he was throwing off gradually a preconceived idea that my entire journey had him for its object, and that though I might not have intended to enter his service, I was bound on some commission either open or mysterious in its nature. I usually availed myself of Mr. Mackeson's complaisant offer to be my interpreter, and this must have assured him very soon that I had no designs of that nature. He rarely spoke of India or the English territories there, but chiefly asked my opinion of his own country, his army, the European officers in his service, and the designs of foreign countries and very distant lands of which he had hitherto heard nothing. Nor did he omit some very odd questions about my own circumstances; for instance, whether I belonged to the caste of the Raja or the Wazír? Each question was conveyed in the fewest words possible, and one followed upon another in such rapid succession that it seemed as though his mind required continual nourishment; that he did not wish for any details, but simply a reply. In this spirit I framed my answers to them, and as I had those answers already at hand, I took care not to delay a moment in uttering them. Short sentences and quick replies are likewise especially needful wherever an interpreter is used, to prevent a conversation becoming intolerably tiresome. He asked me at last whether I should like to see the horses nearer, and on my request so to do, he rose and taking my hand, walked out of the tent, and ordered them to be led up one after the other. A pommel of one of the saddles struck me as particularly worthy of remark, having a ruby two inches square, bearing on it the name of Jehánghír. Dow, in his *History of Hindosthan*, tells us, that when Jehánghír had his name engraved on this beautiful stone, the celebrated Empress Núr Jehán told him that she thought it a pity; to which he answered, "This jewel will more assuredly hand down my name to posterity than any written history. The House of Timúr may fall, but as long as there is a king, this jewel will have its price." Many other names are now engraven on it, the best known being Ahmed Shah's, who found it in the famous peacock throne (Takht-i-Táús), made by Shah Jehán in 1635, at Agra. This stone was stolen from Timúr in the year 1398, at Delhi, and Jehánghír repurchased it. Ranjít Singh told me he had received a splendid pair of pistols from Lord Amherst, and desired that they might be brought. His people searched in various holsters without finding them, until he called out and named the horse on which they were eventually found, a proof of his good memory, and of the bad regulation of his stables. The pistols are studded with gold, and set in bad diamonds; but Ranjít Singh seemed very proud of having received them, as a present from Lord Amherst, and said to me, "When you get home, send me a pair of pistols from your country," which I promised, and, God willing, will not forget to do. As we returned to the tent, I told him I had not seen the most celebrated of his horses, and on his asking which that was, I named Láilí, which had made his name almost as well known in Europe as the foundation of his extensive dominion had done. He promised that I should see it on the morrow. As we seated ourselves he went on: "I was sure you would like to see the famous diamond. Will you look at it now?" for they had brought before us four shields, on which was laid the most superb assortment of jewels; but the celebrated *Kohi-núr*, or Mountain of light, the largest diamond in the world, attracted my admiration above all. It is of the shape and size of a hen's egg, exquisitely white, and brilliant beyond description. It is set in an armlet, having a diamond on either side, for which the Mahá Raja told me he gave 130,000 and 100,000 rupees (13,000*l.* and 10,000*l.*) in Amritsir. Both of these had belonged to Shah Shújah. The history of the *Kohi-núr* deserves to be related, showing as it does the character of Ranjít Singh, if not to advantage, at least so truly that it will be worth while to devote a few words to it in the chapter dedicated to him. Ranjít put this treasure into my hand that I might examine it more narrowly, and I must confess that the thought of the enormous value set by fancy on this single jewel caused me many a deep reflexion. How many thousand poor families might be made happy for the price at which this diamond was estimated! In an instant I looked on it as something of more than earthly value, as the means of happiness; but it could only bless by being parted with, and then it would become so much dead capital in the hands of another; its existence only becoming really valuable while it is being transferred from one to another party, like a bank-note or a bill of exchange. Perhaps, as kings of every age have taken delight in the accumulation of treasures, it is well that they hoard precious stones instead of keeping away gold from the trade and prosperity of their kingdoms, for that is distributed without diminution of its value. This idea brought me to a comparison between jewels, which require a connoisseur and admirer to prize them at their real worth; and gold, which has an intrinsic worth to all men: these in their respective value appeared to me to resemble the nobler gifts of genius and talent. How few can estimate the former, while talent is recognized by all.

Ranjít Singh was much pleased with my long examination of this treasure, and roused me from my reverie by asking me how I liked it. He then pointed with gratified vanity to each particular stone, and gave me its history, particularly that of the great emerald, which in the above-named peacock throne of Delhi, formed the body of a parrot.

Thirty elephants, gaily dressed out, now passed by. The largest, of an immense size, and named Sirdarji, had been lately sent to Ranjít by the King of Nepál, and was ornamented with a splendid gilt howdah and crimson velvet cushions. Red velvet housings fell as low as his knees, trimmed with a gold border and fringe. The long tusks were cut at the end, as is the case with all tame elephants; but this deficiency was supplied by tops of silver gilt, united by a golden chain. Round his ancles were heavy gold bangles, such as the Hindús wear, curiously wrought. The price of this elephant's ornaments, according to the Mahá Raja's account, was 130,000 florins*. The animal was quite black, except the face and trunk, which were painted with various colours. Unluckily, however, his pedigree is ignoble; he does not carry his head high, and instead of feeling proud of his finery, or playing with his chains, he behaves like a plebeian decked out in a court suit.

The Mahá Raja told me that he had 101 elephants, the same number that attends the Governor-General whenever he travels; 1000 saddle horses for his own use, 27,000 for his infantry; for the troops in armour 15,000; for the cavalry 27,000; apprehending that I might not have fully understood him, he went over his story again, which I learnt afterwards was strictly correct. He then told me that he thought I should like to see some of his finest tents, and that he had ordered them to be pitched. I accordingly visited them while he remained seated. Some were made of the wools of Kashmír, others of stuffs woven with silver threads, and I observed that one had a border of pearls, but there were none of any considerable size. A Kashmír shawl was laid down as a carpet for every one. When I returned from my inspection, horses were led up for our use, that we might see the troops to advantage; the seat on one of these inestimably costly saddles is very uncomfortable to a European. Ranjít Singh was quickly on the back of his steed, his shield at back, his like a common Sikh, and his face half hidden by the lower part of the turban which was wrapped over his chin. As we rode towards the troops, we were saluted by the most barbarous and discordant band of music, so called; every musician sounded his instrument as loudly as possible, and no two sounded them in tune. It was lucky for my ears that the drums exceeded them all in loudness, and in front of these the Mahá Raja took his station.

* About 13,000*l.*, reckoning the florin in round numbers at two shillings English or one rupee. The average exchange of Vienna is nine florins, fifty-two creuzers to the pound sterling of England. The silver florin is equivalent to sixty creuzers.—*Ed.*

I never heard so horrible a noise before, and with much difficulty repressed my inclination to laugh outright, it did seem such utter folly to stand where I did, instead of taking to instant flight with my hands to my ears; but I suppressed my own feelings on the occasion as well as I could, and looked straight before me until at a signal from the Mahá Raja, the unearthly din ceased. He then turned to me, his features plainly saying, "There, I am sure you never expected that; you had no idea how great proficients we are in European harmony." He inquired what I thought of his music, and as the reader may suppose, I said it was surprisingly good.

After we had passed the lines, the men presented arms, and the commanding officer dropped his sword. The Mahá Raja inquired for Sultan Mohammed Khan. He was told by one of his suite, that he had been waiting for some time; presently he appeared with his son on foot, and was presented to me by the Mahá Raja in this style:—"This is Sultan Mohammed Khan, the Sirdar of Pesháwar, and brother of Dost Mohammed Khan. At this time I am giving him three lakhs of rupees as Jaghir." Sultan Mohammed Khan is about thirty-six years of age, and was clothed according to the fashion of Kabúl, in long garments of gold brocade, and a yellow shawl wound as a turban about his head. He made a low bow, without uttering a single word, and thus ended the introduction. Sultan Mohammed Khan was one of the fifty brothers of Fatih Khan, the Wazír of Mohammed Shah, who conquered the kingdom of Kabúl for his master, which was occupied by Shah Shúja, the brother of Mohammed Shah. Mohammed Shah, however, put Fatih Khan to death, and thereby lost his throne, the brothers of Fatih Khan immediately breaking out into open rebellion, and dispersing themselves in every part of the kingdom. The most powerful of them is Dost Mohammed Khan, who lives in Kabúl. Two of these brothers have already felt the power of Ranjít's arms, viz., Jabar Khan, who had appropriated to himself Kashmír, and Yár Mohammed in Pesháwar; the first was forced to quit the country where he had taken up arms; the last, unable to defend himself against the men of his own faith, the savage Juff Yusufzei, dwelling in the mountains north of Pesháwar, entered into terms with Ranjít Singh, by which, in return for protection given him against these enemies, he became his vassal. When Yar Mohammed died, General Ventura was in Pesháwar, whither he had gone to receive the horse, his tribute to the sovereignty of Ranjít Singh, and he obeyed the command of the Mahá Raja to put the deceased's brother, Sultan Mohammed Khan, in possession of Pesháwar. Disturbances, however, broke out quickly, and Sultan Mohammed Khan favoured them, in order to get from Ranjít Singh something in exchange for his resignation of Pesháwar. The fact is, that Pesháwar is on the borders of his eldest brother's, Dost Mohammed Khan's territory, and during the latter war of Ranjít Singh against him, the theatre of operations was precisely in the neighbourhood of Pesháwar, rendering the position of Sultan Mohammed Khan, obliged, though a brother and a Mohammedan, to join the standard of Ranjít Singh, one of peculiar difficulty. In return for the resignation of Pesháwar, of which he took immediate possession, Ranjít amused Sultan Mohammed Khan with promises for a long time; and it is but this very day, that Mohammed Khan, after incessant exertions, has obtained a territory, which brings him in a revenue of about three lakhs of rupees. Perhaps, but for my arrival, he would have had to wait still, for the recompense was given to-day, with the evident design of displaying the greatness and generosity of Ranjít Singh before foreign visitors.

Having stationed ourselves in front of the battalions and the artillery, the exercises and manœuvres began, the firing being very regular. The men loaded and fired five times in the minute. An accident then occurred, which was truly original in its nature. The elephants, carrying different persons of the suite, stood in front of the guns. After the first firing, they began to show great symptoms of inquietude, and spreading wide their legs, they trembled all over, and roared in a frightful manner. Presently, in spite of the blows given them by the driver in the face, the *Ankush* causing the blood to follow at every stroke, they wheeled about, and rushed over the plain in all directions, with their tails distended, and trunks lifted high up in the air, putting the assembled multitude to instant flight.

The manœuvring was very indifferent, and consisted chiefly in firing off a quantity of blank cartridges. When the troops had marched away, I took my *rukhsut*, or leave, of the Mahá Raja, and returned to the house highly delighted with the brilliant spectacle I had witnessed, which in originality, splendour of costume, and the addition of the beautiful natural scenery, surpassed anything of the kind I had ever witnessed during the last twenty years of my life.

On my return, I found letters from India, with good wishes for my safe journey, and an invitation from Captain Wade, inviting me to Fírozpoor, and thence to travel with him to Lúdiana. Fírozpoor was in a Sikh state, on the left shore of the Setlej, but has lapsed to the East India Company lately, in consequence of the demise of the last possessor without direct heirs. The captain had been sent to take possession of it, Mr. Mackeson having been despatched to Lahor, to settle some differences which had arisen in consequence of Ranjít Singh claiming Fírozpoor as his property. I would have accepted the invitation gladly, as a means of taking me more speedily to Lúdiana, but then I should have missed seeing both Govindgurh and Amritsir, which lie on the direct road between Lahor and Lúdiana. I therefore declined the offer, with suitable acknowledgments.

In the afternoon Fakír Khalifa Sahib came with another message from the Raja. He inquired, first, whether the review had not fatigued me, to which I answered, that the last five years had pretty well hardened me against fatigue, and that I had brought away with me an impression of surprise at the splendour of Ranjít Singh's court. He then said that the Mahá Raja had desired him to request me to give him some of the medicine I always carried about with me, if it were not asking too great a favour, for he had learned that the powder was sent yesterday by Mr. Vigne, and not by myself. I promised to let him have some as soon as I should get back to Lúdiana.

He told me that the Mahá Raja had given a dose of the pills in the morning to one of his officers, who had not as yet been sensible of any effect from them. I answered, that the mildness of the remedy would perhaps only occasion a slight feeling of improvement, and that if the officer were already in good health, he might not be sensible of any change whatever.

I omitted to mention before, that Ranjít had consulted me in the morning about his own state, complaining of weakness in his right side. His pulse was natural for an old man. I inquired whether the skin were insensible, and hearing that such was the case, I advised him to have some powerful ointment rubbed into it, to excite and invigorate the powers. He then complained of his tongue, over which he has not perfect command, and which feels at the root hardened like wood. I cheered him with the hope that this proceeded from want of activity in the muscles, and would be remedied when the side was irritated.

In proof of his courtesy, I may add here, that while at the review, a plate with about a dozen of the grapes of Kabúl, was brought to him. He asked my permission to eat them; and the manner in which the question was interpreted, made me suppose that in consequence of my advice as to his diet, he was asking my medical opinion. I said, therefore, that I did not think a few grapes could hurt him, He saw where the mistake had arisen, and quickly added, "An invalid must ask pardon whenever he does any thing disallowed."

I had omitted to take a present with me on my first interview, a compliment expected from every visitor, for I could find nothing that I thought likely to be at all valued. General Ventura gave me an opera glass to-day, and I filled an ornamented silver inkhorn, which shut fast with an India rubber stopper, with some "bouquet du Roi." These I carried to him, recommending the last as a remedy for the headach. But the first attracted his attention directly, and he looked through it at the troops. His eye was too weak, however, to enable him to make any use of it.

In the evening we had the dancers again, and among them was a girl of thirteen, who amused us a good deal with her jokes, at the expense of Mr. Forni, who sat there with his grey beard and his foraging-cap, caring nothing about us, or the jests mostly levelled at his beard, and which his bad sight only allowed him to understand very imperfectly. There were also present some dancers of the Mahá Raja's, and they drank an incredible quantity of spirituous liquors, without becoming intoxicated. It is singular, how much of the strongest brandy these girls will swallow, without any effect; the fact is, they are so completely deadened by their course of life, that they seem no longer alive to any excitement.

Saturday, January 16.—The Mahá Raja sent this morning to say, that if I would not remain in Lahor altogether, he hoped at least that I would not go away before the Húli, which falls about the end of February, and draws to Lahor every dignitary of the empire in all their glory. The Húli is a festival celebrated in honour of the god Krishna by Hindús of all classes, and with the wildest sports and dissipation. I had heard throughout Hindústhan of the splendour with which it is always kept at Lahor, and was therefore sorry to miss the chance of seeing it. The fakír came back in two hours, and told me that as the Mahá Raja thought I must be curious to see the festival, he would send the dancing girls with everything necessary, to show me the manner of its celebration. I expressed my obligations; General Allard's garden was fixed on as the locality, and it was agreed we should meet at one o'clock. At the hour appointed we repaired to the spot, the Mahá Raja having already sent everything necessary, not forgetting silver and gold tinsel.

This Hindú festival, as I have said, is in honour of Krishna, and represents the manner in which he and his beloved Sita, with their companions, amused themselves. A quantity of *Singhára* meal dyed yellow, green, red, and blue, is put into large baskets, and mixed up with little pieces of gold and silver tinsel, a number of large pots of water dyed with the same colours, and little water-engines being set near. Every one appears in white garments, and the festival commences, by the dancing girls sitting down, and breaking forth into a song in honour of the feast. The baskets of coloured meal are then introduced, and thin glass balls full of Singhara powder, are distributed to the assembly, which they throw at each other, and being broken with the slightest force discharge their contents on the white dresses, and stain them. Like all games of this description, these begin gently, but soon assume a rougher aspect, each player seizing as many balls as he can, and flinging them at one another. When the glass balls are exhausted, they take the coloured meal, first, as much as the fingers can hold, then by handfuls, and at last they empty the baskets over each other's heads, covering the whole person. The dirtiest part of the entertainment consists in the sprinkling with the coloured waters. In great houses the Húli is often held in the Zenana, and on those occasions the women are allowed to be present. Spirits are drank, and the amusements are then carried far beyond our European ideas of propriety, but the Hindú thinks no harm of them.

In General Allard's garden, built by himself, is a pretty little building. The eagle and Napoleon's flag are displayed on every wall, and here and there are figures representing the soldiers who served under him. In the upper story are a few rooms, adorned with mirrors, and set apart for the females of his family. Before the main building is the tomb of his young daughter, a singular but durable monument, in the Mohammedan taste, but embellished with the cross, the sign of the father's faith, while the style of the tomb shows the mother's.

In the evening the dancers who had performed the Húli all came: they are always carried about in Gárís, or covered vehicles drawn by oxen, and usually escorted by a party of armed police, whom they pay for fear of being robbed of the costly jewels with which they are usually decked. To a European's eye there is nothing more singular than one of these processions going or returning.

Sunday, January 17.—The Shalimár garden is one of the sights of Lahor. There are three famous gardens of this name. One at Delhi, the original from which the others are copied, and which cost, they say, ten millions of florins; a second at Lahor, made by Núr Jehán; and the third and most celebrated of all, at Kashmír, laid out by Jehánghír. Having a leisure day, I begged General Ventura to lend me his carriage to take me there; and accompanied by his brother-in-law Mr. Dubuignon, and Vigne, I set off. The garden is five miles from the city, and the road to it carries one past serais, palaces, and ruins, so numerous and extensive, that they must be seen to be believed. In Europe, the sight of a ruin creates in the mind a feeling of curiosity and surprise, imagination is set to work, and we retrace the strange existence formerly perhaps passed within the walls. The reason is, that ruins are not often seen there, and they carry us back to bygone days and the traditions of history. In India, their great numbers make us pass thousands without any emotion. True, scarcely any of them, except those belonging to the pre-Mohammedan times, are without a history, and the Hindú ruins are stored with the most fanciful of legends; but their number, and sometimes their modern date, interest the spectator otherwise than with us. There may be inhabitants of Lahor now living, who have seen most of those buildings, whose walls are now crumbling in unshapely masses, in their day of pride: here the mind has to reflect on the fallen greatness, the rapidity of time's destructiveness, the swift departure of men and their works; while we, in Europe, look on ruins which are monuments of an age of power, to which nobler and better things have succeeded.

Some bold eminences start up from this chaos of ruins, and interrupt the monotony of the plain. Not that nature has had any thing to do with them, whatever their height or extent may be; they owe their existence to the burning of bricks, and a view of the numberless ruined edifices constructed with this material at once accounts for their appearance here. Near them is a crowd of new palaces, built in the worst taste, the largest of which, belonging to Kripa Rám, (not the former governor of Kashmír,) looks over the midst of this scene of desolation, like a house of cards built in the Colosseum of Rome. Four miles from Lahor the road to the Shalimár leads through the Serái of Núr Jehán, a large building like a fortress, but now entirely in ruins.

The Shalimár is a large building, for the entire garden, about a mile and a half long and a quarter of a mile broad, is in fact an edifice, and not a pleasure ground. The entrance of the building, which is constructed of fine marble, is the prettiest part of it, and is at present occupied by the family of a poor gardener. From this spot the ground falls, and at a quarter of a mile further on is a large reservoir, which is nearly as extensive as a lake. Close to it are several buildings huddled together, some tasteful enough; indeed, the whole might well have served as a model for the pleasure gardens of the age of Louis XIV. The Shalimár is well kept, and many very fine fruits, particularly the Santareh oranges, thrive abundantly. Ranjít Singh frequently passes a day or two in this place.

The Máli laid a beautiful basket of fruit at my feet. I perambulated the garden in all directions, and the buildings in like manner; I determined to have a brisk walk, for my present inactivity, after the constant exercise I had been long accustomed to, caused me sensations of great disquiet, and was even painful to me.

In this garden Núr Jehán was wont to hold yearly fairs, where pleasure became madness. A straw hut, built by Ranjít Singh, has a strange appearance in the midst of so much that breathes of royal magnificence. As we came back I expressed my wish to see General Ventura's garden. The road is dreadful, being over the ruins of the old city, which extended in this direction, from the ancient citadel, the present city, four or five miles in a semi-circle round the Rávi. Large as Lahor is at present, it must formerly have been at least ten times as extensive. We reached the garden with some trouble, a Sikh General having taken a fancy to the place, had pitched his tent there, and his horses prevented our carriage from getting near the gate. The garden is prettily situated; the entrance-hall in the first division is large and handsome; the rooms in the second, or the Zenána, are also pretty; but Jacquemont indulged his fancy very largely, when he wrote that this was one of the fairy palaces of the Thousand and One Nights.

We rode back for a mile along the city wall, and when not far from home, I descried a black fakír dancing with his guitar, and singing praises to Govind Singh. He was standing on a lofty terrace before a handsome tomb, in which he had taken up his abode. His long black robe was lined with red; a black and white belt with astrological signs hung from his right shoulder across the left side, and a high magic cap completed his fantastic array. He had a circle of female auditors. I alighted from the carriage to view this novel spectacle somewhat nearer, and was surprised at the manner in which he danced to the melody of a very fine voice.

On my return home, I found the Fakír Sahib waiting for me, with a request from Ranjít Singh that I would give him a testimonial. After some trouble, I made out that he wanted a writing, in which I was to congratulate both the Mahá Raja and the Company on the strict friendship existing between them, and acknowledge the handsome reception given to myself. I could not help laughing at the idea, and asked the fakír what possible use such a testimonial from an insignificant foreigner, who had nothing to do with the English Government, could be to Ranjít Singh. Nevertheless, without waiting for any further request, I promised to draw up something of the kind, and take his opinion of it on the following morning, when he was to return. In the evening we had a nách again, an entertainment which has no attractions for me, but which they think necessary for the proper reception of every stranger.

Mr. Mackeson started this evening for Fírozpoor, taking with him some letters for me for my European correspondents. I saw him depart with much regret. He is a very amiable, prudent man, and I foresee that my intercourse with Ranjít Singh will not be carried on so easily without him.

Monday, January 18.—I rose early to draw up the paper for Ranjít Singh, and after pondering a little, I wrote down as follows, but, before I had it translated into Persian, I intended to show it to Ventura and the fakír. "When I left my own country to visit the different kingdoms of the world, I made every inquiry how far it would be possible for me to travel. The kingdoms of Lahor and Kashmír, so little known to Europeans, were peculiarly interesting to me. I had heard of the great Mahá Raja of Lahor, who, living in peace and amity with the English East India Company, protected travellers with his power, and received them with distinction at his court, much spoken of in Europe. In consequence of my information, I journeyed to Hindústhan, and finding that the friendship between the two powers was much stronger than I had believed, I asked and obtained the Mahá Raja's permission to visit Kashmír. Throughout my journey I was loaded with kindness by the Mahá Raja; but I was chiefly impressed by the evident confidence and good understanding subsisting between the Company and the Mahá Raja, which is for the happiness of the world, and, like the tree of life, protects and gives security to the whole of India."

When the fakír came, Ventura translated these words to him. He said that the Mahá Raja would like to hear something more about the great friendship between the two countries, and would be pleased to have it written in English by my own hand, so that the Persian translation might be made on the same page. I then wrote these lines:—

"Previously to leaving my own country with the intention of visiting foreign kingdoms, I made inquiries how far a European might be able to penetrate, and hope to enjoy the protection of the sovereigns ruling over them. The kingdom of the Panjáb and Kashmír had particular attractions and interest for me as being, especially the latter, countries little seen by, and still less known to the inhabitants of the western world. In Europe, I had heard of the most powerful Mahá Raja of Lahor, who, living in peace and friendship with the Company Sirdar, not only afforded protection to travellers visiting the Panjáb, but received them with distinction at his court. Upon my arrival in Hindústhan, the accounts which I had heard in the course of my travels, of the friendship subsisting between the two governments were not only confirmed, but proved to me to be much stronger than I had even imagined. Thus encouraged, I asked and obtained the permission of the Mahá Raja to go to Kashmír, and afterwards to present my respects to his Highness at Lahor. From the Mahá Raja I experienced not only the protection and munificence becoming a great king, but his kindness has left a lasting impression upon me. This, as the first Austrian who had ever visited these countries, was particularly gratifying to my feelings, and it was with equal surprise and pleasure, that I observed the close and unreserved friendship established between the Mahá Raja and the British government, which happily spreads its branches over the whole of Hindústhan and the Panjáb, and will every day acquire strength and solidity."

The last words "and will" were added at the urgent request of the fakír. The whole looked rather strange to me, and if it should ever be found among Ranjít's papers, will not be very easily understood. Perhaps the testimonials which were asked of me by all his subordinates, from the governor of Kashmír down to the most humble Thanadar, were sent to him for the purpose of keeping them for a similar motive. To gratify his childish whim, I wrote this in English in my best manner, and affixed to it my large European seal. The fact is, that time hangs heavy on Ranjít Singh's hands; he has always been accustomed to visit all parts of his dominions on horseback, which exercise is now painful to him. Nor can he amuse himself any longer in the Zenána, his feeble health preventing him from occupying his leisure hours with the trifling diversions of the women. Not being able to turn to any mental recreation, he is forced to seek amusement, therefore, from external sources, for the speculations of thought have no charm for him, and to seek amusement in reading, or in being read to, is a thing quite unheard of in India.

I informed the Fakír Sahib to-day, of my wish to leave Lahor on the 20th, and to take three days for my journey to Lúdiana. From Kopartela, the second day's resting-place, I had my dhák arranged by Captain Wade, that is, I had bearers ready at the appointed stations in such relays, that I should make one day's journey of several. General Ventura was to take me to Amritsir in his carriage, and I desired to be furnished by the Mahá Raja with elephants to convey me from Amritsir to Kopartela. The fakír said that he would acquaint Ranjít with my wishes, and that it would take four days to arrange the matter. In the Panjáb every thing is transacted through Ranjít's orders, and nothing can be done without them.

I had hitherto been waiting for my palankeen, which contained the trunk enclosing my uniform. Captain Wade had sent me word that it had left Lúdiana on the 8th, and I could not conceive what could have detained it so long. Anything like a robbery was most improbable, for I have before remarked that, in this respect, the Panjáb is much safer than Hindústhan, the Mahá Raja calling every village near which the robbery takes place, to a very strict account, and making the inhabitants pay the value of things stolen to the loser.

I have forgotten to mention the Shah for a long while. I introduced him to General Ventura, who assigned him a dwelling near his own, and promised, in my presence, that he would take his cause in hand when I left Lahor. Perhaps I shall do well to describe in this place, Ventura's position in the Panjáb, as well as that of the other Europeans in Ranjít's service: the General has been of great service to the Mahá Raja, both in the field and in the training of his forces, but he is blamed for not being sufficiently pliant and refined for a court. None but minions have any influence over Ranjít Singh, and it is to Ventura's honour that he is not one of these. Here and in India he is acknowledged to be a man of high honour, and during a journey he took not long since in Hindústhan, the English Generals and other officers, testified their respect to him most cordially. He has been appointed by the Mahá Raja, Kázi and Governor of Lahor, which gives him the third place at his court. He has to attend the Mahá Raja soon after sunrise every morning, and during the day all sorts of grievances are brought before him. General Avitabile is a Neapolitan, who served some time in Persia, and has lately entered Ranjít's service. A longing after his native land urged him some time ago to revisit Europe, but disgusted by a variety of circumstances which seemed to make his home distasteful, he soon returned to the East, and entered the service of an independent prince. The Mahá Raja gave him at first the post of Governor of the Rekhna Doáb, and the capital of Wazírabad, where he distinguished himself so much by the strong measures he took, that when the difficult post of Peshávar required the presence of an independent resolute man, inaccessible to the influence of the incapable Shír Singh, the Mahá Raja sent him there against his own inclination. The following anecdote will give an idea of his character. The Mahá Raja is always unwilling to inflict the punishment of death or mutilation, but he knows not how to reconcile mildness with the just reward due to crime. While Avitabile was at Wazírabad not long ago, six robbers were taken, professors of the Sikh religion, to whom Ranjít Singh thought himself bound to show forbearance. It was an embarrassing circumstance, this being the second apprehension of the thieves. They were sent to Avitabile, with a command that they should not be allowed to escape again, and the same hour they were hanged. The Mahá Raja sent for Avitabile in high wrath; all his friends trembled for him, and when he appeared before Ranjít, he was asked how he had dared to hang six Sikhs, who had been given into his safe keeping. Avitabile answered, that he thought it the surest means of preventing their escape, and obeying the Mahá Raja's command. The king laughed at this answer; the event was not taken any further notice of:

the Sikh who told me the story seemed to think it a good joke, and all the people regard him with much reverence. Colonel Court quitted the Polytechnic Institution of Paris, of which he was a pupil, in the year 1815. He is a good officer, and well informed, commanding two battalions of Ghorkas in the service of the Mahá Raja, and likewise at this time the French legion at Akora, near Atok.

In the evening we again had a nách, and there was a feast at the Fakír Sahib's, which gave him the opportunity of sending to General Ventura a repast consisting of about 100 lbs. of boiled rice, with butter and sweetmeats in proportion. This, and the daily present of fruit and pastry sent by the Raja, namely, twelve boxes of grapes, baskets of oranges, pears, apples, &c., made up the supper of the dancers, which they ate while squatting on a carpet, over which a cotton cloth was spread.

Tuesday, January 19.—I remained at home all the day and wrote, but not without many interruptions. The Jemidar's son came with his tutor, a well-bred and well-educated man from Kashmír. I have said that this Jemidar is a Brahmin; the tutor is a Mohammedan, and the youth can read and write the Persian, the Panjábí, and the Hindú languages. He wishes much to learn English, and has applied with that view to a man who calls himself an American, but who is really an Irishman, and not belonging to that class called gentlemen, to judge by appearances. He is an officer in the Mahá Raja's artillery. Then came the son of Mehán Singh, with a letter from his father, complaining that the Mahá Raja required, for the ensuing year, a tribute of twenty-two and a half lakhs of rupees from the valley, which, as I very well knew could not be raised in the country; he therefore begged me to intercede with Ranjít for some diminution of the sum demanded. I desired the Munshí to answer this request instantly, saying, that the Governor must have learned by this time, in what manner I had spoken of him to the Mahá Raja; that if he questioned me again, I should repeat the same opinion. I was also convinced that the country could not pay twenty-two and a half lakhs of rupees this year, and Mehán Singh was at liberty to show my letter to Ranjít Singh, or make use of it as he thought best.

In the evening I took a walk with Mr. Fox, and we strolled to a fine monument, one side of which, undermined by an arm of the Rávi, which flows along by the exercising ground, is disjoined from the building, and open towards the west. Of the three lofty cupolas, the one on this side was rent asunder in the middle, and the chasm yawned like some revengeful monster crying towards heaven. The colours were quite fresh, and no one would have supposed that paint could have so well withstood the winds and storms of centuries. We visited many more of such monuments, and the dwelling of a fakír, who has a fancy for sitting by a well, and in this artificial wilderness can always assist the wanderer with a refreshing draught. The sun was just sinking, and the awakening spring filled the breast with those sensations which make the first appearance of the same season so like the commencement of a new life to a European. The feeling is stronger here, in proportion as the powers of vegetation spring up to a renewed existence more swiftly from the slumber in which they have been buried for a briefer space. Here the winter never kills the buds: it merely bends their heads for some days, until the next soft breeze unfolds them into full leaf. With us winter is the death of the year, and spring a tedious regeneration; here, nature is immortal, and her sleep is so light, that the first warm day of sunshine suffices to arouse her.

On my return, I betook myself to the platform in front of the house, and watched the vapours of evening as they veiled the setting sun, and the great city with its brilliant palaces. The horizon was clear in one direction only, viz., where tombs and monuments, minarets and domes, were piled up, a mass of ruins in the artificial desert they have made around them, reminding one of the Egyptian monuments in their natural sands: in both, the quiet abiding-place of those who have gone to their long last rest. The sun was yet red in the heavens, but the eye can gaze on its disk unharmed as it approaches the straight horizontal line formed by the vast Indian waste, which has the effect of a sunset on the boundless surface of the ocean. Single elephants and long trains of camels were bringing for themselves and their working comrades large branches of the fig-tree to the city, and moving along with a measured regular tread. Horses and asses laden with grass were following these, or marching past them at a more rapid pace. Here, a cloud of dust follows a finely dressed Sikh, who was hastening forward on his proud steed, attended by a numerous suite, to a once imperial dwelling; there, Indians were driving their small flocks towards the city, some bearing a new-born kid, others helping onward some aged animal over the uneven ground. They were seeking a refuge against the nightly depredations of the wolf and the hyena, or against man, even worse than these. The poor man has neither friend nor protector in India, he has but hope and patience to bear him onward to a better world. Large parties of crows and jackdaws were flying towards the towers of the city. Everything was seeking rest for the night—all, but the parrots chattering among the trees in the garden, and the sound of the water-wheel worked by oxen, which is accompanied by the cry of the industrious peasant, as it turns heavily round day and night without intermission,—announced departing day. In the distance, the songs of the dancing fakír in honour of the great Govindji, and the accompaniment of his guitar, were still audible.

Such was the scene which I quitted only when night rendered all objects invisible to me, and the cold reminded me where I stood. For some inexplicable reason, my mind has been more depressed to-day than usual. Perhaps this is the effect of rest and leisure, after the necessary labour of my continual journeyings. If so, it is a bad omen for that rest, which, God willing, I trust to enjoy in my own country. It would be well to depart at once, and forget my present temper of mind in trouble and deprivations. But there is a sort of enjoyment in the expression of one's feelings which I cannot resist. Age is always selfish, and I feel life advancing. Should these lines reach home without me, they will suffice to prove how much years must have stolen upon me. I force myself to recollect that there was a time when life was dear to me for the sake of others, and when I looked forward only to home with peace and joy. The stranger, far-distant in place, time, and feeling; the self-banished one, has long given up all claims to happiness for himself, and against his expectation he finds that five years of solitude, toil, and exertion are gone, and that, however outward circumstances may have changed, he is the same in heart as when he once bade a long farewell to Vienna, his fatherland. The past started up to-day like a spectre in the darkness, weighing down my soul with the consciousness that it had destroyed all hope and gladness in me. I must look back to a remote period ere I can forget the long interval of sadness which has intervened; may it have passed for ever, and for that I would gladly relinquish all that I have learned, my travels, my collections, my writing, everything for forgetfulness. A partial forgetfulness, however, is painful, bringing from the past, only what we would most wish blotted out, as the sun shines on the bleached bones of the famine-stricken people of Kashmír, where they lie among the green herbs.

Wednesday, January 20.—The Mahá Raja deputed the Fakír Sahib this morning to express his disappointment at having seen so little of me during my stay in Lahor, more particularly as he heard that my departure was so near at hand. He had not sent for me, because he hoped I should visit him whenever I found it agreeable, and he knew that I desired to see the curiosities of the city. If I had already done this, he trusted that I would not refuse to devote the next fortnight to him. I thanked the Raja for his invitation, but repeated my wish to pay my visit, and take leave of him to-day.

I introduced Mohammed Shah to the Fakír Sahib, and recommended his business to him as well as I could. But I had been in Lahor long enough to see that every man there thinks and acts for himself, and therefore was determined to name the subject to the Mahá Raja himself. Every thing depends on a petitioner seeing the king, wherefore I now begged the Fakír Sahib, who is a most honourable and independent man, and, in this respect, stands almost alone in Lahor, to request an audience for the Shah. In a few hours he returned to me with the information that the Mahá Raja wished to see me on the following day. He had spoken of the Shah, but had received no answer.

Yesterday, I had regulated my watch after taking an observation with the sextant in the presence of the Jemidar's son, who asked me the meaning of what I was doing. I explained it, adding, that I wished to know the distance from Lahor to Calcutta. This morning he visited me again, bringing the astronomer and astrologer of Lahor with him, the last having a large astrolabe and a Sanscrit book in his hand. He seemed very earnest and thoughtful. I had long desired to meet with an individual of this class, and presently asked him if he knew how to use the instrument. He did not understand my question, and I soon discovered that he carried it about with him only as an external sign of his rank. On inquiring the subject of the book, he informed me it was the Sháster; I pointed out a passage and requested him to read it, this however he could not do; all he knew, in short, was to repeat a few passages which he had got by rote and could point out. These people know the latitude of the ancient cities from the Sháster; for instance, they know that Lahor is 32° from Lanka, but where that point commences, or what was the measure of each degree, they were quite ignorant, as also of the number of degrees to the circle. Now, it is quite unimportant from what place the degrees of latitude are reckoned, the Hindús reckon from the middle of the sea, but the reckoning can be worth nothing, if the length of the degree is unknown, and I could not at first understand what made this man come to display his ignorance before me. After a while I found that he wanted to ascertain the latitude of Amritsir for astrological purposes. This, as a city of newly acquired importance, is not mentioned in the Shástor.

The American Irishman came a little later, and brought me a plan of Kandahár. I thanked him for the attention, but observed that I should not make use of any plans, except the map I had myself taken. Besides these, I was honoured with many other visitors, all with petitions of some sort to the Mahá Raja. Having determined to speak for no person who was unknown to me, I was obliged to decline any interference on their concerns, even in the affair of Mr. Forni, which I knew that I could not further. The Mahá Raja had offered him 700 rupees a month if he would manage a powder-mill for him, but Mr. Forni demanded 3000 rupees, and had already been here several months, executing various little services, for which he had never received the smallest recompense. He would be glad now to be dismissed altogether with a sum of a few thousand rupees, but cannot succeed in getting any payment at all. He was very desirous to travel with me, and wished me to speak to the Mahá Raja on the subject, but I assured him that the first was quite impossible, and that I could not do the last. He travelled to Lahor up the Indus, in the company of a German adventurer who wished to enter the service of Ranjít, but could not obtain anything, and is now at Kabúl, whence he wrote the most absurd letter to General Ventura that I ever read, giving himself out for a Russian spy, and offering to perform the same service for him on payment of a salary equal to what he now receives.

Yesterday we had no nách. I was out of spirits, and having generally contrived to animate the evening's conversation, the hours passed heavily on that account. General Ventura thought that I missed the usual amusement, and though I assured him to the contrary, he ordered the performance this evening, and I regretted the repetition of the monotonous, and to me unpleasant noise, not to speak of the unnecessary expense to which it put my kind host.

Thursday, 21st January.—At noon the Fakír Sahib came, with saddle horses and the Mahá Raja's carriage drawn by four horses. The equipage was by no means splendid, though he had received it as a present from the King of England. Lieut. Burnes brought it over for him, and with it five horses. It had become of much importance to England to survey the Indus, and ascertain the possibility of navigating it. That it was navigable in the time of Alexander is evident, but we hear nothing about it in any other age, and the information drawn from the accounts of that time is of the most meagre description. All men acquainted with the history of the last forty years, will understand the humane intentions of the English philanthropists, who desire to give an outlet to the productions of the upper provinces of India, and enable the poor inhabitants to exchange their coarse home-made stuffs for the far better and cheaper goods of England. The Indus has several mouths, and the channel is not only very shallow, according to the last survey, (in fact it has only three feet of water before the rainy season, in the shallowest places of the deepest among its arms,) but the sand is constantly shifting, thus altering the water-way, and in a short time blocking up one arm and forming a new one. The lower Indus is in the possession of three small states, whose princes are called

Amírs of Sindh, viz., Hyderabad, Khyrpoor and Mírpoor. These are Mohammedans, and were it rendered serviceable to them, the Company could no doubt easily induce them to enter into a commercial treaty, when the survey of the Indus shall be completed.

Ranjít Singh had sent a present to the English king, and the occasion of returning this courtesy by a gift, the very nature of which rendered it essential to take advantage of the river, was an excellent pretext for sailing up the Indus. Four large cart-horses, some mares, and one of those huge dray-horses which are sometimes seen in the London streets, and appear to carry death and destruction at their heels, were embarked accordingly, and despatched to Bombay. What, indeed, could be more flattering to Ranjít Singh, than a present so exactly in accordance with his well-known predilection for fine horses; what more natural than that care should be taken not to expose this expensive present to a fatiguing land-journey! To add to the impropriety of such a risk, the Governor of the Bombay Presidency, Sir John Malcolm, added an old coach, lined inside with blue velvet, and coarsely painted without. In 1830, Lieutenant Burnes was commissioned to convey this splendid gift up the Indus to Lahor, and to survey the river on his way. But the Amírs of Sindh were as little to be deceived by the pretext as Ranjít Singh himself; and it certainly did evince great ignorance of the circumstances and affairs of India, not only on the part of the authorities in England, but of those also in Bombay. It would seem almost incredible, indeed, if it stood alone; but, unhappily for the Indian population, there are not wanting evident and repeated proofs how imperfectly acquainted the English Ministry is; nay more, how uninformed with Indian politics even one Presidency is with the affairs of the others.

It was considered most advisable to sail up the Indus, without obtaining the previous permission of the Amírs; hence, when the expedition entered their territories thus unexpectedly, they at first refused to suffer it to proceed, but were at length induced, though against their convictions, to give up their opposition. Now it is most incumbent on such a power as that of the English in India that it should act with vigour, instead of having recourse to subterfuge which everybody can see through, and in this case it would have been far better to have entered into an open negotiation, and communicated its purport to Ranjít Singh. By the method adopted, they ran the risk of provoking Ranjít to take possession of these small states, or at least to impede the whole plan, as far as he could do so. After all, the treaty with the Amírs ended with the usual "I will" of the Company, and therefore it would have been better to have pronounced it at first. What must Ranjít Singh have thought of this way of conveying his presents? The English Ministry could not have been made aware, that thousands of horses are conveyed to and from India through the Panjáb every year; that scarcely a day passes that horses do not leave Calcutta for Lúdiana and Lahor, and that there is not a station in Northern Hindústan where vehicles of various kinds are not kept, which during the fine season travel from Calcutta to the Setlej, drawn by horses, and mounted on four wheels. The Company must have known this, because so far back as 1810, Lord Minto sent a state carriage to Ranjít Singh all the way from Calcutta to Lahor. The Begam Samrú, that extraordinary woman, who rose from a dancing girl, to have the government of an independent principality, bringing in a revenue of 700,000 florins, in like manner sent from Serdhána, her chief town, a present of a state carriage of glass, with four horses, to General Ventura, which as far surpasses in beauty the lumbering vehicle of the Company as the Medicean Venus surpasses the Begam Samrú.

But to the selection made: to send four brewers' horses and a monstrous dray horse to a prince who has a peculiar fancy for the most elegant saddle horses, is something like giving a man who loves the rare flowers which adorn his beautiful hothouse, a cart-load of potatoes. Had it been possible to make a more extraordinary present, Ranjít Singh must have been flattered, nevertheless, by the very idea that it came from the King of England. The mares were forthwith sent to graze, without receiving any further notice, as these animals are very rarely used in the Panjáb. There the plough is drawn by oxen and buffaloes, and horses are never harnessed to waggons. The other gigantic horse was sent to the schoolmaster, to be instructed in the art of dancing with other Panjábi horses; he was found so untractable, however, that all hope of his improvement was eventually relinquished, and he was dressed up like an elephant, and stationed before Ranjít's palace, where at the expiration of a year he departed this life.

Into this state coach I now stept, with Vigne and the Fakír Sahib, while Mohan, whom the Mahá Raja distinguishes on all occasions, stood behind with some officers. Some of the straps had given way, and the coach swung about in the most uncomfortable manner. It happened most unluckily that the place where we were to meet the Mahá Raja was five miles off, the exercising ground extending that distance along the shore of the Rávi. The road was good and well watered: Ranjít Singh's rich and beautiful tents added greatly to the ornamental character of the fine groups of trees which studded the park-like ground. A large Kashmír carpet was spread on that part where the river forms a bend, and four arm-chairs were placed on it. Ranjít Singh was occupied in overlooking the troops while they threw up a field-work. He took my arm and asked me whether they were working properly, to which I replied in the affimative. Perhaps my looks were not quite in unison with my words, as their want of order and regularity made them resemble some seditious multitude, collected for the purpose of destroying rather than constructing field works. Ranjít Singh informed me that he was making a carriage road onward to Amritsir, similar to that which was carried through the ground where we then were. I observed, that he could not possibly do better than make good roads, which would facilitate the movements of his troops, and render their progress from one place to another so rapid and easy, that their numbers would be apparently doubled. Mohan, who acted as my interpreter, caught my idea immediately, but had some difficulty in making it intelligible to Ranjít Singh; when at length he comprehended its purport, after many interrogatories, he answered: "Yes, but I should make it also more easy for an enemy to advance against me." I reminded him that the want of roads had never prevented the subjection of any part of India hitherto, but that it might in like manner have impeded the advance of any force desirous of relieving a threatened point, and in order to act with any efficiency, a regular army must have regular roads. "I wish," he exclaimed, "that you could remain with me. Could you not, at least, postpone your journey for three months?" I said that I appreciated his kindness most sincerely, but that my arrangements were finally completed, and that it was a twelvemonth since I had received any letters from my native land. Very little, moreover, could be accomplished in three months towards the reorganization of his troops.

We now proceeded to a small palace, before which some troops were drawn up, and Ranjít Singh, fatigued with walking, though he leaned on my arm, stood still, and said to Vigne: "Do you understand how to restore a country which is much impoverished?" Vigne did not quite understand Mohan, and I repeated the question, adding in English: "Take care, he means to appoint you his viceroy in the country we have recently quitted." Vigne took my words in jest, and made some reply in a jocular way, which expressed nothing. Mohan, however, translated it into an affirmative, and the Mahá Raja continued: "Do you understand how to govern a country?" This seemed so absurd to Vigne that he laughed outright in Ranjít's face, who asked him again: "What would you do in Kashmír to make it more prosperous?" Vigne was quite unprepared with an immediate reply, and desired Mohan to say as much. The boy not well understanding this, the conversation dropped, as the thoughts of Ranjít had wandered to other subjects. He presently addressed me: "I begin to feel old; I am quite exhausted now, and must be taken to the battery in my palankeen. You will ride in the carriage. What is that carriage worth?" I said that I knew its history, and should like to have the sum it had cost ere it came into his possession. He and the young Raja Híra Singh got into the palankeen, and I mounted the carriage, that he might not be kept waiting, but I ordered that it should remain in the rear of his palankeen. This he would not suffer, but commanded the coachman to proceed. An open tent was pitched for the Raja in front of the building. Two nine-pounders were set on the bank of an arm of the Rávi, and on the opposite side a white spot was painted on an acacia tree; while behind the guns was stationed a company of infantry and a pultun of Gorchelí*.

* Captain Murray, in his Political Reports, calls them Ghorchurs. The above is the more probable name, or perhaps Ghorchelas.—*Ed.*

The palankeen being some few hundred steps behind, I went up to the guns. Both were cast in Lahor, and seemed in excellent order; their carriages were made after English models. I carefully examined every part, and as I stooped to see whether the aim was good, Ranjít Singh came up, and inquired of me if they were good guns. "Very good," I answered.—"Are they properly adjusted?" he inquired. "No," answered I; "they will not hit the tree unless the sight be wrong, and the gunners are perfectly aware of it." He ordered the pieces to be fired, but they hit nothing; two shots more were equally unsuccessful. He said that he should like much to know where the fault lay, and requested me to point them. The fault, I observed, must always rest with the man who laid the guns, and who ought to know better; but I made no doubt if he would allow me three shots, that I should succeed in hitting the mark the third time. I then pointed the piece, stepped aside, and my excellent eyesight did me good service. The tree was about 800 yards distant, and following the ball, I saw it fly straight over the tree; while the other gun, discharged by an officer, dropped the ball in the ground just in front of the tree. My second ball fell in the branches a little too far to the right; while that from the other gun flew away over them. I then pointed the gun the third time, and stepped behind the Mahá Raja. It went off, the ball passing through the trunk, and splitting the tree. "I knew this would be the result," exclaimed Ranjít Singh; while the Gorchelí, who had all drawn near, cried: "Wáh! Núr unallah núr!" To explain the Mahá Raja's words, I must add, that, though without any real faith, he considers it necessary to pretend great devotion to the Sikh religion, and is, moreover, exceedingly superstitious.

Not long ago a Frenchman came to Lahor, and giving himself out for an officer of artillery, desired to enter Ranjít's service. The Mahá Raja, to test his skill, appointed as a trial the same tree, which was to be hit by these guns in three shots. General Ventura clearly explained that success in this trial depended more upon chance than upon the talent of the officer, and therefore endeavoured to dissuade him from requiring such a test, as he might thereby, on the one hand, lose an officer whose services in his army might be very useful; or on the other, he might give some post to a man whose only merit consisted in having luckily hit a tree. But the Mahá Raja adhered to his own opinion; the experiment took place; the officer missed the tree, and lost his hope of emolument. It was evident that Ranjít Singh had entertained an idea that fate would pronounce to him whether I was to be useful to him or not, by the success of my aim at this same tree; his exclamation, "I was certain of it," verified the correctness of my opinion.

When we were seated, both pieces were discharged in our presence several times, but without success. This reminds me of the management of Ranjít Singh's artillery, which is divided into so many Daroga, or batteries, each commanded by an officer, but deficient in regular gunners or carriages; hence, when their service is required in the field, the officer has to find both men and horses. This prevents the artillery from being well served, and the only duty they seem to perform is that of loading and firing as well as they can. The officers of the French legion have drawn the attention of the Mahá Raja to the necessity of keeping this, as well as all the other branches of the army, in an efficient state of equipment and training; at present, those trains only which are attached to the French legion, besides the two batteries of six guns, now in Lahor, are regularly organized.

The guns now fired spherical case, which burst too soon. These had astonished the Mahá Raja beyond measure when he first saw them at a review at Rúpar, during his conference with Lord William Bentinck: after every shot, he rode up to the target, and counted the holes which the balls and fragments of the shivered shell had torn in it. He then observed the fearful havoc such missiles would occasion among irregular troops. He ordered his European officers to provide the same for his artillery, and the first shell which exploded was worth 30,000 rupees to Colonel Court. Ranjít asked me whether I understood anything about them, and on my telling him that I did, he inquired further, perhaps in order to prove my knowledge, how it happened that the shells did not all burst in the same way? I answered, that in a manufacture which was by no means simple and which required the utmost nicety, the fault might lay either in the fuzes being of different lengths, or in the powder being badly made, or of indifferent quality; and then, thinking it a favourable moment to speak a word in behalf of Forni, I told him that he would soon find it necessary to build a regular and well-organized powder manufactory, where the powder might be prepared of the proper strength and quality, and that there was already a man called Forni in Lahor, who thoroughly understood the process. Without answering me, Ranjít ordered a ball ready primed to be brought to us, and I told him that it was very coarsely made. He begged me particularly to say what I thought of the spherical case. I said that this was one of the rarest inventions of modern days, but that one of the most difficult points in gunnery was the management of mortars. It might not only be most dangerous but perfectly useless without a proper knowledge of the due strength of the powder, and the exact measure of the fuze. "Stay with me here," he exclaimed, "a few years to you can signify but little. You are still young: I wish you to go to Amritsir and visit the laboratory, and I will write to the Commandant at Govindgurh, that he must meet you and show you everything there." As I made no reply, he continued, "You must, at all events, go to Amritsir; will you write to me there?" I promised to do so. "I know," he said, "that you came to take leave to-day; but you must give me a few days longer. You must remain until the Basant*." This, I knew, would take place on the 22nd. I therefore told him how happy I was at all times, when it was possible, to comply with his wishes, and that I would remain at Lahor until that time.

"Those are the Gorchelí," he said, pointing to the troops, "of whom I told you that I had 4000." I asked him the meaning of the word. He told me that they had territories which brought them in a revenue of 3000 or 4000 rupees a-piece, and that their horses and entire equipment were also their own. They are, in fact, the remainder of those 69,500 Sikh lords of the Panjáb, brought under the power of Ranjít's authority, and receive from their despotic master an assignment of property which he can take from them whenever he sees fit. I requested leave to inspect them, and never beheld a finer nor a more

* The festival of opening spring.

remarkably-striking body of men. Each one was dressed differently, and yet so much in the same fashion, that they all looked in perfect keeping.

The handsome Raja Sushet Singh was in a similar costume, and reminded me of the time when the fate of empires hung on the point of a lance, and when the individual whose bold heart beat fearlessly under his steel breastplate, was the sole founder of his own fortunes. The strange troop before me was most peculiarly Indian. The uniform consisted of a velvet coat or gaberdine, over which most of them wore a shirt of mail. Others had this shirt made to form a part of the tunic. A belt round the waist, richly embroidered in gold, supported the powder-horn, covered with cloth of gold, as well as the Persian katár and the pistols which many of them carried in addition to those weapons. Some wore a steel helmet, inlaid with gold, and surmounted with the kalga or black heron's plume; others wore a cap of steel, worked like the cuirass in rings: this cap lies firmly on the turban, and covers the whole head, having openings for the eyes. The left arm is often covered from the hand to the elbow with a steel cuff inlaid with gold. The round Sikh shield hangs at the back, fastened with straps across the chest, a quiver at the right side and a bow slung at the back being carried as part of the equipment; a bag made in the belt holds the balls, and a tall bayonet, frequently ornamented with gold, held in the right hand when the man is on foot, and carried over the shoulder when in the saddle, completes the dress. One would suppose that the arms that each man carried would be enough to weigh him down, but this is not the case, and though the Sikhs are anything but strongly-built men, they seemed to bear them with the greatest ease; the black curly beard which hangs as low as the chest giving them an appearance of power which they do not in reality possess. It is a strange sight to a European to see their slippers embroidered in gold covering their naked feet. Some few among them wear high jack boots. When I returned to Ranjít Singh he asked me if I should like to see them fire, and on my requesting to do so, a brass pot was fixed about 100 paces' distant, and one Gorchelí after the other stepped forward to shoot at the mark. One of them hit it every time, and very shortly the poor brass pot was perforated in every part. A fresh one was then set up and the company of regular troops advanced, and were ranged into rank and file, evidently to disadvantage. The number of regular troops which fired were three times that of the Gorchelí, and the Mahá Raja was much amused when in three rounds a few balls only hit the mark; for the men at the wings could scarcely aim at the pot at all. Ranjít Singh saw me smiling, and he observed: "This is the way that regular troops fire, a great inducement, is it not, to turn old warriors into disciplined soldiers?" I said that the Gorchelís would not fire so well if they were in rank and file; the adversary was not the target but the line.

"You have now seen divisions of all my troops," observed Ranjít to me; "tell me what you think of them?" I answered that what I had seen exceeded any thing that I could have anticipated. He still pressed for a more definite answer, and I continued: "The world knows what these troops have done under you. The answer to your question has been given by your cannon from Ladák to Multan, from the Setlej to the heart of Afghánistan." "You evade my question," said Ranjít Singh. I answered that he was a much better judge of soldiers than I.—"Tell me," he persisted, "what you think of my troops compared with those of the East India Company?" "You require me to do so?"—"Yes," he said. Mohan had on an imitation Kashmír shawl of mine, while one of his suite wore a genuine and very beautiful one. I showed him both, saying, "This is genuine, the other an imitation,—which of the two is the best?" He looked at me, and said, after a short pause, "You have expressed my own opinion; but do you believe that a battalion of my army could engage with one of the Company's battalions?" "My answer is already given in my last question. I do not."—"Do you believe," he went on, "that my troops could stand against an attack of a body of Russians." I replied that I thought them able to withstand any force likely to appear west of the Indus at present. Upon which he said, "It is growing late; the sun is low on the horizon, and we are far from the city. I take you at your word, that you will remain for the Basant."

I then left him, and our carriage drove rapidly over the ground, escorted by a party of horsemen, while Ranjít followed slowly in his palankeen at the head of a large division of his troops. He soon dismissed the Gorchelí and his suite, and at once, with a wild and loud cry, the armed horsemen sprang forward, firing off their pieces, and rushing over the plain: they were followed by the guns, which sent forth a salvo as they advanced; next came the elephants in their trappings striding along, and a cloud of dust soon after veiled the whole from sight. Before I reached the house, night had completely enveloped every object in thick darkness.

Friday, January 22.—I forgot to notice yesterday, that I received intelligence that Dr. Henderson was at Atok; I rejoice to learn that the journey had not been too fatiguing for his enfeebled frame, and that there was some probability of my even seeing him in Lahor. The morning brought the Fakír Sahib, and the large elephant to be drawn by Vigne, and the famous horse Láili, that I had inquired for. The Mahá Raja let me know that this horse had cost him 60 lakhs of rupees*, and 12,000 soldiers, having been the occasion of several wars. It was the property of Yár Mohammed Khan of Pesháwar, and Ranjít Singh made the delivery of the animal to him one of the conditions of peace. The cunning Mohammedan, however, who considered this article humiliating to him, evaded it several times by sending another horse under the name of Láili, and it was owing to a plan devised by General Ventura, that it was eventually obtained. He took a company of soldiers as his guard on one occasion when he went to Pesháwar to receive the horse. The Khan would have temporised as before, but he was taken suddenly ill and died, whereupon Ventura put his brother Sultan Mohammed Khan, the same whom I have spoken of as being present at the first review, by the Mahá Raja's command, in possession of Pesháwar, but on condition that Láili should be given up. Sultan Mohammed Khan tried also what evasions would do; but General Ventura made his appearance one morning, attended as usual by his troops, to press the fulfilment of the conditions of his investiture. He entered the reception room, and demanded Láili; and when Sultan Mohammed interposed some fresh obstacle, Ventura suddenly called out

* Six hundred thousand pounds sterling in round numbers.—*Ed.*

to the soldiers, who were posted ready in the courtyard, to come up to him in the palace, and on their appearance he pronounced Sultan Mohammed a prisoner in his own capital, until he chose to surrender Láili. Mohammed was so astounded at this bold step, that he ordered the horse to be brought immediately, and Ventura quitted Peshávar with his costly booty. It is the finest horse belonging to the Mahá Raja, and I could not help mounting a steed that had cost six millions of florins. The bridle and saddle was splendid, and round his knees he has gold bangles: he is a dark grey, with black legs, thirteen years old, and full sixteen hands high. I have heard that at Rúpar, Ránjít Singh showed a brown horse as Láili, but General Ventura assured me that this was the true Láili.

The Fakír told me that the Máha Raja wished to have another paper from me, and that he would have spoken about it yesterday, but feared that I should not understand what he wished. I had seen since my first writing, he said, a great many things, and moreover, I had not said any thing about the friendship of the Company towards him. Several articles had appeared of late in the newspapers of Hindústhan and of Calcutta, which went to show that the English must of necessity soon march to the Indus, and make that river the western boundary of British India, and I fancied that Ranjít Singh had thought a good deal of these articles. Further, he added, the Mahá Raja had permitted me to visit the Durbar in Amritsir, and begged that I would take notice of it, as though I had been there already. Finally, I had said nothing before of my friendship for the Mahá Raja, nor of his for me. I told the Fakír Sahib that I would draw up the memorial without loss of time, make the Múnshí translate it into Persian, and send it to him, that it might be brought into a proper form, requesting him to leave out any thing likely to displease Ranjít Singh, and to assist me with his talent for the most acceptable compliments. The following was the result*:—

"During my stay at Lahor, his Highness the Mahá Raja has honoured me with a review of those regiments which were here by chance, and

* These, and other documents, are copied from the Baron's English originals, with some trifling verbal alterations.—*Ed.*

which, although soldiers only of a year's standing, astonished me by their good appearance and their quick fire: they are decidedly more advanced than recruits of the same standing are in Europe. If I had to proffer my opinion upon the service which may be expected from them, I should say that the troops of the Mahá Raja are fully prepared to dispute the palm of victory in the plains of the Panjáb with any army crossing the Atok. Yesterday the Mahá Raja showed me the practising of artillery, and of his troops at the target. The most distinguished feat of this day, there is no doubt, was the firing of the Gorchelís armed with matchlocks. The Austrians are celebrated for their shooting at the target, but there cannot be a better shot than one of the Gorchelís, who, every time he fired, shot through the vessel placed as the target.

"I must confess that I have been very much surprised at all that I have found in Lahor, notwithstanding I had heard very much of it in India, and if, on my return to Europe, I should give an account of what I have seen of the magnificence of the court and of the army of the Mahá Raja, to his Majesty the Emperor of Austria [this was put in by his expressed wish], he will be very much pleased and astonished with it.

"I have to acknowledge, moreover, the gratitude I feel to the Mahá Raja for having had the kindness to allow me to approach the place known to the whole world for its holiness, and envied to the Panjáb by the whole of Hindústhan, namely, the holy reservoir at Amritsir. For the permission to see it, I feel no less gratitude to the Mahá Raja than for his other numerous favours.

"I have to add, that having spoken in my first letter of the friendship between the Mahá Raja and the Honourable Company only by report, I must now state, that I was long enough in India and the Panjáb to form an opinion of it for myself, and that I am convinced that it is strong, sincere, reciprocal, full of confidence, and without reserve. If it is the wish of the Mahá Raja to preserve it, it is the interest of the British Government to do so also; and whatever the liberty of the press may allow to appear in the newspapers against it, I am sure that it is the desire of the English Government to maintain and fortify it, and, if it were possible, still more to consolidate it. How sincere the Mahá Raja was, I, who experienced the benefit of it, had the clearest proof, since the friendship of Austria with Great Britain caused me to be treated as the friend of a friend. May this friendship always increase for the happiness of the world.

"I have lastly to return my sincere thanks for the friendship of which the Mahá Raja gave me a proof in his wish to retain me at Lahor; and I have only to add, that I hope the Mahá Raja's friendship for me will last as long as mine for him, which is to say, for ever.

"BARON CH. HUGEL.

"Lahor, January 22, 1836."

The Fakír Sahib finding this testimony very good, it was written out in Persian and English, and sealed up, and committed to a very fine bag which I had brought from Kashmír. Yesterday the Mahá Raja having commissioned the Fakír Sahib to make the request, Vigne began a drawing of an English soldier. This morning he went on with his task, and finished a representation of an officer holding the English flag in his left hand, and giving the right to a Sikh, who holds the flag of the French legion, tri-colored, with Govind Singh on horseback, carrying the falcon on his right wrist, as a testimony of friendship. This being quite ready, I waited while my paper was being written out in Persian, that I might present both to Ranjít Singh.

Vigne had much wished to take a drawing of the black fakír; and that no time might be lost, I sent to him while my letter was being transcribed. A droll scene took place when he arrived. The black fakír, or Hindú converted to the Sikh faith, looked with very jealous eyes on the Mohammedan Fakír at the court of the Sikh Mahá Raja. The Fakír Sahib began with all the politeness of a courtier, by telling him that the Mahá Raja not only permitted, but wished the European gentleman to take a portrait of him, the fakír. "The Mahá Raja!" said the black fakír; "and who is he?"—"The holy (Sri) Mahá Ranjít Singh," answered the Fakír Sahib. "I do not know him," continued the other; "and if I did, how can he wish or command as you say? I have nothing to do with him, and have no need of him." The Fakír was astonished and very indignant, but still exceedingly polite. "The Mahá Raja thought that you would not be the only one of his subjects to refuse to treat his friend, a European gentleman, with the courtesy that he himself shows to him."

Mohan, who stood behind my chair, whispered to me, "The beggars are beginning to squabble." "I am not Ranjít Singh's subject," cried the black fakír, "I am a saintly personage, and belong to God, and to nobody else, and you call yourself by a name that you have no title to. You are the Mahá Raja's servant, I shall not do any thing at your bidding, either to go or to stay: I am very angry now, but perhaps I may let him draw me bye-and-by, not because the Mahá Raja wishes it, but because it pleases me."—"It is the same thing on what account you consent, so that you let it be done," returned the Fakír Sahib. And the black devotee soon complied with our requests. When at length the copy was ready, Vigne and I rode out on horseback to the same place where we had met the Mahá Raja yesterday. They were firing away at a tree near the mark of the preceding day, and Ranjít Singh pointed it out directly to me, already shivered in pieces. I had not seen Ranjít looking so well, or so young, as on this occasion. He was in high spirits too, and his hand, before almost lifeless, was to-day quite warm. When the Fakír Sahib presented my letter, he examined the seal carefully, to see that it was unbroken; and having had the contents read over to him, he expressed himself much gratified with it, and ordered it to be given into the custody of the Fakír Azíz ud Din.

Vigne now produced his drawing, and the Mahá Raja was delighted when he found that the Setlej, with Fílor on the one side, and Lúdiana on the other, were represented in it. These are the boundary towns of his own and the Company's territories. Calling one of his grandees to him after the other, he explained to each the allegory of his friendship with England. This thought seemed more flattering to him than any other, and is a good proof of the influence of the Company's empire in India. A better explanation of this will be seen, when we come to treat of Ranjít's power, which, although great in itself, is naturally overrated by the founder of it.

The Fakír Sahib had told me in the morning, that the Mahá Raja had postponed the Basant for a day, in order to prolong my stay. I therefore did not remain long there on the field, the evening drawing on when I first came on the ground. My large suite not allowing me to ride fast, Ranjít Singh gave me his carriage on my return; he himself was carried in a palankeen. In the evening we had the dancing girls again.

Saturday, January 23.—The Basant, literally the spring, is a festival celebrated yearly at this season in Upper Hindústhán and the Panjáb, the *Sirsya* then covering the whole face of the country with its blossoms. This is the first sign of the opening of the year, as the snow-drop is with us. On this day the Mahá Raja betakes himself to a small building not far from the Shalimár, and the whole population of Lahor have orders to show themselves on the road to it. I never saw a more singular-looking assemblage. The Sikhs are the only Hindús of the plain always ready for amusement, and the people of Lahor are especially known for this disposition. I took this road at twelve o'clock, with Khalifa Sahib and Vigne; and as we went on remarked them in succession, some collected in groups, others idly loitering among the ruins, and many moving along on camels, oxen, horses, or elephants, according to their means. On the camels, which were dressed out with collars of shells and little bells, mingled with large tassels, formed of party-coloured wools, and the tails of the Tibet cow, sat three or four men; while from eight to twelve persons were seated in the Munjil, Amári, or Howdah on the elephant's backs. Nor were the palankeens less numerous, or less strange in shape and colour. Large crowds had formed round a talking or a singing fakír; a juggler or an astrologer; a vender of toys or sweetmeats. At another spot, grown-up men were running about the fields with kites, and multitudes of persons were seen following some musicians who were beating their tám-táms, and blowing horns. About half way along, at the balcony of a first story, sat a Sikh Gurú, such as I have already described at Baramulla; and not a Sikh passed him without his "Salám, Mahá Raja," while some bestowed on him a few rupees. All was bustle and mirth, and in every direction we heard the Sikh greeting, "Wáh! Gurúji-ke fatih!" Hail to the conquering Gurú!

The horsemen attending on me were all in light yellow, as well as the whole court: this being the colour of the spring in the Panjáb. We missed our way at one time and got entangled among the ruins, whence we had so much trouble in recovering the direct path, that the Mahá Raja was kept waiting some time for us. On the last mile, three regiments, dressed in yellow, were drawn up like a close fence on both sides. In Europe, this change of uniform would cost a large sum of money, but here the expense is trifling; the white linen is coloured with saffron for the day, and then washed again. The unsightly building where Ranjít Singh held the Basant stood at the end of a close alley. "And why here?" I inquired. "Because it is the will of the Mahá Raja," said the astonished Fakír Sahib. Before it, in two lines, stood thirty elephants, so close to one another that, in order to gain the entrance we were obliged to squeeze in under their trunks, or just before them; but they were so tame and gentle, that there was not the least danger in this. The elephant is a very social animal, and behaves himself in company whether with his equals or with men, with the greatest discretion. It is to be supposed that the Sirdár Hati was among them. We crowded in through a narrow doorway into the interior, for the greatest freedom reigns during the feasts and ceremonies in India, and the people were all pressing forward together. One part of the court was divided from the rest by a kanát, or canvass screen, and there sat Ranjít Singh in an arm-chair under a large tent of Kashmír stuff, yellow like the carpet, himself, and every thing about it. It gave him a look of additional ugliness. Large quantities of the *Sirsya*, and other yellow flowers were scattered about here and there. Vigne and I were the only persons in dark clothes, Mohan being in yellow, according to the prevailing fashion. Here I saw Karak Sing, the Mahá Raja's eldest son, whose exterior promises very little. I was presented to him, but could hardly find time to speak a word, for the Basant began as soon as we had taken our seats, and I found that it was in reality a levée, each person being expected, as at every opportunity here, to offer some present to the Mahá Raja. On his right hand sat Karak Singh; on the left, his favourite, Raja Híra Singh; directly opposite sat Vigne and I on arm-chairs, and more to the left

Sultan Mohammed Khan and his son, who came in after us, and brought with him a present in gold. Behind the king stood the Jemidar, Sushet Singh, and General Ventura, while in the background were a number of the inferior state officers. The Fakír Sahib, Mohan and the Múnshí stood near me. Next came Sirdárs, Rajas, and Khans, from different provinces, all bringing gold, among whom I recognised my friend Ráhim Ullah Khan, the Raja of Rajáwar. The most remarkable figure was Zúlfikar Khan, one of the sons of the brave Mozaffer Khan, the former possessor of Multan, who entered with a proud bold bearing, and then squatted down immediately like the others, his forehead and cheek being marked with a deep scar, which somewhat relieves his excessively plain features. A descendant of one of the Mohammedan Emperors, who strove with Humáyún for the throne, a young man, and now a Sirdár under Ranjít Singh, Zúlfikar Khan appeared to-day before his lord for the first time: he stood for a little while upright, and looked about as much as to say that some of those Sikhs ought to give him one of the arm-chairs. I thought we should have had a scene, for his eyes began to flash, and he did not even incline his head before Ranjít Singh, until two of the masters of the ceremonies, who had their eyes upon him, pressed him down very roughly. As I gazed round the circle, their various forms did not inspire me with much confidence. Most of the Mohammedan Sirdárs sat with their left hand resting on the ground, their right grasping some weapon, which hung at their girdle; and as I watched their eyes sparkling with rage, and their compressed lips, I thought how speedily one cry to arms would have converted this peaceful festival into a scene of blood. The garments they wore were most expensive and gorgeous, those of Ranjit Singh only excepted, who, as usual, was dressed in his plain wrapping-gown. The dancing girls were introduced, all in yellow, and to them the Mahá Raja sent the silver money which had been presented to him.

Presently he ordered silence, and beckoning to Mohan, spoke to him in a low voice: this was a request that I would relate some anecdote of military life. I sent back for answer, that had I known his wish earlier, I would have prepared myself and Mohan, but that with such an inexperienced interpreter, it would be a very tedious undertaking. Ranjít then applied to Zúlfikar Khan, who, without rising, told us a story with the greatest vivacity and eloquence, of being once surprised with thirty men, by a party of five hundred, whom he at last drove back, "carrying away with me *this*," he said, pointing to his scar.

We then broke up, and as Ranjít Singh had heard that the carriage had made its way with some difficulty, he begged me to mount the Sirdár Hati, but I preferred the former conveyance, being well acquainted with the uneasy movements of a plebeian elephant.

On our return the crowd was ten times greater than before, and I cannot give an idea of the pressure caused by horses, oxen, carts with women, camels and elephants, mingled with thousands of men, and threading the ruins which encumber this part of the city. Every moment, as the masses moved along the narrow ways, I expected to see men trodden down and crushed beneath an elephant's foot. But I did not witness any accident at all; and the clouds of dust which were raised by all this throng, can hardly be described. On the road we met one very fine Bactrian camel, here called Baghdádi, and a white dromedary. They were the property of the young Raja Híra Singh; and on Vigne expressing a desire to take a drawing of them, the Fakír Sahib ordered them to General Ventura's house.

I received tidings that Dr. Henderson might be expected to-day, and accordingly he made his appearance in the evening. I most gladly welcomed and presented him to the General, and to the rest of the party. His costume, though different, was not less extraordinary than the garb in which he introduced himself to me in Kashmír, consisting of a species of Polish garment, evidently intended for a figure the reverse of his tall, gaunt stature. I asked him the meaning of this dress, and he told me that his intention had been to proceed from Mozafferabad to Derbund on the Atok, thence to cross that river, and reach the highest pass of the Hindú-khúsh.

This plan he found impracticable, on account of the bands of robbers who infested the country between the two towns; he was therefore obliged to take nearly the same road that I had travelled, and cross the Atok near Ghári, some fifteen miles from the city of Atok.

Thence he wandered to the mountain chain, but the snow prevented him from reaching the point he had contemplated; and he soon found, that in the country of the Yusufzáis he was not in the best of company. He was attacked by a party as he was on his road to Pesháwar, and stripped of everything; but what grieved him most, of the watch and instruments I had lent him. I told him that I had not given them to him with the idea of ever seeing them again, and that he must therefore count them among his own losses. It was lucky for him that he had sewed some gold pieces in a piece of cloth, which he held in his hand while he was being robbed, and with one of these he was able to purchase a woollen coverlet and a coat to protect him from the cold. Thus, he entered Pesháwar, where M. Avitable received him most kindly, and gave him one of his own suits, which as he is short and stout, did not become Henderson particularly well. His throat and arms were thrust out far beyond his clothing, and all the rest would have contained two such men. The pretension to elegance in the whole costume rendered it still more absurd when contrasted with the form and carriage of the poor Doctor.

The Fakír Sahib came again with a message from the Mahá Raja, which he would not deliver until we were alone in a private room. It was to say that he did not know who Dr. Henderson was, he having travelled without his permission in the Panjáb as a fakír. I told him that he was a physician in the Company's service, of the same rank as Mr. M'Gregor, who had lately attended him, and that he was a clever enterprising man, and skilful in his profession.

"But the Mahá Raja desires to know what he travels for?"—"The reason will surprise you; it is that he wishes to discover the sources of the Atok." "What good would it do him if he did find them?"—"Not any, but his vanity would be gratified if he should be the first to do so." The Fakír Sahib seemed to think that Europeans were guilty of many unaccountable follies; but he merely said that the Mahá Raja desired to know how he was to receive him. I answered, "I think it would be best to receive him as though he had travelled with the Mahá Raja's leave."—"But he has not the leave of the Company, the Mahá Raja's friend." "On that account, I think the Mahá Raja should receive him well."—"Why?" "The Company do not allow their servants to pass the Setlej, under the impression that it might be against Ranjít Singh's will, but Dr. Henderson came in full confidence of the good will of the Mahá Raja towards Englishmen; and if he were not kindly received, it would show a want of generosity, and give an idea that Ranjít Singh's friendship was merely a political one. The Company are bound to try Dr. Henderson on the charge of having crossed the Setlej; but I think the Mahá Raja should not make him feel that he is here without leave."—"The Mahá Raja has heard that there is an order to put Dr. Henderson under arrest as soon as he arrives on the left bank of the Setlej;" (this was true, but I was surprised that he had heard it;) "and he wishes to know whether as the Company's friend, he ought not to be angry with those who have angered them, and whether it would not be thought a want of attention towards them, if he took no notice of the matter." "The Company must affect displeasure, but in reality they are very glad that Dr. Henderson undertook this journey; and to notice the order at all, would show, that the spies of the Mahá Raja have been a little too active on the other side of the Panjáb."—"You are right," he said, "I will take your answer to the Mahá Raja."

In the course of an hour he returned, bringing Dr. Henderson the customary present of welcome. I repeated to the Doctor the conversation I had had with the Fakír respecting him, and this present relieved the anxiety he had begun to feel as to his reception.

I reminded the Fakír Sahib that the *Basant* being over, I wished to pay my farewell visit to Ranjít Singh, and also to bring Mohammed Shah with me. He answered, that the first would be bad news to carry to the Mahá Raja.

After the dangers and the want to which Dr. Henderson had been exposed, our cheerful mode of life seemed to give him the idea of a fairy world. He was suddenly transported from toil and need, from solitude and deprivations, to a house with beautiful rooms glittering with lights and mirrors; he was welcomed by friends and acquaintance, and in addition, a richly-furnished table and a dozen dancers invited him to share in the gaiety and amusements of India.

I have not yet said much about these Indian dancing girls. Lahor is the only place where they seem to have any beauty, and where the lavish profusion consequent upon the residence of a court causes their art to be more valued and better paid for. They are not, as sometimes happens in Calcutta, stolen children or slaves*; but the daughters or near relatives of dancers, and their education for their profession usually begins at five years old, and requires an apprenticeship of nine years to perfect them in the song and dance. Although this two-fold art is not in accordance with European tastes, there is certainly a clearness in the voice, and a precision in the step, which surprises, where it does not please, and there is in the Nách of Lahor something peculiarly striking. The women of the Panjáb are renowned throughout India for the singular whiteness of their teeth, which are perfect both in form and regularity. This gives a great charm to the countenance, and they are generally finely formed, with beautiful hands and feet, though their dress does not display their figure to advantage. Their dress consists of coloured silk trousers, fitting tight below, and fastened round the waist by a band and tassels which hang as low as the knee. Over this falls a tunic of white muslin, reaching only half way down the leg, and a shawl is thrown over the figure in coming and going away. Such, in short, is their house costume. When dancing they put on a very wide garment of various colours, mingled with gold, which covers them from the shoulders to the ankles. According to our European ideas, the dancers from Kashmír were the prettiest, with their fair and florid complexions, and their symmetrical forms peculiar to the people of that land. The others were darker skinned, but in

---

* This continues, in spite of every exertion of the authorities throughout India, to be the most prolific source of slavery, and attended with unmitigated evil. If, however, we look narrowly into the history of the class of persons by whom this iniquitous traffic is kept up, it is melancholy to advert to the multitudes, reduced by a far more grievous procedure in the metropolis of the most civilized nation on the face of the earth to the condition of slavery—no less abject—infinitely more destructive of every right principle, under the very eye and cognizance of a great Christian government. The beginning of all good legislation must be at our own doors.—*Ed.*

regularity and beauty of features they far surpassed the Kashmírians. One of them we called Heloise, on account of the enthusiastic expression of her countenance; and she and her aunt had ornaments on them worth from 10,000 to 12,000 rupees; their clothes were sumptuous in proportion, and over them was thrown a Kashmír shawl valued at 1000 rupees more. To destroy the charm of all this, I must add, that there was not a sufficient attention to cleanliness manifested to render a nearer examination of their finery at all desirable. A dancer called Káira, the same whose beauty had caused her to be chosen as a performer on the occasion of the Mahá Raja's interview with Lord William Bentinck, had really a beautiful voice: she sang and danced with most expressive grace, carriage, and sweetness of voice. When one has got over the strangeness of the combination, there is a certain charm in this manner of singing poetry. I shall not soon forget the expression with which the girl sang the words*:—

> Thou art my soul; thou art my world.
> I who please thee here am thy slave.

Throwing herself at the same time at the listener's feet, her features lighted up as though beseeching for a hearing, and her hands clasping his knee, then abruptly starting up with the exclamation:—

> But thou art silent; thy heart is of stone.
> It is cold for me; it will never be mine.

She moved away, her hand raised, and her head thrown back; while she threw an expression of despair into the last line, and seemed to sob out the words. The continued movements of the musicians are also

---

* The Baron's German conveys far more beautifully the style and taste of the original.

> Du bist meine Seele,
> Du bist meine Welt:
> Ich bin Deine Sklavin,
> Die hier sich gefällt.
>
> Allein Du schweigst,
> Dein herz ist von stein,
> Für mich ist es kalt,
> Ach nie werd ich Dein!

in character with the rest of the performance, which begins with the amatory songs, the dancer standing at the far end of the room, having the musicians behind her. She presently steps forward, the soft slow music becomes louder and quicker, as the expression becomes more impassioned; the dancer, describing either hope or fear, moves rapidly from side to side, and the whole usually concludes with an imitation of despair. Their epic poems are always sung seated, and the motion of the dancers is indicative of the vivacity of a narrative. The only songs which require dancing as a part of them, are those of a jocular character, where the joke borders on the verge of impropriety without overstepping it. It is but very seldom that these dancers have the talent of Káira; in general they are, on the contrary, very stupid, and do not properly suit the action to the word, or else act like puppets set on motion by clockwork. Their greatest beauty is the delicacy of their feet and hands, which seem quite peculiar to themselves, and the freedom and grace of their action are inimitable.

I have not mentioned the Shah often, but I saw him daily, and from time to time sent him some of the Mahá Raja's presents. Every morning his confidential servant was despatched to inquire after my health, and I went through the same ceremony of daily asking how he was. Still, I fear, that the ground is too slippery for him to succeed in his object at Lahor.

Sunday, January 24.—This morning the Fakír Sahib came to say that the Mahá Raja wished me to write to him my opinion of the son of the Jemidar Kushál Singh, who has been, as I have already said, appointed a general. This I soon did. The youth has unquestionably a great deal of natural talent, but he wants much instruction, and in my letter I pointed out to Ranjít Singh the danger of raising such a mere stripling to this high rank before he had any sort of experience.

I asked the Fakír whether I could take leave of the Mahá Raja to-day. He could not tell, but he knew that Ranjít Singh wished to see me. I inquired whether I might take Dr. Henderson with me, and he answered, that the Mahá Raja expected his visit. The Commandant of the Artillery in Lahor came in the course of the morning to introduce himself, dressed in the European fashion, with a blue frock coat and pantaloons. Mohan, who came to announce him, told me that the black fellow was dressed out like a nobleman, an odd remark enough, his own skin being very dark, but conveying a great deal of meaning, and explaining much that strikes the observing man as enigmatical in the relation between Indians and Europeans. The Commandant, a Mohammedan in Ranjít's service, who had picked up a few words of English, stepped into the room like some affected dandy, which roused the ire of Mohan, and when he laid hold of a chair and seated himself without waiting for my leave or offer, he cried out: "Why do you dress yourself so like a fool? the tailor cannot make a nobleman of you." The Commandant looked at the boy in astonishment, and though not a little amused at his rudeness, I was obliged to reprove him for it. Mohan wished me much not to leave him behind, but to take him to Europe with me, and the boy's uncommon acuteness would have enabled him to make his way very well. But though much attached to him, I was bound to consider what would be for his real interest. He could not travel to Europe with me without losing his caste for ever, and whatever situation I might afterwards be able to provide him with in India, he would feel himself humbled by his inferiority to Europeans. There is nothing more sure to make a man unhappy than to have a consciousness within him of his own powers, and the inability to make them available. In India, as with us, the conscious superiority which suffers by neglect is generally considered as nothing more than romance. I decided then on recommending him to Ranjít Singh, and on sending him to his court after he had passed a couple of years at some good school. The idea of our separation was very painful to myself. He had greatly contributed to render my journey of some use to me, and often when the wants and discomforts of a fatiguing day had exhausted me and all the rest, his good temper and manner of silencing complaints sufficed to make us all right again. He was very fond of travelling, and the distance of Europe from his home and family made him feel very proud. Youth, with all the hopes of life spread out before it, bears such separations very easily, and looks forward to a certain reunion; while an older man always looks back to what he has lost, and never can regain, and every parting seems to him a final one.

All sorts of testimonials were now required from me. The Shah and his confidential servant, Júni Lál, and various others asked for them, and even the Jemidar Kushál Singh required one from me. The Fakír Sahib came at noon to fetch me in Ranjít Singh's carriage, which conveyed us both, with Henderson and Vigne. My hussar uniform having arrived last evening, I put it on for the occasion. Mohan, Mirza, an escort of soldiers and a numerous suite, attended me. I had sent my Jemidar three days before with some of my baggage and servants to Lúdiana, that I might not have to wait for them there. When we had proceeded a little way, I felt that the single spring was broken, and instead of the coach jolting as before, it had changed even for the worse, and rested entirely on the pole. I told the Fakír Sahib that it would be much better for us to take General Ventura's carriage at once. But no one dared to act against the command of Ranjít Singh, and he had said that they were to bring me in his carriage. What I anticipated, soon happened; ere we reached the city, one side fell down on the wheel so low as to prevent it from turning. It was in vain that I expressed a wish to alight; the horses were forced to drag us onwards with the wheel thus stopped; at length the axle-tree broke, but still we kept our seats. The wheel was tied on, the coach held up by a dozen men, and in this plight we were drawn into the city, and to the palace, where another carriage holding but two persons, and which the Raja had bought of some adventurer, was got ready for us. Vigne and the fakír had recourse to an elephant, Henderson and I got into the carriage. Ranjít Singh was in the same tent, at the end of the exercising ground, where he had received me two days before. As soon as he saw me, he came out to meet me, and surveyed my uniform with much attention, bringing every part within three inches of his eye. He was particularly curious to know what the furred jacket was for, and I told him that where these were worn the weather was so changeable that we were obliged to carry a second coat with us. "How strange," he said, "to carry your wardrobe about with you. Why don't you give this to a servant, instead of troubling yourself with it?" I told him it belonged to the uniform, and that servants were not always at hand; that private soldiers wore the same, only ornamented with worsted instead of gold, and they could not transfer their jacket to anybody. "They might fasten it on their horses," he answered; "do you appear so before your Emperor?" I told him I dared not appear otherwise.

It always strikes an Oriental as unaccountable, that our dresses so often reach no lower than the waist, and Ranjít Singh was puzzled at my present costume, not being able in this instance to attribute it to meanness. He turned me round and round, and seemed to be much pleased with the richness of the uniform. I then presented Dr. Henderson to him. He told him he was glad to see he had arrived safe, asked him some questions about Peshávar, and observing his odd dress, said: "I hear that you are an officer of the East India Company."—"Yes," replied Henderson. "But how is it," inquired Ranjít Singh jocularly, "that you have no other uniform?" I interposed, saying that he must have heard how Dr. Henderson had been plundered. "That," said he, "is the consequence of your travelling as a fakír. But where is your proper uniform?"—"In Lúdiana." "Do me the favour of sending for it, that I may see you in your usual dress. Stay here eight days that you may recruit yourself, and then cross the Setlej again." He then turned to me, saying, "You wish to leave me?"—"I am compelled," I said, "though with much regret." "Stay another week. There are many things in Lahor which you have not seen yet. The French Legion will soon return here. Do not leave me in such haste." I assured him it was a matter of great grief to me, to make so short a stay.—"After travelling for five years," he rejoined, "a week more or less can make no difference to you." "The question does not concern one week but a whole year. If I am not at Bombay in six weeks from this time, I shall be too late for the steamer, and shall be detained a year."—"But as you cannot reach Bombay in six weeks, you had better remain for a year with me than in Bombay." The Fakír Sahib here reminded him of a Persian proverb, "It is no favour to detain a man against his will."—"That is true," said Ranjít Singh, turning towards him, and then presently beckoning, two shields were brought loaded with presents. First, he gave me a musket, saying: "You showed great interest for the corps of Gorcheli*, I hope you will remember them when you return home." He then presented me with a powder flask made of the horn of the buffalo, covered with cloth, and highly ornamented with gold. The Gorcheli carry these at the right side; then the small cartouch-box containing the balls, bullet-mould, and matches, &c. Vigne, who took his leave at the same time, intending to go with me to Lúdiana, received presents also very much like mine.

I had already furnished myself with some of the weapons peculiar to northern India and the Panjáb, namely; the crooked mountain sword; the battle-axe; the short dagger, having a hilt of ivory ornamented with precious stones; the fearful sabre, wielded with both hands; and finally, for the embellishment of the turban, two kalgas, or black heron's plumes, set in gold according to the fashion of the Panjáb and Kashmír. A beautiful horse was now led forward with an enamelled bridle and saddle, and a rich Kashmír saddle-cloth. "What do you think of doing with this horse?" he asked. "I shall ship it for Europe, if possible," I said.—"So I expected, and therefore sought for a Persian horse, because the horses of the Panjáb do not bear the sea voyage." Then lifting up the presents one after the other, he continued: "Here is a khelat and eleven pieces of Pashmina," and first he fastened an ornament of emeralds in my shako, and then gave me a string of pearls, a pair of gold bracelets set with jewels, and 1300 rupees. Then taking up a Persian sword ornamented with gold, he said: "What I have offered you already, was a present made by the Mahá Raja befitting your rank, but I want to give you some memorial of a friend. The King ought to have given a sabre set with precious

* This noble body of household cavalry were divided into two classes by Ranjít Singh,—the Ghorchar Sowárs and Ghorchar Khás, as they are designated by Captain Murray in his political reports to the Supreme Government; the first being paid in money, and the latter by jaghirs: both classes, however, were mounted on the finest horses procurable, the property of the state. The Ghorchar, or Gorcheli, of all classes at Ranjít Singh's death amounted to about 12,800 picked men.—*Ed.*

stones, but I know it will not be less acceptable to you if I give you one which I have drawn and used myself. Take this, show it to all, but never part with it. It is the gift of a friend." I was deeply affected, and answered that I needed nothing to remind me of his generosity, but that his words had given the utmost value to this munificent gift.

He then called Mohan, and said: "Whenever your master leaves you, come to me." I told him that I had made up my mind to consign the boy to his care, knowing that he could reward his merits much better than I, that I had every cause to be satisfied with him, and felt assured that he would be found a most useful servant to the Mahá Raja. But, as he wanted much instruction, I proposed to place him for at least a year, in Captain Wade's school in Lúdiana. "You are right," said the Mahá Raja, "and when he has finished his studies, he shall come back to me. I will not forget him." He gave Mohan two shawls, a turban, and 100 rupees, and delivered a similar present to his care for the Múnshí, who had set off before this for Lúdiana; then calling to a one-eyed ill-looking man whom I had not seen before, he gave him a pair of shawls, observing to me: "This is the Company Sirkár's spy, who gives information about you. He furnishes the Court Akhbár. It is customary to give him a present whenever a stranger is going away." I remarked that this seemed to me a most absurd custom, as the Company and not he, ought to pay him.—"The very same thing happens in Lúdiana," he said, "when a Sikh is sent there by me; it is a mutual understanding, and signifies that we do not feel annoyed at these spies being employed.—Have you anything to ask of me for any person?" I answered, that I felt quite ashamed to have omitted hitherto all mention of the travelling companion who had come with me from Kashmír to Lahor, my friend Mohammed Shah Nakshbandi, but had I recollected that this was the day of my final leave-taking of the Mahá Raja, I would have brought him with me and presented him. "He is a most honourable man," I added, "and was the means of saving some thousands of your subjects, by feeding them during the raging of the famine in Kashmír."—"What does he want?" he inquired. "I will hear his petition," he replied, "and I promise you also to do what I can for him." I thanked him, and beckoning to Mirza to come near; he made his salám to the Mahá Raja, and according to custom offered him two rupees. Ranjít Singh turned to me, "Shall I increase his pay?" This is the usual expression for promotion. I begged him to do so, upon which he summoned his secretary, and ordered him to prepare his commission as a lieutenant. "Here," said he, handing him 100 rupees, "that is for your equipment, and this is your appointment." I then told him that I had learnt the day before that his son, Karak Singh, was here, and that I wished to pay him a visit before I quitted Lahor. "Why?" he asked. "Because," I replied, "I think the eldest son of the Mahá Raja has a right to this mark of respect from me."—"Good; then you must stay here a few days longer." "If it is not agreeable to the Mahá Raja, I will give up my purposed visit."—"Not so, not so, visit him to-morrow morning, before you set off, and now, I will not detain you any longer. Farewell. You will hear from me at Amritsir, for I wish you to visit my laboratory for the artillery there, and the commandant will call on you. Write to me when you get home, and as often as you can." He stood up, took my hand, and returned to his palankeen. Vigne had long wished to take the Mahá Raja's portrait, and I told him when first we came here, that it would be best to choose a day when we visited him, and then to request permission to sketch him while we conversed. He was of opinion that it would be better to ask permission through the fakír; and the natural result of this was, that nothing more was heard of it. He now felt mortified at the idea of leaving Lahor without succeeding in his wish; and at the moment when the Mahá Raja got to the palankeen, he begged Henderson to ask leave for him to take his likeness. Henderson had declined, as being too late to ask the favour, but Vigne exclaiming, "Mahá Raja," and Ranjít turning round, Henderson was obliged to speak out. Ranjít thought for a moment, and then asked how many days he required. "Half an hour only, before I set off to-morrow."—"That is too short a time. Go to Amritsir, and take it there." "How is that possible?" said Vigne.—"The Governor-General has my portrait, and nobody wishes for it.

If you wish to take one, bring me first as an evidence of your skill a likeness of the King of England." Then turning round to us, he said, "Remember that you have always a friend in the Panjáb." I was too much moved to make any reply.

We were soon on our way back to General Ventura's house. I had seen, for the last time, that extraordinary man who acquires such influence over all who approach him, and who had shown to me, since my first appearance in his dominions, continual marks of attention. All that I had heard before had prepared me for much flattery, and Jacquemont's letters had not caused me to set much value on it. In them he represents it to have always been the Mahá Raja's custom to overwhelm Europeans with flatteries, perhaps for the purpose of making himself respected or loved by them, and then to amuse himself with the ridiculous figure they make. But it seemed to me that it would have been a very useless and troublesome comedy to carry on this dissimulation all the time I stayed in Lahor. Jacquemont, though always boasting of Ranjít Singh's friendship, was even disliked by him; and during his residence in Lahor, he was not allowed, whenever my informant was present, to sit in his presence. This happened as a thing of course. Jacquemont's friend, General Allard himself, not presuming, as one of Ranjít's servants, to sit in his presence, except on the ground, always therefore chose rather to stand than thus demean himself.

The Fakír Sahib soon came to me to say, that Ranjít Singh would see the Shah on the following morning, and invited Dr. Henderson to accompany him. I was asked whether the Shah should be offered an arm-chair. I answered that there were no doubt certain rules followed at the Mahá Raja's court, which I should be sorry to infringe through any partiality of my own, but that probably the sanctity of his person might entitle him to the privilege. "The Mahá Raja wishes to know whether you would like him to receive a dress of honour?"—"I think him worthy of the distinction, for he has ever shown himself a friend to Europeans, believing that in so doing, he was gratifying Ranjít Singh." "The Mahá Raja has assigned him a Jaghír."—"Allow me to send for the Shah Sahib," I replied with exultation.

The Shah entered, and the Fakír addressed me again: "The Mahá Raja has assigned to the Shah five villages in Kashmír, and he wishes to know whether the formal assignment shall be prepared in your name."—"I am sure," I said, "that the Shah would rather receive it from the Mahá Raja's hands; but as he cannot forget him, I request that it may be made out in my name, whom otherwise he might forget." The Shah stood up, ready to kiss my hand; I embraced him with feelings of emotion, saying, "The Mahá Raja desires to see you to-morrow. Do not forget to make him every acknowledgment."

As soon as he had left us, I told Ventura and the Fakír that I feared the Mahá Raja might forget his engagement: they promised to do all they could to prevent such a case. The evening drew on, and when my things were nearly packed, the Fakír came again to ask me in Ranjít Singh's name what present I wished to receive from Karak Singh on the morrow, whether a horse for myself, or shawls for Mr. Vigne and myself. I answered, neither; but the Fakír said this was impossible, and as Vigne had told me that he should be busy finishing a drawing, and could not visit Karak Singh, I told the Fakír that I should go alone, and would accept a shawl as a remembrance. We had a nách for the last time. Henderson was enchanted with his reception by Ranjít Singh, and with the conversation he held with him.

Monday, January 25.—The Fakír came at seven o'clock to attend me to Karak Singh; and as Vigne had finished his drawing, he wished to be of the party. The breakfast was ordered at eight, and Henderson came back from his audience in time for it. The Shah had been well received by the Mahá Raja. Henderson soon left us again to pay some visit, and hoped to return shortly; but I did not see him any more. Forni, I was really sorry for; he cried like a child when I took leave of him, at the thought, as he said, of his own ill luck at being compelled to stay behind; but my compassion was much lessened when by his own confession I learned that he possessed 60,000 rupees; a sum quite sufficient to keep him at home; it is clear therefore that he remains here by his own free choice. At the gate I parted from Fox and Dubuignon, the last was in the service of the Begam

Samrú. There he was picked up by General Ventura, who offered him his wife's sister, and, I believe, 500 rupees a month, until he found a situation of the same value, or could gain as much himself. Hitherto, no prospect of either has awaited him, and for nearly a year he has been living on Ventura's hospitality. He is a very pleasing good young man. General Ventura is rich, though his salary is in arrear some 150,000 rupees. Whenever he asks for money, the Mahá Raja says, "What do you require it for? Is not all I have yours?" When Allard quitted the Panjáb, there was also a large arrear due to him, and this may possibly induce him to return*.

One of the commissions with which the Mahá Raja charged the Fakír Sahib yesterday evening, was to ask for a piece of my uniform. I offered him the whole of it, but this he would not accept. He sent an artist at daybreak this morning to paint it, and in writing requested that I would send him, as soon as possible, a dozen ells of the same stuff, or one complete uniform. This artist had a portfolio filled with drawings, some very good. Vigne's was among them, and the artist had been directed to paint a fine Govind Singh on the flag. I was surprised to see how accurately and with what facility he had executed his task.

Karak Singh's residence was in the city. A regular Durbar was held for my visit, and his brother-in-law receiving me at the gate, led me up three flights of stairs to the roof of the house, where Karak

* General Allard served with much distinction in the Imperial army of France, and was regarded as an officer of great personal bravery, high qualifications, and most conciliatory temper. He served under Napoleon in the army of Italy and Spain, in which last country he followed the fortunes of Joseph Buonaparte. Being excluded by his political views from all participation in the Royalist amnesty, he embarked with other officers for Egypt, whence he shortly proceeded to the court of Persia, and was prevailed upon by General Ventura to quit a country where a ten months' residence had satisfied them there was no immediate prospect of employment under Shah Abbás, and finally travelled through Kandahár to Lahor. For some time Ranjít Singh was indisposed to entertain them, from a suspicion that they were not what they represented themselves to be, but English spies. His scruples, however, were at length overcome, and their services engaged in the first instance at a very inadequate salary. How faithfully and ably they have discharged their trust our own countrymen will be ready to testify.—*Ed.*

Singh sat under a canopy, surrounded by a group of Sikhs squatting on carpets. They all stood up as he welcomed me at the head of the staircase and led me to the arm-chair set out for me. Karak Singh is almost imbecile. As soon as he was seated, General Ventura would have withdrawn, but he grasped his right arm with both hands and begged him to stand by him. "Say something," said General Ventura, "this stupid fellow will not speak a word." Our conversation was silly enough. I had nothing better to say, and therefore admired a carpet worked in gold. He said it was from Herát, and desired that it should be packed up for me directly. As soon as the allotted time for the visit was over, and the presents received, I took my leave, glad to have seen and spoken with Karak Singh, in order to judge what might be expected from him, particularly with regard to Ventura. Throughout India the General is supposed to be not on good terms with this Prince, whose poverty of intellect is rarely adverted to; but I was convinced during my visit this morning that this opinion is erroneous.

We left the palace on the elephants which had carried us there, and soon reached the carriage. Mohan had received a present, and was in high spirits at the prospect of his journey homeward. I had now the painful task of bidding farewell to General Ventura, who had acted so friendly a part by me, and to whom I could hardly expect ever to have it in my power to make a suitable return. He is a man of the highest honour: unhappily, as a Modenese, he was not included in the capitulation of the Italian army, which placed all the officers on an equal footing in the Austrian service; young and unemployed, he considered it a duty incumbent on him to enter upon active occupation of some sort, and was thus led to his present station.

The Fakír Sahib embraced me with tears in his eyes, and entreated me to write a few words of remembrance to him, whenever I should find time, which I engaged to do. And now, ere I close the narrative of my travels in the Panjáb, and give an account of my journey from Lahor to Lúdiana, the last military station on the frontiers of British India to the north-west, I shall insert a brief historical sketch of Ranjít Singh and his predecessors, chiefly derived from information communicated by Mr. Prinsep. As the history of this family is intimately connected with that of the Sikhs in general, there are many particulars which have been already alluded to; repetitions, however, have been avoided as far as possible.

Ranjít Singh cannot lay claim to any noble pedigree. Like most Sikhs whose families have distinguished themselves in the field against the supremacy of the Mohammedans, his forefathers are unknown, at least, before the beginning of the eighteenth century. It is only of late and with great difficulty that the Mahá Raja has been able to persuade some of the descendants of the higher castes to embrace the Sikh faith, and we shall show further how much trouble this has occasioned him.

It is not to be wondered at, if we cannot trace the history of Ranjít Singh's ancestors beyond the last pages of history. The first of his family, of whom he knows anything, having been a common Zemindar, or more properly a small farmer, named Disú, a Hindú of the Ját caste, of the Sánsi race, whose entire fortune, at the beginning of the eighteenth century, consisted of three ploughs and a well, the usual method of estimating a cultivator's possessions in the Panjáb, where the rivers are not made available for irrigating the fields, and where without water the best ground is valueless, bearing no crops, in fact nothing but briars. Disú lived in a village called Sukerchák, in the district of Mánjha, in the Jinhat Doáb. Nothing more is known of him, than that he was the father of Nodh Singh, who embraced the Sikh faith; the inducement being his love for Guláb Singh's daughter, a Zemindar of Mejéthia, who made the conversion of Nodh Singh to his own persuasion the condition of his assent to the alliance with his daughter. Nodh Singh, in nowise discouraged, drank the initiatory *Páhul,* and thereupon took the name of Nodh Singh, sold his ploughs and his hereditary patrimony, with which he purchased a horse, and enrolled himself in the Fáizulapúria Misal, the chief of which division, Kápur Singh, resided in Gujrát.

Nodh Singh died in 1750. His son, Charat Singh, married a girl from Guseráoli, a village thirty miles north-west from Lahor, and uniting with his brothers-in-law, Dal Singh and Jodh Singh, who disdained to serve in any subordinate capacity, he formed a band of robbers, whose depredations were so successful that in a short time they required some place of security wherein to stow away their booty. Having therefore the permission of his wife's family, Charat Singh built a *garhi*, or mud fort, at no great distance from Guseráoli, an excellent situation near the high road to Atok, and not very far from Lahor. Their booty increased so rapidly that the attention of Khája Obíed, whom Ahmed Shah Abdáli had left as his Viceroy in Lahor during this period of general disorder, was drawn to the band. He felt how important it would be to seize the first-built stronghold of the Sikhs, and judged that his presence would render the enterprise more effective. In 1762 he led a considerable force in person against the garhi, purposing to drive out Charat Singh, and level the fort with the ground. The design failed, Khája Obíed was forced to flee towards Lahor, and Charat Singh remained in possession of his fort. This result, mainly owing to his own activity and talent, drew so many Sikhs into the service of the successful leader, that he soon found himself strong enough to found another Misal, which he named Sukercbákia, the last in the list of twelve, and registered as having 2500 horse.

In 1764, Ahmed Shah gave up all pretensions to India, and Charat Singh, with all the other Sikh Sirdars, extended his dominion unopposed, among the Mohammedan and Hindú population. In 1774, an opportunity presented itself to the ambitious Charat of still further increasing his power, and he did not fail to seize it. Ranjít Deo, the Hindú Raja of Jamú, enraged at the shameless conduct of his eldest son Brij Ráj, disinherited him in favour of his younger brother Míyan Dalel Singh. Brij Ráj withdrew to the enterprising Charat Singh, and promised to pay him a yearly tribute if he would help him to dethrone his father, and gain possession of the masnad, or throne, of Jamú. Charat Singh gladly agreed to these terms, strengthened himself by an alliance with Jái Singh, the Sirdar of the Ghania Misal, and marched to Jamú. Ranjít Deo collected together all the troops of Chám or Kángra and of Narpoor, the Sikhs of the Banghi Misal, with their Sirdar, Jhánda Singh, co-operating with them. The opposing forces met at the Bassanta river, where Charat Singh lost his life in his forty-fifth year (1774) by the bursting of his own gun. He had raised himself from a common highway robber, or Dharwari, to be the leader of a Misal. He left a widow, Disan, two sons, Mahá Singh and Sahaj Singh, and one daughter, Raj Kúnwar. His territories brought in a revenue of 300,000 florins a-year. The eldest son, Mahá Singh, was ten years old when he succeeded to the chieftaincy, under the guardianship of his mother Disan and Jái Singh. As a trait of Sikh morals we may mention that this Jái Singh, Charat's ally, and the widow, found it the surest means of extricating themselves from the difficulties into which his death had plunged them by causing the Sirdar of the Banghi Misal, who was the most powerful enemy of the orphans, to be murdered. They therefore bribed a Mihtar (the lowest servant in a house), who fired at and mortally wounded Jhánda Singh, with a gun, and then the two Misals under Jái Singh and Disan retired, unmolested by the Banghi Misal, leaving Brij Ráj to his fate. The boy Mahá Singh, however, on the occasion of Brij Ráj leaving his presence, went through the ceremony of the Dosterbadi, which consists in exchanging turbans as a sign of fraternal union. The extreme youth of this Mahá Singh had nearly proved the ruin of the growing power of his house. The chiefs subject to him were mistrustful, and fancied that under Gandha Singh, the successor of the murdered Jhánda, they should have a better chance of enriching themselves. Dharam Singh was the first rebel, and the widow Disan succeeded in driving him out of his possessions, which she immediately confiscated before Ghanda Singh could come to his aid. This success alarmed the other chiefs, and the time appearing favourable, the same year (1776) the marriage of Mahá Singh was celebrated with the daughter of Gajpat Singh of Jhínd, the betrothment having previously taken place. Jhínd, lying at some distance from Guseráoli, on the left bank of the Setlej, Jái Singh, the guardian of Mahá Singh, appeared in the bridal procession (*Barat*) with a formidable attendance, invited from among those Misals which were friendly to him. This marriage was the origin of Ranjít Singh's present claims on Jhínd, which the Company have lately taken possession of as their right, by lapse of heirs.

In 1778 Mahá Singh began his military exploits by storming a fortress, called Rasúlnaggar, belonging to a Mohammedan, and which he thenceforth called Rámnaggar. This conquest so increased his fame that many chiefs, unattached to any of the Misals, ranged themselves under him. Ranjít Singh was born of this Jhind wife on November 2, 1780. Soon after his birth he was attacked with the small-pox. Mahá Singh, to avert the threatened calamity, sent rich offerings to Jwálamúkhi, the place of pilgrimage, and the boy recovered, but lost his left eye by the disease; hence he was called Ranjít Singh Kána, the one-eyed; his face was altogether much disfigured.

The warlike spirit of Mahá Singh sought another opportunity for display, and soon found it at Jamú. Brij Ráj being reconciled to his father, ascended the masnad, or throne, at his death, and Mahá Singh demanded the fulfilment of the treaty made with his father Charat Singh, one of the stipulations binding Brij Ráj to the payment of a yearly tribute. This unreasonable demand Brij Ráj refused to accede to. Mahá Singh forthwith led an army against Jamú, and Brij Ráj, unprepared for resistance, fled to Trikota Devi, a celebrated resort for pilgrims near Jamú, and left that city to its fate. It was then the richest city of the Panjáb; for under the paternal sway of Ranjít Deo, who united to personal bravery a large share of prudence, the richest among the Hindús had all taken refuge there from different parts of the country, to protect their property more effectually against the Sikh robbers and their Mohammedan rulers. Mahá Singh entered the city without meeting any obstruction: this, however, deterred him just as little from plundering it, as the exchange of turbans (the Dosterbadi) had deterred him from making war on Brij Ráj. Laden with booty, he returned at the end of a few days to Guseráoli, the wealth he had acquired gaining him more than adherents sufficient to protect him from his enemies, though not from the reproaches of his old patron and benefactor, Jái Singh, who had preserved his orphan's inheritance in times of no common difficulty. Brij Ráj, also the friend of Jái Singh, was highly incensed both at the unreasonable pretext invented by Mahá Singh for his invasion, and at his disregard of the Dosterbadi. When therefore Mahá Singh returned from his incursion and entered Amritsir, in order to purify himself from his sins in the holy reservoir, and have an interview with this powerful chief, Jái Singh loudly reproved him for his faithless breach of the ceremonial compact. Mahá Singh was perfectly conscious of his criminality, and being deeply sensible also of his numerous enemies, was anxious to be forgiven by the head of the Ghania Misal. He did not think it beneath his dignity to appear as a supplicant before the old man who had protected his childhood, and leaving the chamber where Jái Singh lay stretched on a chárpái, he presently returned with a tray of sweetmeats, knelt down before him, and besought him to name the conditions on which he would again receive him to his friendship and protection. Jái Singh drew the shawl which covered his feet over his head, and turning himself about, said disdainfully, that he desired to hear no more of such *Bhagtia*, romantic nonsense. Mahá Singh left the presence of the implacable chief in a rage, denouncing vengeance. Reinforced by his allies, he appeared suddenly close to Bátála, Jái Singh's capital, and prevented his junction with the troops of Ghánda Singh, Sirdar of the Banghi Misal, which, united together, would have been six times more numerous than any force he could have mustered.

When Jái Singh was informed of Mahá Singh's advance, he sent his eldest son Gur Baksh in all haste against him with a body of 8000 chosen cavalry; but this daring young man fell at the first charge, and his soldiers took to instant flight. It frequently happens that the very accidents which seem to threaten the speedy downfall of a family serve only to increase their power. It was thus with Mahá Singh, whose defeat would have been inevitable, if the forces of the two powerful fraternities, the Banghi and Ghania Misal, who mustered together some 18,000 horse, had united. The rapid advance of Mahá Singh determined the struggle in his favour, and the aged Jái Singh, whose pride was broken by the death of his son, was driven to the humiliating necessity of suing for peace of the youth who owed even his inheritance to his care.

Jái Singh had two younger sons, but all his love and hopes had centred in the eldest; he now transferred his affection to his son's widow, Sada Kúnwar, whose power over him soon became unlimited. Her only child was Mehtáb Kúnwar; and Mahá Singh, to gain over the old Jái Singh and Sada Kúnwar to his interest, proposed the betrothment of his son Ranjít Singh, then five years old, with Mehtáb Kúnwar. This ceremony, called the Mángní, took place in 1785, and the alliance, together with the influence of Sada Kúnwar, insured to Mahá Singh the assistance of one of the most influential Sirdars; while his bold enterprises procured him the ascendancy over all the Sikh confederacy.

In 1791 Mahá Singh was tempted to undertake an expedition, which had well nigh ruined the hopes of his family for ever. His sister, Ráj Kúnwar, was married to Sáhib Singh, who succeeded his father in the Sirdaree of Gujrat in 1791. The moment seemed propitious for Mahá Singh to get his supremacy over this important place acknowledged, nor did his ambitious mind hesitate on the score of any relationship. He thereupon required his brother-in-law to send him a sum of money in token of his subjection to him. Sáhib Singh sought time to prepare himself, and offered to prove that as his father had belonged to the Banghi Misal, Mahá Singh could have no possible right to demand tribute from him. On hearing this, Mahá Singh marched to Sodera, the chief stronghold of Sáhib Singh, and invested it. Sáhib Singh, notwithstanding, had time to solicit assistance of the Banghi Misal, who came to relieve the place, but being too weak to succeed, were eventually repulsed. During the siege Mahá Singh fell sick, and expired in his own city of Guseráoli in 1792, in his twenty-seventh year. His death called into action the talents of Sada Kúnwar, which had an important influence on the destinies of the Panjáb. His only son, Ranjít Singh, was twelve years old, and the numerous enemies of his father seemed only to have awaited his death to seek their revenge; while, in spite of the Sikh custom which made his widow regent of the kingdom under the superintendence of the Díwan Lakhpat Singh, the Minister of her late husband, Sada Kúnwar, the mother-in-law of the young Rajá, managed to get the direction of affairs into her own hands.

The year following, 1793, Jái Singh died. He disinherited both his sons, Bágh Singh and Nidhán Singh, and appointed his daughter-in-law,

Sada Kúnwar, regent for his grandchild, Mehtáb Kúnwar, the wife of Ranjít Singh, to whom he bequeathed his territorial possessions and treasures. The sons had neither talent nor courage to oppose this will. Sada Kúnwar seems to have designed so completely to surround Ranjít Singh, scarcely arrived at boyhood, with the pleasures of youth, that his mind should be rendered almost incapable of being roused to the affairs of government. During her guardianship, he was married for the second time to Raj Kúnwar, the daughter of the Náki chief Khúja Singh. But the pleasures in which he lived had their usual effect of satiating, and the youth turned from them to enter on the sterner duties of the man. This ambitious woman was not only scheming against his health, but she also prevented him from receiving any of the benefits of education; and Ranjít Singh, too late, found himself as ignorant, untutored, and inexperienced, as if he had grown up among brutes. At seventeen years of age he awoke from the stupor in which his senses had been lost; seized on the reins of power, and began his government by sending his guardian Díwan Lakhpat Singh in command of a perilous attempt against Khytal, where he lost his life, not without a suspicion that Ranjít Singh had formed this plan to be rid of him. His own mother was accused of improper conduct, and Lakhpat Singh was supposed to be neither the first nor the last of her admirers. Ranjít Singh having had proof of her guilt, either commanded or at least permitted her to be put to death, and the aged Dal Singh is thought to have been her poisoner. From that time Ranjít Singh carried on the government under the guidance of his mother-in-law.

The two first incursions of Shah Zemán into the Panjáb, took place during his minority, but the third, in 1798, found Ranjít Singh governing his own Misal. He was one of those Sikh Sirdars who retreated as the other advanced, but did homage through a deputy at Lahor. Meanwhile Ranjít Singh withdrew to the left bank of the Setlej into the province of Sirhind, and took advantage of this time, when apprehension of the Afghans was universal, to overrun every town or village which he found too weak to resist him. As soon as the Shah was compelled to hasten homewards to Kabúl, Ranjít Singh returned quickly to his own territories, following the Shah's army without any settled design except that of availing himself of circumstances. The service which gave him Lahor, has been related in another part of this work, as well as the manner in which he possessed himself of the city. His success excited the jealousy of the other Sirdars, and an allied force was levied against him; but a few months saw them dispersed without their having undertaken anything, and Ranjít Singh, whose forces were far inferior, was allowed to breathe freely. This was the last attempt of the Sikh Sirdars to withstand the growing power of Ranjít Singh. They saw that their independence was at an end; but instead of uniting against this artful and powerful prince, each one was in hopes of escaping, by some lucky chance, that ruin which had overtaken the others.

While Ranjít Singh's influence was thus increasing, the Panjáb was divided between Sikh and Mohammedan rulers, the last being as disunited as the former, with regard to any plan for resisting the common enemy of all. Before his cunning policy therefore, without any other warlike enterprise on his part, they all succumbed. Ranjít Singh has always shown an unwillingness to have recourse to arms, not from any want of personal courage, but from his consciousness that while the success of a battle depends on the joint will of a number, that of negotiations depends on the preponderance of one man's talent, and every stratagem is good to him that conduces to his own private ends. His conscience never troubled him whether he robbed the widow or orphan; deprived some unfortunate dependent on his honour of all his property; seized the treasures confided to his care, or claimed the whole fortune of his friend, or even the inheritance of his own son.

In 1805, a storm came from the south, which might have annihilated the precarious power of Ranjít Singh. A battle was fought between the British army in Hindústhan under Lord Lake, and the Mahrattas under their general Jaswant Ráo Holkár, who, after his defeat, betook himself to flight in the direction of the Panjáb. Ranjít Singh had now to choose the lesser of two evils. It might be impossible to oppose Holkár, without much preparation; or a friendly reception might transfer the seat of war to the Panjáb, and the British, once there, might be rather more difficult to remove than any other enemy.

Holkár reached Lahor, and endeavoured by every argument to prevail with Ranjít Singh to join the Maharatta confederacy in hostilities against the British, pleading that the Hindú population had at that time nothing more to fear from the Mohammedans, and that such a powerful coalition might probably decide the fate of India. Ranjít Singh delayed his final answer, in expectation that Holkár's impetuosity would cool down; and the Maharatta leader saw at length that while no partial aid would avail him, it was vain to expect the Sikh nation to espouse his quarrel *en masse*. He therefore concluded a peace with Lord Lake in December, 1805, and both armies retired to Hindústhan.

The history of the three following years offers little matter of interest for Europeans, important as they were for the country, then being gradually overrun by the Sikhs, whose conquests included, besides the north of the Panjáb, the strip of country from the Jamna to the Setlej, called Sirhind and Malwa, of which Ranjít Singh made himself undisputed master. The means by which he gained this large territory were little to his honour, although every praise may be conceded to the views he entertained of reducing the disembodied provinces and tribes to one consistent government. The independent Sirdars, as if under the wand of some enchanter, inevitably implicated Ranjít Singh in their quarrels, and the result invariably turned to the sole aggrandizement of the Sikh. If one of these Sirdars died, so surely did Ranjít seize a part or the whole of the inheritance, whether cities, treasures, or lands. This indeed was a period in the annals of Indian history, when no feeble prince had any prospect of immunity, nor were prescriptive rights, however ancient, secure against the presumptive claims of a self-confident and powerful usurper.

We have already spoken of the treaty between the East India Company and Ranjít Singh, appointing the Setlej as the boundary of their respective states. If it set narrower limits to his kingdom in this direction than he had proposed, the embassy which concluded it was the indirect means of extending his sway in another quarter, and taught him, moreover, the useful lesson of avoiding all contention with the British Government. I allude to the event which took place in the camp of the envoy Mr. Metcalfe, (the present Sir Charles Metcalfe,

Governor of the newly-formed presidency of Agra, and now of Canada,) which, however unimportant in itself, made a deep impression on the sagacious mind of Ranjít Singh. The following was the occasion of this bloody scene: The Mohammedans of the sect of the Súnis in India, have an absurd and superstitious ceremony which concludes their Moharram, during the last ten days of which they erect canopies or *tábuts* of different colours, ornamented with gold and silver, and illuminated by multitudes of lamps, which are carried about on the last day of the feast, in joyful procession, and with loud cries are then burnt or thrown into the water. The ceremony is to commemorate the martyrdom of Hásán and Húsáin, the sons of Ali. The Shiahs consider this as heretical, and use all their influence to prevent the Súnis from holding the procession at all. The spirit of animosity with which the opposite parties are inflamed, is frequently the occasion of loss of life in the more populous Indian cities.

In 1809, the Moharram fell at the end of February, at the same time as the Hindú feast of the Húli, and the Envoy's camp happened to be then in the holy city of Amritsir, Ranjít Singh having made that the residence of his court during the celebration of the Húli. Through some misunderstanding of the orders issued by Mr. Metcalfe, prohibiting his Mohammedan escort from carrying about the Tábut, the procession was proceeding with every demonstration of joy, when the Akáli, enraged at the spectacle of this Mohammedan ceremony profaning the vicinity of their holy reservoir, stirred up the people of Amritsir against the enemies of their faith. Phula Singh headed the fanatical multitude, and with a discharge of fire-arms and fearful cries, they blindly rushed on Mr. Metcalfe's escort, which consisted of two companies of regular sipáhis, and sixteen horsemen only. This small force received the onset of the populace steadily; they soon brought the fanatics to their senses by a close fire; and forming into a line, they in their turn attacked the Akális, and forced them to seek safety in flight. Ranjít Singh meanwhile had been informed of the accident, and hastening to the spot just in time, as he thought, to stay the massacre of every Englishman, beheld the final charge, and the dispersion of the vast crowds of his own subjects. He rode onwards to the Envoy's tent, to request his pardon for the occurrence, and to express his admiration of the conduct of his soldiers. From that time he set about the organization of his own army, perceiving the vast superiority of implicit obedience in the British soldiery, over the fanatical rage and enthusiasm of his irregular troops. He strove to obtain subalterns from the Company's army to discipline his own, but the plan succeeded but very partially among his native army, hitherto unaccustomed to the least control. He perceived now that it was the order and discipline more than the number of the Company's soldiers, which made them so formidable. From finding himself at that time too feeble to act against them, he entertained the thought of connecting himself closely with them, and of enlarging his own power in another direction than Hindústhan. He signed the treaty which bound him to non-interference in those territories on the left shore of the Setlej, or "the golden harvest of Sirhind and Malwa," as the Sikhs call that country, which, but for British interference, could not have eluded his grasp. The extent of this deprivation may be measured from the fact, that of the many Rajas and Sirdars who bear rule there, one only, the Raja of Patiala has a yearly revenue of three millions of florins.

Ranjít Singh being thus shut out from this rich conquest, turned towards the north for his future prey, where several powerful Hindú princes still exercised the sovereign power. He interfered in all their disputes, generally invited by the contending factions; the first act of the drama being opened at Kángra, a fortress considered impregnable by the natives. In 1809, the old Raja Sansar Chand requested his assistance against the powerful Ghorka chief Amar Singh Thápa, promising to receive a body of Sikhs into his fortress. No sooner, however, did these Sikhs make their appearance, than Sansar Chand began to repent of his engagement, and sought a pretext for delay, in the hope that while the Sikhs and Ghorkas were encamped before the place, they would turn upon each other, and relieve him at once of his open enemies, and still more dangerous friends. Ranjít Singh, however, saw through this plan, and therefore ordered his troops, on the refusal of Sansar Chand to admit them, to advance against Kángra. The fire of his batteries was opened on the Sikhs, of whom many were killed and many wounded while climbing the precipitous ascents; but, on reaching the gate of the fortress, to their astonishment it was opened to them, and thus Ranjít Singh became master of Kángra.

From thence he marched into the Jhalandar Doáb, where he robbed the widow of the lately deceased Bhaghái Singh of her Jaghír or fief, while his Díwan appeared before Faizulapura, invited the Sirdar, Bhúp Singh, to an interview, seized him and took possession of his country for Ranjít Singh. And by such enterprises he gained, in addition to their territories, the hoarded treasures of the unfortunate Sirdars, whom he generally left to beggary. So long as this system injured the Sikhs only, it was looked upon by the Hindús as a robbery of one thief by another; and Ranjít Singh was deemed an instrument sent to punish them for their crimes; but when Hindú Rajas lost their lands, and ancient dynasties came to beg their bread, his transgressions began to be viewed in a very different light.

Ranjít Singh was now organizing his army: he divided his infantry into battalions of 300 or 400 men each: he made the artillery a separate corps under a commandant or Darogha; while the cavalry remained under his own command, divided into Ghorchar Khás and Ghorchar Sowár, the last receiving pay and horses from the Government, the former having possessions in land assigned to them.

In 1810, the failure of his attempt on Múltán satisfied him that his army was still very imperfectly disciplined, and the remainder of that year was devoted to its improvement, and to the confiscation of the property of the helpless, which took place even with more faithlessness and less assignable pretext than before. One example out of many may here be cited. Ranjít Singh repaired to Rámnaggar, and summoned Nidhán Singh Atha before him. The chief, remembering how treacherously many of the independent Sirdars had been made captive, answered that he would not come without the security of a Sodi, (Sikh priest), upon which Ranjít Singh forthwith invested his fort of Daskas; but his artillery could do little against it, nor did his shameful impositions on the family of the besieged, who accidentally fell into his hands, avail him more. He therefore sent the Sodi priest, who gave him his word that Ranjít Singh had no design whatever against the freedom of the brave Nidhán Singh Atha, declaring that he only wanted the fortress, for which he would give him a Jaghír in exchange. On this assurance, Nidhán Singh came over in perfect confidence to the enemy's camp, where, in utter disregard of the solemn promise given, he was thrown into chains, and detained six weeks in prison, until the Sikh priests, whose honour was implicated in this affair, sat before Ranjít Singh in Dharna till he had released the prisoner, and given him the stipulated Jaghír. No sooner was Nidhán Singh Atha restored to liberty, than he refused to accept the Jaghír, but avowed to Ranjít Singh that as an honourable man he could not swear fidelity to one so devoid of principle, and quitting the Panjáb, entered the service of Atá Mohammed Khan in Kashmír.

Ranjít Singh felt himself henceforward strong enough to act as master of the whole of the Panjáb. Every Sirdar, no matter what his faith might be, had to pay him tribute, and if he refused to obey a summons to the camp, was deprived of his territory, sent in chains to Lahor, and there detained until the festivals of the Huli, or Dasara, loosed his bonds. In no instance, however, did Ranjít Singh restore the property. Whenever a Sirdar died, Ranjít Singh, according to the Indian usage of supremacy, claimed to be heir to his possessions, and in case the son had not made himself friends beforehand, he never recovered his rights. Under any circumstances, he had to pay a large sum by way of *nazzerána*, for the investiture of the turban at court. The same causes which operated in favour of the extension of the East India Company's dominion, contributed also to give Ranjít Singh unlimited power in the Panjáb. His weaker opponents, by their improvident divisions overrated their own strength, and began hostilities; the alliance of the lesser chiefs was soon broken, who then in cowardly despair, submitted themselves unconditionally to Ranjít Singh, whose sole dependence was on intrigue, the most prompt measures, and an unshaken confidence in his own resources.

About this time, one of the Sirdars gave an answer to him, which shows that his designs were penetrated, and that he could sometimes tolerate bold words. In 1811, he had taken possession of the land belonging to his uncle Nidhán Singh Ghania, nominally for his wife,

Mehtáb Kúnwar, but really for himself, Nidhán Singh being taken captive and shut up in Lahor. Jodh Singh, a Sikh Sirdar, to whom something very similar had already happened, came to Lahor with a body of soldiers, with which he was to attend the Díwan to Múltán, and on taking leave, Ranjít Singh ordered a turban to be given to him as a token of the Mahá Raja's favour. But Jodh Singh begged to be excused, saying, that these were times when every Sirdar must esteem himself favoured by the permission of Ranjít Singh to keep his own turban, and his head into the bargain.

The blind Shah Zemán, came at this same time to Lahor, to interest Ranjít Singh in the affairs of his brother, Shah Shúja, in Kabúl, but he found himself so entirely neglected, that he soon returned to Ráwal Pindí, where they had both taken up their residence temporarily. Shah Shúja made an attempt on Peshávar, in the same year that he had ineffectually sought the aid of Ranjít Singh. The invitation shows how little he could have known Ranjít Singh's character, to suppose that he would be so egregiously foolish as to assist him in uniting the Afghan power under one chief. Neither a yearly tribute, nor the cession of a large province, could offer him any recompense for the prospect opened to him by the civil discords of Afghanistan. These discords made it impossible for the Afghans to assist their co-religionists on the left shore of the Indus, where one small kingdom after the other fell before Ranjít Singh. Shah Shúja's attempt to reconquer his crown was equally unfortunate; he narrowly escaped his enemies on the right shore of the Atok, and when he arrived on the left shore, was made prisoner by Juhán Dád Khan, and sent by him to his brother, Atá Mohammed Khan, in Kashmír. Shah Zemán, the unhappy blind brother of the captive king, had remained in Ráwal Pindí awaiting the issue of the attempt, and had now no better course to take, than to flee to Lahor with his own and his brother's family.

Shah Shúja found means to escape from Kashmír, and in 1813 he came also to Lahor with the Díwan Mokham Chand, Ranjít Singh having told his wife, Vafa Begam, who had accompanied Shah Zemán to Lahor, that it was the best thing her husband could do. Shah

Shúja was infatuated enough to believe that Ranjít Singh meant to grant him some assistance, but he had scarcely entered his own dwelling when the Mahá Raja sent to require him to deliver up the famous *Kohi Núr* diamond. The early history of this jewel is not known. According to the Hindús, it belonged, before the Moghul Emperors owned it, to the Pándús, whose legends remind one of the Cyclops of Roman Mythology. Many believe that it was presented to Shah Jehán by the Amír Jemla, who was at one time a jeweller, and who afterwards farmed the diamond mines in the Dekhan, and that the present had a great influence in making him a Wazír. The French traveller, Tavernier, saw the Kohi Núr in Aurangzíb's possession, ornamenting his small throne, and gives its weight as 420 carats, I believe. The largest diamond in Europe is in the crown of Russia, and weighs 194 carats *.

Nádir Shah seized this with all the other treasures in Delhi, and carried it to Persia, where it became the property of Ahmed Shah Abdáli, when Nádir Shah's tent was plundered after his murder. It remained with the kings of Kabúl until the accession of Shah Zemán; but that unhappy monarch was obliged to flee before his victorious brother, and confiding in the fidelity of Múlla Aushik, took refuge in his castle (1800), and when there he found himself a prisoner, his former friend keeping him until he could deliver him up to his enemies. Shah Zemán having in vain shown the Múlla the baseness of his

* The celebrated Kohi Núr diamond is cut in the rose form, and, when rough, is said to have weighed 900 carats. It is believed to have been found at the Golconda mines about the year 1550. The magnificent Russian diamond is about the size of a small pigeon's egg, and was at one period the eye of a Hindú image, whence it was purloined by a French soldier. After passing through several hands, it came by purchase, eventually, into the possession of the Empress Catherine of Russia, who gave the vendor 90,000*l.* in money, and an annuity of 4000*l.* But the most beautiful, and probably the most perfect diamond hitherto found, is a brilliant brought from India by a Mr. Pitt, which weighs rather more than 136 carats, and was purchased by the Duke of Orleans for 100,000*l.*, who placed it among the crown jewels of France. The average price is 2*l.* per carat in the rough, or 8*l.* when wrought, exclusive of the workmanship; but the values increase as the squares of the weight; diamonds of 1, 2, and 3 carats, being respectively 2, 8, and 18*l.* in the rough; the carat is equal to the 150th part of an ounce troy.—*Ed.*

treachery, concealed all his treasures, and among them the Kohi Núr, in the wall of his chamber, where they remained until the accession of Shah Shúja, in 1803, when he punished Múlla Aushik, and drew the Kohi Nur from its hiding-place. He always carried the stone wherever he went, and had it with him in his flight.

Ranjít Singh now offered him a considerable jaghír for the stone, but the Shah denied having it with him, and the Vafa Begam declared that it had been pledged to a Saraf, or money-changer, for a loan of money. Ranjít Singh was not to be imposed upon by this shallow pretext, and to prevent the jewel being sent away, he instantly ordered guards to be set round the Shah's house, who allowed no one to quit it without submitting to a rigorous search. To bring the unlucky Shah to confession, other means were soon resorted to, and for two days no food was suffered to enter the house; yet even hunger could not make him betray the secret, and Ranjít Singh determined to go more cunningly to work. Letters were brought forward purporting to have been written by the Shah to Fatih Khan in Kabúl, inviting him to invade the Panjáb and liberate him. In consequence of this discovery, instead of the guards hitherto appointed, two companies were posted round his house, and he was informed that he was to be taken to Govindgurh as a state prisoner, every means being taken to alarm and distress him. Shah Shúja saw that he should never regain his liberty, but on condition of giving up this precious stone, and demanded two months, in order to find time, as he said, to redeem it from the Saraf. Ranjít Singh was reluctantly compelled to accede to his terms, and the Shah for a time was left unmolested. Before the expiration of the term, however, his treatment became more harsh, that he might be reminded of the necessity of keeping his word. The Shah saw then that no further delay was possible, and that Ranjít Singh was resolved to have the jewel, even if he put him to death to obtain it. On the last day of the two months he invited the Mahá Raja to come and receive the diamond, and when he appeared with a few attendants, the Shah received him with the dignity peculiar to him, and being seated, remained profoundly silent for an hour. It is not to be wondered at, that Ranjít Singh at last lost all patience, and softly bade one of his attendants to remind the Shah of the purpose of his visit. The Shah did not make any answer, but beckoned to a eunuch, who quitted the room and presently returned with a small packet, which he laid on a carpet spread out between them. Ranjít Singh ordered one of his attendants to open it, and having satisfied himself that it really was what he came for, he instantly left the place, without speaking a word or even saluting the Shah.

This account of the event came from the Shah's own lips, and is naturally given in the darkest colours. It may be perhaps much softened down. It is always excusable to deprive an enemy of the means of creating fresh disturbances. Certainly Shah Shúja was invited to Lahor by Ranjít Singh; he did not come as an enemy but as a guest, and generosity would have required a fallen man to be spared. But at this very time Ranjít Singh had been deceived by the Afghans in the reward promised for his co-operating with them against Kashmír, and it demanded more self-denial than was to be expected in the ignorant enemy of the Mohammedans, had he disregarded the opportunity of seizing this famous stone, which it is pretty sure that the ex-Shah would have applied to some warlike enterprise.

The offer of a jaghír from a Sikh to the former monarch must not be considered according to our European ideas. A rightful, though dethroned king, will be always respected as such in Europe, and particularly so long as there is any chance of his reinstatement; but in India the possessor alone has any claim on respect. Shah Shúja thought to outwit Ranjít Singh, and only irritated him. Sooner or later he must have lost his jewels, which were so well known in India, that every Sirdar, whose country he traversed, would have been on the look-out for them. Once before they had nearly cost him his life. When he was obliged to fly from Pesháwar, in the year 1809 (when Mr. Elphinstone first saw him), the Vafa Begam fled to Mozaffer Khan at Múltán, who invited Shah Shúja to repair to him also, and give him counsel how he could best withstand Ranjít Singh. The Shah soon appeared, but to his astonishment he and his escort were fired on from the fort which he was approaching without the smallest suspicion. It is supposed that the Nawáb acted thus in order to kill the Shah and steal his jewels, or to take him prisoner and deliver him up to Mohammed Shah. Shah Shúja withdrew out of the reach of the guns, and waited until Mozaffer Khan thought better of it, and this soon happened. He came out to the Shah, welcomed him as his guest, and gave him a Jaghír which produced a revenue of 20,000 rupees.

As soon as Ranjít Singh had got the Kohi Núr, he allowed the Shah more liberty; but instead of taking advantage of it instantly, and making his way to the frontiers with the jewels still left to him, he began the same course of intrigues which had occupied his whole life. A letter was very shortly intercepted, written by his Kázi, Shír Mohammed, to Mohammed Azim Khan, the Governor of Kashmír, in which the Kázi proposed to him to murder Ranjít Singh, and unite with his brother Fatih Khan of Kabúl, in a combined attack on Lahor. Ranjít Singh had the writer and the letter both seized and carried before Shah Shúja, who sent them back, desiring that the Mahá Raja would punish the writer as he thought proper. Persuaded that pain would draw a confession from the Kázi that he had acted by the Shah's orders, the guards were commanded to beat him with their shoes and sticks. Fainting under their blows, the poor wretch still took the whole blame upon himself, and was carried to prison, whence the Shah was forced to procure his release by a mulct of 20,000 rupees.

The year following fresh intrigues came to the knowledge of Ranjít Singh, who, knowing that they could only be carried on by the sale of the Shah's remaining jewels, resolved to deprive him of all opportunity of concocting any further mischief. He demanded them; but Shah Shúja, who ought to have known with whom he had to deal, assured him that he had none left. In consequence of this, Ranjít Singh was determined to convince himself of the truth of his statement, and sent Bhái Rám Singh with one of his own wives to the Shah's house, with orders to search it throughout, and to bring him every box and parcel which contained anything of value. His wife penetrated into the innermost recesses of the Zenána, and searched even the wives of the Shah. Everything of value was packed up and carried to Ranjít Singh's palace, where the packets were opened in his presence; he appropriated to himself all articles that took his fancy. But although

Shah Shúja had reason enough to complain of the rapacity of Ranjít Singh, nevertheless this prince did not find all he wanted, the Shah having up to the present time continued occasionally to dispose of jewels, and as lately as 1834, sold one at Amritsir, which the Mahá Raja purchased for 80,000 rupees.

In 1814 the Shah succeeded in sending Shah Zemán and his own wives to Lúdiana in disguise; he soon after made his escape and joined them. He ascribed his success in this plan to his own talents, while Ranjít Singh was very glad to be rid of a guest who cost him a good deal of money, and from whom he thought he had wrested all that he had to give. Shah Shúja and Shah Zemán took up their residence in Lúdiana, where the East India Company allowed the first 50,000 and the last 30,000 rupees a year, and why? their newspapers say, that it seemed to them too hard that the poor Hindús should have to support two kings who had no territories in India. But there is probably some political object in this protection of the kings of Kabúl. Shah Zemán has found consolation for his misfortunes in his religious observances, while Shah Shúja entertains a distant hope of recovering his empire, and squanders large sums in spies, and the hire of soldiers. Since 1814 he has undertaken two expeditions, the first in 1818, a second more recently: both of which have, however, signally failed*.

---

* It is quite impossible for any dispassionate man to read the above account of the character of Shah Shúja and Ranjít Singh, without recurring to our want of better information on questions of vital Political importance to the British Government, on which the issue of great public measures so materially depended. It may be said, that subsequent events, and the fatality which seemed to attach to all the events of Shah Shúja's life, have verified this historical estimate of his vacillating, treacherous, and imbecile mind—and the bloody scenes enacted in the Panjáb, since Ranjít Singh's death, give us likewise an insight into the real nature of the elements compacted together by the faithless procedure of a self-confident individual, regardless of the mode by which he effected his purpose. It cannot be doubted that the publication of this work at an earlier period, coming as it does from an intelligent foreigner, who had no bias or preconceived ideas of necessity to disturb his review of past events, would have exercised a most salutary influence in the highest quarters, and possibly have deterred us from espousing the cause of a prince so utterly destitute of every qualification for the sovereignty to which he was advanced by the powerful aid of the British Government, and in every

I have already spoken of the ill success of the expedition against Kashmír, and the part taken in it by Ranjít Singh, who, although a man of great personal bravery, has never been a successful general. A few words on the siege of Múltán in 1818, will give an idea of the quality of his troops, where he considered himself at the head of a disciplined army, and was moreover reinforced by the brave Ghorkas, or Nepalese troops, who were dismissed after the peace with the East India Company.

The control of the force destined for this expedition was given to the Díwan Misar Chand, who had risen to that rank from a very inferior station. Híra Singh, the Mahá Raja's eldest son, was invested with the nominal command, to avoid giving offence to the Sikh Sirdars by this appointment. After Ranjít Singh's former enterprises against his neighbours, it was unnecessary to make any pretence for attacking Múltán; he proceeded, therefore, on the presumption which gives right to the strongest party, without attempting to palliate his conduct. The army having approached Múltán, Mozaffer Khan, the Nawáb, was required to give a large sum in gold, and five of his best horses, as a tribute. This, however, he declined, clearly seeing that a scene of the same kind would soon be repeated, and, in fact, he had been twice laid under contribution already, (in 1804 and 1807,) and in 1810, he was besieged, though ineffectually, and bought off his enemies with a heavy fine of 180,000 rupees.

According to another account, Mozaffer Khan complied with Ranjít Singh's demand, and as soon as the army had retired with his money and horses, rode after Ranjít Singh, and did him homage as a Zemindar. Ranjít Singh admired the horse he rode very much, and one of his suite in a very uncourteous manner, demanded it for his master.

---

respect so little disposed by previous habits of life or nature to refrain from dabbling in political intrigues with the enemies of his best and greatest friends. Such, no doubt, was the true and proper cause of the fatal insurrection at Kabúl. The whole tenor of Ranjít Singh's conduct to his associate chiefs; their mutual want of faith, and the lawless cunning and heartless disposition of all who exercised any share of power or authority, sufficiently prove the futility of treaties with such parties, however solemnly they may be pledged.—*Ed.*

The Zemindar, enraged at this insolence, rode up to the Mahá Raja's elephant, and with his sabre endeavoured to strike him, but the seat was too high to enable him to reach his person. Ranjít Singh's suite soon came to his help, and forced the Zemindar to defend himself. Many of the Sikhs attacked him, but so dexterously did he manage his horse, that they were all struck to the earth, and they then had recourse to the cowardly expedient of shooting him from behind, when the horse from which he fell was seized by the Mahá Raja's command. This was probably the origin or pretext of the enmity which brought about the siege of Múltán. Mozaffer Khan, aware of the inefficiency of his enemy's guns, and confident in his own bravery, hoped to have witnessed the failure of this attempt against him also. But, like Mohammedans in general, he never thought of inspiring his soldiers with a similar spirit, or of strengthening his fortress. In India, the Mohammedan garrison defending a fortress, believe themselves, each man individually, capable of firing off the guns, and without any precise orders, usually go about from one station or tower to another, serving any of the guns, while the rest of the party seat themselves quietly behind them, and begin talking and smoking. From time to time one gets up, loads the guns chiefly with balls which are not fitted for them, and when they go off, exclaim, Wáh! Wáh! and sit down again to smoke, until another thinks fit to reload and fire. Múltán consists of the town and the fortress or citadel, which is furnished with outworks and a double wall. The former being taken without any bloodshed, the kilah, or citadel, was invested. Each Sirdar and Jaghirdar in Ranjít Singh's army, brought his own arms and ammunition, and fired whenever and at whatever he pleased. Guns and muskets were therefore being discharged on all sides night and day. In two months' time the outer wall of the kilah was nearly destroyed, and several breaches were effected in the inner one, which the besieged were too careless even to repair. Ranjít Singh, though absent, directed the operations of the siege. In May the army was intrenched behind the outer wall, but the Mahá Raja forbad the Díwan Misar Chand to run any risks, for he had not yet recovered the losses he had sustained by his Kashmír expedition, and felt that another check might be productive of the most serious consequences. He even offered to give the Nawáb of Múltán a Jaghír if he would surrender his fortress, a very liberal offer considering that he had nothing left him now, except this citadel badly defended. But Mozaffer Khan refused it, rather than be dependent on Ranjít Singh. On the 2nd of June, a Sikh Akáli called Sadhu Singh, with a few comrades, attacked the Afghans keeping guard between the inner and outer walls, overpowered them, and took this advanced work. He was followed by the Sikh troops, who took the outworks without any loss on their side; those Afghans who made the least resistance were instantly put to the sword. Encouraged by this easy victory, the troops pushed forward, forced their way through the breaches in the walls, and penetrated to the interior, where the besieged were quite unprepared for any attack. The Nawáb, his four sons, and his attendants, valiantly defended his own house: two of the sons fell with their father; the third, Zúlfikhar Khan, lay severely wounded by a sabre; the other, the eldest of the family, whom his father had made Governor of Múltán, was found concealed in a cellar. This rich fortress was thereupon abandoned to indiscriminate pillage.

Ranjít Singh received the news of its surrender with the liveliest expressions of satisfaction, and soon resolved that he would be no loser by the sacking of the fortress. It was well known that great treasures were concealed there, and recollecting how Nádir Shah made every one of his soldiers deliver up the booty he had taken in India at a certain station on the Atok, including all the treasures of Delhi, Ranjít Singh commanded his troops, with the exception of one company left to garrison Múltán, to return to Lahor, where he made officers and soldiers alike give up the spoil. Each of the Nawáb's two sons received a Jaghír.

This year, 1818, Fatih Khan, the faithful servant of Mohammed Shah of Kabúl, was first blinded and then put to death at the command of his ungrateful master. On the death of this great man, whose distinguished talents alone had raised the Shah to the throne of Kabúl, the dynasty of Ahmed Shah fell likewise, principally through the instrumentality of his grandson. By this event Ranjít Singh was freed from the only man whom he had to fear in the west, and he had no sooner heard of it than he marched by Atok to Pesháwar, whence, after several smart skirmishes, he compelled the independent Governor, Yár Mohammed Khan, Fatih Khan's brother, to seek refuge in the mountains. Ranjít Singh, who commanded in person, appointed Juán Dád Khan, to whose perfidy he was indebted for the acquisition of Atok, to be Governor of Pesháwar, and returned to the Panjáb; but Yár Mohammed soon came down from the mountains, and appearing before Pesháwar, obliged Juán Dád to make his escape. He happened during his flight to meet with Shah Shúja, brought by the events in Kabúl to the shores of the Atok, and remained with him so long as there was any prospect of the Shah's reinstatement on his throne; but when the latter was forced to retire to Lúdiana, poorer than before, Juán Dád Khan repaired to Herát, where he was received by Mahmúd Shah.

The power of the Afghan empire terminated with the death of Fatih Khan. It thereupon fell into the separate parts from which it had been formed; one province only, Herát, being left to Mahmúd Shah, a grandson of the great founder, and on this Ranjít Singh first commenced his aggressions. The year following he was engaged in the conquest of Kashmír; and the next in extending his dominion over the Indus to Jellálabad, half-way between Atok and Kabúl. This increase of power was chiefly gained by the soldiers of Allard and Ventura, who both came to Lahor in 1822, and entered the service of the Mahá Raja. The events which occurred from that period up to 1835, are of no particular interest, and some have been touched on elsewhere. In 1835, the army of Dost Mohammed Khan, the brother of Fatih Khan, who had seized on Kabúl, and that of Ranjít Singh, under the command of Ventura, faced each other for some time on the Kabúl river, but neither general desired an engagement. Dost Mohammed Khan soon retreated, and Ranjít Singh contented himself with strengthening his power in this direction, without extending it.

Before I enter into a detailed statement of Ranjít Singh's power, I will say a few words of his person and character. In person he is short and mean-looking, and had he not distinguished himself by his great talents, he would be passed by without being thought worthy of observation. Without exaggeration, I must call him the most ugly and unprepossessing man I saw throughout the Panjáb. His left eye, which is quite closed, disfigures him less than the other, which is always rolling about, wide open, and is much distorted by disease. The scars of the small-pox on his face, do not run into one another, but form so many dark pits in his greyish-brown skin; his short straight nose is swollen at the tip; the skinny lips are stretched tight over his teeth, which are still good; his grizzled beard, very thin on the cheeks and upper lip, meets under the chin in matted confusion; and his head, which is sunk very much on his broad shoulders, is too large for his height, and does not seem to move easily. He has a thick muscular neck, thin arms and legs, the left foot and the left arm drooping, and small well-formed hands. He will sometimes hold a stranger's hand fast within his own for half an hour, and the nervous irritation of his mind is shown by the continued pressure on one's fingers. His costume always contributes to increase his ugliness, being in winter the colour of gamboge, from the *Pagri* (the turban or Sikh cloth, on his head,) down to his very socks and slippers.

The Sikh *pagri* consists of a long narrow piece of linen, in which the hair is wrapped up; and it is so fastened either in the front or a little on one side, that one cannot see either end or knot. It lies down smooth on the head, one end hanging half way down the back. Ranjít Singh hides this end under his upper garment. The *Angraka* (coat) is tied over the chest, and reaches to the knee, and the trousers fall in many folds down to the ancle. Over the whole is worn a mantle lined with skins. The entire costume is, as I have said, of yellow Pashmina, green being worn sometimes by him, but not commonly. In summer he wears white muslin. At the festival of the Basant, he was particularly disfigured by the straw-coloured dress he wore with a slight intermixture of green in it. In earlier days he used to appear in divers ornaments; but this custom he has long discontinued, and I never saw him wear any embroidery, brocade, or rich ornament of any sort.

When he seats himself in a common English arm-chair, with his feet drawn under him, the position is one particularly unfavourable to him; but as soon as he mounts his horse, and with his black shield at his back, puts him on his mettle, his whole form seems animated by the spirit within, and assumes a certain grace, of which nobody could believe it susceptible. In spite of the paralysis affecting one side, he manages his horse with the greatest ease.

If nature has been niggardly to him in respect of personal appearance, denying him the privilege of thereby making a favourable impression on strangers, she has recompensed him very richly by the power which, in common with all remarkable men, he is enabled to exercise over every one who approaches him. He can in a moment take up a subject of conversation, follow it up closely by questions and answers, which convey other questions in themselves, and these are always so exactly to the purpose, that they put the understanding of his respondent to the test, and satisfy him whether the subject is as fully apprehended, and as quickly followed as by his own mind.

With a voice naturally rough and unpleasant, he can assume a tone of much fascination whenever he wishes to flatter; and his influence over the people of northern India amounts to something like enchantment. They believe that he can do whatever he pleases, because higher powers are at his command. For example, I observed a spot on the Atok above the city, the time being at low water, where the river seemed particularly shallow, and I inquired whether it was fordable at any season of the year. They answered that it never had been found practicable. "Why," said I then, "I have been told that the Mahá Raja passed the Atok with an army, and without making use of a bridge. Where about was this?"—"At this very spot." "Is not this then a proof of such possibility?" I inquired.—"The Mahá Raja can do whatever he pleases." "But how came he by this influence?" I asked, and heard a long story about an inestimable jewel, on which was a powerful Mantram or magic prayer engraven, buried under the skin of his right arm, and which gave him power to do whatever he had a mind to effect.

When I smiled at this superstitious fancy, the following instance of the power of a similar Mantram was given me, as having happened in the Dekhan. A Rámúsi Náik, or head of the Rámúsis, a warlike tribe, named Dádji, had dishonoured a female Brahmin. This was in the time of the Peshwa, or chief of the Mahrattas, Mádhú Ráo. The injured party hastened to the Peshwa's wife, Ganga Bháí, related the grievance, took an oath of her that she and her caste should have vengeance on the Rámúsi Náik, and then, not willing to survive dishonour, bit off her own tongue, and expired in the presence of her mistress, who vowed never to perform her ablutions or taste food until Dádji was punished. The youthful Peshwa depended much on this Dádji to support him against his uncle; but the vow must be redeemed; Dádji was therefore summoned under the pretext of some affair of importance to the fortress of Púrander, lulled into security by presents, and separated from his suite. The Peshwa directed his people to seize him, and put him to instant death. The executioner tried to perform his duty, but in vain; he could not even raise a mark on the skin, and knowing from experience that his prisoner's fate could not be sealed so long as this lasted, he sent for a saw, and proceeded to cut off the delinquent's hands and feet. The prospect of such a frightful death made Dádji beg for a knife; having been furnished with one, he slit up the skin of his left arm, and took out a talisman, and then submitted his neck to the executioner, which was completely severed from the body at the first stroke.

The sole aim of Ranjít Singh is the preservation and extension of his own unlimited power; and though his ambitious mind considers all means perfectly allowable to this end, he has never wantonly imbrued his hands in blood. Never perhaps was so large an empire founded by one man with so little criminality; and when we consider the country and the uncivilized people with whom he has had to deal, his mild and prudent government must be regarded with feelings of astonishment. This alone has prevented the necessity of putting to death those numerous independent Mohammedan, Hindú, and Sikh princes, whom he has dethroned, and in most cases beggared, and who might have attempted to regain possession of their territories. It is very remarkable that no attempt of the kind has been made in the Panjáb; and it proves not only the talent of Ranjít Singh, but the little attachment borne by the Indians to their rulers. They can depend on their troops only, and not always on them, for they are mercenaries in the fullest sense of the word, and betake themselves from one service to another without the slightest scruple.

In estimating the character of Ranjít Singh, we must lay aside in a great measure, our own European ideas. Born in a country where everything is permitted to the powerful, and belonging to a sect whose followers are proverbially distinguished by their ignorance and licentious habits, and indulged in every kind of dissipation from his tenderest years by his own mother-in-law, we can hardly wonder at occasional severities. The first use he made of his accession to power, in imitation of his father Mahá Singh, was to poison his own mother, who forfeited her life as a punishment for her dissolute conduct. This was in accordance with their usages; but, after all, we must add, that the story of the poisoning rests entirely on report, and in a country where all the affairs of the Zenána are veiled under the greatest secresy, it is impossible to ascertain the exact truth. The action does not agree with the further development of Ranjít Singh's character, which is assuredly not a barbarous one. I may add, that I never heard the event mentioned with any reprehension in the Panjáb; on the contrary, her punishment seems to have been thought perfectly justifiable.

The extravagances of his early youth must be ascribed to the character of the people around him; nor could it be expected that at such an age he should refrain from indulging in habits which heathen usage is thought fully to justify. Of his favourites at this period, one only is of sufficient importance to be mentioned. This was a Kanchni, or dancer of Lahor, named Mora. During the Húli, when all business is laid aside, and the Hindús of Northern India are sometimes inebriated for weeks, and give themselves up to all kinds of revelry in their Zenánas, Ranjít Singh had as little scruple as any other Sirdar of the Panjáb, to appear openly *mastt*, or drunk, and exhibited himself in the streets of Lahor with several females riding on an elephant; while the people thought none the worse of him for this, and set it down as *his* manner of celebrating the Húli.

This Mora understood the art of pleasing so well, that Ranjít Singh had coins struck in her name, an act of great importance in India, though perhaps done by him as a jest against the Company Sirkár, or

East India Company, who are generally represented in India as an old woman,—the wife, widow, or mistress of the king of England. Suddenly, however, in August, 1811, Mora was carried off in a palankeen to Patháukot, where she still resides; and this is probably the reason why travellers are not allowed to visit that fortress.

Another favourite of Ranjít Singh, is a young Gáur Bráhmin, called Kúshál Ram, who was persuaded by him to embrace the Sikh religion, and take the name of Kúshál Singh. Originally a cook, he rose by degrees to the office of a Jemidar, or house-steward, and finally, to be a Deoriwalla, or great chamberlain, with large estates. With the single exception of a part of the year 1817, he has always preserved the favour of his master. At that period Kúshál Singh was visited by his brother, Rám Lál, from Hindústhan, and Ranjít Singh took the latter into favour also; but when he demanded the abandonment of his faith, Rám Lál escaped beyond the Setlej. In order to draw him back, Ranjít Singh deprived Kúshál Singh of his office and threw him into prison. This had the desired effect, and he returned and assumed the name of Rám Singh. I have written of Kúshál Singh more in detail in my journal, as the absence of Dhyán Singh obliged him to be constantly in attendance at the court during my stay in Lahor.

Raja Híra Singh also is at present in high favour. He is the son of Raja Dhyán Singh, the Deoriwalla, or first chamberlain, who, with his brothers, Guláb Singh and Sushet Singh, received the investiture of Jamú in 1820, when Guláb Singh acted so brave a part in the mountains of Kashmír. The favour he had transmitted from father to son, induced Ranjít Singh, in 1827, to think of procuring a suitable alliance for the youth, then only twelve years old, who was called Raja as well as his father and uncles, the Míyan, or lords, of Jamú. About this time Raja Aurodh, a son of the late Sansar Chand, the Raja of Kangra, a member of an ancient, but since Ranjít Singh's conquests, deeply humbled dynasty, came to Lahor, accompanied by his mother and two sisters. One of these Ranjít Singh demanded as a wife for Raja Híra Singh, which kindled all the pride of the old Brahmin family; but Ranjít Singh had procured a written engagement from Aurodh Chand, promising the hand of both his sisters to whomsoever

Ranjít Singh pleased to grant them. The mother left Lahor secretly with her daughters, and escaping over the Setlej, placed herself and them under the protection of the British authorities, Aurodh Chand soon following them. In order to punish him, Ranjít Singh immediately confiscated his lands on the right shore of the Setlej; and a Khawás, or mistress, of Sansar Chand being induced to leave the family with her children, Ranjít Singh granted the title of Raja to her son, and a part of her father's possessions as a Jaghír, and gave both his sisters away in marriage.

Ranjít Singh has an only son, Karak Singh, born in 1802, his mother being Raj Kúnwar, the daughter of the Sirdar Khuján Singh of Náki, and the second wife of Ranjít Singh, whom he married in 1792, while in his minority. In 1812, Karak Singh was married to the daughter of Jáimal Ghania, the Sirdar whom Ranjít Singh had deprived of his fortress of Páthankot, at whose death, soon after the marriage, he became master of all his territories and large treasures. Ranjít Singh endeavoured early to accustom his son to lead an army and to govern a kingdom; and for that purpose, when ten years of age, he was not only placed at the head of a large force, but received after his expedition against Jamú, the districts of Akhnur and Bimber as a jaghír, which he governed under the control of his mother Raj Kúnwar and the Díwan Bhúj Rám Singh. Karak Singh, notwithstanding, did not fulfil his father's expectations. The contingent of troops which he was bound to furnish were found to be in such a miserable condition, that Ranjít Singh sharply reproved his son, and as repeated complaints of oppression were brought before him for the space of four years, and the troops looked worse and worse, the Díwan was brought to an account, and put in confinement until Ranjít Singh had made the greatest part of his fortune answer for his delinquencies. This event was hastened by the discovery of the too great intimacy existing between the Díwan and Raj Kúnwar, who was placed in restraint in the fortress of Shekopoor, on the ground of her immoral conduct.

Karak Singh has an only son, Nao Nihál Singh, born in February, 1821, and at present in command of Múltán. He is a fine, promising, high-spirited youth. Sada Kúnwar, the mother of Ranjít's first wife,

Mehtáb Kúnwar, of whom I have already spoken, as the chief accessory to his fortunes, thought that her influence over him would be greater than ever, if her daughter had children, but of this there was little probability. What Providence had denied, Sada Kúnwar thought to obtain by artifice, and when Ranjít Singh quitted Lahor in September, 1807, on one of his expeditions for conquest, she set about her projects. Mehtáb Kúnwar, on suspicion of some impropriety of conduct, had been sent to her mother, which facilitated the scheme. On his return in December, Sada Kúnwar presented him with twin sons, as the offspring of Mehtáb Kúnwar. Not one observation escaped Ranjít Singh's lips about the children, whom Sada Kúnwar carried away with her again. It is commonly believed that Sada Kúnwar bought these children of the wives of a carpenter and a weaver, having previously prepared the minds of those within the palace for the accouchement of Mehtáb Kúnwar by a fictitious tale. The children were called Shír Singh and Tára Singh, and the first was adopted by Sada Kúnwar, who had a large independent fortune. When he was thirteen years old he demanded of her, at Ranjít Singh's instigation, a sufficient jaghír, and on Sada Kúnwar referring him to Ranjít Singh, who was bound to provide for him and Tára Singh as his sons, the Mahá Raja answered, that she must take care of them, her large property being amply sufficient to provide for both. On Sada Kúnwar's refusal, Ranjít seized the opportunity of humbling one whose imperious demeanour had long been insupportable to him, and she was ordered to settle the half of her whole fortune on the youths. She refused to obey, but finding herself at this time in a Sikh camp at Shah Dera, not far from Lahor, on the right arm of the Rávi, she had no resource but to have the deed got ready. Scarcely was it executed, when she thought of a way of eluding the promise into which she had been forced, and as a preliminary step to escape from the Mahá Raja's power. This she designed to effect by means of a covered waggon on the following night; but her intentions were betrayed, and she had hardly left the place, when Ranjít Singh's horsemen overtook and brought her back. She was instantly sent into close confinement, from which she has never since been released; while an armed force was despatched to her territories to take possession of all her riches. As quite characteristic of the Panjáb, we may observe, that the only strong fort belonging to Sada Kúnwar that had held out against Ranjít Singh, was Atalgurh, which was defended for some weeks by one of her female attendants. Her territories on the left shore were not surrendered to Ranjít Singh by the English Government until 1828. Had these belonged to her own inheritance, it would not have been so, nor would her deed of transfer have been legal; but as they were given to her in 1808, by Ranjít Singh himself, it was decided that, according to Indian law, he might claim them again, a very erroneous judgment, and one which opens the way to many difficulties, since no right of supremacy can continue thus, as it were, in abeyance. In the affair of Jhínd, for example, the English laid it down as a maxim, that by the treaty of 1808, Ranjít Singh had lost all right of sovereignty in Hindústhan, against which decision he appealed to the above judgment of the year 1828.

We have seen Shír Singh as Governor of Kashmír, and the lucky accident which caused the chief Syud Ahmed to fall into his hands, gave him favour in Ranjít Singh's eyes. He is now the nominal Governor of Pesháwar, while Tára Singh lives quite neglected in Lahor.

Two other sons are given to Ranjít Singh, namely, Kashmír Singh and Pesháwar Singh, youths of fifteen or sixteen years old, who enjoy independent commands. Nothing is known of them, except that they were born in the Mahá Raja's Zenána. The natives, in fact, give themselves no further concern about them.

The men, or rather the machines, about the Mahá Raja's court, according to their rank, are: 1. Raja Dhyán Singh, whom I did not see; he was on his own property near Jamú, hog hunting. 2. Kushál Singh, of whom I have already spoken. 3. Raja Sushet Singh, the brother of Dhyán Singh. 4. Hákim Azíz-ud Dín, the fakír, Ranjít's confidential secretary, through whom all business is transacted. He is a prudent, sagacious Mohammedan, who is employed by him in all difficult affairs. 5. Khalífa Sahib, a fakír, the marshal of his household, an upright and yet versatile courtier, who has acquired the respect both of natives and strangers.

The other grandees of the Sikh court are some with the army and some in their own territories, the feasts of the Húli and the Dasera generally bringing them all to the presence of their prince. The most distinguished among them are, Fatih Singh Aluwála and Harí Singh Nalwa, both of whom I have described more circumstantially in the preceding pages. None of them influence the actions of Ranjít Singh, and though he squanders vast sums on his favourites, they have no power over him. Neither have the foreigners in his service any influence. Their advice is followed when it is good; but it is never taken without trial of its value. Ranjít Singh is always very polite, and when most angry, the object of his displeasure learns it for the first time by his punishment. In this respect he is a master of dissimulation, and many a Sirdar who has left him believing him his friend, has found himself transferred suddenly from the Durbar to a palankeen, carried off to his estate, and there met by an officer appointed by the Mahá Raja to take possession of all his treasures.

There is nothing pleasing in the expression of Ranjít Singh's features; and, though he often laughs, there is nothing of inward gladness in the sound, but rather the expression of something which has just crossed his mind,—a recollection of some past occurence.

Ranjít Singh's policy is to overthrow everything which existed before his time; to raise all the people of the Panjáb to the same social level, and to assign to every Sikh his separate position and estate. Everything must proceed from him: he treats all who lay claim to rank or hereditary estates as his enemies, and has reduced most of them to beggary; while on the other hand he promotes those who have served him well, or with whom he has at some time or other been pleased.

Among a people like the Hindús, there is a great spell in the idea that they may be elevated in a moment to high rank; and the profusion of Ranjít Singh is sometimes as excessive as his covetousness. In his youth treasures were his means, not his end; now he has grown miserly in the extreme. He has laid down a strange principle, that the fortunes of all who are slain by his enemies belong to him. "The man has injured me; his death deprives me of his services," he said, on hearing of the fall of one of his officers. "I must make myself amends." Such a way of proceeding would operate most injuriously on any other people; but it only teaches the Sikh, daring to a fault by nature, to be more circumspect. Other nations need to be spurred on to bravery, the Sikh requires a curb to restrain his reckless impetuosity *.

CONCLUSION OF THE JOURNAL.

I now return to the last page of the journal of my travels in the Panjáb. It was nearly 12 o'clock when we quitted Lahor, a party of horse escorting us, while Júni Lal and Khán Singh had gone on to Amritsir to prepare everything for our reception. Ventura had likewise despatched some of his household to make me comfortable while there, and my servant Hingam † waited for my arrival. The distance between Lahor and Amritsir is twenty-five kos, or thirty-two miles. Two relays of four horses had been stationed for me on the road by order of the Mahá Raja.

Seven miles from Lahor the ruins terminate, giving place to a desert plain, which gives place, when close to Amritsir, to finely-cultivated land. It was already dark when we arrived in the city; and we alighted at a pretty garden of the Mahá Raja's, where the sight of a dinner was not unwelcome, for I had fasted all the day. In the evening the Thanadar of Amritsir came to pay his respects, and brought with him some fruit and sweetmeats, and 700 rupees, in the name of the Mahá Raja. I dismissed him, after giving him notice of my desire to

---

* Such is the individual spirit of all the nobler families of India. Whether they refer it to *Nasíb*, their proper destiny, or to fate, they have frequently exhibited instances of personal gallantry, moral courage, and heroism, worthy of the most patriotic cause; and under a better discipline of mental and moral culture, such as Christianity, and a just, paternal government might ensure, would furnish many bright and beautiful examples of true greatness. These can never be disjoined with any prospect of success or honour to Great Britain.—*Ed.*

† The proper name is more probably Hingan; but this is not very material. —*Ed.*

visit the sacred reservoir at daybreak on the morrow. Then came a shawl merchant, who showed me some letters with orders from London and Paris, and promised to bring me some beautiful shawls at daybreak, to look at.

Tuesday, 26th January.—As I had to travel to-day a distance of thirty kos, from forty to forty-five miles, on elephants, we got up at early dawn, and left the garden at seven o'clock. Khán Singh having to go back to-day, I gave him a testimonial of good conduct, and a present which General Ventura had fixed beforehand; and as I had to give something to everybody, the amount was a very important consideration. In order to reach the city, we were taken round by the external wall of Govindgurh, the famous fortress built by the Mahá Raja. I was sorely afraid that the commandant would have orders to detain me while I explained the manner in which the howitzers should be loaded and prepared, and I was all impatience to quit the spot, greatly as I prized the liberty of being the only European who had been suffered to enter there. It was very possible, however, that some danger might be apprehended by the Mahá Raja, in suffering a European to visit a fortress from which he had hitherto so carefully excluded them, and that this might have caused him to think no more about spherical case-shot and shells.

Govindgurh is a strong post, as it is built in a plain; any other situation would have done quite as well for a fortress, but it owes the present one to Amritsir; the holy tank, and the pilgrims who flock to it, wanted a protection against the persecutions of the Mohammedans, and Ranjít Singh began the works in 1807. It was to have been built on the plan of Ramgurh, with the view of flattering Jodh Singh, the grandson of Jái Singh, whose co-operation in the conquest of Kasúr was required by Ranjít Singh. The protection of the holy tank and of the pilgrims, was a good pretext for erecting a strong place for himself. In 1809, he ordered it to be put into the best state of defence, and continual improvements have made it now a very strong post: rising to a lofty height above the plain, it presents, with its tiers of guns, one over the other, a remarkably imposing aspect. The Indians say that the Mahá Raja's treasure is kept here, and that it consists of 30 lakhs of rupees, or 300 millions of florins, but I suppose this to be an idle fable. I dare say that some treasure of importance is hoarded here, though persons very well informed on the subject have assured me that Ranjít Singh's revenue hardly covers his expenditure. It was in some respects a great error to build this fortress so close to Amritsir. There are no outworks; and vast ruins, of the origin of which I could not gain any satisfactory account, extend to the entrance gate. The very thing which would be an impediment to the settlement of merchants in Europe, has exactly the contrary effect in India. In Europe a merchant would carefully avoid the vicinity of a fortress, which naturally attracts the foe; and in case of a siege, as surely endangers the safety of his property, and the existence of his house. In India it is otherwise. Whenever the fate of the country is in the balance, the property of individuals is destroyed; for a change of rulers invariably brings about a similar change of owners. The object of most importance is to secure property against the bands of robbers, who avoid the neighbourhood of a fortress like Govindgurh. The stronger this point, the more difficult the Indians suppose it of access, and the greater the security it affords them in Amritsir, which is now the richest city in northern India. I felt agitated with various emotions, as my elephant passed the city gate, where the Thanadar was waiting with a numerous deputation of merchants to receive me. How much blood had flowed round the spot upon which I was now treading!

Amritsir is a larger city than Lahor. The wealth of the whole Panjáb seems collected in it, and the great merchants have made it their abode. Under the Mohammedans it was an unimportant place called Chák. It became the holy city of the Sikhs, when their fourth Gurú, Rám Dás, dug a large tank, or *tuldo*, here in the year 1581, which he called Amrita Saras, or the spring of immortality. It was also a place of pilgrimage for all the Hindús, and called Rámdáspúr and Amritsir. But it was only in the latter half of the past century that it acquired importance by the events which occurred in its neighbourhood. Places of pilgrimage are so numerous in India, that they are only noticed by the government for the sake of the tax levied on each pilgrim; and here the assembled crowds being of the lowest classes, they had nothing from which any tax could be levied. It was not until the Mohammedans clearly saw of what importance Amritsir was in the religion of the Sikhs, that they fancied themselves able, by destroying the town, to aim a fatal blow at the faith. The opinion was an absurd one; for persecutions are the very means by which the force of any faith is established; let the mind once embrace the belief of an eternal reward for actions done, and whether in truth or in error, no earthly event can tear it away from the soul. Ahmed Shah Abdáli wanted to chastise the unquiet spirits who called him so often over the Atok, and thought it possible to eradicate the evil by destroying the holy city, where the first open assembly of the Sikhs took place, after the expulsion of his viceroy Khája Obied, in 1762. This assembly or ceremony, called Sarhat Kálsa, was held with great rejoicings. After every Sikh had bathed in the holy purifying water, they met to hold a Gurmatta or council, for the organization of the Sikh confederacy. Their proceedings being carried on with the proper forms, the Aluwála Sirdar carried the battle-axe of the people, called Kalál; the chief of the Nishánwála Misal carried the banner of the faith, or Nishán. These officers, like those of the holy Roman empire, have now ceased to exist. Ranjít Singh did not want them; he has no idea of the policy of keeping the most formidable chieftains near his throne by the concession of such privileges; he is on his own throne, and cares nothing for what may happen after him.

The first general assembly had hardly broken up, ere Ahmed Shah appeared to take a bloody revenge on them. The Sikhs fled in all directions; and after encountering and slaughtering a great part of their number at Kos Ráhira, he returned towards Amritsir. The temple of Harmander (Harí Mander, the temple of Harí or Vishnú) was blown up with gunpowder, the broad stones round the holy tank were torn up and flung into the water, which was choked up with masonry and rubbish; and not content with this profanation, they brought cows to the place, slaughtered them on the heaps of ruins, sprinkled the stones with their blood, and flung their entrails about.

Ahmed Shah had not reached the Atok before a second Gurmatta was held in Amritsir, where the profanation of this sacred spot animated all the spectators to deeds which brought about, perhaps sooner than might otherwise have happened, the downfall of Mohammedan power in the north of India. At the same time the Sikhs began to cleanse their dishonoured tank, and (a rare example for Hindús) it was restored to greater splendour than ever.

Amritsir is the most bustling of all the cities of the Panjáb; in every street the most beautiful productions of India are seen exhibited for sale; and it seemed to me, though the elephants moved on briskly, as though there was no end to the streets. At length I arrived at the chief entrance to the temple, which is very unpretending, and surrounded by houses. Here I pulled off my shoes, and waited some time until Vigne had disengaged himself from his boots. I gave 125 rupees to Júni Lál for distribution in the temple.

The *Tuláo*, or pool, struck me with surprise. It is about 150 paces square, and has a large body of water, which to all appearance is supplied by a natural artesian well. There is no sign of the spring to be seen. It is surrounded by a pavement about 20 or 25 paces in breadth. Round this square are some of the most considerable houses of the city, and some buildings belonging to the temple, the whole being inclosed by gates: although one can look very conveniently from the windows of the houses into this inclosed space, and some of the doors even open into it. There are several stone steps by which the bathers descend into the water, which is as clear as a mirror, a rare occurrence in such places in India. I went entirely round the basin. In the midst of the Tuláo stands the temple of Harí Mander, built on an ísland, and reached by a bridge on the west side. The holiest spot for bathing is on the east side, as they step out of this temple; but before the pilgrim is allowed to bathe there, he must have performed his ablutions in another part of the pool. Opposite to this revered place stand some small buildings, in which Gurús and Fakírs are seated; another which is untenanted is shown as the place where Gurú Rám Dás, the excavator of this bath of immortality, passed his whole life.

Several fanciful-looking structures stand before the western entrance, a lugubrious sound of music proceeded thence, and a Gurú clad in silk appeared seated under the canopy belonging to a throne in the first story, surrounded by a sort of court or levee. The Sikhs in my suite did not treat these Gurús very reverently, though Júni Lál gave one of them a handful of rupees in a platter he held out for them, receiving in return a muttered blessing. Every bather, on returning from his or her ablutions, brings a present for these Gurús, chiefly of fruit or flowers, but I also saw some very large pots containing 200 pounds of Ghí, or clarified butter, and rice standing before their houses, offerings made this morning. The Gurú presented to me and to the superior persons in my suite three leaves of the *Pán*, or Piper betel, to chew, but without the Areca nut: this is a general custom in India. The three-storied house near the Gurú's and before the bridge, is the place of consecration. I inquired whether this ceremony took place often, and with true Indian accuracy, I received for answer, "a thousand times every day." I said that I should like much to see it, and would wait until a neophyte came, but on being told that perhaps on that very day none might come, I understood at once that the thousands were by no means to be taken literally.

All Indian temples have something in them which appeals forcibly to the imagination, and the Harí Mander is particularly mysterious and romantic in its character. It is surmounted by a golden roof, very beautifully and skilfully contrived, and is inlaid with marble, a large door of gold opening into the temple, which is surrounded with little vestibules, the ceilings being supported by richly ornamented pillars. Before the entrance to the bridge are two large banners of red; on one is written, "Wáh! Gurúji-ke fatih!" in white letters; and on the other, the name of Rám Dás. These banners are from thirty to forty ells long, and are stretched on masts and confined with iron chains. Having crossed the bank I entered within the temple; in the centre sat the first Gurú of the Sikh faith on the masnad, or throne of cushions, the wall of the building being ornamented with a handsome carpet worked in gold, while before him lay another of Kashmír shawl stuff. A large circle of devotees and followers had formed around him, leaving an open space which is never encroached upon, it being customary that the Gurú should be viewed from a certain distance with due reverence. Júni Lál laid before me a bag of rupees, that I might present it to the Gurú. The stillness was quite unbroken, and I had time to gaze on the venerable features of the aged man, as his Cháori-burdar waved the fan, made of the Tibet cow's tail, before him. At first, there was to me something striking in the whole scene, but it became wearisome as the silence continued unbroken, the Gurú keeping his eyes intently fastened on the Granth, or Holy Book. I asked Júni Lál whether he would not speak to us, and thereupon the Gurú's master of the ceremonies asked who the great king was, whose good fortune had brought him to the Srí Gurúji, the holy Gurú, (I have forgotten his name.) An agent from Ranjít Singh, whom I had not seen before this, now handed to the servants of the Gurú the bag of rupees, beginning at the same time a long-winded oration, comprehending the creation of the world; the ancient history of India; the great Mahá Raja; the holy Gurú; the Company Sirkár; myself, as the Lord Mahá Raja and the friend of the king; the beloved and holy Gurú Govind Singh; and in short all things possible to be talked about. The speech, uttered with the most rapid and sonorous voice, lasted a whole hour, and as he was then beginning afresh, I told Júni Lál that the day was much too short for such a harangue, and Júni Lál hinted to him to leave off. The Gurú's master of the ceremonies then opened his speech in the fashion of a herald: "Know all men that on this day, the Mahá Raja, Lord Baron Hügel Sáhib Bahádúr, a friend of the Srí Mahá Raja Ranjít Singh, whose friendship with the Company is as eternal as the Sun, which causes the Moon to hide her face in envy, has appeared at the Durbar of the beloved and holy Gurú, receiving from him his blessing and numberless valuable presents." The Gurú then uttered a prayer out of the Granth, still sitting, the gifts were brought, and during the performance of some soft music, I left the Durbar. The valuable gifts consisted of a turban and another cloth, which both together might be worth five rupees. While there, I had heard a strange knocking and hammering, for which I could not at all account, and desirous of seeing what it meant, I took the paved way round the temple on the little island. On the sacred bathing-place was a small vestibule, in which I observed workmen employed in ornamenting it with a pietra dura floor.

The marble walls were smeared with glaring colours representing flowers.

I quitted the temple of Amritsir, and returned to my elephant. The Thanadar, Lena Singh, accompanied me on his elephant a good way out of the city, attended by a servant carrying a double-barrelled gun, and to my surprise on taking it in my hand, I found a new and beautiful Joe Manton, which he, according to custom, offered to me, and which I, of course, refused. Before the gate lay an immense gun formed of metal cast from iron bars. I asked how old it was, and how it came there, and was told by the Thanadar that he had only recently manufactured it, and expected to receive the carriage for it from Lahor. Ranjít Singh's mint is in Amritsir, but I had no desire to visit it, as, to judge from its productions, it must be still in the lowest rank of manufactures, and my time was precious. Ranjít Singh has introduced the standard money of the Company, viz., the rupee, which is the largest silver coin, of equal value to the Calcutta sicca rupee, and the gold mohur of sixteen rupees.

It is thirty kos, or forty miles, from Amritsir to Kopertela, and this distance I travelled on three elephants, which were stationed at certain intervals; the country was well cultivated, and the animals moved along swiftly, but very uneasily for the traveller who is seated on their back. Mohan, Hingam, and Vigne were with me: Júni Lál had another elephant. At each post I was received by the Thanadar with a party of horsemen, who escorted me to the next station. Not far from Kopertela we reached the Beyas or Báás, as it is here called, the Hyphasis of the Greeks. The English have been as unmerciful to many of the Indian names as the natives to this. The ferry-boats were so small, that I thought it advisable to appropriate one to my own use, particularly as the over-heated elephants were not to be restrained from amusing themselves continually with the water, which did not tend to increase the safety of the vessels. When these animals are once in the boats, they know they must not venture to move their feet, and they stand, therefore, as though riveted to the spot, but so long as the Mahút allows them, they never cease filling their trunk with water, and sprinkling themselves all over. I also observed to-day particularly, that when heated by a long march, they can pump the water out of their stomachs by means of their trunk, and refresh their skin with it. They do this so often and so long, that it is inconceivable how they contrive to carry so much water.

The evening had not drawn in when we reached Kopertela, the territory of Fatih Singh Aluwála, a brother of the turban to Ranjít Singh, who has been spoken of in another place. He has some lands under the protection of the British, which are worth about four lakhs of rupees yearly, and others under the dominion of Ranjít Singh, which produce a revenue of three lakhs. In 1825, for a reason which I shall presently explain, he fled from Ranjít Singh to the left shore of the Setlej; but I must first speak of the town through which my road led. Since Avitabile built the Bazár in Wazirabad, a taste has arisen for broad streets, and Fatih Singh has built one in Kopertela, which, if not quite comparable with the Regent's quadrant in London, is at all events, very wonderful for the Panjáb. Some hundreds of masons are still busy with a portion of it. Above the whole, towers a large temple just completed near the palace, and looking very fanciful and picturesque. Half a mile from the place, I observed an unfinished building in the English taste, intended as a substantial summer-house for Fatih Singh, and the subterranean vaults form a Tikána, not unlike the *casemates* of a fortress. A Tikána is a subterraneous abode for the summer, usually from twenty-five to thirty feet beneath the surface, and therefore always cool*. Fatih Síngh's house was roofed in, and only wanted the doors and windows, when Ranjít Singh heard that he was erecting a fortress between Lahor and Lúdiana. He was instantly summoned before the Mahá Raja, but Fatih Singh called to mind how often, under a similar pretext, Ranjít had availed himself of the oppor-

---

* In all the old Mohammedan cities there are still many splendid subterraneous structures of this description. After the city of Ahmedabad was ceded to the British Government in 1818, numerous beautiful halls built of stone, with large reservoirs of water, from 100 to 200 feet in length, and from 50 to 100 in breadth, with broad corridors all round, supported on massive stone pillars richly carved and ornamented, were found beneath the suburbs, which I was informed, served as a luxurious cool retreat to its former wealthy occupants.—*Ed.*

tunity to plunder the possessor of a rich inheritance; he therefore escaped to his lands over the Setlej, though with the utmost difficulty, and only with the guarantee of the British agent for his safety, was he persuaded to return to the Panjáb, where Ranjít Singh gave him a very good reception. They are now quite reconciled, but Fatih Singh is always on his guard. He is reckoned an able tactician, and Ranjít Singh may thank him for that portion of his kingdom, which stretches in a southerly direction across the Panjáb.

On my arrival at Kopertela I found the servants whom I had despatched from Lahor with my beds, &c., &c. The unfinished palace, not touched by Fatih Singh since 1824, was made, with the addition of kanats and carpets, to all appearance tolerably habitable; but a piercing wind blew through it in all directions, and the indefatigable Jwála, with all the pains he took, could hardly succeed in making it sufficiently comfortable. Presents, like those I had received in Amritsir, and provisions of all kinds, were brought to me; but it was late ere I could taste the various productions of my own cook. I had not done so before for some time, and I reckoned on this being the last, intending to dismiss my establishment in Lúdiana, and find my way to Bombay without any attendants.

Wednesday, January 27.—Impatience deprived me of rest. This day was to terminate my Kashmír expedition, and bring me once more to English ground; the change seemed to take me so many months nearer to my own home.

Fatih Singh had sent me word that he should come and visit me this morning; but then I should have had to wait for him, and a long experience had informed me that it was by no means easy to get over an interview appointed by a native Indian of high rank. I therefore rose long before day, and waked Vigne, to whom I would not allow a moment's delay on this occasion. We were both ready before sunrise, but had to wait some time for the elephants, which made it seven o'clock ere we took our way to the fine palace in the centre of the city. I offered some trifling presents to Fatih Singh, who received us with his two sons, and after a short and lively conversation we parted, and I returned to the unfinished palace.

The distance between Kopertela and Felor is thirty-seven kos. We ate our breakfast in haste, and I then got into a palankeen, thinking that I should be conveyed more quickly by that means than on the slow-pacing elephant; but finding myself quite mistaken on that point, I had recourse to the first of three which were stationed in relays to carry me to Felor. The first town we reached was Jhalander, the ancient Jala or Jhíl-Indra*, situated in a richly-cultivated region, where I saw for the first time since we had left the Indus, plantations of mangoes. A crowd of majestic tombs shewed that Jhalander was anciently the residence of a dynasty, namely, that of the Lodi Afghans. The city still numbers 40,000 inhabitants. The Thanadar, who welcomed me with a party of horsemen, desired to escort me through the streets of the city, and as he assured me that it was the nearest way, I could not help myself. My elephant could hardly make his way through the trees in the main street, and when we came to the gate of egress, the large animal could not pass through with the howdah. We dismounted, and as it would have cost me an hour to send him through the city again, I desired the Mahút to try whether the elephant would not bend down in some way. The man brought the creature up to the gate, made him feel it with his trunk, to ascertain its height, and then urged him onward. The elephant really seemed to understand all about it, for bending both his knees as he walked along, he passed safely through with the howdah on his back. Here another elephant was stationed, but it was so much smaller that the howdah would not fit him, and I determined to proceed a little further with the same, which had walked the day before without any burden twenty-seven miles from Amritsir, carrying me the other thirteen miles to Kopertela. To lighten the weight for him now, I made Hingham and Mohan ride on the little elephant with our baggage.

The country hereabout is well cultivated, and after a three hours march, we reached a town called very appropriately Baghwara. It has

* *Jala* is the Sanscrit expression for water. *Jhíl* signifies a tank, or more correctly, the water which a swollen river leaves behind after retiring; or the bed of a dry river, with occasional deep hollows. *Indra* is an Indian god.

15,000 inhabitants, and its gardens, which are very extensive, are succeeded by fields, which, like them, are interspersed with fine trees. An elephant was waiting for me there, but its pace was so tiresome, that I was glad to take on my old friend, who performed seventy kos in two days, the greatest distance ever travelled by an elephant in the same time out of charity to a gentleman. The day's journey with these animals is generally very short, eight or ten English miles being considered a very hard day's work for them. Hence, as beasts of burden, they are of all others most unsuited to the movements of an army. If we consider also the immense quantity of food they require, and the great value of provisions, it will convince us, that in these days, when fire-arms are quite common in India, elephants, whether in peace or in war, are only useful to keep up the state of a prince*.

Just as the sun went down, Felor appeared in the distance with its towers and gate. I observed several Jhils, or pieces of standing water, relics of the ancient bed of the Setlej, which unite with the present stream at the period of extensive inundations. The fort of Felor, built in 1809, by Ranjít Singh, is of little importance, and is garrisoned by 150 men. It stands on the elevated shore of the Setlej. Júni Lál wished me to pass the night there, as the sun had set, but I laughed at such a ridiculous proposal, and alighting from my elephant, mounted another got ready for me, and receiving from the officer who commanded Captain Wade's body-guard, some letters from that gentleman, I resumed my journey and was soon on the left sandy shore of the Setlej.

I took a farewell look at the Panjáb, while the elephant dragged slowly onward through the deep sandy path, and before the darkness overshadowed all things. In thought I bade farewell to the land which had occupied my mind for the last three months, and to the many kind inhabitants who had received me with so much friendly

* The ordinary progress of an elephant is three miles an hour, the quickest rate five; that is, for a continuance: and a great deal of this tardiness is probably due to the unwillingness of the *mahúts*, or drivers, who, to say the truth, have not a very easy task to coax and urge on their charge. The motion of the best elephants at a good pace is like that of a boat in a tumbling heavy sea.—*Ed.*

attention. As the surrounding objects gradually faded into indistinctness with the parting day and distance, so this portion of my life will gradually become less vivid in my remembrance. There are but few indelible impressions graven on the heart, and if men are sooner forgotten than events, feelings vanish before all. I had ample leisure while pacing towards Lúdiana, which is three kos from Felor, to think over that episode in my travels, which had taken me in so wide a circle, from the shore of this river, back to it again. But where were the waves which carried my boat from Biláspoor to Jelakátela? They have disappeared in the ocean, in the gulf of Omán, as the days spent in my journeyings have also gone into the sea of eternity. The fields watered by this stream have borne their fruits meanwhile, and what those days have matured for me in life, is laid up in these pages. As the laws of nature command these waters to roll on continually, till they meet with their equilibrium in the great deep, so does a higher law command man to exercise the power of his mind, until he reposes on the level surface of the bier. Whether I follow this law, or waste my time in idle pursuit, must and will be pronounced by a higher Judge. My own conscience acquits me of reproach on this point.

The spring originating in the dark bosom of the earth, gushes pure and joyful into light; to many a one is it permitted to meander in company through fertile regions, slowly and undisturbed towards the sea; others again there are, whose stormy course carries them over rocks, their appointed destiny being one of continual agitation; some rush down the mountain side, and are soon lost in vapour, after a brief existence and a hurried fall; others creep along the burning desert alone, and disappear without leaving a trace behind them. Some are troubled by the vicinity of a great city, and instead of the pure river, the rich produce of an abundant spring, terminate their existence in a marsh. Only a small number are allowed to purify themselves in the middle of their course in some gentle lake; to rest there awhile after their rapid journey; and then pursue their wanderings softened and improved by its grand quiet majesty. To still fewer is it given to beautify, to fertilize, and to enrich the countries through which they flow. How closely do the various incidents of man's brief and chequered career, resemble the springs in their courses!

Whether, in the designs of Providence, this last blessing was ever awarded me, whether a wide sphere of activity was open to me in the north of India, and whether I have done wrong to decline the chances of promoting a far better order of things which may be in store for millions of our fellow-creatures, it is not for me to decide. Neither vanity, pride, cowardice, idleness, nor any selfish feeling deterred me from embracing the opportunity then offered, and hence I have no cause for regret. At eight o'clock in the evening I was in the hospitable house of Captain Wade at Lúdiana.

BRIEF POLITICAL AND GEOGRAPHICAL REMARKS ON THE KINGDOM FOUNDED BY RANJIT SINGH, AND ON THE PANJAB.

To Europeans, the kingdom founded by Ranjít Singh may seem of little importance, compared with the vast territory of Britain in Asia; but it is by no means insignificant in reality. It extends from the highest chain of the Himálaya, in 35° north latitude, to 28°, and from the 70th to the 79th degree of longitude west from Greenwich. The Setlej and the Ghára are its boundaries to the south and south-east; on the north-east, north, and north-west tower the inaccessible summits of the Himalaya, and the thinly-peopled mountain chains of the Hindú Kúsh; the western boundary is advanced as far as Jellálabad, into the heart of Afghánistan, while on the south-west is the waste on the right bank of the Indus, and mountains almost as desolate. Besides this independent kingdom, Ranjít Singh has large territories on the left shore of the Setlej, which have acknowledged the supremacy of England since the proclamation of May 6, 1809.

Captain Murray calculated the income of the Khálsa or Exchequer, in 1832, the land revenues and tribute from the different territories belonging to Ranjít Singh, to be - - - 124,03,900 rupees.

From Peshávar and the territory, as far as Jellálabad, in round numbers - - -	10,00,000	„
The customs of the Panjáb - - - -	19,00,600	„
The Moharána, a tax on every paper laid before the Mahá Raja for his signature, Moharána signifying the impression of a seal -	5,77,000	„
	158,81,500	„

Or about 159 lakhs.

Captain Murray calculates, moreover, that in the Panjáb there are fiefs which either belong to the ancient families, or have been granted by Ranjít Singh, producing a revenue of 109 lakhs 28,000 rupees, which may be withdrawn at any time by his arbitrary will or command, making his revenue to amount to the large sum of 268 lakhs 9500 rupees, or about two millions seven hundred thousand pounds sterling.

His army is organized thus:—

1. The French legion, clothed and exercised in the European manner - - - - - - -	8000 men
To these were added some regiments of cavalry, who, not receiving their pay regularly, all deserted.	
Gorchelís and Gorcher Khás, cavalry armed with muskets, wearing armour, and paid either in money or lands - - - -	4,000 „
Disciplined battalions - - - - -	14,941 „
Cavalry in various fortresses - - -	3,000 „
Infantry Pultuns (Regiments), equipped variously	23,950 „
Contingent of the Sirdárs in cavalry - -	27,014 „
	80,905 men

To this we may add 34,014 horses, and 101 elephants.

The artillery of Ranjít Singh is considerable, though, with the exception of that portion which is attached to the French legion, it is miserably organized and served.

Captain Murray calculates that there are 376 cannon and 370 *jinjáls*, or long narrow pieces of ordnance which are carried by camels. Of the whole number, probably not fifty would be reckoned serviceable by us. From 4000 to 5000 men are employed in this service; but they are enlisted and discharged, according to the position of affairs, particularly in the case of the Jinsi or heavy artillery. In the field each corps has a battery assigned to it.

Ranjít Singh's kingdom being exclusively his own work, nothing takes place throughout its whole extent without his express commands. He is the soul which animates the entire body. The government of the separate parts, whether they form large provinces or small districts, is very simple. Here, as in every part of India, the produce of the smallest strip of country is regularly estimated, and the Governors and Thanadars have to account for the stipulated sums. How the taxes are levied, matters not to Ranjít Singh; and this, as well as all other duties in their respective districts, is left entirely to the discretion of these Governors. As one may well suppose, they extort as much as possible for themselves into the bargain. If they do not deliver the required sum, they are dismissed, forced to pay the money in arrear out of their own pockets, and on any failure on this point, imprisoned, and often very ill treated. These Governors resort therefore to any method of extortion to raise the required sum; and when it does come to that pitch, that a Governor cannot by any means send in the necessary amount, it may be confidently assumed that the province has been, and is really in a state of utter ruin. To a European such a system of government seems, on a cursory glance, to be framed only for a very brief duration, but the conclusion is erroneous. The exactions are carried to a certain point, and if they exceed this, the people emigrate, and the land is left uncultivated. Hence, the inhabitants, although never meeting with indulgent forbearance, have their capabilities of endurance estimated by the selfish economy of their masters, as a driver takes care not to lay a heavier burden on his beast than he thinks it able to carry. If no particular event happens, this state of things lasts for a long time; but a calamity, like the famine which has visited Kashmír, at one swoop so reduces a country, that it never again recovers its former state of prosperity. We may easily imagine that the produce of each province has been brought down long since to the minimum.

What will become of the Sikh empire after his death, has never occasioned Ranjít Singh a moment's anxiety. Without any religion himself, he has always outwardly conformed to the faith in which he was born, and which happens to suit his plans very well. For this life, for his own life only, he acts and builds up; only desiring that the heterogeneous parts which he has thus bound together, may continue compact while he is alive, and whether the future may see the overthrow of his kingdom, and he may be the first and the last Mahá Raja of the Sikhs, he cares not, so that he may die the king over all his brethren of the faith. His mind is as indifferent to the earthly immortality of fame as to the real immortality of his soul, nor does he take any thought as to who may be his successor. All his sons must be considered as fully adopted, and nothing but his express denial of them can deprive them of the rights acquired by being born in his Zenána. The laws of succession of the Sikh branch to which he belongs, clearly make Karak Singh, his eldest son, the sole heir to his throne.

These Sikh laws of succession are different in different families; but the Sikhs themselves may be divided into two principal classes: the Manhi and the Malna Sikhs; the Manhi Sikhs came from the northern part of the Bári Doab, between the Beás and the Rávi, and have spread themselves over the Panjáb and Sirhind. Their laws of succession are the Bháiband and the Chandaband; the first dividing property equally among brothers, or giving a larger share to the eldest; the last, giving equal portions to the wives of the survivor, when they have sons. The Malna Sikhs, to whom Ranjít Singh belongs, acknowledge the rights of the first-born, giving Jaghírs or fiefs to the younger children.

According to this, Karak Singh's right to the throne is unquestionable, but Ranjít Singh has granted such large estates to his favourites, that it would demand more prudence than Karak Singh possesses, to establish his own power firmly, and at the same time keep the great men of the kingdom obedient to him. These men, however, will probably prefer a simple prince to one more clever and powerful, in order that they may feel, or make themselves quite independent. Kushál Singh, accustomed to obedience, will always serve the successor faithfully, but the three brothers, Rajas of Jamú, who have an army, fortresses, and treasures, with vast territories defended by difficult passes, will no doubt avail themselves of the first opportunity to throw off their yoke. They will seize on Kashmír, which is most accessible from their lands. Shír Singh, on the other hand, will most probably take possession of that portion of the kingdom, where he may happen to be in the command of the army, when Ranjít Singh's death takes place, and thus this disorder and anarchy will prevail, until the whole empire becomes a portion of the vast dominions of British India. Should Ranjít Singh outlive Karak Singh, or should the son of Karak Singh, Náo Nihál Singh, have time to ingratiate himself with the army, it is possible that he may be able to confirm and continue his dominion over the new kingdom.

During the last few years a great change has taken place in the policy of the British in India. The former practice of directly interfering with all the concerns of the nominally independent princes of India, has produced its results; and besides their already acquired dominions, they have made themselves heirs of every man, from the king to the humblest jaghirdar, who dies without male heirs, thus, in a short time annihilating every great family, which would otherwise have been carried on by the practice of adoption. The course of life usual among the rich natives, forbids the long continuance of any lineage, and there is scarcely one Hindú or Mohammedan prince, whose masnad, or throne, is not on the point of lapsing for want of heirs. The Company have now adopted the system of non-interference in the domestic affairs of the native princes, perhaps with the liberal intention of giving them more liberty; but more probably with another end in view. Whoever is well informed on the character of Indian princes, is well aware, that, with very rare exceptions, they are like so many grown-up children who must be guided with leading-strings; and if non-interference with neighbouring states is difficult in Europe, in Asia it is a thing impossible. Such a neutrality in the affairs of the native princes must infallibly, and very shortly produce disorders, which will in a very brief space lead to consequences otherwise requiring the efforts of a whole generation to bring them to maturity. To most of the Indian princes, their present liberties are anything but acceptable, and they are always entreating the English Resident at their court, to prescribe to them, as formerly, all their political and administrative duties, having more confidence in the character and intelligence of the British than in their own Díwans, or Wazírs, but the Residents have such strict injunctions to the contrary, that they dare not give their opinion. The liberties granted to these native princes will end in such an amount of insolence, that disorders will arise calling for the interference of an armed British force. The unquiet land is then impoverished by the forced payments for their maintenance, and the Company finally assume the government, and grant a pension to the imbecile rulers.

This system will explain their different transactions with Ranjít Singh. There would have been no difficulty in concluding with him an offensive and defensive treaty, but during his interview with Lord William Bentinck in 1831, on the English side of the Setlej, such a thing was never suggested. Ranjít Singh invited both the persons to his tent, whom he believed to be agents for the Company, and after much circumlocution, requested that he might be authorized to attack the Amírs of Sindh, who had just before detained Lieutenant Burnes, when on an embassy to him, or that they would join him in a common expedition against them. Envoys from Sindh were then in his tents, and he received permission to remonstrate with them, but no notice was taken of the hints he gave of the riches, the weakness, and the insolence of the Amírs, and a document asked for by himself, setting forth the eternal friendship of the British Government for him, was the only written evidence of the meeting between these high personages. Ranjít Singh had joyfully accepted Lord William Bentinck's proposal for the interview, and he soon surmounted the difficulties which arose on certain points of etiquette, by relinquishing all his claims. The British authorities imagined shortly after this, that Ranjít Singh entertained some apprehension of treachery on the part of the East India Company, and in fact, on the eve of the meeting, the astrologers were ordered to cast his *Saket*, or horoscope, with a view to discover whether he ought to pass the Setlej or not. They pronounced, that Ranjít Singh should take in his hand an apple for an omen, and offer it to the Governor-General as soon as they met; if he accepted it, it would be a certain sign of his friendly dispositions, but if not, Ranjít Singh was instantly to return to his own tents on the right bank of the Setlej. Ranjít Singh did make his appearance accordingly with an apple in his hand, an incident which caused no little surprise among the English, amidst the splendor which characterized this above all former spectacles of a similar kind, when they saw him alight from his elephant, and offer their Governor-General an apple. We may suppose that this singular present was accepted, particularly, when we hear that the predictions of the astrologers had been already made known to Lord William Bentinck. Ranjít Singh may have acted this farce with the apple, partly in compliance with Indian usages, which require that some present be offered each time a superior is approached; and though he would not acknowledge the Governor-General as superior to himself, he may have wished to ingratiate himself by flattery, and hence devised the present of a friendly apple. Another peculiarity of this first meeting was, that Ranjít Singh, seeing the eyes of every one fixed on him, pointed to the great jewel, Koh-i-Núr, which he wore on the occasion, and exclaimed, "This is the Koh-i-Núr," eager in his superstitious fancies to avert from himself to the jewel the gaze which, according to their belief, may bring mischief on the observed. This superstition is like that of the Neapolitan gittatura and contra-gittatura.

A treaty offensive and defensive with the British Government, having a guarantee for the integrity of his possessions, was the only thing that could ensure the dominion of Ranjít Singh. But this would have prevented England from taking immediate advantage of any sudden occurrence which might fall out.

Ranjít Singh's power is not of that nature, that in the event of a war breaking out between two European Governments near or in India, he could turn the scale in favor of either party, but in petty warfare, his cavalry acting as auxiliaries, might serve as the Cossacks in attendance on the regular Russian army.

There can be little doubt, which part Ranjít Singh would embrace, supposing an event, which, however, cannot occur during his lifetime, viz., that two European armies were fighting in the plains of India for the brightest jewel in the crown of England. He would never fight under the banners of England, unless he were quite sure that they would be victorious without his help.

We must not think more meanly of the spirit and talent of Ranjít Singh, because we find his kingdom occupying so small a portion of the vast regions of Asia, nor can we make any comparison between it and the empire of the Mohammedans in India, or the Mahratta power, still less with that of the British. The last, the slow and laborious development of two centuries of government, owes its present supremacy to the folly of Napoleon, who, eager to ruin his opponents, shut out from England a part of Europe, and gave her in return the world for her prize! The Mohammedans invaded a peaceful nation; the Mahrattas burst in upon a divided and unhappy country, like so many robbers, ruined every thing and restored nothing. Hemmed in between the colossal power of England, and the brave Afghan nation, who had so recently pulled down the sovereignty of Delhi, and lifted up themselves into mighty kingdoms, struggling against the hatred of the Hindús, and the contempt of the Mohammedans, Ranjít Singh worked alone, raising by his genius a throne, on which he still reigns, and undisturbed too, over both Hindús and Mohammedans. A few strides more, and he will succeed in extending his kingdom to the deserts of Persia, taking possession of Kabúl, Kandahár, and Ghizni, and will thus revenge the native Hindús, by means of a native-born heathen, on those arrogant and orthodox believers, who have brought so much misery and poverty on their great and beautiful country.

This seems to me the most suitable place for a few remarks on the western boundaries of British India. This splendid inheritance of the British people, founded by bold adventurers, has natural limits in every direction, and only towards the west has any doubt ever been entertained on the subject. Bounded on the south by the vast ocean, on the east and north by impenetrable mountains and forests, towards the west by the Thar, or great Indian desert, there is but a somewhat narrow stripe in the north-west, where the question assumes any difficulty. The perseverance of England has worked its way so far now, that a few thousand square miles more or less, in fixing the limits of her Asiatic dominions, do not seem of much importance.

They who are conversant with the world's history, or who merely cast one glance over the map, will at once appoint the Indus for her boundary. For geographers there is nothing so convenient as a river for a boundary, though two nations are often separated quite otherwise; very different, also, must be the line of demarcation in the north-west of British India, the only point accessible to an enemy. A river boundary is often a very good one, because it frequently seems not so much to divide, as to unite two people together. So far as we yet know of the world, the opposite shores of the same river are always inhabited by the same race of people, and the same language is spoken by them. It may therefore be worth while to inquire more precisely, whether the Indus answers or not to the ideas we have formed of the best boundary to the Anglo-Indian empire.

We trace the Atok, or Indus, from the high mountain chain, rushing like the Jelam in various forms from rock to rock, until it arrives in the plain of Shúsh, at the further extremity of which, near the junction of the Indus with the Kabúl river, the city of Atok is situated. Thence, it re-enters the mountains, and after traversing the salt-hills, it flows through a sandy wilderness and towards its Delta, arrives in a country more or less fertile. From the mountains to the sea it is the Indus which gives life to the whole country; even in the desert a small line of cultivated land appears on its banks, but on the right bank the sandy wilderness soon encroaches on this line, stretching far towards the west; and if the signs of cultivation extend somewhat further on the left bank, the Rávi which is 150 miles broad, enlarges the expanse of desert-land, until in 28° lat. it covers a surface 360 miles broad.

It would be a useless task to enumerate the reasons why the Indus, from its mouths to the junction of the various streams of the Panjáb, cannot form either a line of demarcation or a military boundary. They might be briefly summed up in these two:—1. That an army could not fall back upon its line of operations, which must be on the other side of the desert; and 2. That an army stationed there, would leave all Hindústhán to the enemy's mercy. Nor is any enemy to be reasonably expected in this direction; for though the first Mohammedans from Kandahár and Ghizni marched by this route to Gújerat, they came in detached bodies, while the large armies journeyed to cross the Indus near Atok.

From the meeting of the Panjáb rivers upwards, the right bank forms the termination of a precipitous mountain-chain, scarcely cultivated, and inhabited by wild Afghan tribes. Over these mountains some solitary caravans, but no host could possibly travel; and this part of the Indus would be a very ill-chosen boundary, because it must be left unguarded, in order to unite the troops at whatever point the enemy might make his appearance. This would be Atok, a distance of 300 miles from the junction of the Panjáb rivers. It is the certainty that Atok would be this point, which makes the idea of the Indus being fixed on as the boundary entertained by so many; but the chief thing to be thought of is, how to make it most difficult for an enemy, and most easy for a friend, to arrive at this boundary. Now, it would assuredly be much easier for any detached party to reach the Indus from the west than from the east, from the mouths up to Atok. In fact, the Indus may be called in a measure inaccessible from the Indian side to any troops; the only means of communication open to any large force stationed there, would be by steamers to Bombay, by which it might be made useful in a diversion on the enemy's line of communication. If, however, the fate of India were in the balance, a general would hardly decide on despatching his troops up and down the Indus in steam-vessels, and thus deprive himself of their co-operation in Hindústhan.

History looks with wonder at the fact of Alexander the Great not only finding his way into India, but also having the penetration to fix on the very point from which to depart, whence he could reach it most easily. Just in like manner have other historical writers marvelled, how Vasco de Gama from Mozambique on the east coast of Africa, ever found his way to Calicut, on the coast of Malabar. There is nothing more surprising in such expeditions than in the means by which a humble journeyman finds his way from Vienna to Paris; for in the days of Alexander, the produce of India was carried into Persia and Greece, and the merchant chose not the best and easiest, but the only route. So Vasco de Gama found a pilot, who brought him from Mozambique to the commercial city of Calicut, which was well known there, although the Western World knew nothing about it. We are to wonder at the genius which urged onward those great men, of whom Vasco de Gama was one of the noblest, to enterprises such as this, but not at the consequences which naturally followed them. Many writers have enlarged on these expressions of surprise, finding a vast deal to marvel at in the fact that subsequent conquerors, Sabaktagi, Mahmud Ghiznavi, Timúr, Báber, Nádir Shah, and Ahmed Shah, all followed Alexander's route to India. The reason cannot be made simpler than we find it. It is the only road that an army could have taken.

But granted that the Indus is the boundary of India, that general would indeed be rash who struck his final blow there. No finer field could possibly be chosen for such a purpose, than the plain of the Atok, which is spread out like a vast exercising ground, fifteen or twenty miles in every direction. But what would be the consequences of a battle won there, to the defenders of India? The enemy would retreat to the strong positions in his rear, through a country never cut up by rains, and very difficult to exhaust by any means; and where, if it pleased the conquering army to remain quietly stationed for a twelve-month, it might do so while the rainy season on the other side of the Indus prevented any supplies being transported. What would be the consequences of a lost battle to the British troops? The defeated army would have to make their way through a difficult and most unfruitful country, where one storm of rain might make it quite impossible to send the requisite reinforcements or even beasts of burden through the interminable ravines. The Jelam might be made a rallying point for the army, but from thence, the rivers are so near to one another, and so subject to fearful and sudden inundations, that there would be great danger of losing by a second attack any succour that might have arrived. From the Indus to the Setlej, a retreating army would be at a great disadvantage; every one of their positions might be turned, while in one only direction is there any means of retreat. The difficulty of passing a river with an Indian army, is greatly increased by the number of unarmed men over those who are fit for action; the difference being as ten to one.

Let us now compare this greatly-prized natural boundary of the Indus, with the artificial and despised line of the Setlej. Along both rivers the Indian desert extends as far as Fírozpoor, rendering it all but impossible for any army to traverse it, a few Rajpoot states alone having small outposts there. The natives of these states have been at all times renowned for their courage and ardent love of liberty; and they are quite capable of coping with any force bold enough to attempt the passage of this desert. From the end of this desert and of the arid country near Fírozpoor up to the Himalaya, the line is not above 100 miles, and an army posted behind the Setlej could march more speedily from one point to another than the enemy could on the right bank, who could neither move by the Himálaya nor through the desert. Whichever may be claimed as the boundary of India, the great struggle must be fought in the plain of Sirhind, where the advantages are all on the defending side, and where a battle lost would expose the assailants to as imminent peril as on the banks of the Indus. Of this we have a striking proof in Ahmed Shah, who lost a battle in this same plain of Sirhind, when he first invaded India, and who forthwith escaped over the Atok without stopping to assemble his forces at any other point.

Again, historians wonder that the destinies of Hindústhan should have been decided so often on the plains of Paniput, when they might soon have accounted for the fact, had they traced it to the cause. Much information is to be gained by comparing together events in history which are of a similar nature, for it is not chances which resemble one another, but similarity of causes which bring forth a correspondence in the deeds performed.

When events shall have stretched the boundary of the British dominions to the Indus, their line of defence must necessarily be advanced further westward, into the mountains between Kabúl and Herát, probably as far as Herát itself. But to dwell on this would be to transgress the limits traced for the present work, which has to do only with Kashmír and the Panjáb.

Ere I close my volume, a few words on Alexander's expedition to India may not be out of place. From Central Asia, Sogdiana (Bokhara), and Zariaspa or Bactria (Balkh), he advanced by Bámian to the foot of the northern side of the Hindú Kúsh, the Paropamisus of the ancients, and called by the Macedonians Caucasus. Crossing the Kalú Pass, which is 13,400, and the Gajigak, which is 12,400 feet above the level of the sea, mounting then to the Una Pass, 11,000 feet high, to the east of the Koh-i-Bába, which towers 18,000 feet in height, he was then in the region of the sources of the Indus. Aristobulus (Strabo xv. 691,) says in express terms: "After the setting of the Pleiades, Alexander left the country of the Paropamisadæ, and passed the winter partly in the mountains, partly among the Aspii and the Musicani. The army saw snow continually, and rain for the first time in Taxila." In other words, Alexander began his march from Balkh in the beginning of winter, and crossed the Hindú Kúsh during that season. But from Burnes' Travels, (vol. i., pp. 166, 177,) we find that the passage is closed during the six months of winter, and we shall therefore be more safe in following Arrian, who tells us (vol. iv., pp. 7, 22), that Alexander spent the most severe part of the winter in Zariaspa, quitting Bactria in the beginning of spring to proceed to the conquest of India.

He had already, on his march towards Bactria, journeyed over this same route in an opposite direction, and founded a city called Alexandria, not far from the base of the Paropamisus: the site of this city is now uncertain. Arrian says, without hesitation, that it lay on the south side of the Paropamisus, and we should plainly identify it with the site of the present Kabúl, had he not written further (iv. 22), "that Alexander moved forwards from Alexandria to the city of Nicea and the Kophenes." Kabúl being built on both sides of the Kophenes or Kabúl river. To transfer Alexandria as Diodorus does (xvii. 83), to the north side of the Paropamisus towards Media, and near the present Bámian, is in direct opposition to Arrian (iii. 28), who expresses himself thus, when writing of Alexander's expedition against Bactria, and his passage of the Indian Caucasus in a northerly direction:—"About this time Alexander moved towards the Indian Caucasus, where he built a city, calling it Alexandria. After he had sacrificed to the gods, he went over the Caucasian mountains, &c." Further on (iv. 88), when relating the expedition from Bactria to India, he writes:—"After he had crossed the Caucasus in ten days' march, he arrived at the city of Alexandria, which he had founded on his first expedition against the Bactrians and the Paropamisatæ." It does seem therefore more probable and agreeable to the truth, to conclude, that Nicea was only at a short distance from Alexandria (Kabúl), and was situated on the Logur, the main branch of the Kabúl river, coming from Ghizni. If we call, as Strabo does, (xv. § 12,) the one source of the Kabúl river Kophes, (the Kophenes of Arrian,) and the other Choaspes, transporting Alexandria to the Choaspes or Kabúl, (which is not named by Arrian,) and Nicea to the Kophenes, the difficulty will vanish.

Alexander marched from the Kophenes eastward, having been told that the most fruitful and best populated countries of India were to be sought in the mountains and towards the north; the south and the plain being, on the contrary, parched with heat and infested with wild beasts (Strabo xv. § 12). Arrian does not say anywhere that when Alexander moved along the left bank of the Kophenes, he had crossed the stream; but we find it in Strabo (xv. 697), although he confounds the Choaspes in this passage with the Kophenes; and it is clear that he must on his way to the Indus, have crossed the Gurband, the Káma, and the Lánder. We find in Arrian the passage of three river mentioned, the Kophenes, the Euaspa, and the Guræus.

We cannot, at present, ascertain the position of those cities, which are mentioned by the above-cited authors, by Megasthenes, a Greek, who lived at the court of the Indian King Sandracottus, and by all the Grecian and Roman geographers and historians after them, as having been founded in Alexander's time in the region of the Indus. With rare exceptions, rivers have kept on in one course unmoved; while cities have crumbled near them without any successor rising up over their ashes. The Grecians did also alter names in such a manner, that scarcely one is to be recognised in the original language, and one chief cause of this may be, that the most trustworthy accounts of Alexander's exploits were not composed, as Arrian informs us, until after his death.

The conquest of the city of Nyssa, on the right bank of the Indus, gives us the first instance of an Indian name. It belongs to a mountain in the vicinity of the city called Meros, and although Arrian (xi. 125) assures us that this is a Greek word, we can hardly fail to see that the Greek Meru has been clipped and made up from it.

Alexander moved onwards towards the city of Peucelia, where he crossed the Indus into the plain of Shúsh, and probably in the vicinity of the city of Benares (Atok), above where the Kabúl river joins the Indus. Thence he advanced to Taxila, a city seated in a fruitful plain, between the Indus and the Hydaspes, perhaps the modern Ráwal Pindí. On the left shore of the Hydaspes, or Jelam, was Porus and his army; Alexander forced this passage and built a city on each shore of the river, naming the one Nikí, or Victory, the other Bucephalia, in honour of his horse Bucephalus (Ox-head), who died after the battle. Sir A. Burnes thought he had found this double city in the modern Jalálpoor. We have no means of ascertaining where Alexander passed the Acesines, or Chenáb; for the rock in the bed of the river is no more to be found. The crossing of the Hydraotes, or Rávi, is only mentioned generally, but it may have been in the country of Lahor, since, as we shall presently see, Alexander's progress was in a south-easterly direction. As he pursued his march, it might have happened that if the enemy were stationed near, or some great city presented itself, he was sometimes necessarily compelled to change his route. Now, according to the Greeks, of all the cities in the Panjáb, Sangala was the largest and most formidable. It lay three days' march from the Hydraotes, or Rávi, the distance of Chák, or Amritsir, from Lahor. After storming this city, he proceeded to the Hyphasis (Setlej). That the Hyphasis must be the Setlej and not the Beás, is clear from Diodorus (xvii. 93), who says: That from the Hypkásis to the Ganges (or rather the Jamna) extends a desert of eleven days' march, behind which the King Xandranes stationed himself with an immense force. This is true of the Setlej, or the Ghára rather; but the country on both sides of the Beás is the most fruitful district throughout the Panjáb. Arrian speaks (vi. 14) of the meeting of the Hyphasis with the Chenáb. Alexander was compelled to retire after some sharp combats on the left bank of the Setlej, his troops being overpowered with the fatigues and dangers consequent upon their march through the Panjáb, which took place (a fact scarcely credible) during the rainy season.

Ere he crossed the Hyphasis, however, which he probably did not far from Hari, he raised a monument to the divinity he served most constantly,—his own vanity. Ordering his tent to be enlarged to the double of its original size, and a ditch, fifty feet broad and forty deep, to be made around it, he had weapons, much larger than any man could carry, manufactured for his purpose, with harness for horses far beyond the common weight, and commanded that they should be left behind to astonish and alarm his enemies; and, finally, building up twelve altars fifty yards high, and the same width at the base, in the form of pyramids, he sacrificed on them to the gods, and forthwith crossed the Hyphasis*. Thence he pursued his course, crossing the Hydraotes and the Acesines, and then pitched his tents near the double city of Nicea and Bucephalia on the Hydaspes, or Jelam.

He remained there for some time, repairing the injuries which his towns had suffered from the rains, and occupied with the construction of a fleet destined to convey him down the Hydaspes. To this project Alexander was moved by an expectation that the Hydaspes was one of the branches of the Nile, in which belief he was confirmed by seeing the lotus, or nelumbium, in the Jelam, and the crocodile, or alligator, which is very frequently met with in that river. This made him hope to reach the Mediterranean Sea by means of his ships. Nor should such an idea be considered by us as unworthy of the intellect of Alexander, but rather as a proof of the ignorance of his time in point of geographical knowledge. The opinions of modern days regarding the source of the Nile were not less extraordinary, and especially one theory among many, which made the Nile and the Niger have their rise from the same lake.

As soon as his fleet, which was composed of eighty vessels of thirty rowers each, and nearly 2000 other ships, was ready, he divided his army into three parts, of which one was to march along the right, the second along the left shore of the river, while the third and smallest division

---

* Plutarch says that in his time the Hindús were wont to come from the other side of the Ganges, to sacrifice to the gods on these altars, after the manner of the Greeks.—*Orig.*

embarked with him. While attacking the city near the junction of the Acesines and Hydraotes, Alexander received that dangerous wound in the breast, which was probably the remote cause of his subsequent death; but no sooner had he recovered from its first effects than he resumed his march, and near the spot where the streams of the Panjáb all unite, he founded a large city and harbour, which he also called Alexandria.

As a further detailed account of Alexander's expedition would have no connexion with the design of the present work, I shall merely add a few observations on that portion of it already described. The whole expedition took place between the spring of the year B.C. 327 and the winter of the year B.C. 326, or eighteen months from the first passage of the Indus until the final departure from that river at Patalene. Everything, both in Arrian and Strabo, which relates to the difference of temperature and climate between the upper provinces and the lower Indus is admirably described; but when they write of the religion, government, or manners of the country, their accounts are by no means applicable to any Hindú nation.

I must here take notice of a passage in Arrian (vi. 21), because that author has made a signal mistake in writing of the Etesian winds. The south-west monsoon, which is by them intended to be understood, renders the passage from the mouths of the Indus to the coast of Belúchisthán impossible; the context would explain this to be the case, but at the beginning of the chapter we read that this is the most convenient season for the voyage. *Impossible* should have been substituted for *convenient*, in order to make what comes after intelligible.

I am convinced, from a careful perusal and examination both of all that Arrian and Strabo have written, and of that also related by Ptolemy, Aristobulus, and the mendacious Onesicritus, either that in Alexander's time, neither the Brahmin nor Buddhist faith was known in the Panjáb, or that Alexander and his captains never crossed the Indus, unless we can believe that when their accounts were set down in writing, they had already forgotten all that had been seen and experienced there. Thus, Strabo divides the Indians into seven classes, namely: the Brahmins, the peasants, the shepherds and huntsmen, the handicraftsmen, the warriors, the police, and the courtiers. According to Arrian, the system of castes had no existence (xv. § 44), and the Brahmins ate with Alexander at night, and drank wine. The following passage from Strabo (xv. § 44, p. 714,) shows plainly enough to what faith the natives of the Panjáb belonged at that time. "Aristobulus relates some singular customs of the natives of Taxila. Among these is the custom of casting the bodies of the dead to vultures." Here we have at once a clear proof of the nature of the faith professed in the Panjáb; the worship of the elements, the religion of the Medes, still existing according to the regulations of Zertusht, or Zoroaster, among the Parsees, or fire-worshippers, which declares that the elements are too pure to take up or to destroy a dead body. Arrian says nothing of the Indian funeral rites; for in his accounts of the burning of Kalanus, which nobody would suppose to mean a Brahmin, we cannot understand that he means to describe the burning of the dead as a common custom in the Panjáb. Diodorus (xvii. 104), speaking of a free nation of Indians on the left bank of the Indus, the Oritoni, says: "In regard to their habits, they are like the Indians, but they have one very strange custom; the relations of a dead person carry his corpse naked out of his dwelling, with spears in their hands, set it down in a wood, take away his ornaments, and then abandon it to the wild beasts." This passage would show that all the Indians had not the custom in common; but as Alexander, during his progress through Asia, must have met with it many times, and precisely among the people inhabiting the provinces west of the Panjáb, it would have been a strange thing, had the narratives of Alexander's companions said nothing about a custom existing among the Hindús which so much resembled the Greek funeral rites. In another place (Strabo xv. § 44), Aristobulus says that he has heard how, among some Indian nations it is customary for the women to be burned with the bodies of their deceased husbands; another evidence that this usage, peculiar to the Brahmins, did not exist in the Panjáb.

There are writers who believe that Alexander reached the Ganges.

The story rests upon a letter, which one of his warriors, Kraterus, wrote to his mother Aristopatra, where he tells her that he has seen the Ganges, describes its enormous breadth and depth, and the huge cetaceous animals which live in its waters. It is unnecessary to prove that the whole is a fable, and the letter suppositious. Before he could have reached the Ganges, Alexander must have crossed the Jamna, which has never been asserted.

In order to give some idea of the absurdities invented by the Greeks and Macedonians about the Panjáb, I have here collected the statistical accounts of Arrian, Strabo, and Diodorus. Where the Chenáb and Indus unite, there dwelt the Abastanæ, Xanthæ, Sodræ, Ossadæ, and Massanæ. South of these were the Sogdi, Arachotii (Osii), Drangi, and Subracæ, the last alone opposing Alexander with 60,000 men. Where the Ghára and Chenáb unite in the Báree Doáb, were the Ambræ and Sugambræ, with 80,000 foot and 60,000 horse. Further north on the Hydraotes, or Rávi, were the Oxydracæ, Malli, and Brachmani. In this country dwelt also the Agalassi, who marched against their forces with 40,000 men on foot and 3000 horse. Towards the north, again, were the Sibæ, Sobii, Hiacensi, and Silæ. The Adrastæ, Kathai, Glausæ, or Glausanidæ, inhabited the north-eastern countries of the Panjáb, the Jhalander Doáb. To the east of these, between the Setlej and Jamna, was the King Xandranes with 30,000 horse and 200,000 foot soldiers; 2000 war chariots, drawn by four horses (no Indian custom); and 3000 elephants. Finally, Porus reigned over the great Indian nation, to which no one author has ever given a particular appellation, and who inhabited 300 cities in the Jinhat Doáb, between the Jelam and the Acesines; (the Jinhat Doáb contains about 120 square German miles). The nearest neighbour of Porus on the north was Abisares, King of the Bergindii, whose power was but little inferior to his. King Taxila reigned over the northern part of the Doáb-i Sindi-ságur, which Strabo describes to be as large as Egypt. On the right shore of the Indus reigned the Indian Kings Erix (Curtius viii. 12); Afrikes (Diodorus xvii. 86); Kofacus and Assagetes (Arrian iv. 28); in Strabo occurs the name of the country Bandobene, Gandaritis (Kandahar ?) xv. § 12; and about the Kophenes and its tributaries dwell the Acinacæ, Bazirae, Nicaæ, Hypasii, Aspii, Thyræi, and Arsæi. Strabo (xv. 686) reckons 5000 cities between the Hyphasis and Hydaspes, in the Báree, the Rekhna and the Jinhat Doábs!

For more than two thousand times the earth has performed her circuit round the sun, a period amounting to nearly one-third of the time which has passed since the first creation of mankind; more than 2000 years have elapsed since Alexander crossed the Indus, and we still justly wonder at the undaunted spirit of enterprise which prompted him to the thought of making India pay tribute to Greece. That vast design miscarried, not because the conquest was incomplete—not because the Macedonian hero was too quickly hurried from the world, but because his victories, instead of increasing the power of his kingdom, diminished it; and because he thought that his single will was all that was needed to unite distant empires, each one of which was more powerful than his own hereditary dominions, under his sceptre. Alexander learned for the first time, when the lesson was too late to be of use, that it is easier to conquer a kingdom than to keep possession of it. For it requires, and ever has required, some strong bond of union to keep together a vast monarchy, formed of various nations, when the government has not succeeded, either by power or the right of prescription, in blending the several portions into one whole. In Europe, whether in ancient or modern times, as well as in other countries enjoying European civilization, this union lasts as long as the mutual interests of the individual states require it. But it is otherwise with remote conquered provinces, or with such as stand in a similar degree of subjugation to the mother country. A regularly formed system is there quite necessary to bring the provincial into harmony with the supreme governments; there must be a spirit of order, a careful survey of every addition made to the empire; there must be a central point of real strength; and finally, confidence and persuasion in the power not only of the state, but in each individual part of it. There was nothing of all this to be found in the government of Alexander; his vast conquests only shattered the powers of his kingdom, which on his death fell to the share of different princes, each one more powerful than his successor on the throne of Macedonia.

Two thousand years after Alexander, a people whose native land differs but little from Greece in extent, unconsciously following out his plans, have subdued India. England owes this immense possession neither to her great talent in managing her affairs in Asia, nor to the bravery of her sons in battle against overwhelming numbers; nor to the boldness with which her plans have been carried out. No, it is to the union of intellect and force; the perseverance which followed up the aim, far distant as it often was; their respect for the rights of the vanquished; the co-operation of every individual in the interest of all; the honourable resolution to grant to every British subject without any paltry jealousies, some participation in the riches acquired; India does not belong to the crown alone, nor to the East India Company; it is the property of the British nation, and the foundations of their gigantic empire were laid by their unfailing courage in reverses of fortune, and their bravery in following up success. The power and stability of this Empire are maintained by the strong links uniting the highest powers in the state with the covenanted servants; through the system by which individuals receive regular promotion, the humblest functionary clinging to existing institutions in the sure hope that he is likely to gain much more under the established order of things, than any usurper in a distant land could offer him; and where the highest individual to whom a distant empire in Asia is confided, feels assured, that his commands will be executed so long only as they shall be found in accordance with the principles of the Government at home. This Empire bears the promise within it of a long continuance, inasmuch as the exercise of justice and moderation, the maintenance of law and authority, are qualities peculiar to that mighty race, to whom Divine Wisdom has entrusted the government and happiness of millions of his creatures.
